DATE DUE

Lebanon
a country study

Federal Research Division
Library of Congress
Edited by
Thomas Collelo
Research Completed
December 1987

On the cover: Representing Lebanon's tragic civil strife, a cedar, the national symbol, is shown split in two.

Third Edition, First Printing, 1989.

Copyright ©1989 United States Government as represented by the Secretary of the Army. All rights reserved.

Library of Congress Cataloging-in-Publication Data

Lebanon: A Country Study

(DA Pam; 550-24)
Research completed December 1987.
Bibliography: pp. 245-261.
Includes index.
Supt. of Docs. no.: D 101.22:550-24/987
1. Lebanon. I. Collelo, Thomas, 1948-
II. Library of Congress. Federal Research Division. III. Series.

DS80.L39   1989   956.92   88-600488

Headquarters, Department of the Army
DA Pam 550-24

For sale by the Superintendent of Documents, U.S. Government Printing Office
Washington, D.C. 20402

Foreword

This volume is one in a continuing series of books now being prepared by the Federal Research Division of the Library of Congress under the Country Studies—Area Handbook Program. The last page of this book lists the other published studies.

Most books in the series deal with a particular foreign country, describing and analyzing its political, economic, social, and national security systems and institutions, and examining the interrelationships of those systems and the ways they are shaped by cultural factors. Each study is written by a multidisciplinary team of social scientists. The authors seek to provide a basic understanding of the observed society, striving for a dynamic rather than a static portrayal. Particular attention is devoted to the people who make up the society, their origins, dominant beliefs and values, their common interests and the issues on which they are divided, the nature and extent of their involvement with national institutions, and their attitudes toward each other and toward their social system and political order.

The books represent the analysis of the authors and should not be construed as an expression of an official United States government position, policy, or decision. The authors have sought to adhere to accepted standards of scholarly objectivity. Corrections, additions, and suggestions for changes from readers will be welcomed for use in future editions.

> Louis R. Mortimer
> Acting Chief
> Federal Research Division
> Library of Congress
> Washington, D.C. 20540

Acknowledgments

The authors are grateful to individuals in various agencies of the United States government and private organizations in Washington, D.C., who gave of their time, research materials, and special knowledge of Lebanese affairs to provide data and perspective. The authors also wish to express their gratitude to members of the Federal Research Division who contributed directly to the preparation of the manuscript. These include Helen C. Metz and Richard F. Nyrop, who reviewed the text; Ruth Nieland and Richard Kollodge, who edited chapters; Marilyn Majeska, who managed production; and Barbara Edgerton and Izella Watson, who performed word processing. Others involved in preparation of the book included Andrea T. Merrill, who performed the prepublication review; and Shirley Kessel, who prepared the index. Malinda B. Neale, of the Library of Congress Composing Unit, prepared the camera-ready copy under the supervision of Peggy Pixley.

Special thanks are owed to those responsible for the excellent graphic work in the book. These include David P. Cabitto, who oversaw the entire process; Kimberly A. Lord, who designed the cover and chapter illustrations and who performed the page layout; Greenhorne and O'Mara, which produced the maps; and Harriett R. Blood, who prepared the topography and drainage map. The inclusion of photographs in this study was made possible by the generosity of individuals and private and public agencies. The authors acknowledge their indebtedness to those who provided original work not previously published.

Contents

	Page
Foreword	iii
Acknowledgments	v
Preface	xiii
Country Profile	xv
Introduction	xxi
Chapter 1. Historical Setting	1

Afaf Sabeh McGowan

ANCIENT TIMES	3
The Phoenicians	3
Assyrian Rule	4
Babylonian Rule and the Persian Empire	5
Rule of Alexander the Great	5
The Seleucid Dynasty	5
THE ARAB PERIOD	7
The Arab Conquest, 634–36	7
The Umayyads, 660–750	8
The Abbasids, 750–1258	8
Impact of Arab Rule	8
The Crusades, 1095–1291	10
The Mamluks, 1282–1516	11
OTTOMAN RULE, 1516–1916	12
The Maans, 1120–1697	12
The Shihabs, 1697–1842	13
Religious Conflicts	14
WORLD WAR I AND THE FRENCH MANDATE, 1914–41	17
World War I	17
The Mandate Period	18
World War II and Independence, 1939–41	19
INDEPENDENT LEBANON, 1943–76	21
The Khuri Era, 1943–52	21
The Shamun Era, 1952–58	22
The Rise of Shihabism, 1958–64	24
The Hilu Era, 1964–70	25
The Franjiyah Era, 1970–76	26
The Civil War, 1975–76	29

The Sarkis Administration, 1976-82 32

Chapter 2. The Society and Its Environment 39
As'ad AbuKhalil

GEOGRAPHY 42
    Land 43
    Climate 45
    Rivers and Lakes 47
POPULATION 48
    Migration 50
    The War and Displacement in Beirut 52
    The Palestinian Element 52
SECTARIANISM 53
    Lebanese Confessional "Societies" 55
    Sectarian and Clan Consciousness 56
RELIGION 57
    Tenets of Islam 59
    Muslim Sects 61
    Druzes 65
    Christian Sects 66
    Jews 70
    Others 71
LANGUAGES 71
    Arabic 71
    Other Languages 72
STRUCTURE OF SOCIETY 73
    The Family 73
    Sex Roles 74
    Marriage 75
    Child-Rearing Practices 77
    Impact of War on the Family 78
LIVING CONDITIONS 79
    Prewar Conditions 79
    Wartime Conditions 80
EDUCATION 81
    Primary Education 81
    Intermediate Education 82
    Secondary Education 82
    Technical and Vocational Education 82
    Higher Education 83
HEALTH 84

Chapter 3. The Economy 87
John Roberts

RECENT ECONOMIC HISTORY 93
    Civil War and Partial Recovery, 1974-82 93

Invasion and Trauma, 1982–87 95
THE OFFICIAL ECONOMY IN THE MID-1980s 97
    Balance of Payments 97
    Government Revenues 97
    External Debt and Foreign Exchange 98
    Inflation 99
    The Budget 100
BANKING AND FINANCE 101
    Domestic Banking 101
    The Central Bank 103
    International Banking 105
TRANSPORTATION AND COMMUNICATIONS 106
    Roads 106
    Railroads 109
    Shipping 110
    Aviation 112
    Telecommunications 115
AGRICULTURE 115
    Land and Irrigation 115
    Crop Production 118
INDUSTRY 122
    The State of Industry 122
    Cement 124
    Electric Power and Petroleum Refining 125
AID AND RECONSTRUCTION 127
    Reconstruction and Hope, 1976–82 127
    Arab Reconstruction Aid 128
    Post-Israeli Invasion Reconstruction, 1982–84 131
    Reconstruction and Chaos, 1984–87 133

Chapter 4. Government and Politics 137
As'ad AbuKhalil

THE BASIS OF GOVERNMENT 141
    The Constitution 141
    The National Pact 143
THE PRACTICE OF GOVERNMENT 144
    Zuama Clientelism 144
    The Presidency 146
    The Prime Minister and the Cabinet 147
    The Legislature 149
    The Judiciary 152
    The Bureaucracy 153
POLITICAL PARTIES AND GROUPINGS 154
    Sectarian Groups 155

Minority Parties 166
Multisectarian Parties 167
FOREIGN RELATIONS 170
Syria 171
Israel 173
Palestinians 175
Iran 176
United States 176
Soviet Union 177

Chapter 5. National Security 179
Robert Scott Mason

THE CREATION OF THE ARMY 183
THE LEBANESE POLITICAL-MILITARY SITUATION:
INDEPENDENCE TO 1975 185
The 1948 Arab-Israeli War 185
The Rosewater Revolution 185
The 1958 Civil War 185
The Cairo Agreement and the Prelude to the 1975
Civil War 186
THE 1975 CIVIL WAR 188
The Military Cabinet 189
The Early Stages of Combat 190
Syrian Intervention 192
The Riyadh Conference and the Arab Deterrent
Force 193
The Red Line Arrangement 194
THE INTERWAR YEARS 194
Operation Litani 195
Operations of the United Nations Interim Force
in Lebanon 196
The Ascendancy of Bashir Jumayyil 197
The Missile Crisis 200
The Two-Week War 200
THE 1982 ISRAELI INVASION AND ITS
AFTERMATH 201
Operation Peace for Galilee 201
The Siege of Beirut 204
The Multinational Force 206
The Rise of the Shias 208
The May 17 Agreement 209
The Israel Defense Forces Withdrawal and the
Mountain War 210
The Multinational Force Withdrawal 211

The Bikfayya Accord	212
Events in Southern Lebanon	213
Chaos in Beirut and Syrian Peacemaking Efforts	214
THE LEBANESE ARMED FORCES IN THE 1980s	218
Organization and Command Structure	219
The Army	222
The Air Force and Navy	225
INTERNAL SECURITY AND TERRORISM	226
Suicide Bombings	227
The Hostage Crisis	228

Appendix A. Tables 233

Appendix B. The Contending Sides in the 1975 Civil War 239
Robert Scott Mason

THE LEBANESE FRONT	239
The Phalange Party	239
The Tigers	240
The Marada Brigade	240
The Guardians of the Cedars	240
The Order of Maronite Monks	240
At Tanzim	240
THE LEBANESE NATIONAL MOVEMENT	240
The Progressive Socialist Party	240
The Syrian Socialist Nationalist Party	241
Amal	241
Communist Organizations	242
The Najjadah	242
The Lebanese Arab Army	242
The Baath (Arab Socialist Resurrection) Party	242
Nasserite Organizations	242
Palestinians	243

Bibliography 245

Glossary 263

Index 267

List of Figures
1. Administrative Divisions, 1987 xx
2. Phoenician Colonization and Trade Routes 6
3. Topography and Drainage 46
4. Palestinian Refugee Camps in Lebanon, 1986 54
5. Distribution of Religious Sects, 1983 58

6. Transportation System, 1987 108
7. Economic Activity, 1987 116
8. The Cantons of Lebanon, 1986 156
9. Beirut During the 1975 Civil War 190
10. Lebanon on the Eve of the 1982 Israeli Invasion 198

Preface

Lebanon: A Country Study replaces the *Area Handbook for Lebanon* published in 1973. Like its predecessor, the present book is an attempt to treat in a concise and objective manner the dominant historical, social, economic, political, and national security aspects of contemporary Lebanon. But, like the country, which has undergone radical changes since the mid-1970s, the present study bears little resemblance to the old book; it has been completely revised to reflect the current situation. Sources of information included scholarly books, journals, and monographs; official reports and documents of governments and international organizations; foreign and domestic newspapers and periodicals; and interviews with Lebanese officials and individuals with special competence in Lebanese affairs. Because so much of the literature is polemical, the authors took special pains to separate fact from bias. In addition, because the turmoil that has occurred since 1975 has precluded comprehensive and accurate accounting of economic and demographic statistics, most data should be viewed as rough estimates.

Much of the recent history and much of the political situation in Lebanon are associated with armed conflict. Accordingly, detailed information on these topics is likely to be found in the national security chapter rather than in the chapters on history or government and politics.

Chapter bibliographies appear at the end of the book; brief comments on some of the more valuable sources for further reading appear at the conclusion of each chapter. Most measurements are given in the metric system (see table 1, Appendix A). Because of the complex nature of the fighting during the 1975 Civil War, the rival factions are treated at length in Appendix B. The Glossary provides brief definitions of terms that may be unfamiliar to the general reader.

The transliteration of Arabic words and phrases posed a particular problem. For many words—such as Muhammad, Muslim, and Quran—the authors followed a modified version of the system adopted by the United States Board on Geographic Names and the Permanent Committee on Geographic Names for British Official Use, known as the BGN/PCGN system. The modification entails the omission of diacritical markings and hyphens. In numerous instances, however, the names of persons or places are so wel¹ known by another spelling that to have used the BGN/PCGN system may have created confusion. For example, the reader will find Beirut, Sidon, and Tyre rather than Bayrut, Sayda, and Sur. Furthermore, because press accounts generally use French in the spelling of personal names, the alternate French version is often given when such a name is introduced in each chapter.

Country Profile

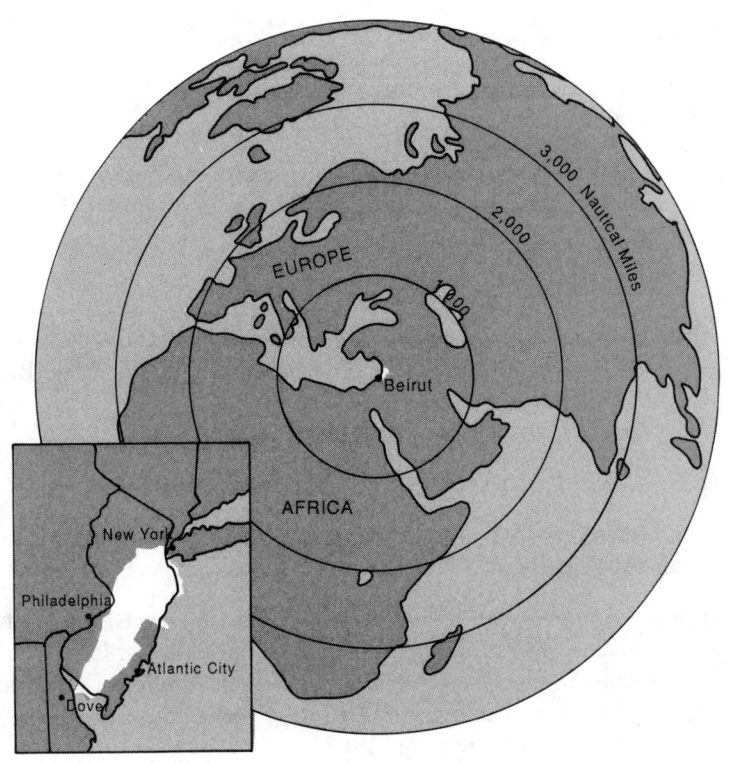

Country

Formal Name: Republic of Lebanon.

Short Form: Lebanon.

Term for Citizens: Lebanese.

Capital: Beirut.

Geography

Size: Approximately 10,452 square kilometers.

Topography: Four major features running roughly from north to south: coastal strip, Lebanon Mountains, Biqa Valley, and Anti-Lebanon Mountains. Several perennial rivers, but none navigable.

Climate: Mediterranean climate with hot, dry summers and cool, wet winters. Weather drier and hotter east of Lebanon Mountains.

Society

Population: Estimated at 2.6 million in 1983, not including about 400,000 Palestinian refugees.

Education: Five-year primary education mandatory. Education system disrupted during and after 1975 Civil War; many children did not attend school.

Literacy: Estimated at nearly 80 percent in mid-1980s.

Health: Drastically reduced health standards because of 1975 Civil War. In 1980s overall shortages of medical staff and facilities. Best health care available in private institutions.

Languages: Arabic official language. French and English also widely spoken. Armenian spoken by Armenian community.

Ethnic Groups: More than 90 percent of population Arab; some Armenians, Kurds, and Jews.

Religion: A variety of Muslim and Christian sects. Muslims included Shias, Sunnis, Druzes, Ismailis, and Alawis. Christians included Maronites, Greek Orthodox, Greek Catholics, Roman Catholics, Jacobites, Armenian Orthodox, Assyrians, and Protestants. Fewer than 100 Jews in 1987.

Economy

Gross Domestic Product (GDP): Estimates in 1985 ranged from L£30 billion to L£43.8 billion (for value of the Lebanese pound—see Glossary); in either case, in real terms GDP no more than half 1974 level. Inflation in 1987 estimated at more than 700 percent, and unemployment estimated at 35 percent.

Agriculture: Diversity of crops grown throughout country. Biqa Valley most productive region, primarily grains but increasingly in late 1980s hashish and opium. Citrus crops grown on coast, especially in south. Tobacco also cultivated in south. Only 11 percent of labor force employed in agriculture in 1980.

Industry: Severely disrupted by civil strife. Employed about 27 percent of labor force in 1980. Cement most important industrial export in 1980s; energy production and petroleum refining also significant.

Currency: Lebanese pound.

Fiscal Year: Same as calendar year.

Transportation and Communications

Railroads: Two standard-gauge lines from Syria: one down coast through Tripoli and Beirut to Az Zahrani; the other through Biqa Valley to Riyaq. Narrow-gauge mountain line from Damascus to Beirut. In 1987 no trains operating on 407-kilometer system.

Roads: Approximately 8,000 kilometers of roads in varying states of disrepair in 1987. Beirut hub of network extending north to Tripoli, south to Tyre, and east through mountains to Damascus. Roads also extending through Biqa Valley and crossing Lebanon Mountains.

Ports: Major ports at Beirut, Tripoli, Sidon, and Tyre. In 1980s numerous smaller, illegal (unofficial) ports operated by militias.

Pipelines: Trans-Arabia Pipeline (Tapline) from Saudi Arabia to Az Zahrani refinery but closed in mid-1980s. Iraq Petroleum Company pipeline through Syria to Tripoli refinery but closed in 1981.

Airports: Main international airport at Beirut; closed intermittently in 1980s. Airport being built at Halat, but not cleared for civilian traffic as of 1987.

Telecommunications: Much infrastructure destroyed during and after 1975 Civil War. International links continued to function in 1980s.

Government and Politics

Government: Central government marginally functional in 1987 and exercised only nominal control. Constitution vests executive power in president of republic, who appoints the cabinet ministers, from whom he selects prime minister. Legislative functions performed by unicameral Chamber of Deputies, elected for four-year terms by universal suffrage. In 1987 no elections had been held since 1972, and only seventy-seven deputies remained out of ninety-nine elected in 1972. Electoral system provided for proportional representation (based on 1932 census) in Chamber of Deputies by religion as well as by region. Chamber of Deputies elects president for six-year term and approves his cabinet appointments. By custom, president a Maronite, prime minister a Sunni Muslim, and speaker of the Chamber of Deputies a Shia Muslim. Judicial system, except for religious courts, based on French model.

Politics: 1975 Civil War, foreign intervention, and internal fighting generally have disrupted politics. Before 1975 many nonideological political parties centered on powerful leaders whose followers were usually of same sect. Since 1975 militias have overtaken parties in importance. New president scheduled to be elected by Chamber of Deputies in September 1988 (see Introduction).

Foreign Relations: In 1987 central government only one of many actors conducting foreign policy. Syria and Israel wielded greatest influence, followed by Iran (especially among some Shias) and Western nations (especially among some Christians).

National Security

Armed Forces: In 1987 consisted of 15,000- to 18,000-man, multisectarian army and small Christian air force (800 men) and navy (450 men). Army had nine brigades organized along sectarian lines, but not all loyal to central government.

Equipment: Lightly equipped with mostly United States, British, and French matériel.

Police: Most internal security personnel assimilated into armed forces by 1987.

Militias: Principal militias, sectarian affiliations, and estimated combat strengths in 1987: Amal (Shia), 6,000 regulars (10,000 reserves); Progressive Socialist Party (Druze), 5,000 regulars (12,000 reserves); Lebanese Forces (Christian), 4,500 regulars (30,000 reserves); Hizballah (Shia), 1,000; and South Lebanon Army (Christian), 1,000.

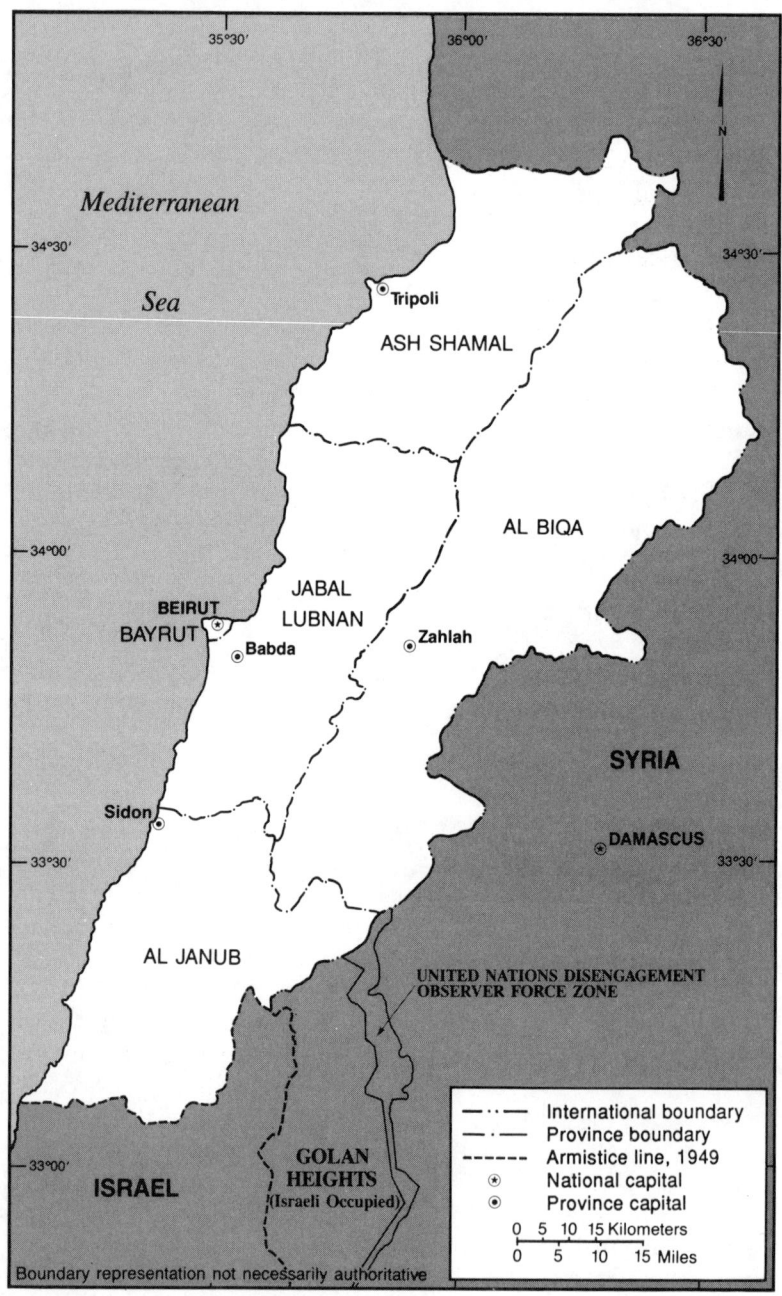

Figure 1. Administrative Divisions, 1987

Introduction

BY THE LATE 1980s, a new term had entered the vocabulary of the popular press—"Lebanonization," a term used to refer to a wide range of political, social, and economic situations whose resolution appeared intractable. Because of Lebanon's deeply complicated ills, which included political factionalization, societal chaos, and economic fragmentation, the term could reasonably be applied to almost any problematic condition anywhere in the world.

What "Lebanonization" failed to denote adequately, however, was the tragedy and suffering of the Lebanese people. As of late 1987, estimates indicated that as many as 130,000 people had lost their lives during civil turmoil, which probably had inflicted at least twice that number of casualties and forced thousands of individuals from their homes. Figures could not show the impact these problems had on the national psyche. By the spring of 1988, Lebanon had experienced nearly continuous warfare of varying levels of intensity for thirteen years, and an entire generation had yet to know peace.

Beginning in the darkest days of the Civil War in 1975 and 1976, tragic events followed almost without interruption. The litany of misfortune includes the Israeli thrust into southern Lebanon in search of Palestinian guerrillas in 1978, the intra-Christian battles of the late 1970s and early 1980s, the deeper Israeli invasion in 1982, the massacres by Christian militiamen of Palestinians in the Sabra and Shatila refugee camps in 1982, the intra-Palestinian clashes of 1983, the fighting in the Shuf Mountains between the Lebanese Army and Druze (see Glossary) militia in 1983 and 1984, the suicide bombings of installations belonging to Western governments in 1983-84, the Amal siege of Palestinian refugee camps in Beirut from 1985 to 1988, and the internecine Shia (see Glossary) Muslim battles of 1988.

In spite of this turmoil, anarchy was a fairly recent phenomenon in Lebanon. Before the Civil War the nation was often regarded as one of only a few truly modernizing Middle Eastern states, and its government was considered a model of pluralism. Some observers regarded Beirut as the jewel of the Arab world, a cosmopolitan city in which Christian and Muslim communities peacefully coexisted. These positive appearances notwithstanding, there were deep—and ominous—divisions in society. Many observers claim that these divisive forces have origins at least centuries old; others believe that the sources of these forces can be traced back even further, perhaps as long ago as ancient times.

As in much of the contemporary Middle East, the area occupied by present-day Lebanon has changed hands frequently (see fig. 1). The Phoenicians, the region's first known inhabitants, were a seafaring people with a penchant for commerce, a cultural trait that has continued through the centuries. But Lebanon's location on the Mediterranean Sea and its bountiful resources, although assets to the Phoenicians, also proved to be liabilities, as they were coveted by a succession of expansionary empires. Before the Christian era, Lebanon was conquered by the Egyptians, Assyrians, Babylonians, Persians, Greeks, and Romans, although it enjoyed brief periods of independence (see Ancient Times, ch. 1).

In addition to the sea, Lebanon's mountainous terrain has figured prominently in its history. The land's mountains, hills, and valleys provided isolated sanctuaries for a variety of people; some sought escape from repression, while others sought the unfettered practice of their religions. Over the centuries the mountains' geographic remoteness has allowed groups such as Druzes and Maronites (see Glossary) to maintain age-old customs and practices.

From ancient times through the Ottoman era to the colonial era, the present-day states of Lebanon and Syria, along with parts of other states, often have been regarded as one area termed *Greater Syria* (see Glossary). And, as this name suggests, Syria has played an influential role in the history of the area. Lebanon and Syria have been linked socially and economically, but especially politically. For example, following the Islamic conquest of the region in the seventh century A.D., the Arab caliph Muawiyah ruled the entire area from his capital at Damascus. Later, under the Ottoman Empire, the pasha, or governor, of Damascus controlled Lebanon through a number of amirs, or princes. After World War I and the defeat of the Ottomans, the Allies granted France mandate authority over both Lebanon and Syria. In the 1980s, Syrian influence in Lebanon persisted because Syria had taken on the role of power broker and was viewed by some observers as the one actor that could bring about peace.

Unlike the populations of many Third World nations that have experienced strife because of racial or ethnic divisions, Lebanon's population is ethnically homogeneous. It is overwhelmingly Arab, and its people speak a common language—Arabic. Lebanon's many conflicts have been the result of sectarianism and political differences. Disputes based on sectarianism were evident as long ago as the 1840s, when Druzes and Maronites clashed in Mount Lebanon (see Glossary). Over the years, confessionalism (see

Glossary) has become more firmly entrenched, as individuals have come to identify with sect and clan rather than with national interest. Modernization and urbanization, which weakened traditional social systems and increased social alienation, contributed to the rise of sectarianism (see Sectarianism, ch. 2). Moreover, the confessional system became legitimated by the National Pact of 1943, which allocated political offices according to sect (see The National Pact, ch. 4). In the 1970s and 1980s, the consequences of the fragmentation of society became clear, as a multitude of groups clashed. But in Lebanon's ever-changing social milieu, today's opponent might become tomorrow's ally.

Before the 1975 Civil War, Lebanon enjoyed a flourishing economy (see Recent Economic History, ch. 3). Tourism, commerce, and other service sectors were all booming. Beirut's banks held large balances of foreign capital, mostly in the form of remittances from expatriates and deposits from West European and Persian Gulf states. As a transshipment point for goods coming from or going to a variety of Arab countries, the government reaped considerable revenues from import and export duties.

Lebanon's wealth, however, was inequitably distributed, much of it concentrated in the hands of a small, predominantly Christian, elite in Beirut. In the opinion of some observers, this maldistribution of wealth contributed significantly to the outbreak of civil strife and the subsequent devastation of the economy.

In the late 1970s and throughout the 1980s, armed conflict and geographic fragmentation kept the economy in ruins. The government, although not bankrupt, was unable to collect sufficient revenues to maintain services and thus was forced to incur huge deficits. Rampant inflation spawned a large-scale black market, industry was almost moribund, and the once-thriving tourism sector was dead. Banks were still functioning, but at greatly diminished levels. Agricultural production, although reduced, continued in areas unaffected by the violence; in some cases, food crops were replaced by hashish and opium. Finally, reconstruction efforts, involving funding by Arab institutions and Western donors, had little impact because calm could not be maintained long enough to allow the implementation of programs.

Lebanon's political structure often was cited by analysts as contributing to hostilities. Political participation was not only circumscribed for all segments of society by the traditional power-broker system, called *zuama* (sing., *zaim*—see Glossary) clientelism, but this system also awarded undue power to Maronites (see *Zuama* Clientelism, ch. 4). The allocation of seats in the legislature, called the Chamber of Deputies, was based on the 1932 census, which counted Christians to Muslims in a six-to-five ratio, and by custom the presidency was set aside for a Maronite, the prime ministry for a Sunni (see Glossary) Muslim, and the speaker of the Chamber of Deputies for a Shia. But as the population makeup changed, Muslims—especially Shias—clamored for greater representation and for reform to reduce the powers of the president; some groups advocated the wholesale restructuring of the political system. After the events of the mid-1970s, the system collapsed, and those parts that continued to function no longer resembled the prewar form. Political power was usurped by sectarian militias or external actors, especially Syria and, after 1982, Israel (see Sectarian Groups; Syria; Israel, ch. 4). In mid-1988 the executive controlled only a small area around the Presidential Palace, the Council of Ministers seldom convened (and, in any case, did not cooperate with the president), and a new Chamber of Deputies had not been elected since 1972. Although reform of the system had been discussed over the years, the multitude of power centers espousing opposing ideologies prevented any meaningful change.

By the late 1970s, the term *national security,* in the commonly understood sense of providing internal security and national defense, could no longer be applied to the Lebanese Armed Forces. In the prewar years, efforts were made to keep the armed forces out of politics, and, for the most part, those efforts succeeded. But during the violence of the mid-1970s, the armed forces fragmented along sectarian lines. In the late 1980s, as only the sixth or seventh most powerful military organization in the country, the armed forces were unable to fulfill their stated missions. In areas where security did exist, it was often the result of a sectarian militia imposing its authority.

* * *

After the research for this book was completed, several events occurred that reshaped Lebanon's political and social structure. The first of these events occurred in September 1988, when, after several failed attempts at convening, the Chamber of Deputies announced that it was unable to elect a new president. Before leaving office, however, President Amin Jumayyil (also seen as Gemayel) appointed the commander of the Lebanese Army, Major General Michel Awn (also seen as Aoun), to head an interim military government. Although he attempted to incorporate non-Christian sects into his cabinet, Muslims quickly renounced the move, and Salim al Huss (also seen as Hoss), the acting prime minister under Jumayyil, formed his own cabinet.

In February 1989, to assert the authority of the state, Awn sent his army to wrest an unofficial (illegally operated) port in Beirut from the Christian Lebanese Forces (LF), a militia headed by Samir Jaja (also seen as Geagea). This operation resulted in a fierce battle in East Beirut between artillery and armored units of the LF and the army. The fighting inflicted great damage on the people and neighborhoods of East Beirut, and soon after the conflict began, Jaja conceded to a cease-fire and agreed to vacate the port.

Following this triumph, Awn sought to extend his control further and ordered the small Lebanese navy to blockade unofficial ports south of Beirut that were run by Druze and Shia militias. Again a bitter confrontation ensued, but in this instance, as had not been the case during the earlier localized, internecine fighting, Syria, which had about 40,000 troops in Lebanon, rallied to the Muslim side. During much of March and April, shells rained down on East and West Beirut, the Shuf Mountains, and the Christian heartland north of Beirut. Observers reported that the fighting was as severe as any battle of the 1975 Civil War or the 1978 Syrian siege of East Beirut. As many as 300,000 people were believed to have fled the bombardments, and many of those who didn't leave were forced to live in basements, often without electricity or water. Reports claimed that all but a few of the several hundred killed and wounded were civilians.

Thus, with rival Christian and Muslim governments and armies in place, and with intrasectarian and intersectarian disputes as common and fierce as ever, prospects for peace seemed remote in early 1989.

May 2, 1989   Thomas Collelo

Chapter 1. Historical Setting

The Temple of Jupiter, built by the Romans in Baalbek

LIKE OTHER AREAS of the Middle East, Lebanon has a heritage almost as old as the earliest evidence of mankind. Its geographic position as a crossroads linking the Mediterranean Basin with the great Asian hinterland has conferred on it a cosmopolitan character and a multicultural legacy.

At different periods of its history, Lebanon has come under the domination of foreign rulers, including Assyrians, Babylonians, Persians, Greeks, Romans, Arabs, Ottomans, and French. Although often conquered, the Lebanese take pride in their rebellions against despotic and repressive rulers. Moreover, despite foreign domination, Lebanon's mountainous terrain has provided it with a certain protective isolation, enabling it to survive with an identity all its own.

Its proximity to the sea has ensured that throughout its history Lebanon has held an important position as a trading center. This tradition of commerce began with the Phoenicians and continued through many centuries, remaining almost unaffected by foreign rule and the worst periods of internal strife.

Lebanon has an Arab culture colored by Western influences. Although Lebanon traditionally considered itself the only Christian country in the Arab world, by the 1970s the Muslim population was greater than that of the Christians, a situation that led to sectarian unrest and struggles for political and economic power.

Ancient Times
The Phoenicians

The area now known as Lebanon first appeared in recorded history around 3000 B.C. as a group of coastal cities and a heavily forested hinterland. It was inhabited by the Canaanites, a Semitic people, whom the Greeks called "Phoenicians" because of the purple (*phoinikies*) dye they sold. These early inhabitants referred to themselves as "men of Sidon" or the like, according to their city of origin, and called the country "Lebanon." Because of the nature of the country and its location, the Phoenicians turned to the sea, where they engaged in trade and navigation.

Each of the coastal cities was an independent kingdom noted for the special activities of its inhabitants. Tyre and Sidon were important maritime and trade centers; Gubla (later known as Byblos and now as Jubayl) and Berytus (present-day Beirut) were trade and religious centers. Gubla was the first Phoenician city to trade actively with Egypt and the pharaohs of the Old Kingdom (2686-2181 B.C.), exporting cedar, olive oil, and wine, while importing gold and other products from the Nile Valley.

Before the end of the seventeenth century B.C., Lebanese-Egyptian relations were interrupted when the Hyksos, a nomadic Semitic people, conquered Egypt. After about three decades of Hyksos rule (1600-1570 B.C.), Ahmose I (1570-45 B.C.), a Theban prince, launched the Egyptian liberation war. Opposition to the Hyksos increased, reaching a peak during the reign of the pharaoh Thutmose III (1490-36 B.C.), who invaded Syria, put an end to Hyksos domination, and incorporated Lebanon into the Egyptian Empire.

Toward the end of the fourteenth century B.C., the Egyptian Empire weakened, and Lebanon was able to regain its independence by the beginning of the twelfth century B.C. The subsequent three centuries were a period of prosperity and freedom from foreign control during which the earlier Phoenician invention of the alphabet facilitated communications and trade. The Phoenicians also excelled not only in producing textiles but also in carving ivory, in working with metal, and above all in making glass. Masters of the art of navigation, they founded colonies wherever they went in the Mediterranean Sea (specifically in Cyprus, Rhodes, Crete, and Carthage) and established trade routes to Europe and western Asia (see fig. 2). Furthermore, their ships circumnavigated Africa a thousand years before those of the Portuguese. These colonies and trade routes flourished until the invasion of the coastal areas by the Assyrians.

Assyrian Rule

Assyrian rule (875-608 B.C.) deprived the Phoenician cities of their independence and prosperity and brought repeated, unsuccessful rebellions. In the middle of the eighth century B.C., Tyre and Byblos rebelled, but the Assyrian ruler, Tiglath-Pileser, subdued the rebels and imposed heavy tributes. Oppression continued unabated, and Tyre rebelled again, this time against Sargon II (722-05 B.C.), who successfully besieged the city in 721 B.C. and punished its population. During the seventh century B.C., Sidon rebelled and was completely destroyed by Esarhaddon (681-68 B.C.), and its inhabitants were enslaved. Esarhaddon built a new city on Sidon's ruins. By the end of the seventh century B.C., the Assyrian Empire, weakened by the successive revolts, had been destroyed by Babylonia, a new Mesopotamian power.

Historical Setting

Babylonian Rule and the Persian Empire

Revolts in the Phoenician cities became more frequent under Babylonian rule (685-36 B.C.). Tyre rebelled again and for thirteen years resisted a siege by the troops of Nebuchadnezzar (587-74 B.C.). After this long siege, the city capitulated; its king was dethroned, and its citizens were enslaved.

The Achaemenids ended Babylonian rule when Cyrus, founder of the Persian Empire, captured Babylon in 539-38 B.C. and Phoenicia and its neighbors passed into Persian hands. Cambyses (529-22 B.C.), Cyrus's son and successor, continued his father's policy of conquest and in 529 B.C. became suzerain of Syria, Lebanon, and Egypt. The Phoenician navy supported Persia during the Greco-Persian War (490-49 B.C.). But when the Phoenicians were overburdened with heavy tributes imposed by the successors of Darius I (521-485 B.C.), revolts and rebellions resumed in the Lebanese coastal cities.

Rule of Alexander the Great

The Persian Empire eventually fell to Alexander the Great, king of Macedonia. He attacked Asia Minor, defeated the Persian troops in 333 B.C., and advanced toward the Lebanese coast. Initially the Phoenician cities made no attempt to resist, and they recognized his suzerainty. However, when Alexander tried to offer a sacrifice to Melkurt, Tyre's god, the city resisted. Alexander besieged Tyre in retaliation in early 332 B.C. After six months of resistance, the city fell, and its people were sold into slavery. Despite his early death in 323 B.C., Alexander's conquest of the eastern Mediterranean Basin left a Greek imprint on the area. The Phoenicians, being a cosmopolitan people amenable to outside influences, adopted aspects of Greek civilization with ease.

The Seleucid Dynasty

After Alexander's death, his empire was divided among his Macedonian generals. The eastern part—Phoenicia, Asia Minor, northern Syria, and Mesopotamia—fell to Seleucus I, founder of the Seleucid dynasty. The southern part of Syria and Egypt fell to Ptolemy, and the European part, including Macedonia, to Antigonus I. This settlement, however, failed to bring peace because Seleucus I and Ptolemy clashed repeatedly in the course of their ambitious efforts to share in Phoenician prosperity. A final victory of the Seleucids ended a forty-year period of conflict.

The last century of Seleucid rule was marked by disorder and dynastic struggles. These ended in 64 B.C., when the Roman

Lebanon: A Country Study

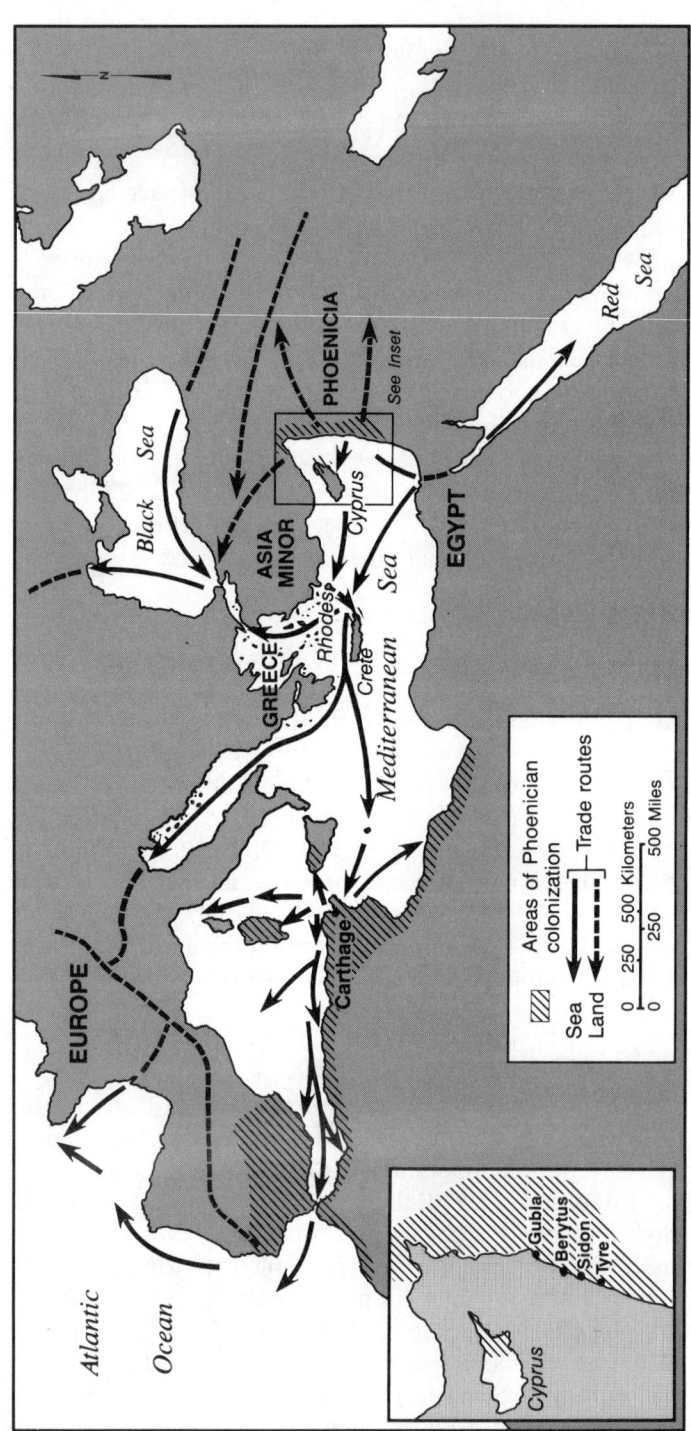

Figure 2. Phoenician Colonization and Trade Routes

general Pompey added Syria and Lebanon to the Roman Empire. Economic and intellectual activities flourished in Lebanon during the Pax Romana. The inhabitants of the principal Phoenician cities of Byblos, Sidon, and Tyre were granted Roman citizenship. These cities were centers of the pottery, glass, and purple dye industries; their harbors also served as warehouses for products imported from Syria, Persia, and India. They exported cedar, perfume, jewelry, wine, and fruit to Rome. Economic prosperity led to a revival in construction and urban development; temples and palaces were built throughout the country, as well as paved roads that linked the cities.

Upon the death of Theodosius I in A.D. 395, the empire was divided in two: the eastern or Byzantine part with its capital at Constantinople, and the western part with its capital at Rome. Under the Byzantine Empire, intellectual and economic activities in Beirut, Tyre, and Sidon continued to flourish for more than a century. However, in the sixth century a series of earthquakes demolished the temples of Baalbek and destroyed the city of Beirut, leveling its famous law school and killing nearly 30,000 inhabitants. To these natural disasters were added the abuses and corruptions prevailing at that time in the empire. Heavy tributes and religious dissension produced disorder and confusion. Furthermore, the ecumenical councils of the fifth and sixth centuries A.D. were unsuccessful in settling religious disagreements. This turbulent period weakened the empire and made it easy prey to the newly converted Muslim Arabs of the Arabian Peninsula.

The Arab Period
The Arab Conquest, 634-36

The followers of the Prophet Muhammad, the founder of Islam, embarked on a movement to establish their religious and civil control throughout the eastern Mediterranean from their base in the Arabian Peninsula. Their determination to conquer other lands resulted both from economic necessity and from religious beliefs, which imbued them with contempt for death.

Calling for a jihad (holy war) against non-Muslims, the Prophet's successor, Caliph Abu Bakr (632-34), brought Islam to the area surrounding Lebanon. Dividing his forces into three groups, he ordered one to move in the direction of Palestine, one toward Damascus, and one toward the Jordan River. The Arab groups under General Khalid ibn al Walid defeated the forces from Constantinople in 636 at the Battle of Yarmuk in northwestern Jordan.

The Umayyads, 660-750

After the Battle of Yarmuk, Caliph Umar appointed the Arab Muawiyah, founder of the Umayyad dynasty, as governor of Syria, an area that included present-day Lebanon. Muawiyah garrisoned troops on the Lebanese coast and had the Lebanese shipbuilders help him construct a navy to resist any potential Byzantine attack. He also stopped raids by the Marada, a powerful people who had settled in the Lebanese mountains and who were used by the Byzantine rulers to prevent any Arab invasion that would threaten the Byzantine Empire. Concerned with consolidating his authority in Arabia and Iraq, Muawiyah negotiated an agreement in 667 with Constantine IV, the Byzantine emperor, whereby he agreed to pay Constantine an annual tribute in return for the cessation of Marada incursions. During this period some of the Arab tribes settled in the Lebanese and Syrian coastal areas.

The Abbasids, 750-1258

The Abbasids, founded by the Arab Abul Abbas, replaced the Umayyads in early 750. They treated Lebanon and Syria as conquered countries, and their harshness led to several revolts, including an abortive rebellion of Lebanese mountaineers in 759. By the end of the tenth century, the amir of Tyre proclaimed his independence from the Abbasids and coined money in his own name. However, his rule was terminated by the Fatimids of Egypt, an independent Arab Muslim dynasty.

Impact of Arab Rule

Arab rule under the Umayyads and Abbasids had a profound impact on the eastern Mediterranean area and, to a great degree, was responsible for the composition of modern Lebanese society. It was during this period that Lebanon became a refuge for various ethnic and religious groups. The presence of these diverse, cohesive groups led to the eventual emergence of the Lebanese confessional (see Glossary) state, whereby different religious communities were represented in the government according to their numerical strength (see The Basis of Government, ch. 4).

The ancestors of the present-day Maronites (see Glossary) were among the Christian communities that settled in Lebanon during this period (see Christian Sects, ch. 2). To avoid feuds with other Christian sects in the area, these followers of Saint John Maron moved from the upper valley of the Orontes River and settled in the picturesque Qadisha Valley, located in the northern Lebanon Mountains, about twenty-five kilometers southeast of Tripoli.

A Roman temple in the mountain village of Bayt Miri
Courtesy Lebanese Information and Research Center (Magnin)

Lebanon: A Country Study

Lebanon also became the refuge for a small Christian group called Melchites, living in northern and central Lebanon. Influenced by the Greek Christian theology of Constantinople, they accepted the controversial decrees of the Council of Chalcedon, the fourth ecumenical council of the church held in 451. As a result of missionary activity by the Roman Catholic Church, some were later drawn away from this creed and became known as Greek Catholics because Greek is the language of their liturgy. They lived mainly in the central part of the Biqa Valley.

During the Arab era, still another religious faith found sanctuary in Lebanon. After Al Hakim (996–1021), the Fatimid caliph of Egypt, proclaimed himself an incarnation of God, two of his followers, Hamza and Darazi, formulated the dogmas for his cult. Darazi left Egypt and continued to preach these tenets after settling in southern Lebanon. His followers became known as Druzes (see Glossary); along with Christians and Muslims, they constitute major communities in modern Lebanon.

Under the Abbasids, philosophy, literature, and the sciences received great attention, especially during the caliphate of Harun ar Rashid and that of his son, Al Mamun. Lebanon made a notable contribution to this intellectual renaissance. The physician Rashid ad Din, the jurist Al Awazi, and the philosopher Qusta ibn Luqa were leaders in their respective disciplines. The country also enjoyed an economic boom in which the Lebanese harbors of Tyre and Tripoli were busy with shipping as the textile, ceramic, and glass industries prospered. Lebanese products were sought after not only in Arab countries but also throughout the Mediterranean Basin.

In general, Arab rulers were tolerant of Christians and Jews, both of whom were assessed special taxes and were exempted from military service. Later, under the Ottoman Empire, the practice developed of administering non-Muslim groups as separate communities called *millets*. In the late-1980s, this system continued; each religious community was organized under its own head and observed its own laws pertaining to matters such as divorce and inheritance (see The Judiciary, ch. 4).

The Crusades, 1095–1291

The occupation of the Christian holy places in Palestine and the destruction of the Holy Sepulcher by Caliph Al Hakim led to a series of eight campaigns, known as the Crusades, undertaken by Christians of western Europe to recover the Holy Land from the Muslims. The first Crusade was proclaimed by Pope Urban II in 1095 at the Council of Clermont-Ferrand in France. After taking

Historical Setting

Jerusalem, the Crusaders turned their attention to the Lebanese coast. Tripoli capitulated in 1109; Beirut and Sidon, in 1110. Tyre stubbornly resisted but finally capitulated in 1124 after a long siege.

Although they failed to establish a permanent presence, the Crusaders left their imprint on Lebanon. Among the conspicuous results of the Crusades, which ended with the fall of Acre in 1291, are the remains of many towers along the coast, ruins of castles on hills and mountain slopes, and numerous churches.

Of all the contacts established by the Crusaders with the peoples of the Middle East, those with the Maronites of Lebanon were among the most enduring. They acquainted the Maronites with European influences and made them more receptive to friendly approaches from Westerners. During this period the Maronites were brought into a union with the Holy See, a union that survived in the late 1980s. France was a major participant in the Crusades, and French interest in the region and its Christian population dates to this period.

Bitter conflicts among the various regional and ethnic groups in Lebanon and Syria characterized the thirteenth century. The Crusaders, who came from Europe, the Mongols, who came from the steppes of Central Asia, and the Mamluks, who came from Egypt, all sought to be masters in the area. In this hard and confused struggle for supremacy, victory came to the Mamluks.

The Mamluks, 1282–1516

The Mamluks were a combination of Turkoman slaves from the area east of the Caspian Sea and Circassian slaves from the Caucasus Mountains between the Black Sea and Caspian Sea. They were brought in by the Muslim Ayyubid sultans of Egypt to serve as their bodyguards. One of these slaves, Muez-Aibak, assassinated the Ayyubid sultan, Al Ashraf Musa, in 1252 and founded the Mamluk sultanate, which ruled Egypt and Syria for more than two centuries.

From the eleventh to the thirteenth century, the Shia (see Glossary) Muslims migrated from Syria, Iraq, and the Arabian Peninsula to the northern part of the Biqa Valley and to the Kasrawan Region in the mountains northeast of Beirut. They and the Druzes rebelled in 1291 while the Mamluks were busy fighting European Crusaders and Mongols, but after repelling the invaders, the Mamluks crushed the rebellion in 1308. To escape from repression and massacres by the Mamluks, the Shias abandoned Kasrawan and moved to southern Lebanon.

The Mamluks indirectly fostered relations between Europe and the Middle East even after the fall of the Byzantine Empire. The

Lebanon: A Country Study

Europeans, accustomed to luxury items from the Middle East, strongly desired both its raw materials and its manufactured products, and the people of the Middle East wished to exploit the lucrative European market. Beirut, favored by its geographical location, became the center of intense trading activity. Despite religious conflicts among the different communities in Lebanon, intellectual life flourished, and economic prosperity continued until Mamluk rule was ended by the Ottoman Turks.

Ottoman Rule, 1516–1916

The Ottoman Turks were a Central Asian people who had served as slaves and warriors under the Abbasids. Because of their courage and discipline they became the masters of the palace in Baghdad during the caliphate of Al Mutasim (833–42). The Ottoman sultan, Salim I (1516–20), after defeating the Persians, conquered the Mamluks. His troops, invading Syria, destroyed Mamluk resistance in 1516 at Marj Dabaq, north of Aleppo.

During the conflict between the Mamluks and the Ottomans, the amirs of Lebanon linked their fate to that of Ghazali, governor (pasha) of Damascus. He won the confidence of the Ottomans by fighting on their side at Marj Dabaq and, apparently pleased with the behavior of the Lebanese amirs, introduced them to Salim I when he entered Damascus. Salim I, moved by the eloquence of the Lebanese ruler Amir Fakhr ad Din I (1516–44), decided to grant the Lebanese amirs a semiautonomous status. The Ottomans, through two great Druze feudal families, the Maans and the Shihabs, ruled Lebanon until the middle of the nineteenth century. It was during Ottoman rule that the term *Greater Syria* was coined to designate the approximate area included in present-day Lebanon, Syria, Jordan, and Israel.

The Maans, 1120–1697

The Maan family, under orders from the governor of Damascus, came to Lebanon in 1120 to defend it against the invading Crusaders. They settled on the southwestern slopes of the Lebanon Mountains and soon adopted the Druze religion. Their authority began to rise with Fakhr ad Din I, who was permitted by Ottoman authorities to organize his own army, and reached its peak with Fakhr ad Din II (1570–1635).

Although Fakhr ad Din II's aspirations toward complete independence for Lebanon ended tragically, he greatly enhanced Lebanon's military and economic development. Noted for religious tolerance and suspected of being a Christian, Fakhr ad Din attempted to merge the country's different religious groups into one

Lebanese community. In an effort to attain complete independence for Lebanon, he concluded a secret agreement with Ferdinand I, duke of Tuscany in Italy, the two parties pledging to support each other against the Ottomans. Informed of this agreement, the Ottoman ruler in Constantinople reacted violently and ordered Ahmad al Hafiz, governor of Damascus, to attack Fakhr ad Din. Realizing his inability to cope with the regular army of Al Hafiz, the Lebanese ruler went to Tuscany in exile in 1613. He returned to Lebanon in 1618, after his good friend Muhammad Pasha became governor of Damascus.

Following his return from Tuscany, Fakhr ad Din, realizing the need for a strong and disciplined armed force, channeled his financial resources into building a regular army. This army proved itself in 1623, when Mustafa Pasha, the new governor of Damascus, underestimating the capabilities of the Lebanese army, engaged it in battle and was decisively defeated at Anjar in the Biqa Valley. Impressed by the victory of the Lebanese ruler, the sultan of Constantinople gave him the title of Sultan al Barr (Sultan of the Mountain).

In addition to building up the army, Fakhr ad Din, who became acquainted with Italian culture during his stay in Tuscany, initiated measures to modernize the country. After forming close ties with the dukes of Tuscany and Florence and establishing diplomatic relations with them, he brought in architects, irrigation engineers, and agricultural experts from Italy in an effort to promote prosperity in the country. He also strengthened Lebanon's strategic position by expanding its territory, building forts as far away as Palmyra in Syria, and gaining control of Palestine. Finally, the Ottoman sultan Murad IV of Constantinople, wanting to thwart Lebanon's progress toward complete independence, ordered Kutshuk, then governor of Damascus, to attack the Lebanese ruler. This time Fakhr ad Din was defeated, and he was executed in Constantinople in 1635. No significant Maan rulers succeeded Fakhr ad Din II.

The Shihabs, 1697–1842

The Shihabs succeeded the Maans in 1697. They originally lived in the Hawran region of southwestern Syria and settled in Wadi at Taim in southern Lebanon. The most prominent among them was Bashir II, who was much like his predecessor, Fakhr ad Din II. His ability as a statesman was first tested in 1799, when Napoleon besieged Acre, a well-fortified coastal city in Palestine, about forty kilometers south of Tyre. Both Napoleon and Al Jazzar, the governor of Acre, requested assistance from the Shihab leader; Bashir, however, remained neutral, declining to assist either combatant. Unable to conquer Acre, Napoleon returned to Egypt, and the death of Al Jazzar in 1804 removed Bashir's principal opponent in the area.

When Bashir II decided to break away from the Ottoman Empire, he allied himself with Muhammad Ali, the founder of modern Egypt, and assisted Muhammad Ali's son, Ibrahim Pasha, in another siege of Acre. This siege lasted seven months, the city falling on May 27, 1832. The Egyptian army, with assistance from Bashir's troops, also attacked and conquered Damascus on June 14, 1832.

Ibrahim Pasha and Bashir II at first ruled harshly and exacted high taxes. These practices led to several revolts and eventually ended their power. In May 1840, despite the efforts of Bashir, the Maronites and Druzes united their forces against the Egyptians. In addition, the principal European powers (Britain, Austria, Prussia, and Russia), opposing the pro-Egyptian policy of the French, signed the London Treaty with the Sublime Porte (the Ottoman ruler) on July 15, 1840. According to the terms of this treaty, Muhammad Ali was asked to leave Syria; when he rejected this request, Ottoman and British troops landed on the Lebanese coast on September 10, 1840. Faced with this combined force, Muhammad Ali retreated, and on October 14, 1840, Bashir II surrendered to the British and went into exile.

Religious Conflicts

On September 3, 1840, Bashir III was appointed amir of Mount Lebanon (see Glossary) by the Ottoman sultan. Geographically, Mount Lebanon represents the central part of present-day Lebanon, which historically has had a Christian majority. Greater Lebanon, on the other hand, created at the expense of Greater Syria, was formally constituted under the League of Nations mandate granted to France in 1920 and includes the Biqa Valley, Beirut, southern Lebanon (up to the border with Palestine/Israel), and northern Lebanon (up to the border with Syria). In practice, the terms *Lebanon* and *Mount Lebanon* tend to be used interchangeably by historians until the formal establishment of the Mandate.

Bitter conflicts between Christians and Druzes, which had been simmering under Ibrahim Pasha's rule, resurfaced under the new amir. Hence, the sultan deposed Bashir III on January 13, 1842, and appointed Umar Pasha as governor of Mount Lebanon. This appointment, however, created more problems than it solved. Representatives of the European powers proposed to the sultan that Lebanon be partitioned into Christian and Druze sections. On December 7, 1842, the sultan adopted the proposal and asked Assad Pasha, the governor (*wali*) of Beirut, to divide the region, then

The palace at Bayt ad Din, built by Bashir II in the early nineteenth century Courtesy Lebanese Information and Research Center

known as Mount Lebanon, into two districts: a northern district under a Christian deputy governor and a southern district under a Druze deputy governor. This arrangement came to be known as the Double Qaimaqamate. Both officials were to be responsible to the governor of Sidon, who resided in Beirut. The Beirut-Damascus highway was the dividing line between the two districts.

This partition of Lebanon proved to be a mistake. Animosities between the religious sects increased, nurtured by outside powers. The French, for example, supported the Christians, while the British supported the Druzes, and the Ottomans fomented strife to increase their control. Not surprisingly, these tensions led to conflict between Christians and Druzes as early as May 1845. Consequently, the European powers requested that the Ottoman sultan establish order in Lebanon, and he attempted to do so by establishing a *majlis* (council) in each of the districts. Each *majlis* was composed of members who represented the different religious communities and was intended to assist the deputy governor.

This system failed to keep order when the peasants of Kasrawan, overburdened by heavy taxes, rebelled against the feudal practices that prevailed in Mount Lebanon. In 1858 Tanyus Shahin, a Maronite peasant leader, demanded that the feudal class abolish its privileges. When this demand was refused, the poor peasants revolted against the shaykhs of Mount Lebanon, pillaging the shaykhs' land and burning their homes.

Foreign interests in Lebanon transformed these basically sociopolitical struggles into bitter religious conflicts, culminating in the 1860 massacre of about 10,000 Maronites, as well as Greek Catholics and Greek Orthodox, by the Druzes. These events offered France the opportunity to intervene; in an attempt to forestall French intervention, the Ottoman government stepped in to restore order.

On October 5, 1860, an international commission composed of France, Britain, Austria, Prussia, and the Ottoman Empire met to investigate the causes of the events of 1860 and to recommend a new administrative and judicial system for Lebanon that would prevent the recurrence of such events. The commission members agreed that the partition of Mount Lebanon in 1842 between Druzes and Christians had been responsible for the massacre. Hence, in the Statute of 1861 Mount Lebanon was separated from Syria and reunited under a non-Lebanese Christian *mutasarrif* (governor) appointed by the Ottoman sultan, with the approval of the European powers. The *mutasarrif* was to be assisted by an administrative council of twelve members from the various religious communities in Lebanon.

Direct Ottoman rule of Lebanon remained in effect until the end of World War I. This period was generally characterized by a laissez-faire policy and corruption. However, a number of governors, such as Daud Pasha and Naum Pasha, ruled the country efficiently and conscientiously.

Restricted mainly to the mountains by the *mutasarrifiyah* (district governed by a *mutasarrif*) arrangement and unable to make a living, many Lebanese Christians emigrated to Egypt and other parts of Africa and to North America, South America, and East Asia. Remittances from these Lebanese emigrants to their relatives in Lebanon have continued to supplement the Lebanese economy to this day.

In addition to being a center of commercial and religious activity, Lebanon became an intellectual center in the second half of the nineteenth century. Foreign missionaries established schools throughout the country, with Beirut as the center of this renaissance. The American University of Beirut was founded in 1866, followed by the French St. Joseph's University in 1875 (see Education, ch. 2). An intellectual guild that was formed at the same time gave new life to Arabic literature, which had stagnated under the Ottoman Empire. This new intellectual era was also marked by the appearance of numerous publications and by a highly prolific press.

The period was also marked by increased political activity. The harsh rule of Abdul Hamid II (1876–1909) prompted the Arab nationalists, both Christians and Muslims, in Beirut and Damascus to organize into clandestine political groups and parties. The Lebanese, however, had difficulties in deciding the best political course to advocate. Many Lebanese Christians were apprehensive of Turkish pan-Islamic policies, fearing a repetition of the 1860 massacres. Some, especially the Maronites, began to contemplate secession rather than the reform of the Ottoman Empire. Others, particularly the Greek Orthodox, advocated an independent Syria with Lebanon as a separate province within it, so as to avoid Maronite rule. A number of Lebanese Muslims, on the other hand, sought not to liberalize the Ottoman regime but to maintain it, as Sunni (see Glossary) Muslims particularly liked to be identified with the caliphate. The Shias and Druzes, however, fearing minority status in a Turkish state, tended to favor an independent Lebanon or a continuation of the status quo.

Originally the Arab reformist groups hoped their nationalist aims would be supported by the Young Turks, who had staged a revolution in 1908–1909. Unfortunately, after seizing power, the Young Turks became increasingly repressive and nationalistic. They abandoned many of their liberal policies because of domestic opposition and Turkey's engagement in foreign wars between 1911 and 1913. Thus, the Arab nationalists could not count on the support of the Young Turks and instead were faced with opposition by the Turkish government.

World War I and the French Mandate, 1914–41
World War I

The outbreak of World War I in August 1914 brought Lebanon further problems, as Turkey allied itself with Germany and Austria-Hungary. The Turkish government abolished Lebanon's semiautonomous status and appointed Jamal Pasha, then minister of the navy, as the commander in chief of the Turkish forces in Syria, with discretionary powers. Known for his harshness, he militarily occupied Lebanon and replaced the Armenian *mutasarrif*, Ohannes Pasha, with a Turk, Munif Pasha.

In February 1915, frustrated by his unsuccessful attack on the British forces protecting the Suez Canal, Jamal Pasha initiated a blockade of the entire eastern Mediterranean coast to prevent supplies from reaching his enemies and indirectly caused thousands of deaths from widespread famine and plagues. Lebanon suffered as much as, or more than, any other Ottoman province. The blockade deprived the country of its tourists and summer visitors, and remittances from relatives and friends were lost or delayed for months. The Turkish Army cut down trees for wood to fuel trains or for military purposes. In 1916 Turkish authorities publicly executed twenty-one Syrians and Lebanese in Damascus and Beirut, respectively, for alleged anti-Turkish activities. The date, May 6, is commemorated annually in both countries as Martyrs' Day, and the site in Beirut has come to be known as Martyrs' Square.

Relief came, however, in September 1918 when the British general Edmund Allenby and Faysal I, son of Sharif Husayn of Mecca, moved into Palestine with British and Arab forces, thus opening the way for the occupation of Syria and Lebanon. At the San Remo Conference held in Italy in April 1920, the Allies gave France a mandate over Greater Syria. France then appointed General Henri Gouraud to implement the mandate provisions.

The Mandate Period

On September 1, 1920, General Gouraud proclaimed the establishment of Greater Lebanon with its present boundaries and with Beirut as its capital. The first Lebanese constitution was promulgated on May 23, 1926, and subsequently was amended several times; it was still in effect as of late 1987. Modeled after that of the French Third Republic, it provided for a unicameral parliament called the Chamber of Deputies, a president, and a Council of Ministers, or cabinet. The president was to be elected by the Chamber of Deputies for one six-year term and could not be reelected until a six-year period had elapsed; deputies were to be popularly elected along confessional lines. The first and only complete census that had been held in Lebanon as of 1987 took place in 1932 and resulted in the custom of selecting major political officers according to the proportion of the principal sects in the population (see The Basis of Government, ch. 4). Thus, the president was to be a Maronite Christian, the prime minister a Sunni Muslim, and the speaker of the Chamber of Deputies a Shia Muslim. Theoretically, the Chamber of Deputies performed the legislative function, but in fact bills were prepared by the executive and submitted to the Chamber of Deputies, which passed them virtually without exception. Under the Constitution, the French high commissioner still exercised supreme power, an arrangement that initially brought objections from the Lebanese nationalists. Nevertheless, Charles Dabbas, a Greek Orthodox, was elected the first president of Lebanon three days after the adoption of the Constitution.

At the end of Dabbas's first term in 1932, Bishara al Khuri (also seen as Khoury) and Emile Iddi (also seen as Edde) competed for the office of president, thus dividing the Chamber of Deputies. To break the deadlock, some deputies suggested Shaykh Muhammad al Jisr, who was chairman of the Council of Ministers and the Muslim leader of Tripoli, as a compromise candidate. However, French high commissioner Henri Ponsot suspended the Constitution on May 9, 1932, and extended the term of Dabbas for one year; in this way he prevented the election of a Muslim as president. Dissatisfied with Ponsot's conduct, the French authorities replaced him with Comte Damien de Martel, who, on January 30, 1934, appointed Habib as Saad as president for a one-year term (later extended for an additional year).

Emile Iddi was elected president on January 30, 1936. A year later, he partially reestablished the Constitution of 1926 and proceeded to hold elections for the Chamber of Deputies. However, the Constitution was again suspended by the French high commissioner in September 1939, at the outbreak of World War II.

World War II and Independence, 1939-41

After the Vichy government assumed power in France in 1940, General Henri-Fernand Dentz was appointed high commissioner of Lebanon. This appointment led to Iddi's resignation on April 4, 1941. Five days later, Dentz appointed Alfred Naqqash (also seen as Naccache or Naccash) as head of state. The Vichy government's control ended a few months later when its forces were unable to repel the advance of French and British troops into Lebanon and Syria. An armistice was signed in Acre on July 14, 1941.

After signing the Acre Armistice, General Charles de Gaulle visited Lebanon, officially ending Vichy control. Lebanese national leaders took the opportunity to ask de Gaulle to end the French Mandate and unconditionally recognize Lebanon's independence. As a result of national and international pressure, on November 26, 1941, General Georges Catroux, delegate general under de Gaulle, proclaimed the independence of Lebanon in the name of his government. The United States, Britain, the Soviet Union, the Arab states, and certain Asian countries recognized this independence, and some of them exchanged ambassadors with Beirut. However, even though the French technically recognized Lebanon's independence, they continued to exercise authority.

General elections were held, and on September 21, 1943, the new Chamber of Deputies elected Bishara al Khuri as president. He appointed Riyad as Sulh (also seen as Solh) as prime minister and asked him to form the first government of independent Lebanon. On November 8, 1943, the Chamber of Deputies amended the Constitution, abolishing the articles that referred to the Mandate and modifying those that specified the powers of the high commissioner, thus unilaterally ending the Mandate. The French authorities responded by arresting a number of prominent Lebanese politicians, including the president, the prime minister, and other cabinet members, and exiling them to the Castle of Rashayya (located about sixty-five kilometers east of Sidon). This action united the Christian and Muslim leaders in their determination to get rid of the French. France, finally yielding to mounting internal pressure and to the influence of Britain, the United States, and the Arab countries, released the prisoners at Rashayya on November 22, 1943; since then, this day has been celebrated as Independence Day.

The ending of the French Mandate left Lebanon a mixed legacy. When the Mandate began, Lebanon was still suffering from the religious conflicts of the 1860s and from World War I. The French authorities were concerned not only with maintaining control over the country but also with rebuilding the Lebanese economy and social systems. They repaired and enlarged the harbor of Beirut and developed a network of roads linking the major cities. They also began to develop a governmental structure that included new administrative and judicial systems and a new civil code. They improved the education system, agriculture, public health, and the standard of living. Concurrently, however, they linked the Lebanese currency to the depreciating French franc, tying the Lebanese economy to that of France. This action had a negative impact on Lebanon. Another negative effect of the Mandate was the place given to French as a language of instruction, a move that favored Christians at the expense of Muslims.

The foundations of the new Lebanese state were established in 1943 by an unwritten agreement between the two most prominent Christian and Muslim leaders, Khuri and Sulh. The contents of this agreement, later known as the National Pact or National Covenant (al Mithaq al Watani), were approved and supported by their followers.

The National Pact laid down four principles. First, Lebanon was to be a completely independent state. The Christian communities were to cease identifying with the West; in return, the Muslim communities were to protect the independence of Lebanon and prevent its merger with any Arab state. Second, although Lebanon is an Arab country with Arabic as its official language, it could not cut off its spiritual and intellectual ties with the West, which had helped it attain such a notable degree of progress. Third, Lebanon, as a member of the family of Arab states, should cooperate with the other Arab states, and in case of conflict among them, it should not side with one state against another. Fourth, public offices should be distributed proportionally among the recognized religious groups, but in technical positions preference should be given to competence without regard to confessional considerations. Moreover, the three top government positions should be distributed as follows: the president of the republic should be a Maronite; the prime minister, a Sunni Muslim; and the speaker of the Chamber of Deputies, a Shia Muslim. The ratio of deputies was to be six Christians to five Muslims.

From the beginning, the balance provided for in the National Pact was fragile. Many observers believed that any serious internal or external pressure might threaten the stability of the Lebanese political system, as was to happen in 1975.

Lebanon became a member of the League of Arab States (Arab League) on March 22, 1945. It also participated in the San Francisco Conference of the United Nations (UN) and became a member in 1945. On December 31, 1946, French troops were completely withdrawn from the country, with the signing of the Franco-Lebanese Treaty.

Independent Lebanon, 1943-76

The history of Lebanon during the 1943-76 period was dominated by prominent family networks and patron-client relationships. Each sectarian community had its prominent family: the Khuris, Shamuns, Shihabs, Franjiyahs, and Jumayyils for the Maronites; the Sulhs, Karamis, and Yafis for the Sunnis; the Jumblatts, Yazbaks, and Arslans for the Druzes; and the Asads and Hamadahs for the Shias.

The Khuri Era, 1943-52

Lebanon's first president after independence was Bishara al Khuri, elected in 1943 for a six-year term; reelected in 1949 for a second term, he became increasingly imperial in his actions. According to his opponents, his regime was characterized by a narrow political structure supported by a strictly sectarian framework, and it did little to improve the economy.

In June 1952 an organization called the Social National Front (SNF) was formed by nine deputies led by Kamal Jumblatt (also seen as Junblatt), head of the Progressive Socialist Party; Camille Shamun (also seen as Chamoun), former ambassador to Britain; Emile Bustani, a self-made millionaire businessman; and other prominent personalities. This front dedicated itself to radical reform, demanding that the authorities end sectarianism and eradicate all abuses in the governmental system. The SNF founders were encouraged by people claiming to be dissatisfied with the favoritism and corruption thriving under the Khuri regime.

On May 17, 1952, the front held a meeting at Dayr al Qamar, Shamun's native town. The meeting was attended by about 50,000 people and turned into a mass rally. The speakers criticized the regime and threatened rebellion if the president did not resign. On July 23 the Phalange Party (see Glossary), led by Pierre Jumayyil (also seen as Gemayel), also voiced its discontent with the regime. On September 11 the SNF called for a general strike to force the president to resign; the appeal brought all activities in the major cities to a standstill. This general strike is sometimes referred to as the "Rosewater Revolution" because of its nonviolence. President Khuri appealed to General Fuad Shihab (also seen as Chehab) the army chief of staff, to end the strike. However, Shihab refused to become involved in what he considered a political matter, and on September 18, Khuri finally resigned.

The Shamun Era, 1952-58

On September 23, 1952, the Chamber of Deputies elected Camille Shamun to succeed Khuri. In the spring of 1953, relations between President Shamun and Jumblatt deteriorated as Jumblatt criticized Shamun for accommodating himself to the traditional pattern of Lebanese politics and for toning down the radical ideals that had led to the change of government in 1952. The balance between religious communities, provided for in the National Pact, was precariously maintained, and undercurrents of hostility were discernible. The Muslim community criticized the regime in which Christians, alleging their numerical superiority, occupied the highest offices in the state and filled a disproportionate number of civil service positions. Accordingly, the Muslims asked for a census, which they were confident would prove their numerical superiority. The Christians refused unless the census were to include Lebanese emigrants who were mainly Christians, and they argued that Christians contributed 80 percent of the tax revenue.

The 1956-58 period brought many pressures to bear on Lebanon. First, there was general unrest in the Arab world following the Suez Canal crisis and the abortive attacks on Egypt by Britain, France, and Israel. More specifically, however, political struggles occurred in two fields: rivalry among Lebanese political leaders who were linked to religious or clan groups and their followers; and the ideological struggle causing polarization between Lebanese nationalism and growing pan-Arabism.

President Gamal Abdul Nasser of Egypt became the symbol of pan-Arabism after the 1956 Suez crisis and the 1958 merger of Egypt with Syria to form the United Arab Republic. He had great influence on Lebanese Muslims, who looked to him for inspiration. In this period of unrest, the Lebanese authorities, most of whom were Christians, insisted on two things: maintaining the country's autonomy and cooperating with the West. Christians considered their friendly relations with the West as the only guarantee of Lebanon's independence. President Shamun's refusal to respond favorably to pan-Arab pressures was in direct opposition to the stand of several prominent Sunni leaders, who devoted themselves to Nasser and the pan-Arab cause.

In 1957 the question of the reelection of Shamun was added to these problems of ideological cleavage. In order to be reelected, the president needed to have the Constitution amended to permit a president to succeed himself. A constitutional amendment required a two-thirds vote by the Chamber of Deputies, so Shamun and his followers had to obtain a majority in the May–June 1957 elections.

Shamun's followers did obtain a solid majority in the elections, which the opposition considered "rigged," with the result that some non-Christian leaders with pan-Arab sympathies were not elected. Deprived of a legal platform from which to voice their political opinions, they sought to express them by extralegal means. The conflict between Shamun and the pan-Arab opposition gained in intensity when Syria merged with Egypt. Pro-Nasser demonstrations grew in number and in violence until a full-scale rebellion was underway. The unrest was intensified by the assassination of Nassib Matni, the Maronite anti-Shamun editor of *At Talagraph*, a daily newspaper known for its outspoken pan-Arabism. The revolt almost became a religious conflict between Christians and Muslims.

This state of turmoil increased when, in the early hours of July 14, 1958, a revolution overthrew the monarchy in Iraq and the entire royal family was killed. In Lebanon jubilation prevailed in areas where anti-Shamun sentiment predominated, with radio stations announcing that the Shamun regime would be next. Shamun, realizing the gravity of his situation, summoned the ambassadors of the United States, Britain, and France on the morning of July 14. He requested immediate assistance, insisting that the independence of Lebanon was in jeopardy.

Furthermore, he invoked the terms of the Eisenhower Doctrine, which Lebanon had signed the year before. According to its terms, the United States would "use armed forces to assist any [Middle East] nation . . . requesting assistance against armed aggression from any country controlled by international communism." Arguing that Lebanese Muslims were being helped by Syria, which had received arms from the Soviet Union, Shamun appealed for United States military intervention. The United States responded, in large measure because of concern over the situation in Iraq and the wish to reassure its allies, such as Iran and Turkey, that the United States could act. United States forces began arriving in Lebanon by midafternoon of July 15 and played a symbolic rather than an active role. In the course of the 1958 Civil War, in which United States forces were not involved, between 2,000 and 4,000 casualties occurred, primarily in the Muslim areas of Beirut and in Tripoli. At the end of the crisis, the Chamber of Deputies elected General Fuad Shihab, then commander in chief of the Lebanese Army, to serve as president.

The Rise of Shihabism, 1958-64

President Shihab, having cultivated nonpartisanship during the 1958 Civil War, enjoyed considerable support from the various political factions. However, his initial appointment to the cabinet of a large number of Muslim leaders, such as Rashid Karami, Sunni leader from Tripoli, whom he asked to form a reconciliation government, led to sharp reactions by the Phalange Party. Shihab was obliged to reapportion the balance in the cabinet on the basis of "no victors, no vanquished." He instituted electoral reform and increased the membership of the Chamber of Deputies from sixty-six to ninety-nine, thus enabling leaders of the various factions in the civil war to become active members of the legislature. He was determined to observe the terms of the National Pact and to have the government serve Christian and Muslim groups equally. This policy, combined with Shihab's concept of an enlightened president as one who strengthened the role of the executive and the bureaucracy at the expense of the *zuama* (sing., *zaim*—see Glossary), or traditional leaders, was later referred to as "Shihabism." Shihab also concentrated on improving Lebanon's infrastructure, developing an extensive road system, and providing running water and electricity to remote villages. Hospitals and dispensaries were built in many rural areas, although there was difficulty in staffing them.

In foreign affairs, one of Shihab's first acts was to ask the United States to withdraw its troops from Lebanon starting on September 27, 1958, with the withdrawal to be completed by the end of October. He pursued a neutral foreign policy with the object of maintaining good relations with Arab countries as well as the West. Many observers agree that his regime brought stability and economic development to Lebanon and that it demonstrated the need for compromise if the Lebanese confessional system of government were to work. At the same time, however, it showed that in times of crisis the only solution might be to call on an outside power to restore equilibrium.

The Hilu Era, 1964-70

Shihab was succeeded by Charles Hilu (also seen as Helou), who was selected president by the Chamber of Deputies on August 18, 1964. President Hilu, a journalist, jurist, and diplomat, was known for his high moral and intellectual qualities. Despite his efforts to promote Lebanon's development, during his tenure the Arab-Israeli June 1967 War, in which Lebanon did not participate, had serious repercussions on all aspects of Lebanese life. The most significant impact was the increased role of Palestinian guerrilla groups in the struggle against Israel and the groups' use of Lebanon as a base of operations. The Palestinian presence impinged on the effort to maintain the confessional balance, for it tended to pit Muslim Lebanese against Christian Lebanese. On the whole, the former group initially viewed the Palestinian guerrillas as upholding a sacred cause that deserved full-scale support. The latter, who strongly favored Lebanese independence, tended to be more concerned with the effects of unrestricted guerrilla activity on Lebanese security and development. They feared both Israeli reprisals and the general undermining of governmental authority within Lebanon if curbs were not imposed on the guerrillas. The Hilu government did its best to satisfy the conflicting demands made on it by guerrillas, Arab governments, Israel, and the internal political and religious elements.

The Chamber of Deputies elections of 1968 and the subsequent disagreements over forming a cabinet had already receded into the background when Israel launched a raid on Beirut International Airport on December 28, 1968. This attack set the stage for the government crises that marked Lebanese life for the next five years, until the Arab-Israeli October 1973 War. Moreover, it highlighted the delicate balance of internal political forces in Lebanon and the connection between that balance and the extent to which Lebanese identified with the Arab position in the Arab-Israeli conflict.

Periodic clashes between the guerrillas and the Lebanese Army continued throughout the late spring, summer, and fall of 1969. In the late summer of 1969, several guerrilla groups moved to new bases, better located for attacks against Israel. Israel regularly raided these bases in reprisal for guerrilla raids on its territory. In October the Lebanese Army attacked some guerrilla camps in order to restrict their activity, an action that led to several demonstrations in support of the guerrillas.

On November 2, 1969, the Lebanese commander in chief and Yasir Arafat, the head of Al Fatah, the leading faction within the Palestine Liberation Organization (PLO), agreed in Cairo to a cease-fire. The secret Cairo Agreement set limits on Palestinian guerrilla operations in Lebanon and helped to restore calm.

The Lebanese government's efforts to curtail guerrilla activities continued through late 1969 and 1970. Migration from southern Lebanon, particularly of large numbers of Shias, increased, primarily because of inadequate security against Israeli shelling and raids along with lack of economic opportunity. In Beirut the migrants, estimated to exceed 30,000, often could not find adequate shelter and met with indifference on the part of predominantly Christian military leaders. These problems resulted in occasional clashes between the migrants and government forces.

To deal with the problems caused by the fighting in the south, a governmental committee was formed, and funds were allocated for Al Janub Province (see fig. 1). On January 12, 1970, the government announced a plan to arm and train Lebanese civilians in southern villages and to fortify the villages against Israeli raids. This action was apparently the result of an intentional government policy to avoid committing the army to action in southern Lebanon, presumably for fear of polarizing the religious groups that composed the army—mainly Christian Maronite officers and Muslim or Druze enlisted personnel. But the problem was exacerbated by increasing activity by Palestinian guerrillas operating from southern Lebanon into Israel and by Israeli reprisals.

On January 7, 1970, General Emil Bustani, the army commander, was replaced by General Jean Njaim, suggesting a government effort to take a harder line toward the guerrillas and to defend southern Lebanon more actively. Clashes between the army and the guerrillas recurred, but southern Lebanese villagers continued to protest governmental inaction. After several bloody clashes between the guerrillas and the Lebanese Army and a nationwide general strike in May 1970, the government approved additional appropriations for the defense of the south, and it pressed the guerrillas to abide by the Cairo Agreement and to limit their activity.

The Franjiyah Era, 1970-76

By the summer of 1970, attention turned to the upcoming presidential election of August 17. Sulayman Franjiyah (also seen as Franjieh), who had the backing of the National Bloc Party and the center bloc in the Chamber of Deputies, was elected president

*President
Sulayman Franjiyah
Courtesy Mokhless Al-Hariri
The Georgetown
Design Group, Inc.*

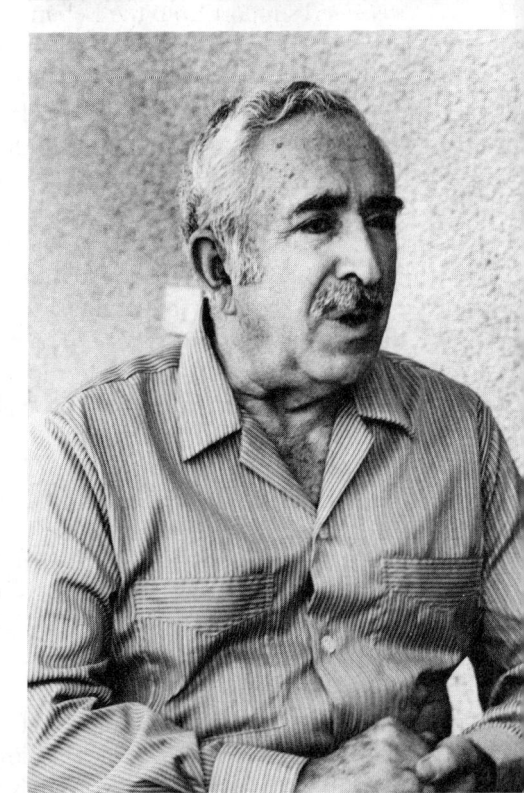

*One of Franjiyah's
prime ministers,
Rashid Karami
Courtesy Mokhless Al-Hariri
The Georgetown
Design Group, Inc.*

by one vote over Ilyas Sarkis, head of the Central Bank, who had the support of the Shihabists (those favoring a strong executive with ties to the military). Franjiyah was more conservative than his predecessor, Hilu. A Maronite leader from northern Lebanon, he had a regional power base resulting from clan allegiance and a private militia. Although Franjiyah had a parochial outlook reflecting a lack of national and international experience, he was the choice of such persons as Kamal Jumblatt, who wanted a weaker president than Sarkis would have been. Franjiyah assumed office on September 23, 1970, and in the first few months of his term the general political atmosphere improved.

The expulsion of large numbers of Palestinian guerrillas from Jordan in late 1970 and 1971, as a result of severe clashes between the Jordanian army and the PLO, had serious repercussions for Lebanon, however. Many of the guerrillas entered Lebanon, seeing it as the most suitable base for launching raids against Israel. The guerrillas tended to ally themselves with existing leftist Lebanese organizations or to form various new leftist groups that received support from the Lebanese Muslim community and caused further splintering in the Lebanese body politic. Clashes between the Palestinians and Lebanese right-wing groups, as well as demonstrations on behalf of the guerrillas, occurred during the latter half of 1971. PLO head Arafat held discussions with leading Lebanese government figures, who sought to establish acceptable limits of guerrilla activity in Lebanon under the 1969 Cairo Agreement.

The Chamber of Deputies elections in April 1972 also were accompanied by violence. The high rate of inflation and unemployment, as well as guerrilla actions and retaliations, occasioned demonstrations, and the government declared martial law in some areas. The government attempted to quiet the unrest by taking legal action against the protesters, by initiating new social and economic programs, and by negotiating with the guerrilla groups. However, the pattern of guerrilla infiltration followed by Israeli counterattacks continued throughout the Franjiyah era. Israel retaliated for any incursion by guerrillas into Israeli territory and for any action anywhere against Israeli nationals. An Israeli incursion into southern Lebanon, for example, was made in retaliation for the massacre of Israeli Olympic athletes in Munich in September 1972. Of particular significance was an Israeli commando raid on Beirut on April 10, 1973, in which three leaders of the Palestinian Resistance Movement were assassinated. The army's inaction brought the immediate resignation of Prime Minister Saib Salam, a Sunni Muslim leader from Beirut.

Historical Setting

In May armed clashes between the army and the guerrillas in Beirut spread to other parts of the country, resulting in the arrival of guerrilla reinforcements from Syria, the declaration of martial law, and a new secret agreement limiting guerrilla activity.

The October 1973 War overshadowed disagreements about the role of the guerrillas in Lebanon. Despite Lebanon's policy of noninvolvement, the war deeply affected the country's subsequent history. As the PLO's military influence in the south grew, so too did the disaffection of the Shia community that lived there, which was exposed to varying degrees of unsympathetic Lebanese control, indifferent or antipathetic PLO attitudes, and hostile Israeli actions. The Franjiyah government proved less and less able to deal with these rising tensions, and by the onset of the Civil War in April 1975, political fragmentation was accelerating.

The Civil War, 1975-76

The spark that ignited the war occurred in Beirut on April 13, 1975, when gunmen killed four Phalangists during an attempt on Pierre Jumayyil's life. Perhaps believing the assassins to have been Palestinian, the Phalangists retaliated later that day by attacking a bus carrying Palestinian passengers across a Christian neighborhood, killing about twenty-six of the occupants. The next day fighting erupted in earnest, with Phalangists pitted against Palestinian militiamen (thought by some observers to be from the Popular Front for the Liberation of Palestine). The confessional layout of Beirut's various quarters facilitated random killing. Most Beirutis stayed inside their homes during these early days of battle, and few imagined that the street fighting they were witnessing was the beginning of a war that was to devastate their city and divide the country.

Despite the urgent need to control the fighting, the political machinery of the government became paralyzed over the next few months. The inadequacies of the political system, which the 1943 National Pact had only papered over temporarily, reappeared more clearly than ever. For many observers, at the bottom of the conflict was the issue of confessionalism (see Glossary) out of balance—of a minority, specifically the Maronites, refusing to share power and economic opportunity with the Muslim majority.

The government could not act effectively because leaders were unable to agree on whether or not to use the army to stop the bloodletting. When Jumblatt and his leftist supporters tried to isolate the Phalangists politically, other Christian sects rallied to Jumayyil's camp, creating a further rift. Consequently, in May Prime Minister Rashid as Sulh and his cabinet resigned, and a new government was formed under Rashid Karami. Although there were many calls for his resignation, President Franjiyah steadfastly retained his office.

As various other groups took sides, the fighting spread to other areas of the country, forcing residents in towns with mixed sectarian populations to seek safety in regions where their sect was dominant. Even so, the militias became embroiled in a pattern of attack followed by retaliation, including acts against uninvolved civilians.

Although the two warring factions were often characterized as Christian versus Muslim, their individual composition was far more complex. Those in favor of maintaining the status quo came to be known as the Lebanese Front. The groups included primarily the Maronite militias of the Jumayyil, Shamun, and Franjiyah clans, often led by the sons of *zuama*. Also in this camp were various militias of Maronite religious orders. The side seeking change, usually referred to as the Lebanese National Movement, was far less cohesive and organized. For the most part it was led by Kamal Jumblatt and included a variety of militias from leftist organizations and guerrillas from rejectionist Palestinian (non-mainstream PLO) organizations (see Appendix B).

By the end of 1975, no side held a decisive military advantage, but it was generally acknowledged that the Lebanese Front had done less well than expected against the disorganized Lebanese National Movement. The political hierarchy, composed of the old *zuama* and politicians, still was incapable of maintaining peace, except for occasional, short-lived cease-fires. Reform was discussed, but little headway was made toward any significant improvements. Syria, which was deeply concerned about the flow of events in Lebanon, also proved powerless to enforce calm through diplomatic means. And, most ominous of all, the Lebanese Army, which generally had stayed out of the strife, began to show signs of factionalizing and threatened to bring its heavy weaponry to bear on the conflict.

Syrian diplomatic involvement grew during 1976, but it had little success in restoring order in the first half of the year. In January it organized a cease-fire and set up the High Military Committee, through which it negotiated with all sides. These negotiations, however, were complicated by other events, especially Lebanese Front-Palestinian confrontations. That month the Lebanese Front began a siege of Tall Zatar, a densely populated Palestinian refugee camp in East Beirut; the Lebanese Front also overran and leveled Karantina, a Muslim quarter in East Beirut. These actions finally brought the main forces of the PLO, the Palestine Liberation Army (PLA), into the battle. Together, the PLA and the

Lebanese National Movement took the town of Ad Damur, a Shamun stronghold about seventeen kilometers south of Beirut.

In spite of these setbacks, through Syria's good offices compromises were achieved. On February 14, 1976, in what was considered a political breakthrough, Syria helped negotiate a seventeen-point reform program known as the Constitutional Document. Yet by March this progress was derailed by the disintegration of the Lebanese Army. In that month dissident Muslim troops, led by Lieutenant Ahmad Khatib, mutinied, creating the Lebanese Arab Army. Joining the Lebanese National Movement, they made significant penetrations into Christian-held Beirut and launched an attack on the presidential palace, forcing Franjiyah to flee to Mount Lebanon.

Continuing its search for a domestic political settlement to the war, in May the Chamber of Deputies elected Ilyas Sarkis to take over as president when Franjiyah's term expired in September. But Sarkis had strong backing from Syria and, as a consequence, was unacceptable to Jumblatt, who was known to be antipathetic to Syrian president Hafiz al Assad and who insisted on a "military solution." Accordingly, the Lebanese National Movement successfully pressed assaults on Mount Lebanon and other Christian-controlled areas.

As Lebanese Front fortunes declined, two outcomes seemed likely: the establishment in Mount Lebanon of an independent Christian state, viewed as a "second Israel" by some; or, if the Lebanese National Movement won the war, the creation of a radical, hostile state on Syria's western border. Neither of these possibilities was viewed as acceptable to Assad. To prevent either scenario, at the end of May 1976 Syria intervened militarily against the Lebanese National Movement, hoping to end the fighting swiftly. This decision, however, proved ill conceived, as Syrian forces met heavy resistance and suffered many casualties. Moreover, by entering the conflict on the Christian side Syria provoked outrage from much of the Arab world.

Despite, or perhaps as a result of, these military and diplomatic failures, in late July Syria decided to quell the resistance. A drive was launched against Lebanese National Movement strongholds that was far more successful than earlier battles; within two weeks the opposition was almost subdued. Rather than crush the resistance altogether, at this time Syria chose to participate in an Arab peace conference held in Riyadh, Saudi Arabia, on October 16, 1976.

The Riyadh Conference, followed by an Arab League meeting in Cairo also in October 1976, formally ended the Lebanese Civil War; although the underlying causes were in no way eliminated, the full-scale warfare stopped. Syria's presence in Lebanon was legitimated by the establishment of the Arab Deterrent Force (ADF) by the Arab League in October 1976. In January 1977, the ADF consisted of 30,000 men, of whom 27,000 were Syrian. The remainder were token contingents from Saudi Arabia, the small Persian Gulf states, and Sudan; Libya had withdrawn its small force in late 1976. Because of his difficulties in reforming the Lebanese Army, President Sarkis, the ADF's nominal commander, requested renewal of the ADF's mandate a number of times.

Thus, after more than one and one-half years of devastation, relative calm returned to Lebanon. Although the exact cost of the war will never be known, deaths may have approached 44,000, with about 180,000 wounded; many thousands of others were displaced or left homeless, or had migrated. Much of the once-magnificent city of Beirut was reduced to rubble and the town divided into Muslim and Christian sectors, separated by the so-called Green Line (see Glossary).

The Sarkis Administration, 1976-82

In December 1976 Sarkis appointed as prime minister Salim al Huss (also seen as Hoss), who chose a cabinet of technocrats that was authorized to rule by decree for six months (later extended). One of the first tasks this government faced was the reorganization of the army, most of whose members had deserted during the Civil War to join one of the various factions. Although the intention of the Cairo Agreement was to station Lebanese military units in southern Lebanon, instead the ADF controlled the area only to the Litani River, leaving the region south of it in the hands of the Palestinians. So strong was their presence that certain areas became known as Fatahland, after the main PLO grouping. Relations with Syria and the problem of the Palestinians in southern Lebanon remained central concerns for Lebanon throughout the period from 1976 to 1982.

The degree of cooperation between the Sarkis administration and Syrian authorities varied, depending on external circumstances in the region. Initially, recognizing its dependence on Syria and Syrian military forces to preserve the peace, the Lebanese government generally cooperated. By late 1977, however, as a result of the Egyptian-Israeli peace negotiations and Syria's consequent rapprochement with the PLO, Lebanese-Syrian relations cooled. In its own role and in its use of the ADF, Syria found itself in an awkward position because it could not fully exert its authority in Lebanon unless it succeeded in disarming both the Lebanese Christian militias and the PLO. However, it was not prepared to pay

*The remains of Tall Zatar, a Palestinian refugee camp on the outskirts of Beirut, after it was besieged by Christian militiamen
Courtesy UNRWA (Myrtle Winter Chaumany)*

the political and military price for doing so and consequently was obliged to maintain a large army in Lebanon, causing a serious drain on Syria's economy.

Relations between Lebanon and Syria deteriorated further when fighting occurred between the ADF and the Lebanese Army in East Beirut in February 1978, followed by a massive ADF bombardment of Christian sectors of Beirut in July. President Sarkis resigned in protest against the latter action but was persuaded to reconsider. Syrian bombardments of East Beirut ended in October 1978 as a result of a UN Security Council cease-fire resolution that indirectly implicated Syria as a party to the Lebanese Civil War. To strengthen its influence over the Sarkis government, Syria threatened several times, in late 1978 and early 1979, to withdraw its forces from Lebanon. But after a relatively cordial meeting between presidents Sarkis and Assad in Damascus in May 1979, Syria stated that the ADF—which by then had become a totally Syrian force—would "remain in Lebanon as long as the Arab interests so require."

From early 1980 onward, Syria became increasingly preoccupied with its domestic difficulties, leaving the Sarkis administration with a freer hand. However, significant ADF action against the Phalange Party militia, headed by Bashir Jumayyil, took place around Zahlah (fifty kilometers east of Beirut) in late 1980 and April 1981. This military threat to its Christian ally caused Israel to intervene, and it shot down two Syrian helicopters over Lebanon. Syria, in turn, introduced SA-2 and SA-6 surface-to-air missiles into Lebanon; the resulting "missile crisis" threatened to cause a regional war, but this possibility was averted through the mediation efforts of other Arab nations and the United States (see The Missile Crisis, ch. 5).

Relations with the Palestinians were complex and interrelated with influences in southern Lebanon. In the early days of the Civil War, the relative peace in southern Lebanon had attracted Lebanese refugees from other areas. After the Palestinians left the area to fight elsewhere, Christian militias, led by Lebanese Army officers supported by Israel, took control of a large part of the south. Israel had forged this link in 1977 with Lebanese officers as part of its "Good Fence" policy to prevent a Palestinian presence near Israel's northern border (see Operation Litani, ch. 5).

However, conflicting interests were at work in southern Lebanon. On the one hand, the Sarkis government saw an opportunity to regain control of the area. On the other hand, the Palestinians, who objected to Syrian efforts to confiscate their heavy weapons and control their activities in the rest of Lebanon, felt they would have greater freedom to operate in the south. For their part, the Syrians wished to eliminate Israeli influence there, while the Israelis wanted direct contact with the population of southern Lebanon and wished to keep both the Syrians and the Palestinians out of the area.

As early as 1977, fighting occurred in the south between the Christian militia under Major Saad Haddad and the Palestinians, who had reinfiltrated the area and were receiving Syrian assistance. The resulting large-scale destruction in the southern area, which Haddad had renamed "Free Lebanon" and which was inhabited mainly by Shia Muslims and Maronite Christians, caused the migration of approximately 200,000 people, or one-third of the population.

To clarify the provisions of the October 1976 Cairo Agreement (preceded by an earlier 1969 agreement) concerning Palestinian activity in southern Lebanon, representatives of Lebanon, Syria (in the guise of the ADF), and the Palestinians held a conference at Shtawrah in July and August 1977. The resulting Shtawrah Accord basically endorsed the Syrian position, which called for the Palestinians to withdraw fifteen kilometers from the Israeli border, with this area to be occupied by the Lebanese Army, and charged the ADF with protecting the southern coastal area. Execution of the agreement, however, was difficult because neither the

The United Nations Interim Force in Lebanon was set up following the 1978 Israeli incursion into southern Lebanon.
Courtesy United Nations

Palestinians nor the Lebanese Army wished to make the first move, and Israel was apprehensive of increased Syrian influence in the area.

The situation in the south was exacerbated by the entry of the Israel Defense Forces (IDF) into southern Lebanon in retaliation for a March 11, 1978, Palestinian guerrilla attack on an Israeli bus near Tel Aviv, in which several people were killed. The IDF staged an all-out attack, and more than 25,000 troops occupied positions as far north as the Litani River and remained in Lebanon for three months. The UN called on Israel to withdraw, and the United Nations Interim Force in Lebanon was sent to replace the Israelis, who withdrew in stages. When Israel withdrew from southern Lebanon in June, Haddad's South Lebanon Army (SLA—formerly the Free Lebanon Army) took over most of the areas Israel had previously controlled.

Throughout the Sarkis administration, various shifts were also occurring in domestic politics. Prime Minister Huss, a moderate Sunni Muslim, was unable to form a national unity government, as requested by Sarkis in the spring of 1978, but remained in office for two more years. In October 1980, Shafiq al Wazzan, another moderate Sunni and chairman of the Supreme Islamic Council, became prime minister. His government experienced even greater difficulties in holding office, with more than half of the Chamber of Deputies refusing to endorse his cabinet. The inability of the Lebanese Army to maintain any effective control over the country was a major factor contributing to the weakness of these Lebanese governments.

Additional shifts occurred among Lebanese military and political groups. The Shias continued to grow in importance, and in 1980 clashes broke out in the south between Amal, the Shia military arm, which was becoming increasingly a political instrument, and Al Fatah, a part of the PLO (see Sectarian Groups, ch. 4). On the Christian side, the Lebanese Front experienced severe internal disagreements. In July 1980 Bashir Jumayyil and his Phalangist militia scored a resounding triumph over the Tigers, the militia of the National Liberals under Camille Shamun and his son Dani. This victory paved the way for Jumayyil's subsequent prominence. Israeli support of the Lebanese Front was curtailed in 1981, as a condition set by the Lebanese National Movement and by Syria for any attempt at an overall resolution of the Lebanese situation.

Lebanon's security deteriorated significantly in late 1981 and the first half of 1982. There were continuous clashes in West Beirut, Tripoli, and southern Lebanon during this period. In September automobile bombings occurred in West Beirut, Sidon, and Tripoli, along with a campaign of terror against foreign diplomats. These violent incidents were followed by terrorist attacks against Muslim and Christian religious leaders in April 1982. The result of these large-scale breaches of the peace was a growing disillusionment on the part of Lebanese Muslims with the ability of the Lebanese National Movement, the PLO, or Syria (through the ADF) to control matters in areas where they were nominally in charge. As a consequence, more moderate and conservative Sunni and Shia figures gained leadership opportunities; a number of them overtly favored the Lebanese government's reestablishing its authority over the country. Shaykh Muhammad Mahdi Shams ad Din (also seen as Chamseddine), vice chairman of the Higher Shia Islamic Council, for example, requested that the Lebanese Army be sent in to quell fighting between the Shia Amal and the PLO in the south, the Biqa Valley, and parts of West Beirut. Clashes in Tripoli, the largest Sunni city, during this period also resulted in requests that the Lebanese Army enter the area.

The general discontent with the situation on the part of various elements of the population provided a favorable opportunity for the Phalange Party's efforts in the 1982 presidential campaign. Bashir Jumayyil saw himself as a leading candidate because the Phalange Party had established its political power by overwhelming the Shamun militia in 1980 and had the largest Lebanese militia, by that time called the Lebanese Forces (see Sectarian Groups, ch. 4). However, Bashir's close ties to Israel and his proposals for eliminating both the ADF and the PLA from the Lebanese scene understandably met with sharp opposition from Assad and Arafat, both of whom considered Jumayyil's brother Amin more acceptable. This, then, was the situation in Lebanon when Israel invaded on June 6, 1982, purportedly in retaliation for the assassination attempt on the Israeli ambassador to London (see The 1982 Israeli Invasion and Its Aftermath, ch. 5).

* * *

There are several important scholarly works on Lebanon. Philip K. Hitti's *Lebanon in History* remains the best single source for the ancient and medieval periods. The modern period is well covered in David C. Gordon's *The Republic of Lebanon,* John B. Christopher's *Lebanon: Yesterday and Today,* Don Peretz's *The Middle East Today,* and *Middle East Contemporary Survey* (volumes 1-7). An excellent account of the Mandate period is found in Stephen H. Longrigg's *Syria and Lebanon under French Mandate.* The latest unrest and civil war in Lebanon is covered in David Gilmour's *Lebanon: The Fractured Country,* Helena Cobban's *The Making of Modern Lebanon,* and Itamar Rabinovch's *The War for Lebanon, 1970-1983.* (For further information and complete citations, see Bibliography.)

Chapter 2. The Society and Its Environment

A street scene showing a church and a mosque, houses of worship for the two dominant religions in Lebanon

SINCE THE MID-1970s, Lebanon has been convulsed by the protracted tragedy of civil strife among the numerous segments and factions of its multiethnic and multisectarian society. The violent civil war of the mid-1970s was followed by incursions, invasions, and occasional occupation by the armed forces of foreign powers and organizations. Throughout the 1970s and 1980s scores of thousands of Lebanese fled their homeland, thousands more were killed, and the warring communities tended to become ever more intransigent in their demands for social autonomy. In the late 1980s, the social systems remained severely fragmented, and a national society could not be said to exist. Prior to the 1975 Civil War some features of social change reflected an underlying trend toward modernization. Decline of kinship ties, social differentiation, rapid urbanization, and an improvement in living standards were all at play, but only within a fragmented social context in which the process of modernization lacked national uniformity. Furthermore, the tension between the forces of continuity and change retarded the pace of modernization, especially when the Lebanese political system did not adapt by expanding the scope of political representation and expression.

Generally speaking, Lebanese society was a traditional one that was exposed to forces of modernization in its urban centers. While some parts of the capital, Beirut, were undergoing a rapid process of modernization, a great influx of villagers to the cities created a "ruralizing" effect. Not only were the forces of change weakened by the value systems of the newcomers, but migration also led to social alienation in the so-called "belt of misery." This area was inhabited mostly by Shias (see Glossary) who were driven out of southern Lebanon in the 1960s by the deteriorating political and security conditions resulting from the Israeli-Palestinian war of attrition. Moreover, the prosperity of Beirut and prospects of jobs lured skilled and unskilled laborers.

Lebanon did not come into existence until 1920, when the French—governing the region under a League of Nations mandate—annexed the peripheral coastal area, the Biqa Valley, the northern region, and Jabal Amil (southern Lebanon) to the *mutasarrifiyah* (district) of Mount Lebanon (see Glossary) to create Greater Lebanon. Before the creation of the republic, Lebanon was politically and socially fragmented among the various Ottoman *vilayets*

41

(provinces) and the confessional (see Glossary) communities that sought refuge in its rugged mountains to avoid persecution.

Lebanese society is divided into numerous sects that are separated from each other by recognizable geographical lines of demarcation and perhaps even more by fear and suspicion. Some communal groups have resisted the changes associated with secularization and modernity by identifying more closely with their own sects and by vehemently opposing the existing political system. In 1987, after twelve years of civil war, Lebanon continued to be confessionally organized. Furthermore, the military battles had reinforced the distances between sects by causing demographic changes through the eviction of members of a whole sect from one region to another. This movement has not only affected Christian-Muslim relations but also sects of the same faith.

Finally, the war had weakened the loose bonds of national loyalty and the feeling of belonging to one society. Although some Lebanese still believed in the efficacy of restoring the unity of a society that would comprise all sects, voices of religious fanaticism and self-interest rejected national and political integration within a system of mutual tolerance. This lack of consensus on national issues partly accounted for the continuation of war and conflict in Lebanon in the late 1980s.

Geography

Lebanon's mountainous terrain, proximity to the sea, and strategic location at a crossroads of the world were decisive factors in shaping its history. The political, economic, and religious movements that either originated in the region or crossed through it to leave an imprint upon Lebanese society give form to that history.

The country's role in the region, as indeed in the world at large, was shaped by trade. The area, formerly part of the region known as Greater Syria (see Glossary), served as a link between the Mediterranean world and India and East Asia. The merchants of the region exported oil, grain, textiles, metalwork, and pottery through the port cities to Western markets. The linkage role of Lebanon was further enhanced by the nomads of the Syrian and Arabian deserts who visited the cities of Syria to trade. The caravans developed limited routes that often led to the coastal cities of Tripoli, Beirut, Sidon, or Tyre. This created a merchant class and brought wealth to the inhabitants of the region. The trade between East and West led to the development of a cosmopolitan culture in Lebanon's port cities, whose inhabitants became known for their multilingualism, flexibility, moderation, and commercial acumen.

The Society and Its Environment

Lebanon was also affected by regional political conflicts and social movements. The wealth of the region attracted powerful rulers who coveted its resources. The strategic location was also attractive; it was used either as a defensive position against enemies approaching the Arab hinterland or as a stepping-stone toward Lebanon's neighbors. Over the centuries, members of the nomadic tribes of the Arabian Peninsula sought a more prosperous life in Lebanon. To this day, many Lebanese families take pride in tracing their descent to ancient tribes of Arabia. Moreover, refugees belonging to minority sects have settled in its virtually inaccessible mountain valleys. Hence, the region became a melting pot of cultural and social interaction among diverse groups. In a social culture where blood lineage assumed primacy as a source of identification and affiliation, the contrast between the new Arab immigrant tribes and the settled inhabitants of the land frequently produced conflicts.

Land

The area of Lebanon is approximately 10,452 square kilometers. The country is roughly rectangular in shape, becoming narrower toward the south and the farthest north. Its widest point is eighty-eight kilometers, and its narrowest is thirty-two kilometers; the average width is about fifty-six kilometers.

The physical geography of Lebanon is influenced by natural systems that extend outside the country. Thus, the Biqa Valley is part of the Great Rift system, which stretches from southern Turkey to Mozambique in Africa. Like any mountainous country, Lebanon's physical geography is complex. Land forms, climate, soils, and vegetation differ markedly within short distances. There are also sharp changes in other elements of the environment, from good to poor soils, as one moves through the Lebanese mountains.

A major feature of Lebanese topography is the alternation of lowland and highland that runs generally parallel with a north-south orientation. There are four such longitudinal strips between the Mediterranean Sea and Syria: the coastal strip (or maritime plain), western Lebanon, the central plateau, and eastern Lebanon (see fig. 3).

The extremely narrow coastal strip stretches along the shore of the eastern Mediterranean. Hemmed in between sea and mountain, the *sahil*, as it is called in Lebanon, is widest in the north near Tripoli, where it is only 6.5 kilometers wide. Fifty kilometers south at Juniyah the approximately 1.5-kilometer-wide plain is succeeded by foothills that rise steeply to 750 meters within 6.5 kilometers from the sea. For the most part, the coast is abrupt and rocky. The shoreline is regular with no deep estuary, gulf, or natural harbor. The maritime plain is especially productive of fruits and vegetables.

The western range, the second major region, is the Lebanon Mountains, sometimes called Mount Lebanon, or Lebanon proper before 1920. Since Roman days the term *Mount Lebanon* has encompassed this area. *Anti-Lebanon* was the term used to designate the eastern range. Geologists believe that the twin mountain ranges once formed one range. The Lebanon Mountains are the highest, most rugged, and most imposing of the whole maritime range of mountains and plateaus that start with the Amanus Mountains, or Nur Mountains, in northern Syria and end with the towering massif of Sinai. The mountain structure forms the first barrier to communication between the Mediterranean and Lebanon's eastern hinterland. The mountain range is clearly defined and has natural boundaries on all four sides. On the north it is separated from the Nusayriyah Mountains of Syria by the Nahr al Kabir (the Great River); on the south it is bounded by the Litani River, giving it a length of 169 kilometers. Its width varies from about 56.5 kilometers near Tripoli to 9.5 kilometers on the southern end. It rises to alpine heights southeast of Tripoli, where Al Qurnat as Sawda (The Black Nook) reaches 3,360 meters. Of the other peaks that rise east of Beirut, Jabal Sannin (2,695 meters) is the highest. Ahl al Jabal (People of the Mountain), or simply *jabaliyyun,* has referred traditionally to the inhabitants of western Lebanon. Near the southern end, the Lebanon Mountains branch off to the west to form the Shuf Mountains.

The third geographical region is the Biqa Valley. This central highland between the Lebanon Mountains and the Anti-Lebanon Mountains is about 177 kilometers in length and 9.6 to 16 kilometers wide and has an average elevation of 762 meters. Its middle section spreads out more than its two extremities. Geologically, the Biqa is the medial part of a depression that extends north to the western bend of the Orontes River in Syria and south to Jordan through Al Arabah to the Gulf of Aqaba, the eastern arm of the Red Sea. The Biqa is the country's chief agricultural area and served as a granary of Roman Syria. The word *Biqa* is the Arabic plural of *buqaah,* meaning a place with stagnant water.

Emerging from a base south of Homs in Syria, the eastern mountain range, or Anti-Lebanon Mountains, is almost equal in length and height to the Lebanon Mountains. This fourth geographical region falls swiftly from Mount Hermon to the Hawran Plateau in Syria, whence it continues through Jordan south to the Dead Sea. The Barada Gorge divides the Anti-Lebanon Mountains. In the northern section, few villages are on the western slopes, but

The Society and Its Environment

in the southern section, featuring Mount Hermon (286 meters), the western slopes have many villages. The Anti-Lebanon Mountains are more arid, especially in the northern parts, than the Lebanon Mountains and are consequently less productive and more thinly populated.

Climate

Lebanon has a Mediterranean climate characterized by a long, hot, and dry summer and cool, rainy winter. Fall is a transitional season with a gradual lowering of temperature and little rain; spring occurs when the winter rains cause the vegetation to revive. Topographical variation creates local modifications of the basic climatic pattern. Along the coast, summers are hot and humid, with little or no rain. Heavy dews form, which are beneficial to agriculture. The daily range of temperature is not wide, although temperatures may reach above 38°C in the daytime and below 16°C at night. A west wind provides relief during the afternoon and evening; at night the wind direction is reversed, blowing from the land out to sea.

Winter is the rainy season, with major precipitation falling after December. Rainfall is generous but is concentrated during only a few days of the rainy season, falling in heavy cloudbursts. The amount of rainfall varies greatly from one year to another. Occasionally, there are frosts during the winter, and about once every fifteen years a light powdering of snow falls as far south as Beirut. A hot wind blowing from the Egyptian desert called the *khamsin* (Arabic for fifty) may provide a warming trend during the fall but more often occurs during the spring. Bitterly cold winds may come from Europe. Along the coast the proximity to the sea provides a moderating influence on the climate, making the range of temperatures narrower than it is inland, but the temperatures are cooler in the northern parts of the coast, where there is also more rain.

In the Lebanon Mountains, the gradual increase in altitude produces colder winters with more precipitation and snow. The summers have a wider daily range of temperatures and less humidity. In the winter, frosts are frequent and snows heavy; in fact, snow covers the highest peaks for much of the year. In the summer, temperatures may rise as high during the daytime as they do along the coast, but they fall far lower at night. Inhabitants of the coastal cities, as well as visitors, seek refuge from the oppressive humidity of the coast by spending much of the summer in the mountains, where numerous summer resorts are located. Both the *khamsin* and the north winter wind are felt in the Lebanon Mountains. The influence of the Mediterranean Sea is abated by the

Lebanon: A Country Study

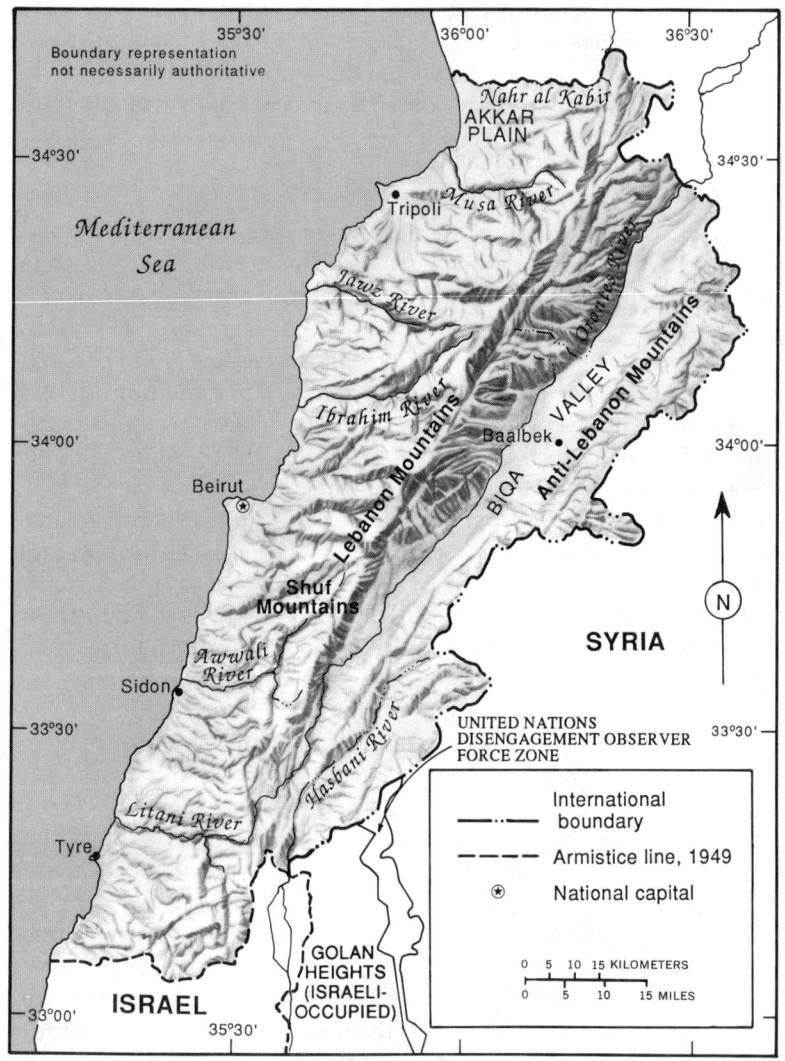

Figure 3. Topography and Drainage

altitude, and, although the precipitation is even higher than it is along the coast, the range of temperatures is wider and the winters more severe.

The Biqa Valley and the Anti-Lebanon Mountains are shielded from the influence of the sea by the Lebanon Mountains. The result is considerably less precipitation and humidity and a wider variation in daily and yearly temperatures. The *khamsin* does not occur in the Biqa Valley, but the north winter wind is so severe that the inhabitants say it can "break nails." Despite the relatively low altitude of the Biqa Valley (the highest point of which, near Baalbek, is only 1,100 meters), more snow falls there than at comparable altitudes west of the Lebanon Mountains.

Because of their altitudes, the Anti-Lebanon Mountains receive more precipitation than the Biqa Valley, despite their remoteness from maritime influences. Much of this precipitation appears as snow, and the peaks of the Anti-Lebanon Mountains, like those of the Lebanon Mountains, are covered with snow for much of the year. Temperatures are cooler than in the Biqa Valley.

Rivers and Lakes

Although the country is well watered and there are many rivers and streams, there are no navigable rivers, nor is any one river the sole source of irrigation water. Drainage patterns are determined by geological features and climate. Although rainfall is seasonal, most streams are perennial. Most rivers in Lebanon have their origins in springs, which are often quite large. These springs emerge from the permeable limestone strata cropping out at the 915- to 1,524-meter level in the Lebanon Mountains. In the Anti-Lebanon Mountains few springs emerge in this manner. Other springs emerge from alluvial soil and join to form rivers. Whatever their source, the rivers are fast moving, straight, and generally cascade down narrow mountain canyons to the sea.

The Biqa Valley is watered by two rivers that rise in the watershed north of Baalbek: the Orontes flowing north (in Arabic it is called Nahr al Asi, the Rebel River, because this direction is unusual), and the Litani flowing south into the hill region of the southern Biqa Valley, where it makes an abrupt turn to the west. The Orontes continues to flow north into Syria and eventually reaches the Mediterranean in Turkey. Its waters, for much of its course, flow through a channel considerably lower than the surface of the ground. The Barada River, which waters Damascus, has as its source a spring in the Anti-Lebanon Mountains.

Smaller springs and streams serve as tributaries to the principal rivers. Because the rivers and streams have such steep gradients and are so fast moving, they are erosive instead of depository in nature. This process is aided by the soft character of the limestone that composes much of the mountains, the steep slopes of the mountains, and the heavy rainstorms. The only permanent lake is Buhayrat al Qirawn, about ten kilometers east of Jazzin. There is one seasonal lake, fed by springs, on the eastern slopes of the

Lebanon Mountains near Al Yammunah, about forty kilometers southeast of Tripoli.

Population

The lack of official statistics makes a demographic analysis of Lebanese society a difficult task. Because of the precarious and delicate sectarian arrangement in the body politic, the government has deliberately avoided conducting a comprehensive update of the 1932 census. Christian communities, primarily the Maronites (see Glossary), fear that the numerical preponderance of Muslims would eventually strip them of their privileges by changing the foundations of political representation. When the French Mandate government conducted the 1932 census, it enumerated 861,399 Lebanese, including those living abroad, most of whom were identified as Christians. The distribution of parliamentary seats among the confessions was based on the findings of the 1932 census; the ratio of six Christians to five Muslims, including Druzes (see Glossary), has been retained.

The government has published only rough estimates of the population since 1932. The estimate for 1956, for example, showed that in a total population of 1,411,416, Christians accounted for 54 percent and Muslims, 44 percent. The estimate was seriously contested because it was based on figures derived from a government welfare program that tended not to include Muslims in areas distant from Beirut. After the 1950s, the government statistical bureau published only total population estimates that were not subdivided according to sect. Consequently, the census became a highly charged political issue in Lebanon because it constituted the ostensible basis for communal representation (see The National Pact, ch. 4).

Conducting a census during the 1970s and 1980s was clearly impossible because of the war. The United States Department of State 1983 estimate for the population of Lebanon was 2.6 million. The figures included Lebanese nationals living abroad and excluded Palestinian refugees, of whom there were nearly 400,000. A 1986 estimate by the United States Central Intelligence Agency of the confessional distribution of the population showed 27 percent Sunnis (see Glossary), 41 percent Shias, 7 percent Druzes, 16 percent Maronites, 5 percent Greek Orthodox, 3 percent Greek Catholics, and many smaller groups. However, these data were, at best, informed estimates subject to revision.

In the absence of a reliable countrywide population census, the most useful information on population came from a 1984 survey conducted in the Greater Beirut region by a team of specialists from the American University of Beirut. An examination of the age composition of the resident population of Beirut in the 1983–84 period revealed a relatively young population in which 41.5 percent were less than 20 years of age. There appeared to be a decline in fertility over the last decade for the resident population of Beirut.

The sex distribution of the 1983–84 Beirut resident population indicated an overall sex ratio of 95.5 males per 100 females. The extreme deficiency observed for males in the age-group twenty through forty-nine may be the result of two factors: the large emigration of men in these ages, mostly to Persian Gulf countries, and a high rate of war-related mortality.

A 1983 World Health Organization study contained some statistics on the demographic characteristics of Lebanon for the period 1960 through 1981, the last year for which figures were available in 1987. Although the reliability of the figures could not be established, the figures revealed some interesting trends. During this period, the crude birth rate declined perceptibly, as did the crude death rate. Surprisingly, life expectancy rose despite the war. The fertility rate continued to decline during the war, but there was little change in the age structure of the population. Total population increased, although at a slower rate than in the prewar period, and there was a dramatic increase in urban population because of the continued influx to the cities. The rate of increase of population density slowed, however, as a result of the war and the consequent emigration of large numbers of Lebanese.

Although accurate figures of Beirut's population in the mid-1980s were lacking, the city's dominant demographic position was unquestioned. Beirut has featured prominently in Lebanese society as a port city throughout its history and as the major population center of the country since at least the beginning of the Mandate period in 1920. Its role in maritime trade brought prosperity to its inhabitants. The creation of the state of Israel in 1948 benefited Beirut, which replaced the Israeli port of Haifa as a center for Arab trade with the West. Until the 1950s, Beirut was inhabited primarily by non-Maronite Christians and Sunni Muslims. In the 1950s, a wave of immigrants from all parts of Lebanon and from all sects sought the lure of economic prosperity and the readily available government services of Beirut. The civil strife that began in the 1970s has reinforced the sectarian demographic divisions in the city.

Other major cities in Lebanon include Tripoli, Sidon, Tyre, Baalbek, and Zahlah. Tripoli, the capital of Ash Shamal Province, has a majority Sunni population and a Christian minority. Sidon, the capital of Al Janub Province, also has a Sunni majority, with a sizable Christian community. Tyre, in Al Janub Province, has a diverse sectarian composition. Although the majority of its inhabitants are Shias, the city has always included Christians of various sects. Baalbek, in Al Biqa Province, has a Shia majority and a Christian minority. Zahlah, the capital of Al Biqa Province, has a predominantly Christian population.

Migration

An important characteristic of the Lebanese is their migratory spirit, which can be traced back to the Phoenicians, who were known for their exploratory expeditions. Substantial emigration occurred between 1860 (after some 10,000 Christians were slain in a conflict with Druzes) and 1914. During this period, approximately 330,000 Lebanese emigrated from what is now Syria and Lebanon. Between 1900 and 1914, the annual rate was about 15,000. The rate dropped sharply during World War I and immediately thereafter but resumed a net annual emigration rate of about 3,000 between 1921 and 1939. Those who had emigrated by 1932 included 123,397 Maronites, 57,031 Greek Orthodox, and 26,627 Melchites, but only 36,865 Muslims and Druzes. Following World War II, the rate decreased somewhat until 1975; thereafter the Civil War caused the emigration of hundreds of thousands of Lebanese. In much of the pre-Civil War period, the proportion of Christian Lebanese emigrants to Muslims and Druzes was as high as six to one.

Rural to urban migration has also been a strong social force within Lebanon. Villagers have moved to the cities, Beirut in particular, to seek improved living conditions or to escape the horrors of war and poverty. The new city dwellers were known for maintaining ties to their home villages. Because of Lebanon's small size and short travel distances, many could continue to spend vacations and weekends in their villages, especially during harvest time. The newcomer to Beirut usually took up residence near fellow villagers and coreligionists. In the case of many Shias, the massive movement to the so-called "belt of misery," which denoted the southern and, until 1976, the eastern suburbs of Beirut, led to deep social resentment since affluent Maronite districts were adjacent to poor Shia districts. In fact, one of the first fronts of the war in 1975 was that between the Shia neighborhood of Shayah and the Christian neighborhood of Ayn ar Rummanah. The road that separated these neighborhoods became known as the Green Line (see Glossary), which in the 1980s designated the line separating Christian East Beirut from predominantly Muslim West Beirut (see fig. 9).

*Palestinian refugees on a pathway in Ar Rashidiyah camp
Courtesy UNRWA
(George Nehmeh)*

More than twelve years of turmoil have resulted in considerable compulsory and voluntary displacement of ordinary people. Hundreds of thousands of Lebanese left their country, some as permanent emigrants, others for what they hoped would be temporary exile. How many left is not known, but Lebanon has the dubious distinction of being the only developing country that the World Bank (see Glossary) believes has actually witnessed a negative population growth rate in recent years. Lebanon's inability to hold a proper census, even in time of peace, means there are only estimates for the country's population. Whereas the population was thought by World Bank and International Monetary Fund (IMF—see Glossary) sources to have grown by around 70 percent to 2.77 million over the 25 years to 1975, by 1984 the population was thought to have declined to 2.64 million.

There has been considerable internal migration as well. Again, it is not possible to quantify this precisely. But the repeated redrawing of militia lines of control, and the repeated fears of members of one community living in enclaves dominated by people of a different religious, national, or political persuasion, make it not unreasonable to suppose that as much as a third of the country's inhabitants in late 1987 had moved to new homes since 1975. It might also be argued that as many as half the people have at some stage moved away from their family homes for a while to escape the persistent violence. Such developments have had profound socioeconomic consequences. A disproportionate number of males have emigrated, while men presumably also account for the majority of those who have died in the years of conflict. Thus there has been a steady increase in the number of women entering the work force and in female-headed households.

The War and Displacement in Beirut

On the eve of the Civil War in 1975, it was evident that the demographic expansion of Beirut and its suburbs had occurred at the expense of the rest of the country. Between 1960 and 1975, the population of Greater Beirut almost tripled, from 450,000 to 1,250,000. In 1959, about 28 percent of all Lebanese lived in Beirut, but this figure ballooned to more than 50 percent in 1975. Lebanon's service-based economy acted as an agent for Western industries and Arab markets alike, leading to the centralization of firms and resources in Beirut, which served as a transit point.

Two factors changed the demographic composition of Beirut in the 1970s. The first was the dramatic growth, starting in 1973, of labor emigration to the Persian Gulf countries. At one point, the outflow included about half the entire work force of Beirut. The second was the series of battles that engulfed the city in a ferocious war. As for the levels of internal migration of various sectarian and ethnic groups at different times during the Civil War, three patterns can be discerned in terms of scope and duration: heavy migration, fast and temporary (the exodus from Beirut when it was besieged by the Israeli Army in 1982); heavy migration, fast and permanent (the eviction of Palestinians and Shias from East Beirut in 1976 and the eviction of Christians from the Shuf Mountains in 1983); and the slow and intermittent migration of individuals and families.

The Palestinian Element

After the creation of the state of Israel in 1948, between 100,000 and 170,000 Palestinian refugees entered Lebanon. They were mostly Muslims and nearly all Arabs, but they also included some Armenians, Greeks, and Circassians. During their first two decades in Lebanon, the Palestinian refugees emerged as politically powerful players (see The Hilu Era, 1964–70, ch. 1). The number of Palestinians in Lebanon swelled as a result of the war between the Palestine Liberation Organization (PLO) and the Jordanian Army and the subsequent expulsion of several thousand Palestinian guerrillas from Jordan in 1970.

In 1987 a large number of Palestinians still lived in or around camps administered by the United Nations Relief and Works

The Society and Its Environment

Agency (UNRWA) for Palestine Refugees in the Near East. In 1975 there were sixteen officially designated UNRWA camps in Lebanon, but in 1975-76 the Maronite militias evicted thousands of Palestinians from the suburbs of East Beirut and demolished their camps. By 1986 there were only thirteen camps in Lebanon (see fig. 4). Many relatively well-off Palestinians lived outside the camps. In 1984 the United States Department of State estimated that 400,000 Palestinians were living in Lebanon, whereas the PLO claimed the figure to be as high as 600,000.

Sectarianism

In 1987 the dominant culture among the various communities was an Arab culture influenced by Western themes. Lebanon's shared language, heritage, history, and religion with its Arab neighbors, however, tended to minimize the distinctiveness of the Lebanese culture. Ethnically, most Lebanese are Arabs, many of whom can trace their lineage to ancient tribes in Arabia. This ethnic majority constitutes more than 90 percent of the population. Muslim and Christian Lebanese speak Arabic, and many of their families have lived in what is now Lebanon for centuries. Moreover, the difference in dialects in Lebanon is a function of geographical location and not of confessional affiliation. Minority non-Arab ethnic groups include Armenians, Kurds, and Jews, although some members of these groups have come to speak the language and identify with the culture of the majority.

Despite the commonalities in Lebanese society, sectarianism (or confessionalism—see Glossary) is the dominant social, economic, and political reality. Divisiveness has come to define that which is Lebanon. Sects should not be viewed as monolithic blocs, however, since strife within confessional groups is as common as conflict with other sects. Even so, the paramount schismatic tendency in modern Lebanon is that between Christian and Muslim.

Sectarianism is not a new issue in Lebanon. The disintegrative factors in society preceded the creation of modern Lebanon in 1920. Before that date, historical Lebanon, or Mount Lebanon, was shared primarily between the Druzes and the Maronites. The two communities, distinguished by discrete religious beliefs and separate cultural outlooks, did not coexist in peace and harmony. Rather, the Druzes and Maronites often engaged in fierce battles over issues ranging from landownership, distribution of political power, foreign allegiances, and petty family feuds. At least twice in the last two centuries, the conflicts between the two confessional communities developed into full-scale civil wars, which were only ended by the intervention of foreign powers. The Lebanese sectarian

Lebanon: A Country Study

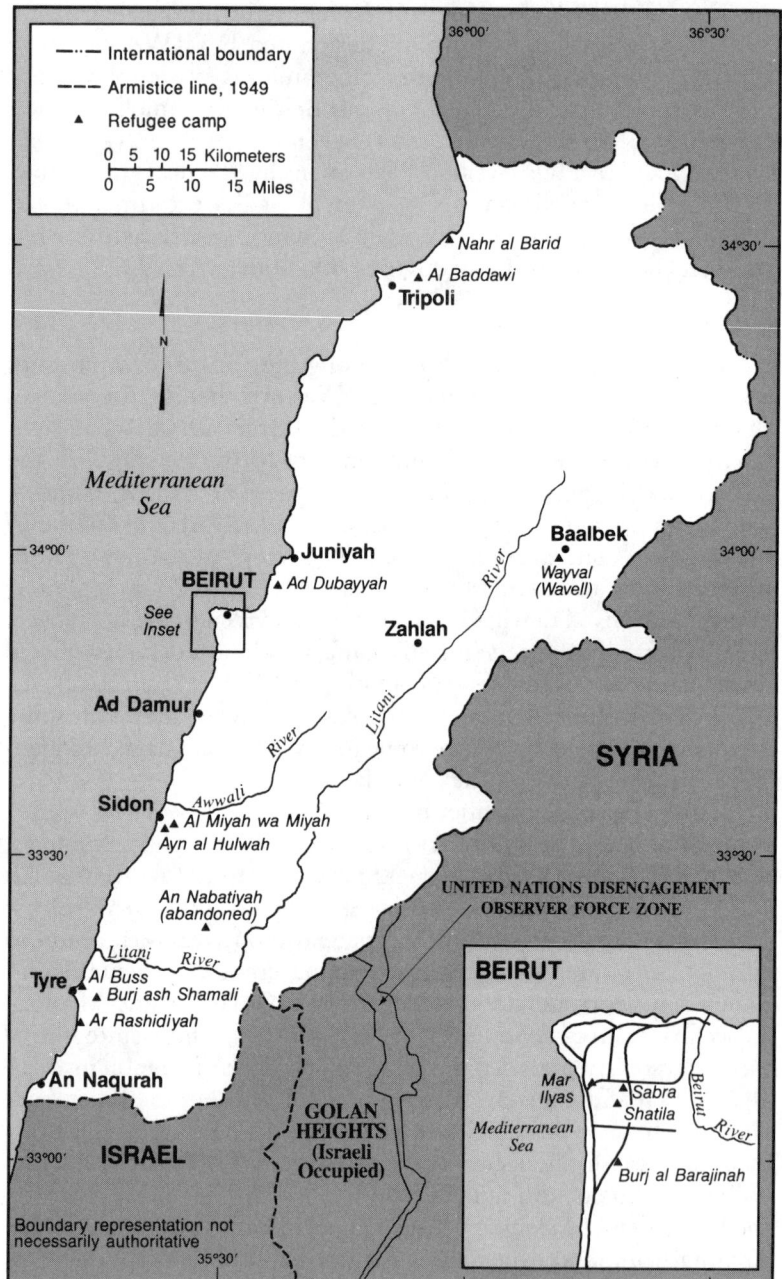

Figure 4. Palestinian Refugee Camps in Lebanon, 1986

problem became more acute in 1920, when the French authorities annexed territories to Mount Lebanon to form Greater Lebanon. Although the new state comprised diverse confessional communities, a political system favoring the majority Christians was established by the French (see The Mandate Period, ch. 1).

Lebanese Confessional "Societies"

The Lebanese confessional "societies" reflect the tensions at the heart of Lebanese society. Although Muslims and Christians have lived together in Lebanon for centuries, their deep disagreements over the Lebanese political formula and state make it unrealistic to treat all Lebanese as members of one social unit.

Since the creation of the republic, the Lebanese have disagreed over the identity of the new state. Although Muslims, specifically the Sunnis, were inclined toward a close association with Greater Syria and the Arab world, Christians, particularly the Maronites, opted for linking Lebanon culturally and politically to the Western world. Christians were not opposed to economic cooperation with Arab countries, to which Lebanon exported most of its products, but they insisted on distinguishing Lebanon's foreign policy from that of its Arab neighbors. The question was not whether Lebanon should be Arab, since as early as 1943 the National Pact (the governing formula) declared Lebanon as having "an Arab face." Rather, the postindependence debate was really over how Arab Lebanon should be. This debate was exacerbated in the 1950s by Egyptian president Gamal Abdul Nasser's pan-Arab activism on the one hand and Lebanese president Camille Shamun's (also seen as Chamoun) pro-Western administration on the other hand.

The controversy over the identity of Lebanon extended beyond the political realm to encompass questions of culture and literature as these were presented in school textbooks. Muslims in general, as well as the Greek Orthodox, insisted that Arab and Islamic culture and literature should be emphasized, whereas Uniate Christians (those in full communion with the Holy See in Rome but separately organized and adhering to an Eastern Rite) refused to commit Lebanese education to what they considered an inferior culture. The Maronite political movement viewed Lebanon's culture as distinctively Lebanese in its origins and values.

Regardless of sectarian affiliation, Lebanon has no civil code for personal matters. Lebanese citizens therefore live and die according to sectarian stipulations. Each sect has its own set of personal status laws that encompass such matters as engagement, marriage, dowry, annulment of marriage, divorce, adoption, and inheritance. These laws are binding on the individual, whether the individual is a practicing member of the sect or not. The confessional system of personal status laws strengthens the role of communal religious leaders and impedes the evolution of Lebanese nationalist or universalist secular ideas.

The economic history of Lebanon has been marred by an unequal distribution of national income and misallocation of benefits and funds. The central government tended to regard the regions that were annexed to what was Mount Lebanon in 1920 as marginal parts of Lebanon. Furthermore, the centralization of government in Beirut worsened the conditions of the rural areas, luring many Lebanese to crowded, confessional-community, poverty belts around the metropolitan center. The central government's neglect of southern Lebanon, particularly, contributed to a feeling of humiliation by the Shias, who in 1987 constituted the largest sectarian community.

The economic situation in peripheral Lebanon, which geographically comprises Al Janub Province, Al Biqa Province, and the Akkar region in Ash Shamal Province, differed sharply from that around Beirut. Economic exploitation was more evident in these areas, where feudalistic production patterns dominated. The land was divided among a small elite, and working conditions on the large estates were harsh. In addition, state services were scarce outside the capital. Beirut and its suburbs became politically and socially explosive when people from the impoverished periphery migrated to the city and came in contact with the affluent city dwellers.

Sectarian and Clan Consciousness

Lebanon's somewhat peculiar political system has reinforced sectarian identification and consciousness. The tendency of the individual to identify with his or her sect as the major political unit has characterized the sectarian composition of political parties (see Sectarian Groups, ch. 4). That most militias in the 1980s were organized along purely sectarian lines, or that the army's brigades were also divided among the sects, indicated the primacy of sectarian consciousness (see The Army, ch. 5).

In the late 1980s, there were other associational affiliations in Lebanon. Shia families in the Biqa Valley were organized into clans (*ashair*) that have existed for centuries. The politics of the region entailed typical clan feuds, alliances, and themes of revenge, which local politicians exploited. The rise in sectarian consciousness among Lebanese generally did not necessarily conflict with clan solidarity.

Another pervasive primordial tie that characterized the Lebanese was their fealty to a group of traditional leaders (*zuama;* sing., *zaim*—see Glossary). The system of fealty involves utmost allegiance and loyalty (including support in election times) by a certain family to a certain *zaim* in return for services and access to power brokers (see Zuama Clientelism, ch. 4). The relationship between the two parties is maintained by a system of obligations and political commitment. This system, a vestige of feudal Lebanon, fostered a bond of fidelity between peasants and the feudal lord. *Zuama* clientelism provides the individual *zaim* with undisputed leadership of a local community, which sometimes encompasses a whole sect (such as the *zuama* of Al Assad in southern Lebanon in the first half of the twentieth century). In the 1980s, the *zuama* were in many cases the direct descendants of the great feudal families of the past.

A new development in Lebanon after 1975 was the rise of an elite that included a new stratum of emerging street leaders who enjoyed power by virtue of sheer military force, individual charisma, or even direct descent from *zuama* families. All three characteristics applied to the late Bashir Jumayyil (also seen as Gemayel) (see The Ascendancy of Bashir Jumayyil, ch. 5). This stratum typically included young and dynamic sons of *zuama*, street thugs, and a rising elite of Muslim religious clerics.

Religion

Divisions within the Christian and Muslim faiths were considerable, but most observers accepted the Christian-Muslim dichotomy as the most salient in Lebanese society. Even so, identification by religious affiliation often blurs subtle social and economic considerations.

Religion in Lebanon is not merely a function of individual preference reflected in ceremonial practice of worship. Rather, religion is a phenomenon that often determines social and political identification. Hence, religion is politicized by the confessional quota system in distributing power, benefits, and posts (see The Basis of Government, ch. 4).

A sectarian group binds its members together on the basis of their professed allegiance to the teaching of the faith and their common location within the sectarian social and political map (see fig. 5). Ethnicity does not strictly apply to Lebanon's confessional communities, since more than 90 percent of all Lebanese are ethnically and linguistically Arabs. But the distinctiveness of Lebanon's confessional communities approximates the notion of sect to that of ethnicity. The exceptions are Kurds, Armenians, and Jews, who constitute ethnic groups in the classical sense. In sum, an understanding of the Lebanese mosaic requires an awareness of ethnicity and confessionalism because the similarity between the two concepts has become clearer in present-day Lebanon, where

Lebanon: A Country Study

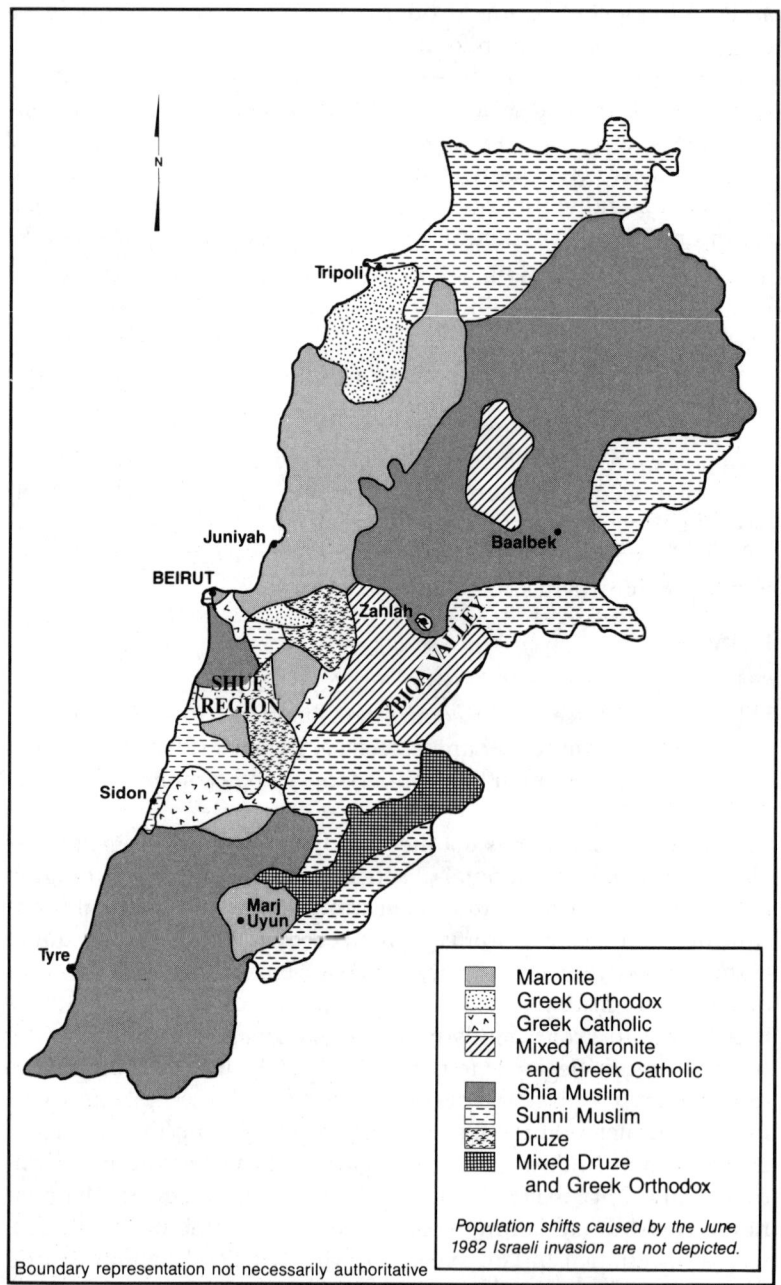

Figure 5. *Distribution of Religious Sects, 1983*

The Society and Its Environment

each sectarian group has its own agenda, political culture, and leaders.

The exact number of Lebanon's sects has always been disputed. In 1936 the French Mandate established the first official law regarding sects in Syria and Lebanon. The sects were enumerated as follows: nine patriarchal sects, one Latin church, the Protestant sect (including eleven Christian denominations), and five Muslim sects (Sunni, Shia, Druze, Alawi, and Ismaili). At that time, the Muslims rejected their division into separate sects, and consequently they were excluded from the appendix of the law that recognized sects.

Following independence, only non-Muslims were included in a 1951 law enumerating officially recognized sects in the following order: Maronites, Greek Orthodox, Greek Catholics, Armenian Orthodox (Gregorian), Armenian Catholics, Syrian Orthodox (Jacobites), Syrian Catholics, Chaldean Catholics, Nestorian Assyrians, Latins (Roman Catholics), Protestants, and Jews. The law specified that each sect was free to manage its *waqf* (religious endowment) properties, as well as its personal status laws for its members. The Alawi and Ismaili sects were considered numerically insignificant, which left them without legally sanctioned institutions. Other Muslim sects—Sunnis, Shias, and Druzes—were considered still covered by the provisions of Ottoman law.

Tenets of Islam

In A.D. 610 Muhammad (later known as the Prophet), a merchant belonging to the Hashimite branch of the ruling Quraysh tribe in the Arabian town of Mecca, began to preach the first of a series of revelations granted him by God through the angel Gabriel. A fervent monotheist, Muhammad denounced the polytheism of his fellow Meccans. Because the town's economy was based largely on the thriving pilgrimage business to the Kaabah shrine and numerous other polytheist religious sites located there, this vigorous censure eventually earned him the bitter enmity of the town's leaders. In 622 he and a group of followers were invited to the town of Yathrib, which came to be known as Medina (from Madinat an Nabi—The Prophet's City). The move, or *hijra* (known in the West as the Hegira), marks the beginning of the Islamic era and of Islam as a force in history. The Muslim calendar, based on the lunar year, begins in 622. In Medina, Muhammad continued to preach, eventually defeated his detractors in battle, and consolidated both the temporal and the spiritual leadership of all Arabia in his person. He entered Mecca in triumph in 630.

After Muhammad's death in 632, his followers compiled those of his words regarded as coming directly and literally from God as the Quran, the holy scripture of Islam. His other sayings and teachings and precedents of his personal behavior, recalled by those who had known him during his lifetime, became the hadith. Together they form the sunna, a comprehensive guide to the spiritual, ethical, and social life of the orthodox Muslim. The *shahada* (literally, testimony or creed) succinctly states the central belief of Islam: "There is no god but God [Allah], and Muhammad is the Prophet of God." This simple profession of faith is repeated on many ritual occasions, and its recital in full and unquestioning sincerity designates one a Muslim.

Like Judaism and Christianity, Islam is a monotheistic religion that acknowledges the absolute sovereignty of God. The word *Islam* means submission (to God), and one who submits is a Muslim. Muhammad is the "seal of the prophets"; his revelation is said to complete for all time the series of revelations received by Jews and Christians.

The duties of the Muslim form the five pillars of the faith. These are the recitation of the creed *(shahada)*, daily prayer *(salat)*, almsgiving *(zakat)*, fasting *(sawm)*, and pilgrimage (hajj). These religious obligations apply to all Muslims, although there are slight variants in the beliefs of Shias as opposed to Sunnis (see Muslim Sects, this ch.). The believer is to pray in a prescribed manner after purification through ritual ablutions each day at dawn, midday, midafternoon, sunset, and nightfall. Prescribed body movements accompany the prayers, which the worshiper recites while facing toward Mecca. Whenever possible, men pray in congregation at the mosque under a prayer leader or imam, and on Friday, the holy day, they are obliged to do so. In the early days of Islam, the authorities imposed *zakat* as a tax on personal property proportionate to one's wealth; this was distributed to the mosques and to the needy. The fourth pillar occurs in the ninth month of the Muslim calendar, Ramadan, a period of obligatory fasting throughout the daylight hours in commemoration of Muhammad's receipt of God's revelation, the Quran. Finally, all Muslims at least once in their lifetime should if possible make the hajj to the holy city of Mecca to participate in special rites held there during the twelfth month of the lunar calendar.

A Muslim stands in a personal relationship to God; there is no clergy in orthodox Islam. Those who lead prayers, preach sermons, and interpret the law do so by virtue of their superior knowledge and scholarship rather than because of any special prerogative conferred by ordination.

The Society and Its Environment

Sunni and Shia Muslims differ over the fundamental issue of succession. The Prophet neither designated his successor nor decreed how a successor should be chosen. Some members of the Muslim community (umma) believed Muhammad's successor should be a close blood relative of the Prophet, i.e., Ali, who was a member of the Hashimite line, the Prophet's cousin, and the husband of Fatima, Muhammad's sole surviving daughter. Other Muslims believed such kinship was not a necessary prerequisite and held that the caliph (from *khalifa*—successor) should be chosen by the community. A split in the ideally egalitarian and harmonious umma developed over this issue. The rift subsequently generated the two major divisions of Islam: Shia, from Shiat Ali (the party of Ali); and Sunni, from men of the sunna and *jamaa*, meaning community (those who favored a leader chosen by the community).

Muslim Sects

Sunnis

Orthodox Sunni Muslims are those who regard the Quran, supplemented by the traditions of the Prophet, as the sole and sufficient embodiment of the Muslim faith. They do not recognize the need for a priesthood to mediate the faith to the community of believers. Thus, Sunnis have no "church" and no liturgy. The Sunnis, especially the Wahhabis of Saudi Arabia, stand for the original simplicity of Islam and its practices against later innovations.

Religious leadership of the Sunni community in Lebanon is based on principles and institutions deriving partly from traditional Islam and partly from French influence. Under the Mandate, the French established the Supreme Islamic Council at the national level, headed by a grand mufti, and the national Directorate of Waqfs; these institutions continued to exist in the mid-1980s. The French also established local departments of *waqfs*, which staffed and maintained hospitals, schools, cemeteries, and mosques. In addition, the *waqfs* managed the funds that supported these operations. The funds were obtained partly from direct donations and partly from income derived from real property given to the community as an endowment.

Shaykh is an honorary title given to any Muslim religious man in Lebanon. As a result of the 1975 Civil War and the intensification in sectarian mobilization and identification, the religious leaders of the Sunni community assumed a more political role, especially with the advent of Islamic fundamentalism in Lebanon. As of 1987, the Sunni mufti, Shaykh Hasan Khalid, was the most powerful Sunni leader; he headed what was called the Islamic Grouping,

Lebanon: A Country Study

which was composed of all Sunni traditional leaders (see Sectarian Groups, ch. 4). The Sunni ulama (learned religious men) of Lebanon emulated the Shia practice of combining temporal and religious power in the person of the imam.

In 1987 the majority of Lebanese Sunnis resided in urban centers. It is estimated that more than two-thirds of them lived in Beirut, Sidon, and Baalbek. The few rural Sunnis lived in the Akkar region, the western Biqa Valley, around Baalbek, and in the Shuf Mountains. Their typical occupations were in trade, industry, and real estate. Large Sunni families enjoyed political and social significance. The most prominent of them were the Sulhs, Bayhums, Dauqs, Salams, and Ghandurs in Beirut; the Karamis, Muqaddams, and Jisrs in Tripoli; and the Bizris in Sidon. It is estimated that 702,000, or 27 percent, of the Lebanese population as of 1986 were Sunnis.

Non-Arab Sunnis include the Kurds, of whom there are only a few in Lebanon, concentrated mainly in Beirut. They originated in the Taurus and Zagros mountains of Iraq, Iran, Turkey, and Syria. The Kurds of Lebanon tended to settle there permanently because of Lebanon's pluralistic society. Although they are Sunni Muslims, Kurds speak their own language.

Shias

Leadership of the Shia community is held by the imam, a lineal male descendant of Ali. A son usually inherited the office from his father. In the eighth century, however, succession became confused when the imam, Jafar as Sadiq, first named his eldest son, Ismail, his successor, then changed his mind and named a younger son, Musa al Kazim. Ismail died before his father and thus never had an opportunity to assert his claim. When Jafar died in 765, the imamate devolved on Musa. Those Shia who followed Musa are known to Western scholars as the Twelver Shias or Imami Shias. The part of the community that refused to acknowledge Musa's legitimacy and insisted on Ismail's son's right to rule as imam became known as Ismailis. The appellation *Twelver* derives from the disappearance of the twelfth imam, Al Mahdi al Muntazar, in about 874. He was a child, and after his disappearance he became known as a messianic figure, Al Mahdi, who never died but remains to this day hidden from view. The Twelver Shias believe his return will usher in a golden era.

In the mid-1980s, the Shias generally occupied the lowest stratum of Lebanese society; they were peasants or workers except for a small Shia bourgeoisie. The Shias were concentrated chiefly in the poor districts of southern Lebanon and the Biqa Valley. From these rural areas, stricken by poverty and neglected by the central

The Society and Its Environment

government, many Shias migrated to the suburbs of Beirut. Some Shias emigrated to West Africa in search of better opportunities. As of 1986, the Shias constituted the single most numerous sect in the country, estimated at 1,066,000, or 41 percent of the population.

Shias of Lebanon, most of whom were Twelver Shias, lacked their own state-recognized religious institutions, independent of Sunni Muslim institutions, until 1968, when Imam Musa as Sadr, an Iranian-born cleric of Lebanese ancestry, created the Higher Shia Islamic Council in Lebanon. Sadr was elected chairman of the council, which was supposed to represent Lebanese Shias both at the political and at the religious levels. The council included as members all Shia clerics, as well as deputies, state employees, ministers, writers, professionals, and most noted Shias residing in Lebanon. Sadr, as chairman for life, continued to head the council until 1978, when he "disappeared" in Libya while on a state visit. He reportedly was kidnapped and killed by Libyan authorities for unknown reasons. Shia leaders in Lebanon as of 1987 still refused to acknowledge Sadr's death. While the chairmanship of the council was preserved for Sadr's awaited "return," in 1987 Shaykh Muhammad Mahdi Shams ad Din (also seen as Chamseddine) was the vice chairman of the Higher Shia Islamic Council. Moreover, a new Shia leader emerged in the early 1980s in Lebanon. Shaykh Muhammad Husayn Fadlallah, the spiritual guide of Hizballah (Party of God), became the most important religious and political leader among Lebanon's Shias (see Sectarian Groups, ch. 4).

Ismailis

In the late 1980s, there were only a few hundred Ismailis in various parts of Lebanon. The Ismailis are Shias known as Seveners because they believe Ismail was the seventh imam.

The Ismaili sect is divided into two branches: the Mustalian branch is found primarily in the Yemen Arab Republic (North Yemen), and the Nizari branch is found in the Iranian district of Salamiya, Afghanistan, Soviet Central Asia, India, the Chitral and Gilgit areas of Pakistan, and East Africa. The Ismailis split into two branches over a succession dispute. The current Nizari imam is a revealed ruler and is well known, even in the West, as the Agha Khan.

Ismaili beliefs are complex and syncretic, combining elements from the philosophies of Plotinus, Pythagoras, Aristotle, gnosticism, and the Manichaeans, as well as components of Judaism, Christianity, and Eastern religions. Ismaili tenets are unique among

Shias during ashura, *the commemoration of the martyrdom of Husayn*
Courtesy As'ad AbuKhalil

Muslims. Ismailis place particular emphasis on *taqiyya,* the practice of dissimulation about one's beliefs to protect oneself from harassment or persecution. Ismaili beliefs about the creation of the world are idiosyncratic, as is their historical ecumenism, toleration of religious differences, and religious hierarchy. Furthermore, the secrecy with which they veil their religious beliefs and practices (together with the practice of *taqiyya*) makes it extremely difficult to establish what their actual religious beliefs are. Their conceptions of the imamate also differ greatly from those of other Muslims.

Alawis

Several thousand Alawis were scattered throughout northern Lebanon in 1987. Lebanese Alawis have assumed more significance since the rise to power of the Alawi faction in Syria in 1966, and especially since the Syrians established a military presence in Lebanon in 1976.

The Alawis are also known as "Nusayris" because of their concentration in the Nusayriyah Mountains in northwestern Syria. They appear to be descendants of people who lived in this region at the time of Alexander the Great. When Christianity flourished in the Fertile Crescent, the Alawis, isolated in their little communities, clung to their own pre-Islamic religion. After hundreds of years of Ismaili influence, however, the Alawis moved closer to

Islam. Furthermore, contacts with the Byzantines and the Crusaders added Christian elements to the Alawis' new creeds and practices. For example, Alawis celebrate Christmas, Easter, and the Epiphany, and they use sacramental wine in some ceremonies. For several centuries, the Alawis enjoyed autonomy within the Ottoman Empire, but in the mid-nineteenth century the Ottomans imposed direct rule. Regarding the Alawis as infidels, the Ottomans consistently persecuted them and imposed heavy taxation. During the French Mandate, the Alawis briefly gained territorial autonomy, but direct rule was reimposed in 1936.

Alawis claim they are Muslims, but conservative Sunnis do not recognize them as such. In the early 1970s, however, Imam Sadr declared the Alawi sect a branch of Shia Islam. Like Ismaili Shias, Alawis believe in a system of divine incarnation. Unlike Ismailis, Alawis regard Ali as the incarnation of God. Because many of the tenets of the faith are secret, Alawis have refused to discuss their faith with outsiders. Only an elect few learn the religion after a lengthy initiation process; youths are initiated into the secrets of the faith in stages. Alawis study the Quran and recognize the five pillars of Islam.

Alawis do not set aside a particular building for worship. In the past, Sunni government officials forced them to build mosques, but these were invariably abandoned. Only the men take part in worship.

Druzes

In 1987 more than half of Lebanese Druzes resided in rural areas. Druzes were found in the Shuf, Al Matn, Hasbayya, and Rashayya regions; those who chose to live in an urban setting resided in Beirut and its suburbs in confessionally marked neighborhoods. The Druze elite consisted of large landowning families.

The religion of the Druzes may be regarded as an offshoot of Ismaili Islam. Historically it springs from the Fatimid caliph of Egypt, Al Hakim (996-1021 A.D.), who considered himself the final incarnation of God. His close associates and followers Hamza and Darazi (hence the name *Druze*) spread the new doctrine among the inhabitants of southern Lebanon and founded among them a sect that non-Druzes called "Druze" and Druzes called "Unitarian." The Druzes believe that Al Hakim is not dead but absent and will return to his people. Like the Ismailis, they also believe in emanations of the deity, in supernatural hierarchies, and in the transmigration of souls.

The Druzes are religiously divided into two groups. Those who master the secrets and teaching of the sect and who respect its dictates in their daily life are referred to as *uqqal* (the mature) and are regarded as the religious elite. Believers who are not entitled to know the inner secrets of the religion and who do not practice their religion are called *juhhal* (the ignorant).

The leadership of the Druze community in Lebanon traditionally has been shared by two factions: the Jumblatt (also seen as Junblatt) and the Yazbak family confederations. The community has preserved its cultural separateness by being closely knit socially. The Druzes constituted about 7 percent of the population (182,000) in 1986. Shaykh Muhammad Abu Shaqra was the highest Druze religious authority in Lebanon in 1987, holding the title of *Shaykh al Aql.*

Christian Sects

There are several Christian sects in Lebanon, of which a few are non-Arab. Each Christian sect has its own cultural distinctiveness, and many claim patriarchs.

Maronites

The Maronites are the largest Uniate, or Eastern, church in Lebanon and represent an indigenous church. Maronite communion with the Roman Catholic Church was established in 1182, broken thereafter, and formally reestablished in the sixteenth century. In accordance with the terms of union, they retain their own rites and canon law and use Arabic and Aramaic in their liturgy as well as the Karshuni script with old Syriac letters. Their origins are uncertain. One version traces them to John Maron of Antioch in the seventh century A.D.; another points to John Maron, a monk of Homs in the late fourth and early fifth centuries. The words *maron* or *marun* in Syriac mean "small lord."

In the late seventh century, as a result of persecutions from other Christians for the heterodox views they had adopted, the Maronites withdrew from the coastal regions into the mountainous areas of Lebanon and Syria. During the Ottoman era (1516–1916) they remained isolated and relatively independent in these areas. In 1858 the Maronite peasants revolted against the large landowning families. The revolt was followed by a further struggle between the Druzes and Maronites over landownership, political power, and safe passage of community members in the territory of the other. The conflict led France to send a military expedition to the area in 1860. The disagreements diminished in intensity only after the establishment of the Mandate in 1920 and a political formula whereby all sects achieved a degree of political representation.

A woman in a Christian village works at home to help support her family. Courtesy United Nations (B. Cirone)

The Maronite sect has been directed and administered by the patriarch of Antioch and the East. Bishops are generally nominated by a church synod from among the graduates of the Maronite College in Rome. In 1987 Mar Nasrallah Butrus Sufayr (also seen as Sfeir) was the Maronite patriarch.

Besides the Beirut archdiocese, nine other archdioceses and dioceses are located in the Middle East: Aleppo, Baalbek, Cairo, Cyprus, Damascus, Jubayl-Al Batrun, Sidon, Tripoli, and Tyre. Parishes and independent dioceses are situated in Argentina, Brazil, Venezuela, the United States, Canada, Mexico, Côte d'Ivoire, and Senegal. There are four minor seminaries in Lebanon (Al Batrun, Ghazir, Ayn Saadah, and Tripoli) and a faculty of theology at Holy Spirit University at Al Kaslik, which is run by the Maronite Monastic Order. The patriarch is elected in a secret ceremony by a synod of bishops and confirmed by the pope in Rome.

In 1986 it was estimated that there were 416,000 Maronites in Lebanon (including an unknown number abroad), or 16 percent of the population. Most Maronites have historically been rural people, like the Druzes; however, unlike the Druzes, they are scattered around the country, with a heavy concentration in Mount Lebanon. The urbanized Maronites reside in East Beirut and its suburbs. The Maronite sect has traditionally occupied the highest stratum of the social pyramid in Lebanon. Leaders of the sect have considered Maronite Christianity as the "foundation of the

Lebanon: A Country Study

Lebanese nation.'' The Maronites have been closely associated with the political system of independent Lebanon; it was estimated that in pre-Civil War Lebanon members of this sect held 20 percent of the leading posts.

Greek Catholics

Greek Catholics are the second largest Uniate community in Lebanon. They emerged as a distinct group in the early eighteenth century when they split from the Greek Orthodox Church. Although they fully accept Catholic doctrines as defined by the Vatican, they have generally remained close to the Greek Orthodox Church, retaining more of the ancient rituals and customs than have the Maronites. They use Arabic and follow the Byzantine rite. In Lebanon, when one speaks of Catholics, one is referring to this group, not to Roman Catholics or Maronites.

The highest official of the church since 1930 has been the patriarch of Antioch, who resides at Ayn Traz, about twenty-four kilometers southeast of Beirut. The patriarch is elected by bishops in a synod and confirmed by the pope in Rome, who sends him a pallium (a circular band of white wool worn by archbishops) in recognition of their communion. Greek Catholic churches, like those of the Greek Orthodox, contain icons but no statues.

The Greek Catholics live primarily in the central and eastern parts of the country, dispersed in many villages. Members of this sect are concentrated in Beirut, Zahlah, and the suburbs of Sidon. They have a relatively higher level of education than other sects. Proud of their Arab heritage, Greek Catholics have been able to strike a balance between their openness to the Arab world and their identification with the West, especially the United States. Greek Catholics constituted 3 percent of the population (78,000) in 1986.

Roman Catholics

Catholics who accept the full primacy of the Holy See and follow the Latin rite comprised less than 1 percent of the population in the 1980s. The Lebanese refer to them as Latins to distinguish them from Uniate groups. The Latin community is extremely variegated, since both laity and clergy, including large numbers of foreigners, are mainly Europeans. As Roman Catholics, they acknowledge the supreme authority of the pope in Rome, venerate the Virgin Mary and the saints, and recognize the seven sacraments of baptism, confirmation, the Eucharist (the sacrament of the Lord's Supper), confession and penance, ordination, matrimony, and extreme unction (given when facing the danger of death). Members of the clergy are celibate.

The Society and Its Environment

Greek Orthodox

The Greek Orthodox adhere to the Eastern Orthodox Church, which is actually a group of autocephalous churches using the Byzantine rite. Historically, these churches grew out of the four Eastern patriarchates (Jerusalem, Antioch, Alexandria, and Constantinople), which, beginning in the fifth century, diverged from the Western patriarchate of Rome over the nature of Christ. The final split took place in 1096. From that time, with the exception of a brief period of reunion in the fifteenth century, the Eastern Church has continued to reject the claim of the Roman patriarchate to universal supremacy and has also rejected the concept of papal infallibility. Doctrinally, the main point at issue between the Eastern and Western churches is that of the procession of the Holy Spirit. There are also divergences in ritual and discipline.

Originally a peasant community, the Greek Orthodox include many freeholders, and the community is less dominated by large landowners than are other Christian denominations. In present-day Lebanon, the Greek Orthodox have become increasingly urbanized, and they form a major part of the commercial and professional class of Beirut and other cities. Many are also found in the southeast, the Shuf Mountains, and the north, near Tripoli. They are both highly educated and well versed in finance. The sect has become known for its pan-Arab orientation, possibly because it exists in various parts of the Arab world. The church has often served as a bridge between Lebanese Christians and the Arab countries. Members of the sect constituted 5 percent of the population, or about 130,000, in 1986.

Jacobites

The Jacobites, or Syrian Monophysites, often referred to as Syrian Orthodox, take their name from Jacob Baradeus, who spread the teachings of the church throughout Syria in the sixth century. The doctrinal position of the Jacobites is that after the incarnation, Christ had only one divine nature. This is contrary to the orthodox Christian position that states Christ had both a human and a divine nature. The church follows the Syriac liturgy of St. James and has an independent hierarchy under the patriarch of Antioch, whose seat was formerly at Mardin in Turkish Kurdistan and is now at Homs in Syria. As of 1986, there were only a few thousand Jacobites in Lebanon.

Armenian Orthodox or Gregorian

The Gregorian Church was organized in the third century and became autocephalous as a national church in the fourth century. In the sixth century, it modified the formulations of the Council of Chalcedon of 451 that confirmed the dual nature of Christ in one person. Instead, the Gregorian Church adopted a form of Monophysitism that believes in the single divine nature of Christ, a belief that is slightly different from the belief of the Copts and the Syrian Orthodox. The Armenian Orthodox Church has five patriarchs, of whom the catholicos of Etchmiadzin in the Armenian Soviet Socialist Republic is the most revered. It also has an Armenian liturgy.

The Armenians in Lebanon were refugees who had fled Turkey during and after World War I. In 1987 they resided in Beirut and its northern suburbs, as well as in Anjar in the Biqa Valley. They are admired for their skills as craftsmen and for their diligence, characteristics which have enabled them to gain prominent economic positions. Politically, Armenians advocate compromise and moderation.

Assyrian or Nestorian Church

The Assyrians are the remnants of the Nestorian Church that emerged with the Christological controversies in the fifth century. The Nestorians, who have a Syriac liturgy, stressed that Christ consisted of two separate persons, one human and one divine, as opposed to having two natures in one person. Their doctrine was condemned by the Council of Ephesus in A.D. 431. Subsequently, those Nestorians who accepted this doctrine formed an independent church, which has only a few thousand members in Lebanon.

Protestants

The Protestants in Lebanon were converted by missionaries, primarily British and American, during the nineteenth and twentieth centuries. They are divided into a number of denominations, the most important being Presbyterian, Congregational, and Anglican. Typically, Lebanese Protestants are well educated and belong to the professional middle class. They constitute less than 1 percent of the population and live primarily in Beirut.

Jews

Lebanese Jews historically have been an integral part of the Lebanese fabric of confessional communities. In 1947 they were estimated to number 5,950. After the creation of the state of Israel in 1948, Lebanese Jews did not feel compelled to emigrate because they enjoyed a prosperous status in Lebanese society and had been granted equal rights by law with other citizens. Moreover, they suffered no harm during the anti-Zionist demonstrations of 1947 and 1948. However, the intensification of the Arab-Israeli conflict

The Society and Its Environment

politicized attitudes toward local Jews, who were often associated with the policies of Israel. In the early 1950s, their synagogue in Beirut was bombed, and the Lebanese Chamber of Deputies witnessed heated debates on the status of Jewish officers in the Lebanese Army. The discussions culminated in a unanimous resolution to expel and exclude them from the Lebanese Army.

During the June 1967 War, Lebanese authorities stationed guards in Jewish districts when hostility toward Lebanese Jews became overt. Several hundred chose to leave the country; until 1972 Jews were free to leave the country with their money and possessions. During the 1975 Civil War, the PLO and Lebanese leftist-Muslim forces posted militia in the Jewish neighborhood of Wadi Abu Jamil, which housed what remained of the dwindling Jewish community, estimated to number fewer than 3,000. Nevertheless, the rise of Muslim fundamentalists, especially in the aftermath of the Israeli invasion of 1982, constituted a real threat to Lebanese Jews. Organizations such as the Khaybar Brigades and the Organization of the Oppressed of the Earth claimed responsibility for kidnapping and killing several Lebanese Jews between 1984 and 1987. As of 1986, it was estimated that only a dozen Jews remained in West Beirut and some seventy others in East Beirut.

Others

In addition to the above-mentioned sects, in 1987 there were a number of small religious and ethnic communities that numbered only in the hundreds. Such groups comprised Chaldean Catholics, Bahais, Armenian Catholics, Copts, Turkomans, and Circassians.

Languages

Arabic

Arabic is the official language, as well as the religious language for Muslims, Druzes, and some Christian communities. Like Hebrew and Aramaic, it is a Semitic language. One of the earliest recorded instances of Arabic is found in an Assyrian account of a war fought with Arabs between 853 and 626 B.C. Arabic inscriptions in various alphabets have been found in the Arabian Peninsula. By the time of the Prophet Muhammad, Arabic had developed into a refined literary language. The Arab conquest brought it to Lebanon.

In Lebanon, as elsewhere in the Arab world, there are essentially two forms of Arabic—colloquial, of which there are many dialects, and classical. Classical Arabic, uniform throughout the

Arab world, is chiefly a written language. It is also used for public speeches, poetry recitations, and radio and television broadcasts. Modern Standard Arabic has been developed from the classical language of the Quran, the Islamic scripture; the syntax has been slightly simplified, the vocabulary considerably expanded, and the literary style made less complex.

The classical Arabic language is the principal unifying factor in the Arab world. It is revered by Arabs as the symbol of their unity, as a sacred language, and as the vehicle of a great literature. They think of it as their original language and of their spoken dialects as corruptions.

Lebanese colloquial Arabic developed from the Syrian Arabic dialect, which includes the Arabic spoken by Jordanians, Palestinians, Syrians, and Lebanese. It has been influenced by Aramaic, which preceded it in the area. Within Lebanon, the dialect changes from region to region, and the dialect of the Druzes is regarded as distinctive.

Colloquial dialects are seldom written, except for some novels, plays, and humorous writings. However, a call for the adoption of the spoken language to replace the classical as the national language emerged in the 1960s among Maronite political and intellectual circles. The movement, which was championed by the prominent Lebanese poet and political activist Said Aql, attracted a number of supporters by 1975, with the rise of a right-wing trend to dissociate Lebanon from its Arab ties. Nevertheless, few took the movement seriously, apart from a handful of writers who wrote in colloquial Arabic.

Proposals also exist for improving the Arabic alphabet and for updating Arabic vocabulary to include scientific and technological terms. In written Arabic, short vowels and doubled consonants are not indicated but must be supplied from the context.

Scholars tend to adopt foreign words without changing them and use them in both Arabic and Roman alphabets. The language academies in Cairo and Damascus, apprehensive of this practice, have achieved a certain amount of success in forming new words from old Arabic roots.

Other Languages

Armenian is an Indo-European language, distantly related to English, although a large part of its vocabulary is derived from Arabic and Turkish. When the Armenians were converted to Christianity in the fifth century, they acquired an alphabet based on Greek and developed a classical literature, which differed considerably from modern Armenian. Modern Armenian literature flourishes today in the Armenian Soviet Socialist Republic and to a lesser degree in Lebanon, where a printing and publishing industry is active. Armenians are strongly attached to their language, which is important as a means of maintaining their identity.

Assyrian, a Semitic language, is a modern spoken form of ancient Syriac, a dialect of Aramaic. The Assyrians increasingly use Arabic as their spoken language, but Syriac continues to be used for religious purposes.

French and English are the most widely used Western languages. Although French is not an official language, almost all government publications appear in French as well as in Arabic. Since World War II, United States influence, and consequently the importance of English, has increased. Some Lebanese authors choose to write in French or English, and fluency in these languages generally marks the educated man and woman. The Lebanese Arabic dialect, particularly in Beirut, has acquired some French words. Arabic literary style, especially in poetry, has also been influenced by the style of Western languages.

Structure of Society

In 1987 Lebanese society was riddled with deep social, economic, political, and sectarian divisions. Individual Lebanese were primarily identified with their family as the principal object of their loyalty and the basis of marriage and social relationships as well as the confessional system. This, in turn, tended to clash with national integration and cohesion. Society was divided not only into diverse sectarian communities but also into socioeconomic strata that cut across confessional lines.

The Family

The primacy of the family manifests itself in all phases of Lebanese life, including political, financial, and personal relationships. In the political sphere, families compete with each other for power and prestige, and kin combine forces to support family members in their quest for leadership. In business, employers give preference to hiring relatives, and brothers and cousins often consolidate their resources in operating a family enterprise. Wealthy family members are expected to share with less prosperous relatives, a responsibility that commonly falls to expatriate and urban relatives who help support their village kin.

In the personal sphere, the family has an equally pervasive role. To a great extent, family status determines an individual's access to education and chances of achieving prominence and wealth. The family also seeks to ensure an individual's conformity with accepted standards of behavior so that family honor will be maintained. An individual's ambitions are molded by the family in accordance with the long-term interests of the group as a whole. Just as the family gives protection, support, and opportunity to its members, the individual member offers loyalty and service to the family.

The traditional form of the family is the three-generation patrilineal extended family, consisting of a man, his wife or wives, their unmarried children of both sexes, and their married sons, together with the sons' wives and children. Some of these groups live under one roof as a single household, which was the norm in earlier generations, but most do not.

The family commands primary loyalty in Lebanese society. In a study conducted by a team of sociologists at the American University of Beirut in 1959, loyalty to the family ranked first among both Christians and Muslims, among both males and females, and among both politically active and noncommitted students. Next to the family in order of importance were religion, nationality or citizenship, ethnic group, and finally the political party. The results of this study probably reflected the attitudes of the Lebanese in 1987. If anything, primordial ties appear to have increased during the 1975 Civil War. The rise of Islamic and Christian fundamentalism encouraged the development of ethnic and familial consciousness. Among Maronites, there has always been an emphasis on the family; for example, the motto of the Phalange Party is "God, the Fatherland, and the Family."

The family in Lebanon has been a means through which political leadership is distributed and perpetuated. In the Chamber of Deputies of 1960, for example, almost a quarter of the deputies "inherited" their seats. In the 1972 Chamber of Deputies, Amin Jumayyil (who became president in 1982) served with his father, Pierre Jumayyil, after inheriting the seat of his uncle Maurice Jumayyil. Because "political families" have monopolized the representation of certain sects for over a century, it has been argued that family loyalty hinders the development of a modern polity.

Sex Roles

The family in Lebanon, as elsewhere in the region, assigns different roles to family members on the basis of gender. The superior status of men in society and within the narrow confines of the nuclear family transcends the barriers of sect or ethnicity. Lebanese family structure is patriarchal. The centrality of the father figure stems from the role of the family as an economic unit, in which the father is the property owner and producer on whom the rest of the family depend. This notion prevails even in rural regions of Lebanon where women participate in peasant work. Although the inferior status of women is undoubtedly legitimized by various religious texts, the oppression of women in Arab society preceded the advent of Islam. The roles of women have traditionally been restricted to those of mother and homemaker. However, since the 1970s Arab societies have allowed women to play a more active role socially and in the work force, basically as a result of the manpower shortage caused by heavy migration of men to Persian Gulf countries. In Lebanon the percentage of women in the labor force has increased, although the Islamic religious revival that swept Lebanon in the 1980s reasserted traditional cultural values. As a consequence, veils and *abas* (cloaks) have become more common among Muslim women. Among Christians, the war enabled women to assume more independent roles because of the absence of male family members involved in the fighting.

Notwithstanding the persistence of traditional attitudes regarding the role of women, Lebanese women enjoy equal civil rights and attend institutions of higher education in large numbers (for example, women constituted 41 percent of the student body at the American University of Beirut in 1983). Although women have their own organizations, most exist as subordinate branches of the political parties.

Marriage

In the past, marriage within the lineage, especially to first cousins or other close paternal kin, was the rule. This provided the woman the security of living among the people with whom she had been raised and also tended to keep property inheritance within the family. Among Muslims, there is traditional preference for marriage to a patrilineal first cousin; in some conservative Muslim villages, the choice is considered obligatory. In Roman Catholic canon law the marriage of persons within the same bloodline or of persons within the third degree of collateral relationship is explicitly forbidden. In Lebanon a dispensation for such marriages can be obtained, and they are not uncommon.

Although permitted under Muslim law, polygyny is generally regarded as both impractical and undesirable because of the additional economic burden it places upon the household and because of the personal complications it entails. Polygynous families consist of a man, up to four wives, and their children. A man rarely has more than two wives, one of whom is sometimes much younger than the other, and is married after the children of the first wife are almost fully grown. The two wives may live with their children in different rooms of the same house, or they may reside in separate abodes. A survey of families in Beirut, made in the early 1960s, indicated that there was more than one wife in only 3 percent of the Muslim families interviewed.

Other than the marriage of close relatives, such as first cousins, a factor that often enters into the choice of a marriage partner is interest in expanding family resources. A man from the leading family of a particular lineage, especially an influential and wealthy lineage, is apt to choose a wife from another such lineage within his own religious community to improve the position of his immediate family group.

The general practice in both Christian and Muslim villages is to find a partner within the village, preferably the closest eligible relative within the family. This practice has been considerably weakened in villages close to cities, where marriages outside the family and outside the village occur more often and where first cousin marriage occurs only occasionally.

Marriage is more a matter of recognizing adult status and of joining interests than of romantic attachment. Men marry to have sons who will continue their lineage, work their land, and do honor to their house. Women marry to attain status and to bear sons for protection in their old age. Most women marry.

Age at marriage varies. In some villages girls tend to marry in their late teens; boys, in their early twenties. Urban youths marry somewhat later. Among educated families, young men frequently postpone marriage for many years, some of them waiting until their late thirties or early forties.

Christians and Druzes do not enter into a formal marriage contract; Muslims, however, do. After the announcement of the engagement of a Muslim couple, and before the wedding takes place, a formal contract is drawn up. The marriage is legal once the contract is signed. The contract notes the consent of the couple to marry and specifies the bride-price, a payment by the young man to his fiancée's family. In traditional Muslim society, the bride-price represented a substantial amount of money, or its equivalent in land, or a combination of both. In the 1980s, however, except in remote villages, only a token gift was made. The bride is expected to provide a dowry, usually in the form of furnishings for a new household.

Premarital and extramarital sexual relations are frowned upon throughout society. In the village there are strong sanctions against sexual relations outside marriage, and such relationships are rare because every potential female partner is enmeshed in the network of kinship ties that reinforce these sanctions. Improper conduct toward an unmarried woman damages the honor of her lineage.

The reversion to traditional values in the 1980s affected the dress of many Shia women. Courtesy As'ad AbuKhalil

Her father and brothers will seek redress, which can take the form of killing the woman and the man involved, killing the man or driving him from the village, or a settlement between the two lineages. If redress is not obtained, open strife between the two lineages may occur.

Child-Rearing Practices

The major reason for marrying is procreation. A wife without children, or even one without male children, is an object of sympathy. Also, among those Christians not under the Holy See and among Muslims, she is threatened with divorce. The importance placed on having sons is reflected in the festivities attendant upon birth. At the birth of a child, the father will give a feast; if the child is a boy, the feast will be more lavish and the guests more numerous. It is always made clear within the family that male children are preferred and are given special privileges.

When the first boy is born to a married couple, friends no longer address them by their given names alone but call them by the name of their son; for instance, "father of x" and "mother of x." They continue to be addressed by the name of their firstborn son, even in the event of his death. With respect to naming children, traditionally one male in every generation is given the name of his grandfather to pay respect to the older man and to honor his memory after his death.

Child-rearing practices in Lebanon are characterized by the severe discipline imposed by the father and overprotection by the mother, who strives to compensate for the rigidity of the father. In Arab society parental control does not stop at age eighteen (when a child is considered independent in most Western societies) but continues as long as the child lives in the father's residence or until the child marries. Furthermore, the practice of the father and mother making major decisions on behalf of their offspring pertains to marriage, especially the son's marriage; the daughter comes under the control of her in-laws. Arranged marriages are still practiced widely across the socioeconomic and sectarian spectrum.

Children are not trained to be independent; they expect their father to care for them as long as they are loyal and obedient. Punishment can be in the form of intimidation (*takhjil*, literally to incite fear and shame) or physical punishment. A study of the impact of the war noted a decline in parental authority because of the extensive involvement of young men in armed militias.

Impact of War on the Family

The protracted Civil War has made the task of conducting empirical research on marriage habits almost impossible. Available statistics indicate that familial and marital habits differ among sects. Christian families tend to be smaller than Muslim—particularly Shia—families. According to a 1970 survey, the average Lebanese Christian family excluding Maronites had 3.57 children, the Sunni 4.38, and the Shia 5.01. A striking aspect of marriage habits in Lebanon, especially after 1975, was the impact of recession on marriage. The high cost of living and housing and the difficulty in finding employment caused men to marry later. In the past, Lebanese men and women married at an early age, but in the 1980s in Beirut the average age for marriage was 31 years for men and 22.5 for women. Economic difficulties also forced more families to resort to birth control, so that the size of the average Lebanese family has declined appreciably.

A study conducted in 1983 indicated, however, that marriage was common among the population of Greater Beirut, with only 10 percent or less of the population remaining single at ages above 40. A majority of females age twenty-five or older were married; a majority of males age thirty or older were also married. Moreover, very few adult males or females were separated or divorced. The percentage of widows forty years of age or younger was considerably higher than that for males of the same age. Marriages based on personal choices of the spouses as opposed to family-arranged marriages increased with the gradual elimination of traditional

The Society and Its Environment

boundaries between the sexes. However, family-arranged marriages continued to be practiced across geographical and social boundaries. They were preferred among the economic elite of the cities as a means of preserving wealth and status within the same extended family or within the same social group.

One study conducted in the early 1980s on the impact of the war on family structure concluded that there was a clear decline in divorce. This probably occurred because of the huge costs involved: payment of deferred dowry, alimony for children, and support of the woman during the prescribed period during which she may not remarry.

Living Conditions

Prewar Conditions

On the eve of the 1975 Civil War, Lebanon's general standard of living was comfortable and higher than that in any other Arab country. Regional variations existed in housing standards and sanitation and in quality of diet, but according to government surveys most Lebanese were adequately sheltered and fed. Known for their ingenuity and resourcefulness in trading and in entrepreneurship, the Lebanese have shown a marked ability to create prosperity in a country that is not richly endowed with natural resources. Economic gain was a strong motivating force in all social groups.

Many problems affecting the general welfare before the war stemmed from high prices and the massive rural exodus to the cities. This exodus has been linked to unproductive farms, fragmented landholdings, and a distinct preference of most Lebanese for urban living and for urban occupations. The population increase in the cities, especially in Beirut, created severe housing shortages for those unable to pay the high rents for modern apartments. It also aggravated the problems of urban transportation and planning. The high cost of living, which had been steadily rising since the 1950s, further diminished the purchasing power of small rural incomes and threatened the consumption patterns of low- and middle-income groups in the cities. Of special concern were high rents, school fees, and the price of food and clothing. Many urban households lived on credit, and indebtedness was widespread in some parts of the countryside.

In urban centers, where the Western influence was most apparent in the 1980s, there had been a tremendous increase in modern apartment buildings that had almost erased the scenes of traditional-style houses with red-tiled roofs. The government did not take action during the construction boom of the early 1970s to protect these remnants of Lebanon's culture. In rural Lebanon, houses with flat earthen roofs were the most common. The size and shape of the house indicated one's economic status.

Wartime Conditions

The disruption of Lebanon's modernization by the war has not been adequately measured. A social data sheet on Lebanon prepared by the World Bank in 1983, however, illustrated some trends. Women's share of the labor force progressed very slowly from 3.4 percent in 1960 to 19.9 percent in 1981, probably because of strong traditionalist resistance within the family. The same data indicated a sharp decline in the percentage of the labor force employed in agriculture, from 38 percent in 1960 to only 11 percent in 1980. There was no corresponding rise in industrial activity, however; the industrial labor force only increased from 23 percent to 27 percent. Most of the labor force was still employed in the service sector. Other indexes such as energy consumption, automobiles per thousand population, radios and television sets per thousand population, and newspaper circulation also documented Lebanon's pace of modernization. What these figures did not indicate was the disproportionate levels of modernization among various communities and regions.

As for the impact of the war in general on public life, radical adjustments had to be made by inhabitants of neighborhoods that were subjected to intense fighting. The people of Beirut, in particular, adjusted to shortages of all kinds: water, electricity, food, and fuel. The wartime living situation started to deteriorate in the spring of 1975. During lulls in the fighting, remnants of the central government attempted to resume services to the population, but the task was impossible because of the harassment by militia members. The government then resorted to rationing water and electricity. It was particularly hampered by the sharp decline in the payment of bills by consumers. According to one employee in the Beirut electric company, only 10 percent of all customers paid their bills. The rest either declined to pay or simply hooked up to utility supply cables.

One of the most difficult periods in the struggle for survival among Lebanese and Palestinians occurred during the siege of Beirut by Israel in 1982. To pressure the PLO to surrender, the Israeli Army, aided by the Christian Lebanese Forces, ensured that no food or fuel entered the city.

The war scarcely left a house or building in Beirut intact or free from shrapnel damage. The Lebanese, however, soon adjusted to the new situation either by living in bombed-out apartments or by fixing damaged parts of their residence. Some displaced people from southern Lebanon who could not afford to rent in Beirut or even in its suburbs chose to live in deserted apartments and hotels in areas close to the Green Line, which separated West Beirut from East Beirut. The situation in many Palestinian refugee camps was particularly oppressive. Some camps along the coastal road had come under Israeli fire during the invasion of 1982, and others in the Beirut area had been destroyed by Christian militias during the war or had come under Shia attack in the mid-1980s (see Chaos in Beirut and Syrian Peacemaking Efforts, ch. 5).

Education

The Lebanese, along with the Palestinians, had one of the highest literacy rates in the Arab world. The rate was estimated at nearly 80 percent in the mid-1980s, but like most other spheres of Lebanese life, communal and regional disparities existed. In general, Christians had a literacy rate twice that of Muslims. Druzes followed with a literacy rate just above that of Sunnis. Shias had the lowest literacy rate among the religious communities.

The war adversely affected educational standards. Many private and public school buildings were occupied by displaced families, and the state was unable to conduct official examinations on several occasions because of intense fighting. Furthermore, the departure of most foreign teachers and professors, especially after 1984, contributed to the decline in the standards of academic institutions. Admissions of unqualified students became a standard practice as a result of pressures brought by various militias on academic institutions. More important, armed students reportedly often intimidated—and even killed—faculty members over disputes demanding undeserved higher grades.

In the 1980s, there were three kinds of schools: public, private tuition-free, and private fee-based. Private tuition-free schools were available only at the preprimary and primary levels, and they were most often sponsored by philanthropic institutions. Many private fee-based schools were run by religious orders.

Public schools were unevenly distributed among Lebanon's districts. The Beirut area had only 12.9 percent of the country's public schools, but a large number of Lebanon's private fee-based schools were concentrated in or near Greater Beirut (see table 2, Appendix A).

Primary Education

In 1987 five years of primary education were mandatory and available free to all Lebanese children. The curriculum of grades one through five was mostly academic, and Arabic was the major language of instruction. French and English were also major languages of instruction in private schools, although foreign languages were taught in public schools as well. No certification was awarded upon completion of the primary cycle. At the end of the fifth grade, the student qualified for admission to the four-year intermediate cycle or to the seven-year secondary cycle.

Intermediate Education

Intermediate education was a four-year cycle, consisting of grades six through nine for intermediate schools and one through four for vocational schools. Three different tracks were offered at this level: lower secondary was a four-year academic course designed to prepare the student for the baccalaureate examination; the upper primary track consisted of three years similar to lower secondary and a fourth year of preparation for entering vocational schools or teacher training institutes; and vocational study was a three-year practical course for less skilled trades. At the end of this cycle, students received an academic, technical, or professional certificate.

Secondary Education

Secondary education consisted of grades eleven through thirteen for academic programs or years one through three for vocational programs. Three tracks were available at this level. The secondary normal track consisted of three-year training programs for prospective primary and intermediate school teachers. A teaching diploma was awarded to students of teacher training schools who passed examinations at the end of the twelfth school year. The secondary vocational track prepared students for careers in such fields as business, commerce, tourism, hotel management, electronics, construction, advertising, nursing, telecommunications, automobile mechanics, and laboratory technology. Finally, the secondary academic track offered concentrations in philosophy (liberal arts curriculum), mathematics, and experimental sciences. The Baccalaureate I certificate was awarded to students who passed the official examination given at the end of the twelfth school year, and the Baccalaureate II was awarded to students who passed official examinations at the end of the thirteenth school year. The Baccalaureate II was necessary for admission to institutions of higher education in Lebanon. Many of the courses taken during the year were comparable to those at the college freshman level.

Technical and Vocational Education

In 1987 around 130 technical and vocational training institutes existed in Lebanon. Seventeen of these were state run, and the remaining 113 were private. Eighty-six of the private institutes were in the Greater Beirut area. Major public institutes included the Industrial Technical Institute, the Technical Institute for Tourism, and the Technical Teachers Institute.

Higher Education

In 1987 there were sixteen colleges and universities in Lebanon, and all but the Lebanese University were privately owned (see table 3, Appendix A). The Lebanese University, established in 1952, was under the Ministry of Education. It had two main branches—one in East Beirut and the other in West Beirut—and smaller branches in the provinces of Ash Shamal, Al Janub, and Al Biqa. University faculties (departments) included law, political science and management, engineering, literature and humanities, education, social sciences, fine arts, journalism and advertising, business administration, and agriculture. The language of instruction was Arabic, and one foreign language was required by all faculties.

Beirut Arab University was established in 1960 and was officially an Egyptian-sponsored institution under the auspices of the Maqasid Society of Beirut. All affairs were controlled by Alexandria University in Egypt. Approximately 85 percent of the students enrolled at Beirut Arab University in the 1980s were non-Lebanese, coming primarily from Persian Gulf countries. Arabic was the primary language of instruction.

St. Joseph's University, established in 1875, was administered by the Society of Jesus and had strong ties to the University of Lyons in France. St. Joseph's University had branches in Tripoli, Sidon, and Zahlah. French was the primary language of instruction, although some courses were offered in English. Faculties in 1987 included theology, medicine, pharmacy, dentistry, engineering, law and political science, economics and business administration, and letters and humanities.

The American University of Beirut (AUB) was initially established in 1866 by the Evangelical Mission to Syria. In 1987 final authority over the affairs of AUB rested with the board of trustees, whose permanent office was in New York City. The university was incorporated under the laws of the state of New York. The faculty of arts and sciences awarded bachelor's and master's degrees; the faculty of medicine awarded bachelor's and master's degrees in science, master's degrees in public health, and certificates in undergraduate nursing and basic laboratory techniques; the faculty of engineering and architecture awarded bachelor's and master's degrees in engineering as well as bachelor's degrees in architecture; the faculty of agriculture and food sciences awarded master's degrees in all departments, as well as doctorates in agronomy. English was the language of instruction at AUB.

Health

Before 1975 Lebanon boasted advanced health services and medical institutions that made Beirut a health care center for the entire Middle East region. The war, however, caused enormous problems. Emergency medicine and the treatment of traumatic injury overwhelmed the health care sector during the 1975 Civil War. Indeed, the problems in health care continued into the 1980s. A World Health Organization study conducted in 1983 found that the private sector dominated health care services and that public sector health organizations were in chaos (see table 4, Appendix A). The weakened Ministry of Public Health maintained little coordination with other public sector health agencies, and over two-thirds of the ministry's budget (US$58.5 million in 1982) flowed to the private sector through inadequately monitored reimbursements for private hospital services. As of 1983, there were about 3.2 hospital beds (0.23 of them public) for every 1,000 persons, but control over the quality of hospital and medical services was minimal, and many public and private hospital beds were unoccupied. There was about 1 doctor for every 1,250 inhabitants, but nurses and middle-level technical personnel were scarce. Furthermore, health personnel were concentrated in Beirut, with minimum care available in many outlying areas. The Ministry of Public Health, as well as other government and private agencies, operated small clinics and dispensaries, but few such centers existed in Beirut. Nowhere in Lebanon was there a health center that delivered a full range of primary health care services.

Although epidemiology is central to public health programs, the WHO delegation found that government health services in Lebanon lacked appropriate epidemiological reporting techniques. At the local or community level, health personnel, especially doctors, rarely reported diseases to the health department, although they were legally obliged to do so for some diseases. A similar situation existed with respect to health establishments such as clinics, dispensaries, and hospitals. Consequently, not only was there a conspicuous absence of health records but, where available, they were often incomplete.

Because of the lack of adequate data, only cautious inferences based on partial data and observations and interviews by the WHO mission can be made concerning the incidence of disease. Respiratory infections and diarrheal diseases headed the list of causes of morbidity, and infectious diseases were endemic.

The American University of Beirut campus
Courtesy Aramco World

Malnutrition was reported to be restricted to groups living in particularly difficult situations, such as the Palestinian and Lebanese refugees. Studies on the growth and illness patterns of Lebanese children, initiated in 1960, indicated a stable 5 to 10 percent of undernutrition (defined as low weight and height for age) in children under five. Various sources reported a high incidence of mental retardation among children, with cases occurring in clusters and seemingly related to consanguineous marriages in certain communities.

* * *

Rare are the books that are devoted exclusively to the study of Lebanese society. The small collection of such books includes Nura Alamuddin and Paul Starr's *Crucial Bonds,* Halim Barakat's *Lebanon in Strife,* Joseph Chamie's *Religion and Fertility,* Dominique Chevallier's *La Société du Mont Liban à L'époque de la Révolution Industrielle en Europe,* Anne Fuller's *Buarij: Portrait of a Lebanese Moslem Village,* Samir Khalaf's *Lebanon's Predicament* and *Persistence and Change in 19th Century Lebanon,* Fuad I. Khuri's *From Village to Suburb,* Sami Nasib Makarem's *The Druze Faith,* Huda Zurayk and Haroutune Armenian's *Beirut 1984: A Population and Health Profile.* Salim Nasr and Claude Dubar's *At Tabaqat al Ijtima'iyyah fi Lubnan* (Social Classes in Lebanon), and Pierre Rondot's *At Tawa'if fi ad Dawlah al*

Lubnaniyyah (Sects in the Lebanese State) are two valuable Arabic sources. Albert H. Hourani's *Minorities in the Arab World* is a classic treatment of this subject, and Robert C. Betts's *Christians in the Arab East* gives a useful account of Christian denominations.

Also useful are some general works on Lebanon that contain relevant information. These include Helena Cobban's *The Making of Modern Lebanon,* David C. Gordon's *Lebanon: The Fragmented Nation* and *The Republic of Lebanon,* Albert H. Hourani's *Syria and Lebanon,* Michael C. Hudson's *The Precarious Republic,* and Kamal S. Salibi's *The Modern History of Lebanon.* (For further information and complete citations, see Bibliography.)

Chapter 3. The Economy

An olive press, symbolizing the agricultural productivity of Lebanon

AS THE LEBANESE state fragmented, so too did the national economy. Many observers have argued that because of this fragmentation, there was not one economy in the late 1980s, but several. Areas held by some militia groups, most notably the Maronite (see Glossary) Christian heartland controlled by the Lebanese Forces, appeared well on their way to becoming de facto ministates. These militias were successfully usurping basic functions of government such as taxation and defense.

Despite the fragmentation, there were still some shreds of the official economy. In late 1987 the main port of Beirut and Beirut International Airport were subject to intermittent government regulation. The Central Bank (also cited as Bank of Lebanon or Banque du Liban) maintained sizable financial reserves, although these declined sharply in the mid-1980s. There were spiraling budget deficits as the government attempted to reestablish the credibility of its security forces and maintain at least some social services.

Measuring the government's impact, however, was another matter. Although the government's financial role in the economy was growing, its role in the daily economic affairs of the Lebanese people was declining. The importance of the official economy in the late 1980s depended on where one lived and how one felt politically. But the economic collapse could not be separated from the human tragedy. For example, two of the most salient facts of life in Beirut in February 1987 were the collapse of the Lebanese pound to less than one-hundredth of a United States dollar and the request by Palestinian religious authorities for a ruling on whether or not it would be permissible for the besieged refugees in the camps at Burj al Barajinah and Shatila to eat their dead. In a country where violence had become endemic, where some 130,000 people had been killed and a further 1 million—a third of the population—had been injured, calculating the impact of the central government on the economy would be impossible.

In the years that followed the outbreak of the 1975 Civil War, political developments dominated economic affairs. Improved security conditions—such as from late 1976 to early 1978, or from September 1982 to January 1984—yielded considerable economic benefits, as relative peace enabled the recovery of commerce. Peace-keeping forces—Syrian, Israeli, United Nations, United States, and West European—brought with them favorable economic conditions in the communities where they were stationed. But the positive effects were frequently shortlived. For example, when Syrian troops entered Beirut in February 1987 (the first time a recognized power had attempted to enforce its authority in the capital since the February 1984 collapse of the Lebanese Army), there was a brief flurry of guarded economic optimism. The upswing of the Lebanese pound lasted only three weeks. But overall instability was the norm from 1975 to mid-1987, and it became clear that nothing short of a total change in the country's political and security structure—in effect, the end of sectarian partitions and militia rule—would lead to any sustained revival of what had once been one of the world's most vibrant economies.

By 1987 Lebanon had entered an era where reliable statistics on the state of the economy were usually absent. Lebanese economists were sometimes able to compile a few indicators, but the numbers were often based on incomplete data. But even without complete statistics, the downward trend of the national economy was obvious.

Bearing testimony to this trend, the Lebanese National Social Security Fund reported in May 1986 that 40 percent of the 500,000-strong private sector work force was unemployed. Industry was running at barely 40 percent of capacity, and per capita income was down to around US$250 a year in 1986, five times lower than eleven years earlier.

In 1985 estimates of the gross domestic product (GDP—see Glossary) varied from L£30 billion to as high as L£48.3 billion (for value of the Lebanese pound—see Glossary). In either case, GDP was no more than half of what it was in real terms in 1974.

Although the collapse of GDP began with the start of the Civil War, the fall of the Lebanese currency began much later. On the eve of the war, it required only L£2.3 to buy a United States dollar. Currency values declined over the next several years, but it was not enough to destroy the basic Lebanese confidence in the pound, which was backed by substantial holdings of gold and foreign exchange. Whereas in 1981 the exchange rate had averaged L£4.31 to the dollar, by the end of 1982, with the new government of President Amin Jumayyil (also seen as Gemayel) in office, the exchange rate was back to L£3.81 to the dollar.

The pound, however, began depreciating rapidly in the aftermath of further Beirut clashes in early 1984 and the withdrawal of the Multinational Force (MNF) of peacekeeping troops from the capital. Although there was widespread currency speculation, the Central Bank could do little to investigate this problem became of Lebanon's tough banking secrecy laws.

The economic prosperity of Beirut can be seen in this photograph taken before the 1975 Civil War.
Courtesy Aramco World

Between January and December 1984, the pound lost just under half its value against the dollar, while in 1985 the trend gained speed, resulting in a further 60-percent erosion in value. The Central Bank was widely criticized, especially by the commercial banks, for failing to act decisively to halt the pound's slide. But even greater criticism was directed against commercial bankers and leading politicians, who were constantly accused of speculating against the national currency.

By 1986 the country was on the verge of hyperinflation as the pound lost almost 85 percent of its already shrunken value during the course of the year. On February 11, 1987, the currency crashed through the psychologically important barrier of L£100 to the dollar and continued its fall. By August the pound was trading at more than L£250 to the dollar. Compounding the problem was that these events occurred after a year in which the dollar had fallen sharply against most major international currencies.

The fundamental principle of the Lebanese banking system had been a freely convertible pound. Citizens were free to hold foreign currency accounts in their banks, and remittances received from friends and family living abroad could be processed with relative ease through banking channels. As the pound began its decline, the importance of foreign currencies (particularly the United States dollar) grew, and a "twin currency" economy emerged. Complex systems were soon set up to circumvent the banking system, not for fear of governmental interference but to prevent the loss of deposits or of letters of credit through bank robberies. In the twin currency economy, foreign cash and drafts on bank accounts held outside the country became increasingly common. It became impossible, however, to calculate how much foreign cash was entering the country once transfers began to bypass the banking system. But it was clear that most people were not receiving enough to retain their pre-1975 living standards.

By 1987 ordinary Lebanese were living in a very strange economy. Public services functioned according to the ability of the government to pay staff, the ability of different groups to tap into utilities (with or without official permission) and the ability of local groups (with or without official help) to keep services operational. The costs of basics, such as gasoline, home fuel oil, and cooking gas were all subject to government price restraints, yet prices could double or triple in times of shortages, as roads between refineries, gasoline pumps, and fuel depots were cut. People found the government price controls ineffective, and the struggle to secure vital goods and commodities reflected not so much a free market as a

The Economy

free-for-all. By 1987 a dozen years of conflict had shown that economic control, as well as political power, came from the barrel of a gun.

By the late 1980s, years of conflict had distorted the economy. Total GDP was down, but the proportion of GDP contributed by the government was up. The national currency collapsed, and the country began sustaining balance of payments deficits. One commentator noted that 1986 marked the first time since the Civil War started in 1975 that Lebanon had suffered economic hardship to such an extent that it had affected the middle classes as well as the traditional urban poor. Another observer argued that Lebanon, once the model of modernity in the Middle East, was being threatened with "de-development."

Recent Economic History
Civil War and Partial Recovery, 1974-82

Lebanon traditionally has had a dynamic economy. In the years leading up to the Civil War, the country enjoyed high growth rates, an influx of foreign capital, and steadily rising per capita income. Although imports were often five or six times greater than exports, earnings from tourism, transit trade, services, and remittances from abroad counterbalanced the trade deficit.

In 1973 (the last prewar year for which detailed figures were available in late 1987), GDP at current prices totaled US$2.7 billion, compared with just US$1.24 billion in 1966. In 1974 GDP rose to around US$3.5 billion because of an increase in the value of the Lebanese pound. Per capita GDP rose from around US$560 in 1966 to US$1,023 in 1973 because productivity increased faster than population growth and because the Lebanese pound gained ground against the dollar.

The Lebanese economy was healthy in the years leading up to the Civil War. The service sector grew fastest during this period. Commerce grew at almost the same rate and by 1973 accounted for almost one-third of GDP. The growth of commerce had important implications because customs duties were a major part of government revenues, sometimes amounting to nearly half of the government's total income. The Lebanese pound was strong, credit was easy, and there was a balance of skilled and unskilled labor. Internal markets were protected, and Lebanese industry was finding increasingly useful outlets abroad, notably in the Persian Gulf countries.

The petrodollar boom that followed oil price increases by the Organization of Petroleum Exporting Countries after the

Arab-Israeli October 1973 War led to a period of expansion for Lebanon. Lebanese banks became major channels for soaring Arab oil revenues. In addition, Arab, West European, and American bankers bought shares in Lebanese financial institutions to secure a share of the profits.

Economic development, however, was uneven. The government was so wedded to free enterprise that it essentially failed to reduce economic and social inequities in various communities. President Fuad Shihab (also seen as Chehab) made some effort to remedy these inequities by pursuing development projects in the traditionally neglected south and north (see The Rise of Shihabism, 1958–64, ch. 1). But the center of the country—Beirut and the central Biqa Valley—was riding a seemingly never-ending economic boom.

The impetus for socially oriented economic development declined under Shihab's successor, Charles Hilu (also seen as Helou), and disappeared entirely under President Sulayman Franjiyah (also seen as Franjieh) (see The Hilu Era, 1964–70; The Franjiyah Era, 1970–76, ch.1). The consequences of economic neglect were felt in the late 1970s and the 1980s, as Shias (see Glossary), who had migrated from the south and the outlying reaches of the Biqa Valley, made their increasingly militant presence felt in Beirut, transforming the southern half of the city into a new, Shia canton, to rank alongside overwhelmingly Christian East Beirut and predominantly Muslim (i.e., Sunni and Druze—see Glossary) West Beirut (see Sectarianism, ch. 2).

The first nineteen months of the Lebanese Civil War (April 1975–November 1976) witnessed widespread destruction of infrastructure and services, mostly in Beirut. Industry sustained direct damage valued at between L£5 and L£7 billion. Indirect damage was valued at between L£972 million and L£2.23 billion. Some 250 industries, capitalized at L£1 billion, were destroyed, and as much as one-fifth of industry's fixed capital was lost. After the first nineteen months of fighting, losses amounted to L£7.5 billion (L£6.2 billion sustained by the private sector and L£1.3 billion by the public sector), according to the Beirut Chamber of Commerce and Industry.

Post-1976 recovery was limited, with industrial production approaching only two-thirds of prewar levels. Further clashes in 1978 again hampered production. Although in 1980 industrial output in current financial terms appeared to exceed prewar levels, inflation had rendered such comparisons almost meaningless. In 1979 the newly established Council for Development and Reconstruction (CDR) unveiled a L£22 billion reconstruction program to span five years, backed by Arab aid (see Aid and Reconstruction, this ch.). Only some of the proposed reconstruction work was initiated, however.

Instability ruined the tourist industry. The Civil War included the notorious battle of the hotels, in which the Phoenicia, St. Georges, and Holiday Inn—all major luxury hotels—became fiercely contested militia strongpoints (see The Early Stages of Combat, ch. 5). A score of smaller establishments suffered the same fate, as fighting ripped through the heart of the capital. Because the hotels were close to the Green Line (see Glossary), which divided the warring factions, they were forced to remain closed for business when the fighting stopped (see fig. 9).

After the war, there were indications that a less centralized industrial economy might emerge. The cities of Zahlah, Sidon, and Tripoli, for example, enjoyed a boom. But growth in these cities reflected fragmentation of the country as much as economic revival.

Lebanon's ability to export industrial goods was damaged by internal unrest and external pressures. The good reputation once enjoyed by Lebanese clothing manufacturers was undermined by imports of cheaper garments that were relabeled and reexported as "Lebanese." By the end of 1981, Iraq had halted all imports of Lebanese garments, and Egypt had frozen preferential terms for Lebanese industrial exports because of false labeling. Although the Egyptian and Iraqi measures were rescinded in 1982, they were symptomatic of the pressures that Lebanon faced throughout the 1980s.

Events elsewhere in the region also had an impact on Lebanon. A tripling of world fuel prices between 1973 and 1981 reduced the country's competitive edge. When Syria imposed restrictions on transit trade, freight forwarders found it increasingly uneconomic to ship goods to Persian Gulf destinations via Beirut. The prices of imported raw materials were higher than ever, while export markets were increasingly restricted. Thus, even before the Israeli invasion of 1982, the Lebanese economy was in bad shape.

Invasion and Trauma, 1982-87

Lebanon, torn by its sectarian and political disputes, was further cursed by invasion and a seemingly endless intermingling of internally and externally inspired conflict from 1982 onward. Beirut suffered grievously between June 6, 1982, when Israeli troops first crossed the Lebanese border, and September 16, when they completed their seizure of West Beirut. Normal economic activity was brought to a standstill. Factories that had sprung up in the southern suburbs were damaged or destroyed, highways were torn up, and houses were ruined or pitted by artillery fire and rockets. Close to 40,000 homes—about one-fourth of all Beirut's dwellings—were destroyed. Eighty-five percent of all schools south of the city were damaged or destroyed. The protracted closure of Beirut's port and airport drastically affected commerce and industry. By 1984 the World Bank (see Glossary) and the CDR agreed that Beirut would require some US$12 billion to replace or renovate damaged facilities and to restore services that had not been properly maintained since 1975.

In a December 31, 1982, national broadcast, President Amin Jumayyil called for the world to launch a new "Marshall Plan" to help reconstruct Lebanon. A series of conferences were held with major potential aid donors. A number of reconstruction projects were launched with support from the World Bank, the United States, and France. Roads began to be repaired, ports were cleared of debris, and schools and hospitals were built or rebuilt. But nothing was done on the grandiose scale Jumayyil had originally envisaged.

It became clear that Saudi Arabia and the Persian Gulf countries were not prepared to provide Lebanon with major reconstruction funds until the World Bank and other Western financial institutions had taken the lead in the reconstruction effort. And repeated breakdowns of fragile truces meant that from 1984 to 1987 there were no real opportunities for large-scale reconstruction efforts.

Still, financial and business circles were optimistic between September 1982 and January 1984 because Western-backed reconstruction plans seemed attainable under the presidency of Amin Jumayyil. But the mood did not last. Economic progress was insufficient to override the recurrence of sectarian strife, and the government seemed ineffective in reconstruction and reconciliation. When Beirut was again divided in February 1984, and the troops of the ill-fated MNF evacuated, a turning point was reached. From that point on, it became impossible to ignore the downward spiral of the Lebanese economy.

Foreign banks began selling and moving out. The decline of the Lebanese pound intensified, and hyperinflation set in. Public debt soared, and only drastic cutbacks in government purchases, which were virtually restricted to oil, ensured an overall balance of payments surplus in 1985.

By 1986 the inflation rate was well over 100 percent. Government revenues from taxation and customs duties continued to erode. And one account declared that at the end of 1986 "currency speculation and black marketeering have become the principal areas of business activity." Economic control was falling into the hands of those who possessed hard currency. The militias' tight grip on customs revenues gave them increasing control over what was left of the national economy; and their strength increased as the central government's control over national finances weakened. Although the Central Bank was still the guardian of one of the highest volumes of per capita foreign assets in any developing country, the government's ability to use these assets to reconstruct the country's shattered financial system or national economy was doubtful.

The Official Economy in the Mid-1980s
Balance of Payments

Before the early 1900s, Lebanon generally had a balance of payments surplus. After that, however, the balance of payments situation fluctuated considerably. In 1983 the Central Bank reported a deficit of US$933 million; a year later, the deficit was set at about US$1.4 billion. But in 1985 there was an overall current account surplus of US$381 million as Central Bank foreign assets rose and the government purchased fewer weapons. Progress was not maintained, however; by the end of May 1986, the Central Bank estimated a US$407 million deficit, comprising a US$583 million Central Bank shortfall and a US$176 million surplus at the commercial banks. Central Bank governor Edmond Naim complained that the shortfall was caused by pressure from the government to finance runaway public expenditure and a failure to do anything about the state's withering revenue base.

Public debt soared as the government's formal revenue sources—taxes and customs receipts—dried up. In 1984 the government spent about US$1.6 billion more than it obtained in revenues. The deficit had to be financed by borrowing US$840 million from the Central Bank and by selling treasury bonds. In 1985 the situation deteriorated even further, and by August the Chamber of Deputies had approved a budget based on US$611 million in government revenues. However, state revenues that year amounted to only US$224 million. The principal reason for the deficit was the persistent failure to secure receipts from customs duties. Public debt reached US$931 million by the end of 1986, and by the end of March 1987 it had increased even more.

Government Revenues

In the pre-Civil War days, receipts from customs duties accounted for nearly half of total government income. In 1984 customs receipts fell to US$69.4 million, barely one-third their 1983 level. The Ministry of Finance stated that customs receipts should be ten times higher than they were in 1984 to meet its targets for this revenue source. Instead, they fell further—to US$24.3 million in 1985. In 1986 total government spending was estimated at US$413 million against income of barely US$23 million. Of this already paltry sum, customs receipts amounted to just US$9.7 million.

In the mid-1980s, the government still had assets to cover its financial obligations. A November 1985 report listed as the nation's principal assets its gold reserves (about US$10 billion in foreign exchange reserves) and holdings in its Intra Investment Company (see Banking and Finance, this ch.). In addition, the report said, there were more than US$440 million in public sector deposits with the Central Bank, about US$200 million in secured debts owed to the state, and about US$86 million in various Central Bank assets. Against this, however, domestic public debt totaled US$2.5 billion, while foreign debt totaled US$200 million.

Some of the government's assets were unusual. By virtue of its Intra Investment Company holdings, the government had an important stake in the Casino du Liban, a famed nightclub at Juniyah. The casino also epitomized the way in which government had become dependent on militia deals to secure financing. In 1986 the casino reached an agreement with the Lebanese Forces (LF) militia under which the LF would close all illegal gambling houses under its control in exchange for a monthly income of US$1.2 million. At that time the casino's earnings were about US$2 million a month, of which 40 percent was paid in royalties to the government.

External Debt and Foreign Exchange

Lebanon had many economic problems in the 1980s, but foreign debt was not one of them. As late as 1986, the total official foreign debt was estimated at no more than US$250 million. The Bank of International Settlements put the country's external bank indebtedness at US$1.7 billion at the end of 1985, a decline from US$1.78 billion in 1984 and US$1.8 billion in 1983. Of the 1986 total, US$356 million was short-term (one-year) debt. The Organization for Economic Co-operation and Development put total external debt, excluding International Monetary Fund (IMF—see Glossary) credits, at US$938 million at the end of 1984. Long-term debt amounted to US$481 million, and total debt servicing, excluding IMF credit, amounted to US$268 million.

Total foreign reserves greatly exceeded debt. Throughout the 1980s, the Central Bank maintained a tight grip on the country's gold reserves and tried to do the same with its foreign currency reserves. The government held 9,222,000 ounces of gold, officially valued on the bank's books at US$42.23 an ounce and ostensibly

Business in Beirut, in one form or another, managed to continue throughout years of civil strife.
Courtesy Mokhless Al-Hariri/The Georgetown Design Group, Inc.

worth only US$389 million. In reality, however, it was worth at least US$3 billion.

In 1984 foreign exchange reserves, valued at US$1.9 billion in 1983, declined to US$652 million. In 1985 the reserves fell further to around US$300 million early in the year but recovered sharply to US$945 million in November. Then, at the start of 1986, there was a run on the Lebanese pound, and reserves plunged to US$300 million in March. The Central Bank attempted to counter falling reserves by forcing banks to increase their statutory reserves and take up subscriptions of treasury bills.

Inflation

Statistics from the General Labor Federation of Lebanon (Confédération Générale des Travailleurs du Liban) showed that for the first three months of 1985, there was a cost of living increase of 30 percent. The statistical directorate at the prime minister's office, however, put the increased cost for a single person living at subsistence level at 100 percent over the same period. The federation's statistics showed an 86-percent inflation rate in the 12 months ending June 1986, with food prices showing the highest increases. At the end of 1986, the federation estimated that during the first 10 months of 1986, the cost of living for a family of

Lebanon: A Country Study

5 had risen by 150 percent. Monthly expenditure on basic items—excluding education, rent, and medical expenses—had risen from L£5,652 to L£14,083. Overall, the federation estimated that 1986 had witnessed a 226-percent increase in prices. By March 1987, the federation was reporting a 250-percent inflation rate, with food prices having increased 300 percent over the previous 12 months.

Periodically, the government ordered wage increases, such as the 25-percent increase for all state employees enacted on January 1, 1986, but the increases did not keep up with inflation. In the anarchic circumstances of Lebanon, no amount of governmental action could resolve the underlying problem of inflation.

The Budget

The government of Amin Jumayyil had to face the seemingly insuperable problem of securing revenues and curtailing expenditures in 1987. Sectarian politics made the problem even more complicated. On the revenue side, the government lost its power to collect customs receipts because the militia forces controlled the unofficial, or illegal, ports. (Illegal ports are those not under the control of the Lebanese government; no official customs duties are collected at these ports.) Militia activity also hampered the government's ability to collect direct taxes and even to collect utility fees for electricity, water, and telecommunications. During good years, however, the government was successful at collecting revenues in some areas around Beirut. But in other parts of the country, and sometimes in the Beirut area, the militias were the only revenue collectors, imposing their own tax systems on areas under their control. This situation was extensive in the area controlled by the LF. The LF set up an organization in 1980 to supervise revenue collection from approximately eight illegal ports under its control. The LF also imposed levies on a variety of private retail establishments, from hotels and restaurants to gasoline stations and shops.

On the spending side, the biggest problem confronting the government throughout the 1980s was subsidies. It had long subsidized bread and sugar, and it was reluctant to remove these subsidies, which benefited the poorest groups. Instead, the government targeted fuel subsidies. In November 1985, Minister of Finance Camille Shamun (also seen as Chamoun) issued a decree abolishing state subsidies on gasoline. Prices at the pump almost doubled but were still less than US$1 per gallon. (The ministry still faced a cumulative deficit of US$365 million for fuel imports at the end of 1985, equivalent to about half the national budget. Actual fuel imports that year cost US$509 million.) The price increases triggered one-day general strikes throughout the country, but the

The Economy

collapse of international oil prices a few weeks later helped bring prices back down.

The question of fuel subsidies, however, remained unresolved. In 1986 the IMF told the government that raising local petroleum prices would be the most effective way of curbing the runaway budget deficit. The Central Bank also pushed to abolish fuel subsidies, and it informed the Ministry of Industry and Petroleum that it would stop payments for oil imports unless the ministry took action to reduce the deficit on its oil account, which the bank predicted would reach US$55 million that year.

In January 1987, the government increased fuel prices by 72 percent, but prices were still far from realistic. Before the price increase, consumers paid about seven cents per liter for gasoline. After the increase, they paid twelve cents per liter—still less than half the price commonly found in the United States, a country with one of the lowest gasoline prices in the world. In effect, such prices meant that gasoline was rationed and that when it was available, there would be an illegal surcharge. The pricing system also fostered a flourishing trade in illegal petroleum exports. Nonetheless, in June 1987 the government again rejected the possibility of terminating state subsidies on petroleum products.

Banking and Finance
Domestic Banking

Banking was one of the great strengths of the Lebanese economy before civil strife began in 1975. Between 1920 and 1964, the Bank of Syria and Lebanon, a French private bank and primarily a commercial enterprise, performed the central banking functions of being the sole issuer of notes and the holder of the government's accounts. The bank's charter expired in March 1964.

Until 1964 banks were totally unregulated. There were no special banking laws, no central bank, and no restrictions on the opening of new banks. No rules governed minimum reserve ratios, and banks were not even asked to produce regular balance sheets. This situation led to the creation of many small banks.

In April 1964, the Central Bank was established and given responsibility for controlling the Lebanese pound, for issuing notes, and for acting as the government's banker. Although prohibited from engaging in normal commercial banking, it had the authority to regulate commercial banks.

In 1966 the Lebanese-owned Intra Bank collapsed, precipitating a banking crisis. Intra Bank accounted for about 10 percent of total bank deposits and about 40 percent of deposits with

Lebanese-owned banks. (Observers believed that the Intra Bank crisis was brought on by Lebanese politicians who had manipulated fiscal affairs to their own gain.)

Intra Bank's collapse was followed by its restructuring, with the Central Bank and the Lebanese government taking major shareholdings. The successor organization, officially called the Intra Investment Company but often referred to as "Intra," became a major shareholder in various institutions, notably Middle East Airlines, the national flag carrier. The main banking arm was Bank Al Mashrek, in which Intra held an 84-percent share following Intra's acquisition early that year of a 42-percent share held previously by the J.P. Morgan Overseas Capital Corporation.

By 1985 the Central Bank held the biggest single share in Intra—27.75 percent. The government of Kuwait held 19 percent; the government of Lebanon, 10 percent; the National Bank of Kuwait, 3.75 percent; the government of Qatar, 3.25 percent; and various private shareholders (many of them from the Persian Gulf), 36.25 percent. The value of the Central Bank and Lebanese government shares in the Intra Investment Company in late 1985 was estimated at more than US$116 million.

Throughout the mid-1980s, however, the Central Bank was engaged in disputes with the Intra Investment Company's management, a wrangle that sometimes appeared to be almost a personal feud between Central Bank governor Naim, a guardian of financial orthodoxy, and Roger Tamraz, arguably Lebanon's most controversial and daring entrepreneur. Tamraz had been elected chairman of Intra following the company's August 1983 general meeting. He had a highly personal managerial style and had engaged in questionable business ventures in 1983 and 1984. The Central Bank became concerned and challenged Intra's policy on foreign bank acquisitions. The Central Bank wanted a new board of directors elected and wanted Intra run by Central Bank representatives and Persian Gulf shareholders. In August 1986, when Tamraz's three-year term was due to expire, the government demanded a shareholders meeting and initiated legal proceedings against him over his chairmanship. Tamraz responded by calling a shareholders meeting for December 29, 1986, the first to be convened since he became chairman.

At the meeting, which was held in East Beirut without representatives from 80 percent of the stockholders or Persian Gulf representatives, a new board was elected, with Tamraz at the helm. The outcome should have been a moment of triumph for Tamraz, but it was not. His tactics aroused concern from Intra's staff and the Central Bank, which claimed that Tamraz had pressured some

The Economy

representatives to miss the election meeting. Two weeks later, Tamraz resigned. In losing his position at Intra, Tamraz also lost much of his official influence with Middle East Airlines (see Transportation and Communications, this ch.). Nevertheless, he did hold onto one very important position: chairmanship of Bank Al Mashrek. Although the events of early 1987 were a major setback to Tamraz in his quasi-public roles, his own business interests remained substantial, and he was still a very potent force on the financial and commercial scene. Tamraz was replaced by Jamil Iskandar, a businessman who had been on Intra's board in 1983.

In the face of the Intra-Central Bank controversy, domestic banks fared poorly and were plagued by nonperforming loans. One local banker claimed that at the end of 1985 nonperforming loans accounted for 45 percent of his bank's total loan portfolio, compared with 25 percent a year earlier. Banking costs rose while fierce competition in a depressed market resulted in excessively high interest rates. In addition, there were more than 50 bank robberies in 1985, entailing known losses of US$800,000.

To overcome the problem, some domestic banks increased their overseas activities. The Intra Investment Company, for example, bought commercial interests of the Paris-based Banque Stern and a small Swiss bank, the Banca di Particepiazioni e Investimenti. In 1986 it also sought to purchase the four Egyptian branches of the local Jammal Trust Bank.

On paper, however, the banks did not appear to be doing too badly. Total assets of the commercial banks rose from about L£100 billion at the end of 1984 to about L£162 billion a year later. About 70 percent of these holdings were believed to be in foreign currency, which meant that in December 1984 assets amounted to about US$11.3 billion and almost US$9 billion a year later.

The Central Bank

Throughout years of the most appalling political, economic, and social suffering, the Central Bank was the only institution that preserved its reputation for essentially sound management. Since 1964 the Central Bank had been the guardian of the country's financial orthodoxy. It embodied the business beliefs common to a variety of Lebanese citizens, from merchants and bankers to the traditional Christian and Muslim political leaders.

From 1974 onward, successive bank governors constantly had to determine how much the Central Bank should squeeze commercial banks in order to secure revenue for the government through the sale of treasury bills. Securing revenue this way provided the bank with some of its more anxious movements as it saw its share of public debt climb steadily, particularly in the mid-1980s.

The Central Bank's activities eventually became controversial, and key issues needed to be addressed. There was the question of whether the bank should use the country's still considerable reserves for reconstruction and development projects (see Aid and Reconstruction, this ch.). There was also the issue of the extent to which the bank should continue propping up the Lebanese pound in the face of currency speculation, widely believed to involve leading Lebanese politicians.

Still, the Central Bank functioned with surprising efficiency, despite its location in the middle of the West Beirut battleground and despite the vicissitudes of the 1970s and 1980s. It reported a L£1.2 billion profit for 1984, essentially from domestic lending operations. In 1985 the profits were L£2.6 billion and in 1986, L£4.9 billion. As customary, the bank kept 20 percent of its profits for reserves and sent 80 percent to the treasury. Although profits appeared respectable when measured in United States dollars, they showed that the bank was losing the battle to maintain its own real income or that of the government. Thus profits, calculated at year-end rates, were US$137.5 million in 1984, US$124.2 million in 1985, and just US$56.4 million in 1986.

Although the Central Bank was keeping the government solvent, it eventually reached a watershed in 1986. At the start of the year, public debt totaled L£53.4 billion (about US$3 billion), of which the bank's share was 25 percent. By May, however, its share had ballooned to 44 percent. Bank loans to the state rose by 41 percent in the first 10 months of 1986 to total L£22 billion, compared with L£15.6 billion at the start of the year. Concern over the bank's funding of public debt grew, causing undersubscription of treasury bills. At the same time, the Central Bank imposed new regulations that angered the commercial banks.

Prime Minister Rashid Karami intervened in May 1986 by helping to negotiate a new agreement in which the size of commercial banks' statutory reserves was reduced, as was the amount of deposits that they had to keep in the form of treasury bills. The agreement, unfortunately, came at a time of renewed clashes between Shia Amal militiamen and Palestinians in the southern Beirut refugee camps. The clashes pushed down the value of the pound even further at a time when the Central Bank accord with the commercial banks had been expected to strengthen the currency (see Chaos in Beirut and Syrian Peacemaking Efforts, ch. 5).

The measures negotiated by Karami proved insufficient either to restore faith in the currency or to end the dispute between the commercial banks and the Central Bank. The Central Bank imposed tighter controls in December 1986. It raised the statutory reserve to 13 percent, increased the volume of bank deposits to be kept in treasury bills, and banned loans in local currency to nonresidents (unless they were for trade purposes). The bank also forbade nonresident banks from receiving deposits, providing credits, or opening accounts in Lebanese pounds. Understandably, the commercial banks opposed the new rules. Before the announcement, only nine of the eighty-two commercial banks then operating were in violation of regulations. But under the new measures, sixty-three banks would have to increase reserves and treasury bill purchases to be in compliance.

The commercial banks protested. They believed that the Central Bank's attempts to force them to cover the budget deficit were preventing them from undertaking more profitable activities. In January 1987, the Central Bank softened its position. Its new policy meant that the largest banks were obliged to keep no less than 45 percent of their deposits in treasury bills, on top of the 13 percent required as statutory reserves. This left the banks with limited funds for productive lending.

The Central Bank's actions did little to improve the national currency, boost the economy, or ease relations with the commercial banks. Just a few weeks later, on February 11, 1987, it took L£100 to buy a single United States dollar. The subsequent deployment of Syrian Army units in West Beirut temporarily reversed the situation, improving the rate to L£85 to US$1, but on March 3 the pound lost 20 percent of its value in a single day's hectic trading. The Central Bank accused commercial banks of attempting to hoard foreign currency and of acting in league with speculators. But the Lebanese Bankers' Association blamed the Central Bank for failing to stabilize the market when the dollar began to move and for selling dollars too late.

International Banking

Many international banks pulled out of Beirut in the 1980s. For example, the First National Bank of Chicago sold its local interests to local investors for US$7.5 million in 1982. But the replacement institution, First Phoenician Bank, ran into liquidity problems in 1984, when the managing director, Waji Muawad, allegedly absconded with US$13 million of the bank's funds. Bank Al Mashrek initiated takeover proceedings in 1985.

In 1985 Bank Al Mashrek also bought two branches of the British Standard Chartered Bank. Banque Libano-Française bought the Toronto-based Bank of Nova Scotia's local operation. The

Moscow Narodny Bank closed its branch, handing over its local business to Bank Handlowy for the Middle East, the local subsidiary of Warsaw's Bank Handlowy. The Chase Manhattan Bank and Bank of America both closed their Beirut operations, the former handing over its business to Banque Sabbag et Française pour le Moyen Orient. By the end of 1986, only two United States banks were still operating in Lebanon—Citibank and American Express International.

The British Bank of the Middle East (BBME), the second largest foreign bank in Lebanon, resisted the trend as long as possible. In 1976 the bank's headquarters in Bab Idris had been the target for one of the biggest heists in history. Losses of cash and contents of safe-deposit boxes amounted to about US$24 million. BBME recovered and maintained operations, however, and opened branches in East Beirut as that part of the city became a distinct entity. At the start of Amin Jumayyil's presidency, BBME's future appeared promising. Its assets stood at L£1.3 billion (about US$315 million). But the growing insecurity of 1984, the kidnapping of two senior managers, and a robbery in West Beirut in 1985 prompted the management to close down four of its six branches in the Greater Beirut area at the end of 1985. Thereafter, the bank maintained a single branch in West Beirut, another in East Beirut, and a third in Tripoli.

Transportation and Communications

Lebanon's mountainous terrain limits transportation between different parts of the country. Transportation has also been limited by warfare in the 1970s and 1980s; by militia control of key ports, highways, and access points; by the destruction of the country's former railroad network; and by the near-destruction of its aviation links with the rest of the world.

Roads

In 1987 Lebanon had some 8,000 kilometers of roads and a highway network, most of which was in various states of disrepair. There were three routes of overwhelming importance, each radiating from Beirut. To the north was the road to Tripoli, Lebanon's second largest city, a route that also passed through such major towns as Juniyah and Jubayl. To the east, crossing the Lebanon Mountains, was the highway to Damascus, passing through the key town of Shtawrah. And to the south was the road to Sidon and Tyre (see fig. 6). Lebanon possessed a second north-south road axis, running along the length of the Biqa Valley. Roads in the northern valley converged on the Beirut-Damascus highway at Shtawrah and

The Economy

linked the important market towns of Baalbek and Zahlah with the primary road network. The southern valley's local road network also centered on Shtawrah at its northern end.

Cross-mountain routes, which linked the northern Biqa Valley with Juniyah and Tripoli and the southern valley with Sidon, were of relatively little importance in times of peace. In the 1980s, however, ordinary travelers have used these routes to circumvent roadblocks on the major roads, and drug dealers have used them for transport (see Crop Production, this ch.). Private militias have also used them to secure lines of communication between the coast and outlying areas. Minor cross-border routes into Syria have also been important entry routes from time to time for Palestinian and sometimes Iranian fighters entering Lebanon. These roads have also served as exit points for produce funneled via Lebanon onto the Syrian black market.

After its establishment in 1961, the Executive Council for Major Projects (Conseil Exécutif des Grands Projets) drew up a plan for a 241-kilometer highway network. The plan was to transform the three main routes from Beirut into four-lane, divided highways through the construction of new roads or the expansion of existing ones. But because of bureaucratic delays, little was done before the outbreak of the Civil War in 1975, although some roads were upgraded. A drive to complete the project was undertaken in 1980; the US$1.6 billion program continued, well into the mid-1980s, albeit somewhat haphazardly in view of the uncertain security conditions.

By 1987 most of the sixty-five kilometers of the Lebanon section of the Beirut-Damascus highway, including a difficult stretch through the Lebanon Mountains, approximated international highway standards. The government hoped to be able to implement plans drawn up by consultants from the Federal Republic of Germany (West Germany) for a full highway link between Beirut and the Syrian border. Likewise, most of the northern coastal highway to Tripoli was complete, except for the final section from Tripoli to the Syrian border. Work on the southern coastal highway lagged, however. Some sections between Beirut and Sidon had been completed, but there was little progress on the stretch between Sidon and Tyre.

The existence of new highways did not necessarily mean they were available for use. For example, during much of the early 1980s stretches of the northern coastal highway were blocked off by local Christian militias who found it easier to regulate traffic on the old coast road.

Lebanon: A Country Study

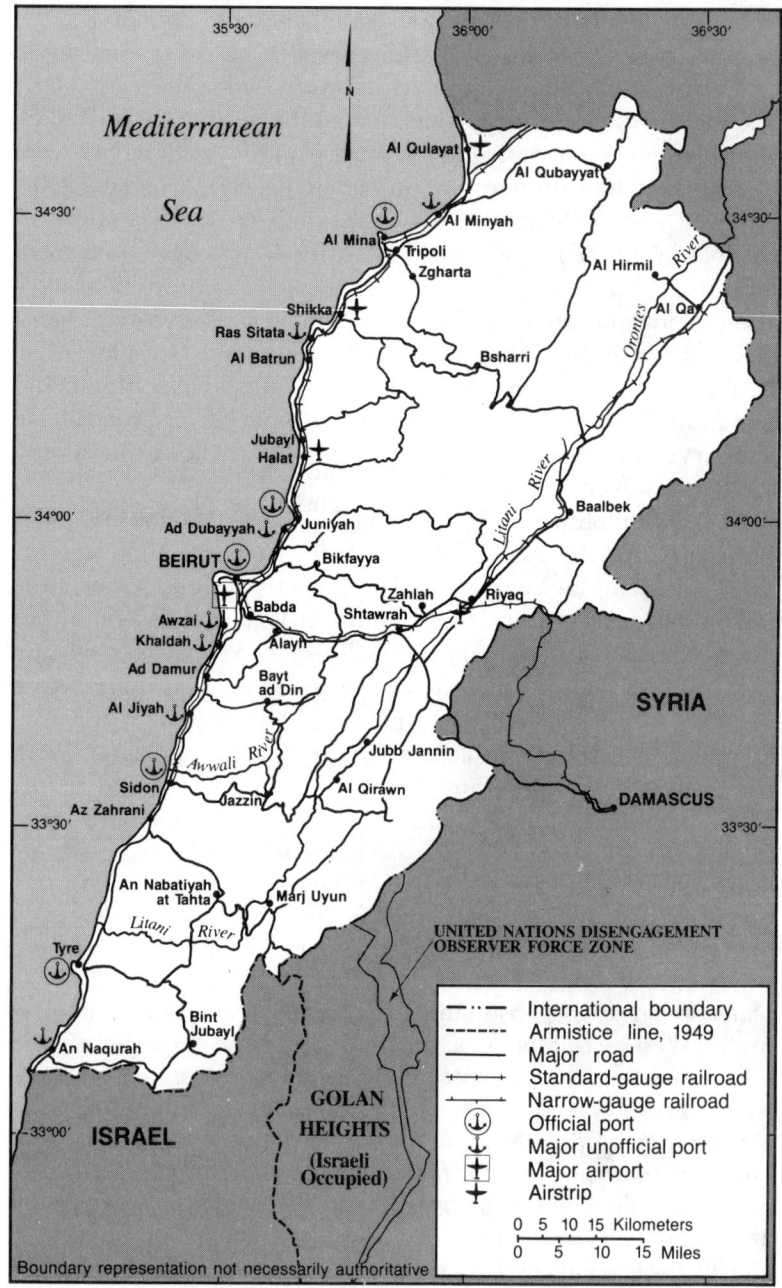

Figure 6. Transportation System, 1987

The Economy

Although the government traditionally allotted high priority to road building and maintenance, the rehabilitation of the country's network has been badly hampered by war. Some roads, however, have been repaired at the behest of Syrian military authorities. In the south, in the area in which United Nations (UN) troops were stationed, roads were built and renovated. And along the Israeli border, but within Lebanon itself, Israel constructed a series of earth roads in the late 1970s and early 1980s designed to facilitate troop deployments.

The collapse of the central government necessitated the development of ad hoc transportation systems. Successive attempts to revive Beirut's public bus system after the 1975-76 fighting failed as a new fleet of French-built buses were turned into barricades in subsequent conflicts, including the 1982 Israeli invasion. In some parts of the country, business enterprises ran buses or trucks to ferry their employees to work, but there was no coherent national transportation system. Shared taxis became the most common form of public transport. Taxis could be hired to carry travelers from one town to another, but taxi service might not be available if militia groups declared a blockade along a particular route. Such blockades also affected deliveries of key products, such as food supplies, fuel, and goods intended for import or export. Travel became prohibitively expensive for ordinary Lebanese when roads were closed. Keeping the roads open became the responsibility of a series of armed forces: the militias, the Lebanese government forces, the UN forces, and, repeatedly, the Syrian Army. From time to time, responsibility lay with Israeli, Palestinian, United States, and West European troops.

Railroads

Lebanon used to have a patchwork railroad system. From the central Syrian railroad depot of Homs, two standard-gauge lines entered Lebanon. One line passed down the coast to Tripoli and Beirut and ended just north of the southern oil terminal at Az Zahrani; the other came down the Biqa Valley to Riyaq, near Shtawrah. A narrow-gauge, mountain railroad running from Beirut through Riyaq to Damascus linked these two lines. The coastal line was still being used for occasional fuel shipments from the Tripoli refinery to Beirut in the late 1970s, but the line's southern section to Az Zahrani was cut in several places just south of Beirut. French companies had begun limited repairs on the damaged line but had to stop as renewed violence erupted in February 1984. The Biqa Valley line, antiquated already in the 1960s, finally went out of commission during fighting in 1975-76. Finally, the Beirut-Damascus line was verging on obsolescence even before the outbreak of war.

By 1987 it was believed that no trains were functioning anywhere on Lebanon's 407-kilometer system, and the prospects for the rail system's recovery were poor. Canadian consultants studied a possible revival of the coastal line in 1983, but security conditions made rehabilitation impossible. If the railroads are ever revived, the coastal line will get priority.

Shipping

There are no navigable rivers in Lebanon, but there is some coastal shipping. Before 1975 the port of Beirut was a major entrepôt for the Middle East, especially for goods bound for Damascus and Amman. In 1974 approximately 3.4 million tons of goods were unloaded at the Beirut docks, 668,000 tons were loaded, and 932,000 tons of transit goods were handled. When the Civil War began, however, the port became a major battleground. Battles also took place there in subsequent clashes between 1978 and 1987. Despite strenuous efforts to restore the port to full working order, by 1987 it had yet to regain anything like its former prominence.

Between the start of the Civil War in 1975 until 1983, the port's best year was 1980, when some 2.7 million tons of cargo were unloaded, 248,056 tons were loaded, and 209,080 tons were handled in transit. The Israeli siege of Beirut led to a drastic drop in port activity in 1982, when goods handled fell to less than two-thirds of the 1980 level.

The shipping industry did not fare well in 1983, the last full year in which the central government could claim to control both halves of the national capital. Although cargo unloaded recovered somewhat to about 2.5 millions tons, cargo loaded was only 105,640 tons, and transit cargo dwindled to a mere 87,415 tons.

The port was closed for five months following the division of the city in February 1984, resulting in lost revenues of around US$30 million. The closure was the longest in the port's history. When the port reopened in July, the Jumayyil government tried to improve conditions by taking over the port's fifth basin, previously controlled by the LF, and closing another LF-controlled illegal port at Ad Dubayyah. These gains were purely temporary, however. In 1986 the LF regained control of the fifth basin, which the government allowed to be run by a new company owned partly by the LF. The government also allowed the company to run the illegal port at Ad Dubayyah and the official port of Juniyah. The establishment of the new company was really little more than legalization

The Economy

of an essentially illegal operation since the LF already controlled the ports and was denying the government customs revenues.

Illegal, or unofficial, ports—those not under the control of the government—developed in the 1970s. By the 1980s, they had become Lebanon's principal purveyors of imports. These ports, mainly controlled by the principal militia groups, were used for a wide variety of imports, ranging from basic necessities to military supplies from Israel and Libya. As of 1987, as many as twenty illegal ports, mostly controlled by militias, were in operation.

The volume of goods discharged at the illegal ports cannot be measured exactly. Nevertheless, two prominent Lebanese economists, Marwan Iskandar and Elias Baroudi, noted in a 1983 analysis of Lebanese port activity that the 19-percent drop in cargo unloaded at the legal Beirut port in 1981 did not necessarily reflect a drop in total imports—a large proportion of imports came through illegal ports. Observers believed an extremely effective central government would be needed to transfer or return revenues from the ports to the national treasury.

With rival militias flanking the port of Beirut and periodically forcing its closure, Lebanon's other ports might have been expected to pick up some of the slack (see table 5, Appendix A). Traffic at Tripoli did rise steadily from 1975 to 1979 but declined thereafter. It suffered from fighting in 1983 between Palestinian and Syrian forces in the northern section of the port of Tripoli and because of the increasing effectiveness of Lebanon's illegal ports. In late 1985, however, after Syrian forces had imposed calm, traffic at Tripoli grew to 50,000 tons per month by January 1986.

Lebanon's other traditional ports at Tyre and Sidon also have had troubled histories. Tyre suffered during the Civil War, during the Israeli invasions of 1978 and 1982, and during other Israeli military actions. Sidon was similarly afflicted, escaping only the 1978 assault. Both ports have also witnessed some internal conflict. After Israel's 1984 pullout from much of Lebanon, however, Tyre appeared to enjoy a revival of its local economy. Although Sidon suffered from further Shia-Palestinian conflict, it recovered modestly, and its export trade increased in early 1987.

Israel has persistently intervened in Lebanese maritime affairs. Its actions ranged from dispatching gunboats to positions off Beirut, a fairly common occurrence, to closing ports under Israeli control, such as Tyre and Sidon in 1984. From time to time, Israeli forces searched ships bound to or from Lebanese ports. In 1984, late 1986, and early 1987, Israel also stopped several ships ferrying passengers between Larnaca in Cyprus and Juniyah, the principal port of the Maronite heartland. Israel claimed that the ships were being used to infiltrate Palestinian guerrillas into Lebanon and warned that the Larnaca-Juniyah link would be closed altogether if the vessels continued to carry Palestinian fighters.

Aviation

For years, Middle East Airlines (MEA) was the star of Lebanese international communications. It had bought out two other private airlines, Air Liban and Lebanese International Airlines, and developed a style and service second to none. By the early 1970s, despite the loss of ten of its airplanes during an Israeli commando raid on Beirut International Airport in December 1968, it had become a model for oil-rich Arab states seeking to establish their own national carriers.

MEA represented the best of Lebanon. It reflected close Franco-Lebanese relations: Air France had a 30-percent stake in the venture, and Intra Investment Company held the principal 62.5-percent shareholding. Its chairman from 1952 to 1978, Shaykh Najib Alamuddin, scorned sectarianism and ran MEA as a socially and religiously integrated operation. This tradition of integration continued after 1978.

By 1975 MEA had become the country's largest employer, providing work for 5,600 people. Although the airline survived the Civil War, it was unable to regain the ebullience that had characterized its prewar operations. MEA survived the 1975–76 fighting by leasing many of its aircraft and flight crews to other Arab airlines and by operating on routes between the Persian Gulf and Western Europe that did not require refueling in Beirut. Nonetheless, losses were heavy, totaling US$12.8 million during the first 10 months of the Civil War. As fighting intensified in 1976, hope for full recovery diminished. During the quieter years of the late 1970s, however, the airline regained momentum. Old routes were reestablished, although in April 1977 MEA lost the right to fly to Damascus, as Syrian-Lebanese relations became strained. (The Damascus right was finally reinstated in August 1985.)

The airline was almost back to normal in the late 1970s and posted a US$2.4 million profit in 1980. But fresh fighting closed Beirut International Airport in the spring of 1981, and passenger traffic dropped. At the same time, an important long-term leasing agreement with Saudia, the national air carrier of Saudi Arabia, came to an end. MEA's revenues fell 32 percent, and fuel bills rose 21.6 percent; the net result was a massive US$19 million loss. Nonetheless, the airline's ambitions remained undimmed, and in October 1981 MEA signed an order to buy five Airbus A310 aircraft, with options on another fourteen.

*The result of an Israeli attack
on a Middle East Airlines jetliner
Courtesy United States Navy (Robert Feary)*

Then came the 1982 Israeli invasion, and Beirut International Airport was closed for 115 days. Five MEA Boeing 707s were damaged so badly they had to be written off; six others were also damaged, but less severely. Company hangars and offices, occupied by the Israelis, were also hit. Passenger volume plunged from 936,618 million in 1981 to 634,919 million in 1982. Losses for the year reached US$49.2 million.

There was little improvement in 1983. The airport was closed for thirty-two days in August and September and for another seventeen days in December. Faced with the prospect of a record US$54.6 million loss, in November the airline terminated its agreement to buy the Airbuses. Airport closures persisted in Beirut, grounding the airline, and in August 1985 a Boeing 720 was destroyed and a 707 badly damaged by gunfire. The airline's all-Boeing fleet was depleted to just three 747s, five 707s, and nine 720s. In January 1987, another 707 was destroyed when the airport came under artillery fire. The aircraft was not insured because of the high war-risk premium, and MEA had to absorb the loss.

By October 1985, MEA had become the only airline serving Beirut, and passenger traffic was down to only 1,200 to 1,300 daily—the lowest level since 1953. Despite falling passenger volumes and a 50-percent reduction in the airline's route network, MEA still held out hopes for recovery and negotiated in 1985 with Boeing, McDonnell-Douglas, and Airbus Industrie for new aircraft. High fuel costs meant that the airline needed a new generation of fuel-efficient aircraft, but the company lacked the funds to purchase them outright and could not borrow money to pay for them because lenders did not have confidence in the airline.

Between 1965 and 1975, Lebanese entrepreneur Munir Abu Haydar had turned a small freight carrier called Trans Mediterranean Airways (TMA) into the largest all-cargo airline in the Middle East. But instability at Beirut International Airport forced TMA to shift operations to Sharjah in the United Arab Emirates in the 1970s and 1980s. TMA suffered a blow, however, in mid-1985 when Saudi Arabia forbade TMA and several other airlines to overfly the kingdom. Iraq, too, had banned TMA from entering its airspace, and the airline was effectively grounded. TMA formally suspended services in August 1985, and began selling off its fleet, which, at the start of the year, had consisted of eight Boeing 707s. The airline, however, was able to sell only one of its aircraft.

The airline asked the government for a US$10.6 million bailout loan, but the government was slow to respond, and bankruptcy became a distinct possibility. Discussions on a merger with MEA began as TMA's financial position steadily deteriorated; its routes were cut, and competition from state-subsidized airlines mounted. The MEA board responded cautiously to merger suggestions and waited to see if the government favored the idea. Then in mid-1986, Jet Holdings, a company with which Intra Investment Company chairman Tamraz was closely involved, effectively took control of TMA and assumed responsibility for its US$7.5 million debt.

Aviation politics in Lebanon were increasingly partisan in the 1980s. Maronite concern about access to Beirut International Airport had prompted efforts to develop an alternative airstrip at Halat, a military airfield twenty kilometers north of Beirut, to serve East Beirut and the Maronite heartland. The project was carried out under the supervision of Jet Holdings. By early 1986, the Halat runway had been extended to 2,600 meters. Tamraz sought to involve MEA in the venture, which he believed might begin with charter service to Larnaca and Athens. But MEA refused to operate flights from Halat because the Ministry of Transport had delayed recognition of the airfield's civilian status. After the government set up a committee to study a plan to turn military airfields, as well as Halat, into civilian airports, Beirut International Airport reopened in May 1987. But without resolution of the Halat dispute, the outlook for MEA—an airline that had once set world standards for service—was in doubt.

Telecommunications

The country's telecommunications system suffered severely from the violence that occurred after 1975. Damage to equipment from 1975 to early 1982 was estimated at about US$150 million. At the time of the Israeli invasion of 1982, the Directorate of Posts, Telephone, and Telegraph was in the middle of a US$325 million 2-year rehabilitation project aimed at installing 32 new electronic exchanges and adding 220,000 new lines. Although new telex facilities had become operational in February 1982, only a few of the new telephone exchanges were in operation when Israel began its siege of Beirut in June. The invasion froze improvements in the telecommunications system, although Lebanese authorities, with United States financial assistance, were able to carry out extensive repair work during the comparative calm of 1983. The Republic of Korea (South Korea) financed and repaired some 81,700 telephone lines around Beirut in 1983 during that period, and a local subcontractor carried out extensive repair work in East Beirut for the United States Federal Electric Corporation until funds dried up in 1984.

Agriculture

The variety of Lebanon's agricultural lands, from the interior plateau of the Biqa Valley to the narrow valleys sweeping down to the sea, enables farmers to grow both European and tropical crops. Tobacco and figs are grown in the south, citrus fruits and bananas along the coast, olives around the Shuf Mountains and in the north, and fruits and vegetables in the Biqa Valley (see fig. 7). More exotic crops include avocados, grown near Jubayl, and hashish, a major crop in the Biqa Valley. Local wines, even those produced in times of war, have won international prizes. Since 1975, however, Lebanon's fertile land has not been fully exploited because of almost constant warfare. In addition, the livestock production, which had made up a significant part of total agricultural production before the war, fell off drastically, especially after the 1982 Israeli invasion.

Land and Irrigation

Almost one-fourth of Lebanon's land is cultivable—the highest proportion in the Arab world. Most of these 240,000 hectares are rain fed, but in 1982 some 85,000 hectares were reported to be under irrigation, 20 percent more than in 1970. Another source estimated that in the mid-1980s 400,000 hectares (including marginal land) were cultivable, with about one-fourth of this irrigated. In 1981 the UN's Food and Agriculture Organization (FAO)

Lebanon: A Country Study

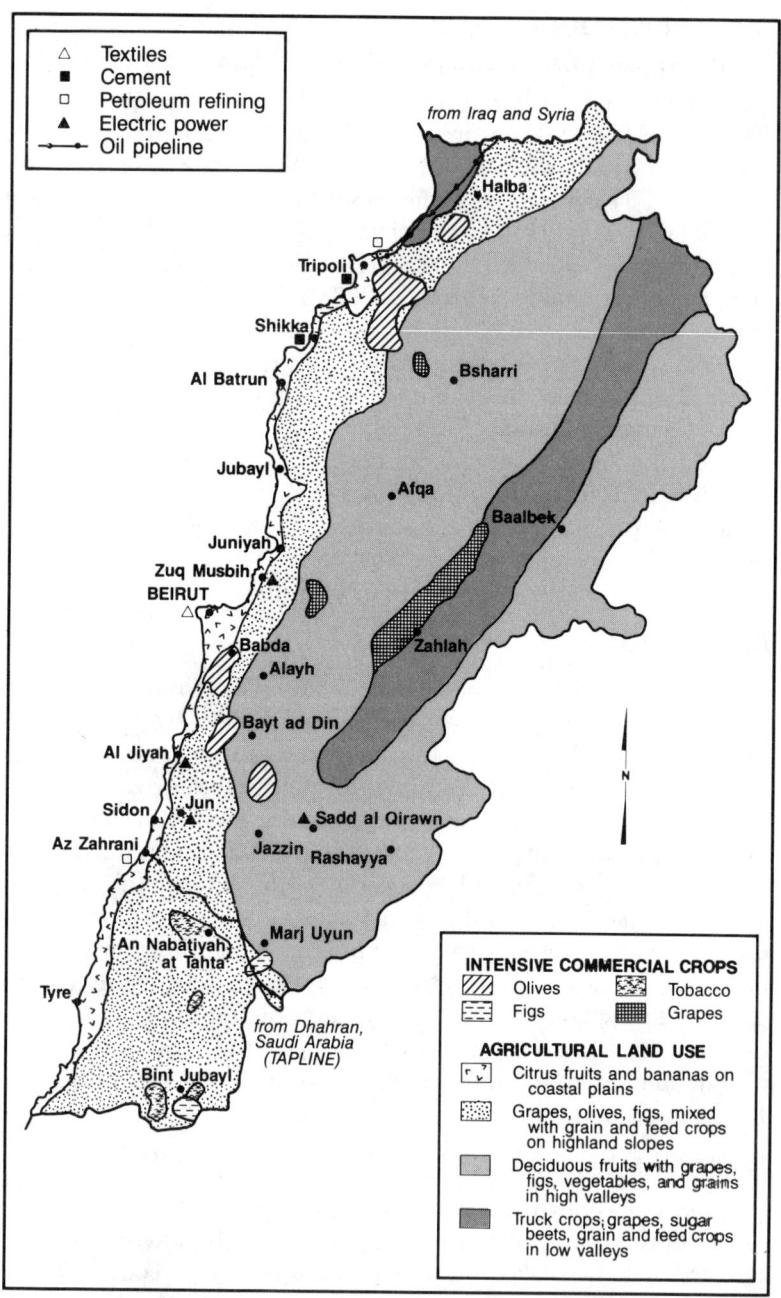

Figure 7. *Economic Activity, 1987*

The Economy

estimated that around 108,000 hectares were permanently cultivated and that 19,300 hectares had been reclaimed for cultivation since the inception of the 1963 Green Plan, a project designed to reclaim 15,000 hectares over 10 years. The FAO estimated that no fewer than 280,000 hectares of land in various parts of the country were reclaimable for agricultural production.

In the early 1980s, the government prepared plans to irrigate an additional 60,000 hectares, and by 1984 studies were under way on 6 major irrigation projects, all designed to be carried out as part of the 1982–91 reconstruction plan. The biggest project, to be implemented by the Litani Water Authority, was for irrigation of some 15,000 hectares of high land (between 500 and 800 meters above sea level) in southern Lebanon over an 8-year period, scheduled to start in 1990. Observers reported in 1986 that the government planned to increase the amount of irrigated land, through various dam and irrigation schemes, from 65,000 hectares to 125,000 hectares.

In the late 1970s and early 1980s, Lebanese officials reported that small tributaries of the Hasbani River were being diverted into Israel near the northern town of Metulla (see fig. 3). Independent water analysts stated that after the 1982 invasion, Israel engaged in a much more serious diversion of Lebanese waters by attaching stopcocks at a pumping station on the Litani River. The stopcocks were designed to switch at least part of the flow—which is generated entirely within Lebanon—to Israel via a specially constructed pipeline.

Lebanon's land tenure system is characterized by many small holdings, but the number has declined over the years. In 1961 about 127,000 farms were reported operating. The partial census of 1970, however, recorded some 75,000 farm holdings, of which 46 percent were smaller than 2 hectares while only 12 percent had 10 hectares or more. In 1981–82 there were some 64,000 active farms, with only 50 in the 100- to 1,000-hectare range.

Landholding patterns were also affected by massive population movements in the 1970s and 1980s. Lebanon's internal refugees strove assiduously to maintain title to their lands, many of which came to be controlled by rival sectarian or political groups. A case in point was in southern Lebanon. After the 1978 Israeli invasion, many Muslim landholders fled to other parts of Lebanon, hoping to reclaim their land following Israel's withdrawal. But instead of handing the land over to the United Nations Interim Force in Lebanon (UNIFIL), as was expected, Israel turned it over to the Christian South Lebanon Army (SLA). The effect was to dispossess many of the former landholders.

Two important socioeconomic trends made it difficult to evaluate the farming structure in the 1980s. The first trend was consolidation of holdings, as Beirut-based professionals began buying up small farms before the 1975 fighting. The war may have slowed this development, however, because it complicated long-distance supervision of land. At the same time, the trend toward large families, especially in the south, made the old system of dividing holdings among male offspring less feasible, although in many cases this factor was offset by the migration of males to the city or emigration abroad. Even elderly farmers acknowledged that the old land inheritance system had to be changed. But the pace of such change could not be monitored easily in the troubled conditions of the 1980s.

The number of farms dropped during the war, resulting in more tracts of untilled land rather than in more ownership transfers. Small freeholders who chose to continue farming often lived in poverty. Even before the 1975 Civil War, the average annual income for the head of an agricultural household was estimated at L£500, compared with L£1,100 for a counterpart working in industry or L£8,060 in the services sector. One report noted that 56 percent of those engaged in agriculture in southern Lebanon, most of whom were landowners, also had second jobs in the late 1960s.

Crop Production

The impact of war and sectarian politics on Lebanese agriculture was unclear. It is obvious, however, that the Civil War did take its toll on the production of most crops (see table 6, Appendix A).

Although there was a recovery from 1979 to 1981, it was not sustained, as the 1982 Israeli invasion disrupted production in the southern half of the country, especially along Israel's so-called "security zone." Even in the relative calm between 1978 and 1981, about 1,100 hectares of tobacco were destroyed, 300 hectares of agricultural land were abandoned because of land mines, and 51,000 olive trees and 70,000 fruit trees were destroyed, according to the United Nations High Commissioner for Refugees.

Regional politics also played a major role in the fortunes of Lebanon's crop production. For example, in 1984 fruit exports reached their lowest level since 1962, in part because Syria had restricted imports of Lebanese produce. Syria imposed these restrictions not only to prevent the sale in Syria of Israeli produce available in Al Janub Province but also to pressure the Lebanese government to abrogate its May 1983 peace agreement with Israel (see The May 17 Agreement, ch. 5). Indeed, Israel's flooding of the market in Al Janub Province with various agricultural products, especially bananas, caused some to claim that Israel was "dumping" surplus produce on a market that could not afford produce imported from any other country.

The collapse of the Lebanese pound in 1984–85 also had a major impact on crop production. On the one hand, the collapse improved Lebanon's ability to compete in foreign markets; indeed, exports of agricultural products, notably fruits and vegetables, increased in 1985. On the other hand, local consumption slumped as fruit and vegetable prices rose an average 85 percent during the year. The fall of the pound also sparked price increases for seeds, fertilizers, feeds, and insecticides.

Tobacco played a major role in the economy of southern Lebanon before the Civil War. The Administration for Tobacco and Tombacs (Régie des Tabacs et Tombacs), a state monopoly, dominated tobacco marketing. Claiming that the marketing arrangements benefited only the largest tobacco growers, in 1973 about 10,000 small planters demonstrated in Sidon against the low prices being paid for their crops. Economic conditions thus helped alienate from the state the predominantly Shia south, a factor that contributed to the troubles of the later 1970s and 1980s. Henceforth, restructuring of the monopoly became a persistent demand of the southern Lebanese, Shia and Christian alike.

The Israeli invasion of 1978 badly affected tobacco production for several years, as dividing lines between militia groups hampered gathering and marketing of the crop. Planters found it difficult to get their crops to the reception sheds set up by the Administration of Tobacco and Tombacs in Bint Jubayl because the sheds were in the center of the border strip from which Israeli forces had declined to withdraw following their pullout from southern Lebanon on June 13, 1978. According to some sources, SLA leader Saad Haddad, to whom Israel had formally handed over control of the border strip in 1979, sometimes seemed deliberately to hinder farmers from getting crops to market in areas controlled by the UNIFIL or Muslims.

The purchase prices of the Administration for Tobacco and Tombacs failed to keep pace with inflation. In 1985, for example, the government raised prices by only 10 percent, although production costs rose by at least 40 percent and the increase in the cost of living was even higher.

Citrus crops also suffered from years of fighting. Citrus fruits are grown on the coast, particularly in the southern half of the country. Between 1965 and 1972, yields rose steadily from 19 to 27.4 tons per hectare. Citrus played a vital role in agriculture, accounting for as much as half of total agricultural output. But the Civil War destroyed some 4,000 hectares of orchards around Ad Damur, and urban sprawl led to the loss of orchards around Tyre and Sidon. Nonetheless, production increased to a record 365,000 tons in 1981. A three-year decline in production followed in the wake of the 1982 Israeli invasion and the loss of more citrus-growing land.

The Biqa Valley, with 40 percent of the country's cultivable land, is the most productive agricultural region. It, too, has suffered from war and foreign occupation. By 1987 Syrian troops had been in the Biqa Valley for more than eleven years. During that time, they clashed with Palestinians, Christians, Israelis, and Shias. The 1982 Israeli invasion and the arrival of the Iranian Pasdaran (Revolutionary Guards) also brought economic hardship to the valley.

Declining wheat production was one indication of the collapse of traditionally productive agriculture in the Biqa Valley. In ancient times, the valley had been part of Rome's Syrian granary, providing wheat for the empire's eastern provinces and for Rome itself. But as time went by, with arable land limited, pressure grew for intensive, high-value cropping. In modern times the amount of land devoted to wheat decreased—from 68,000 hectares in 1968 to around 50,000 hectares between 1972 and 1975. Still, some two-thirds of the field crop acreage in the Biqa Valley was devoted to grains, primarily wheat and barley.

The 1975 Civil War prompted drastic changes in wheat production. From 1977 to 1979, the Lebanese devoted 45,000 hectares to wheat. In 1982 the amount fell to 23,000 hectares, in 1983 to 20,000 hectares, in 1984 to 17,000 hectares, in 1985 to 14,000 hectares, and in 1986 to 13,000 hectares. Production plummeted from a record 76,000 tons in 1974 to 9,000 tons in 1987. A major reason for declining wheat production was an increase in the production of more profitable crops: hashish and opium poppies.

Hashish had long been grown in the region around Al Hirmil in the northern Biqa Valley. Before the Civil War, the government had encouraged local farmers to grow sunflowers instead, but these efforts were blunted by the onset of civil strife and by wealthy *zuama* (sing., *zaim*—see Glossary) and politicians who controlled the illegal export market. Hashish became a major cash crop in the 1970s and 1980s. Annual production rose from about 30,000 tons at the start of the Civil War to around 100,000 tons in the early 1980s, when hashish was grown on an estimated 80 percent of agricultural land around Baalbek and Al Hirmil.

By the mid-1980s, Lebanon had became one of the world's most prominent narcotics trafficking centers. Before 1975 much of this trade was exported by air from small airstrips in the Biqa Valley.

Goats are used for their milk, meat, and hair.
Courtesy United Nations (J.K. Isaac)
A large poultry farm near Beirut
Courtesy United Nations

After the valley came under Syrian control, the drug crop left the country by sea through Christian-controlled ports to Cyprus or it went overland to Syria; sometimes it went through Israel to Egypt, reputed to be the world's largest hashish consumer.

The production and sale of hashish undoubtedly brought some prosperity to the Biqa Valley, but financial benefits and overall gains to the economy were not easily quantifiable. Before the 1982 Israeli invasion, the Palestine Liberation Organization (PLO) was believed to have been earning about US$300 million annually from hashish trafficking. Christian middlemen were profiting, as were Shia growers and Syrian smugglers. And one reporter argued that the crop was worth "billions of dollars to the worldwide Lebanese underworld network."

Growers not only planted more drug-producing crops but also sought to increase the value of their crop. By March 1987, according to a report prepared by the United States House of Representatives Foreign Affairs Committee, the high profitability of opium had caused extensive replanting in the Biqa Valley. The report stated that "with the breakdown of law and order in Lebanon, production, processing, and trafficking are on the rise, and a great deal of hashish production in the [Biqa] Valley has been supplanted by opium, in recognition of the more lucrative heroin trade. It is estimated that up to half the land available for drug cultivation in the [Biqa] Valley is now being used for opium, where previously only marijuana was grown for hashish, largely destined for the Egyptian market. Numerous processing labs are known to exist, both in Lebanon and to a lesser extent in Syria." The report did not estimate the magnitude of production but said, "It is clear that opium production in the [Biqa] Valley has increased dramatically while hashish production has dropped sharply."

Industry

The State of Industry

Lebanese industry expanded rapidly in the late 1960s and early 1970s. By 1974 industry accounted for an estimated 20 percent of GDP, up from 13 percent in 1968, and industrial exports amounted to 75 percent of total exports. This growth was characterized by a proliferation of small industries and was fueled by easy credit, a strong local currency, abundant and cheap supplies of skilled and unskilled labor, subsidized electric power, and trade protection at home and expanding markets abroad, particularly in the Persian Gulf countries.

The Economy

By 1974 an estimated 130,000 people were employed in industry, and the total nominal capital of industrial establishments stood at around US$1.1 billion. The textile industry alone employed some 50,000 people. A further 20,000 were employed in the furniture and wood products industry and some 15,000 in the leather products industry.

Years of strife changed all this. In 1981 the Lebanese Industrialists Association reported a 25-percent decline in industrial capacity, and more than 70 percent of all industrial capacity was believed to have been idle for at least 500 days during the previous 6 years. Layoffs were heavy, with industrial employment in 1981 about half of what it was in 1974. The Union of Textiles Manufacturers estimated that in 1981 the industry employed only 12,000 workers and that less than half of the 1,200 prewar factories were still in business. One of the country's biggest factories, a knitting plant in the Beirut port duty-free zone that had once employed 10,000 workers, was destroyed. National Cotton Mill (Filature Nationale du Coton), the biggest weaving and spinning factory in the Middle East, laid off all but 450 of its workers. In Tripoli, Lebanon's largest compressed wood factory was closed in 1981, with the loss of 600 jobs. One of its problems was that it could not compete with the import of wooden products through the illegal ports.

Following the 1975-76 fighting, the government could no longer afford to try to revive the economy through export subsidies. Even when capital was available, industries were reluctant to use it to expand capacity or modernize machinery. One commentator noted that producers tended to concentrate on improving profits rather than productivity.

Civil strife and disorder continually hampered production, and the financial climate was rarely conducive to investment. The comparative calm of 1977-82 allowed considerable decentralization of Lebanese industry, and Zahlah, Shtawrah, Sidon, and the coastal strip under the control of the Phalange Party (see Glossary) all enjoyed a limited economic boom. In the far north, remote villages in the Akkar region began to prosper because of their distance from the country's principal areas of conflict.

The collapse of business confidence that accompanied the political debacles of 1984 closed hopes for sustained recovery. The Central Bank's tight fiscal attitude limited the money available for investment (see Banking and Finance, this ch.). Capital investment in industry shrank rapidly in both real and nominal terms, which reflected pessimism over the future of Lebanese industry. For example, investment fell from US$147.4 million in 1980 to US$94

Lebanon: A Country Study

million in 1983. By 1984 investment was down to a meager US$34.9 million and to only US$10.6 million in 1985. In addition, industrial production fell 3.7 percent to US$250 million in 1984.

In April 1986, Central Bank governor Naim offered to allow the statutory reserves and treasury bonds held by specialized banks to be used as credit for industry. Although some industrial credits appeared to be available at reduced interest rates, it was clear that economic measures alone would not revitalize the nation's fragmented industries.

Cement

Cement was Lebanon's biggest single industrial export in 1980, accounting for 15.5 percent of industrial exports. Sales to Syria at that time accounted for about 40 percent of all cement exports. In early 1981, however, exports to that country came to a complete standstill because the Syrians, then in the middle of a major program to construct their own cement works, could not reach agreement with the two principal Lebanese cement works on the terms and conditions of cement sales. Thus cement exports to Syria in 1981 totaled only L£34 million, down from L£119 million a year earlier. Overall cement exports dropped to L£201 million but recovered to L£227 million in 1982 as alternative export markets were found. Lebanon's principal cement works in 1982 were situated in the north, away from the fighting around Beirut, so the industry could continue exporting by sea from Tripoli and over land by truck.

In early 1983, when the country's political status showed signs of stabilizing, the Lebanese Cement Company (Société des Ciments Libanaises—SCL) secured a US$36 million syndicated loan to finance a planned US$79.3 million expansion program. Production was expected to increase to 250,000 tons a year, and unit costs were expected to decrease through a change in power supply from oil to coal (with the company running its own generating stations). The reported purchase of a 30-percent stake in the company's parent, Eternit Libanaise, by Prince Abdallah al Faisal, eldest son of the former king of Saudi Arabia, heightened international confidence in the industry's prospects.

But Syria's decision to terminate Lebanese cement imports, the return of instability, and difficulties in finding fresh export markets destroyed prospects for the revival of the cement industry. In July 1983, SCL laid off 300 workers at its Shikka works as it became clear that the industry faced disaster. By the end of 1983, the scope of the disaster was starkly apparent: total cement exports amounted to only L£27.5 million—an 88-percent drop from the 1982 level.

In the early 1980s, the Jumblatt family established the Siblin Cement Company, building a factory near Sidon to provide cement for the local construction industry. The Siblin plant, built with Romanian technical assistance and with a production capacity of 300,000 tons per year, was formally opened just before the Israeli invasion of June 1982. The plant was badly damaged during the fighting, and it was not until 1986 that work to get the plant back into commission could begin in earnest. A fresh injection of L£15 million in capital from local entrepreneur Rafiq Hariri made the company Lebanon's largest shareholding venture.

Electric Power and Petroleum Refining

There were widespread problems confronting the power and refining industries in the mid-1980s. The two industries are closely related because Lebanon relies primarily on oil-fired stations for electricity. By 1984 approximately 71 percent of the country's electric power output came from oil. Although the overburdened power stations suffered continual maintenance problems, the country managed an impressive recovery in this sector following the 1975–76 fighting.

Before the Civil War, eleven major power stations, linked in a common distribution network, supplied most of the country's electricity. In 1974 Electricity of Lebanon (Electricité du Liban—EDL), the state power organization, produced 1.7 billion kilowatt-hours of electricity, while smaller power companies produced a further 296 million kilowatt-hours. In this period, 41.5 percent of power was hydroelectric.

Heavy fighting in 1976 damaged several thermal power stations and transmission lines, so that hydroelectric power accounted for 70 percent of the country's total power output of 1 billion kilowatt-hours that year, 2.25 billion kilowatt-hours in 1980, 2.4 billion kilowatt-hours in 1982, and 2.8 billion kilowatts-hours in 1983. But this impressive increase masked severe strains on the system.

Israeli strikes against southern Lebanon in July 1981 damaged the Az Zahrani refinery, which provided fuel for Al Jiyah, the nation's biggest power plant. Electricity had to be purchased from Syria, but by then this was not a serious problem because most of the major Lebanese and Syrian power grids had been united under a project launched in 1977. Lebanon's ability to import electricity from Syria proved especially important after the 1982 Israeli invasion. During the invasion and siege of Beirut, the lines from Al Jiyah were completely cut. On several occasions after that, fighting in the Israeli-controlled area interrupted power transmission. At the end of 1983, all eight high-tension lines connecting the Al

Jiyah and Litani power stations (at Jun and Sadd al Qirawn) with the national grid were out of service. The Zuq Musbih power station, located north of Beirut, had to fill the gap, but the supply had to be rationed.

Lebanon had long sought to expand power generation capacity. The European Investment Bank financed the installation of three 60-megawatt units at Al Jiyah and two 125-megawatt turbines at Zuq Musbih under a 1977 program. A 1981 expansion program, assisted by the European Community (EC), achieved additional increases in capacity at both stations. In late 1985, Austria agreed to finance construction of a new 75-megawatt steam turbine power station south of Tripoli. The plants, however, were frequently overloaded in the mid-1980s, especially when even one of them was out of service. Constant operation of the Zuq Musbih plant during troubled times in the south meant that regular maintenance could not be carried out.

EDL estimated in 1986 that the annual cost of meeting Lebanon's electricity demand for the next 7 years would be US$150 million. It was not clear where this money would come from. Throughout the Civil War, EDL had suffered from financial problems and had found it difficult to collect current and overdue payments from its customers. Illicit tapping of power lines cut into revenues, and the transmission and distribution system badly needed updating. Nonetheless, EDL continued to supply power to most of the country most of the time.

The government's problems in financing oil imports caused problems for the country's petroleum refineries at Tripoli and Az Zahrani. Oil supplies came primarily from Iraq and Saudi Arabia, but deliveries were erratic, coming sometimes by pipeline, sometimes by ship. Political considerations forced the line from Iraq to close in the early 1970s. The latter reopened but closed again in 1981. The Saudi Trans-Arabian Pipeline (Tapline) to Az Zahrani closed down in the mid-1980s.

Deliveries by ship posed problems. Refineries seldom had more than a few weeks' supply in stock and often they had only a few days' supply. The oil storage tanks in the East Beirut suburb of Dawra caught fire on at least two occasions in the 1980s during clashes. Some petroleum and products, however, entered the country through the illegal ports.

The Az Zahrani refinery, owned by a United States consortium, the Mediterranean Refining Company (Medreco), a joint venture between Mobil and Caltex, suffered from Israeli assaults and from its exposed position in Al Janub Province. It was on the fringe of Syrian-controlled territory and did not enjoy the protection of

The Economy

UNIFIL troops stationed nearby. Operating conditions of the refinery, located in guerrilla-held territory, were already difficult but became untenable as the area switched from Palestinian to Israeli control in 1982. The flow of oil from Saudi Arabia was constantly interrupted, largely because the Lebanese government failed repeatedly to pay its oil bills promptly. After years of problems, the company ended operations on September 30, 1986, handing over its assets to the Lebanese government without compensation.

In 1973 the Lebanese government nationalized the oil refinery at Tripoli, formerly owned by the Iraq Petroleum Company (IPC). But unlike many Third World nationalizations, this move did not reflect any change in the country's fundamentally capitalist approach to business in general and foreign investment in particular. It was administratively necessary after Baghdad had nationalized the much more important IPC installations within Iraq itself and after Syria had taken over IPC's trans-Syrian pipeline and terminal at Baniyas, Syria. IPC disputed the Tripoli takeover, and the Lebanese government offered compensation. The matter was referred to arbitration but remained unresolved in the late 1980s.

The Tripoli Oil Installation, as the new state concern was called, comprised a 35,000 barrel per day (bpd—see Glossary) refinery and a small spur of the old IPC pipeline through Syria. Until 1976 Iraqi crude continued to reach Tripoli via the refinery and was used primarily to meet domestic oil requirements. Normally, the refinery met about one-third of the country's gasoline requirements and about half of its other fuel needs. But in 1976, the Iraqis ceased pumping crude to the main Syrian export terminal at Baniyas and thus halted direct supplies to Lebanon. With the start of the Iran-Iraq War in September 1980, the pipeline was reactivated. Although Lebanon reached an agreement with Baghdad in November 1981 to reactivate the Tripoli spur, the deal collapsed when Syria announced the following April that it would not allow Iraq to use the pipeline. The Iraqis agreed, instead, to pipe 3,000 bpd of crude to Dortyol in Turkey and then ship it to Tripoli by tanker. Heavy fighting between rival Palestinian groups in late 1983 badly damaged the refinery. It was not until August 1984 that repairs were completed and production was resumed at an initial rate of 20,000 bpd. Iraq again agreed to provide crude by tanker, and between 1984 and 1987 the refinery ran on varying mixtures of Iraqi and Saudi crude.

Aid and Reconstruction

Reconstruction and Hope, 1976-82

After nineteen months of fighting in 1975 and 1976, reconstruction was necessary but the prospects for reconstruction were seemingly hopeless. The Council for Development and Reconstruction (CDR) was founded after the war and entrusted with preparing and implementing a comprehensive reconstruction plan. The government gave it authority to negotiate with foreign governments for economic assistance and to implement reconstruction projects or authorize other government agencies to do so. Its creation was a bold step, and the CDR worked hard to honor its mandate.

In December 1978, the CDR produced a US$7.4 billion reconstruction plan, designed to rebuild the country's shattered infrastructure over an 8-year period. The program was to be largely financed by external assistance, with the government providing only 10 to 25 percent of the total. But it was not until November 1979 that the Arab states, at a summit meeting in Tunis, agreed to furnish Lebanon with US$2 billion in aid over a 5-year period.

The CDR produced its first annual work plan, which spelled out the program's implementation schedule. Projected spending for the project in 1980 was just over US$296 million, well below what would be necessary if the entire plan were to be completed within its supposed eight-year time frame. In conformity with Arab donor state wishes, half was earmarked for the south, divided equally between infrastructure development (such as port, road, hospital, and housing repairs) and social projects.

Nevertheless, the CDR was at least able to make a brisk start on reconstruction. At the end of April 1981, it reported that about half of the US$741 million in available funding was being used, with 32.3 percent going for loans to the public sector, 29.1 percent designated as liquid resources for projects being implemented, and 17.3 percent for expenditures on projects under way.

Lebanon was receiving reconstruction aid fairly regularly in 1981, although some donors were behind in some of their disbursements. Other international sources also provided assistance. The United States Agency for International Development (AID) provided approximately US$5.7 million for a variety of projects that year, including technical assistance for the CDR, housing repair grants, housing authority loans, and various health projects. And as far back as October 1980, Lebanon had signed an agreement with the United Nations International Children's Emergency Fund (UNICEF) to carry out US$43.5 million worth of social projects in the south, using reconstruction funds channeled through the CDR. The United Nations Development Program (UNDP) also provided around US$4 million worth of reconstruction projects.

Arab Reconstruction Aid

The Arab aid approved at the 1979 Tunis summit meeting was the key to Lebanon's reconstruction program. During the five-year

*A father and son make brass trays in a shop near Tripoli.
Courtesy United Nations (B. Cirone)*

period from 1980 through 1984, the seven Arab members of the Organization of Petroleum Exporting Countries were to provide specific sums annually. The program got under way late, so that in 1980 just US$168.2 million of an intended US$400 million was actually disbursed. The pace quickened in 1981, however, with the arrival of US$202.9 million. The cease-fire in southern Lebanon from July 1981 until the Israeli invasion the following June provided an opportunity to step up disbursements, but, in fact, they declined. During the first half of 1982, only the United Arab Emirates made any effort to meet its commitment, paying some US$13 million, presumably its regular first-quarter payment.

The Arab states reacted to the Israeli invasion by virtually discontinuing aid. By November 1982, almost three years into the program, the Ministry of Finance had reported receiving just US$384.2 million of an expected US$1.2 billion. Some aid did trickle in during late 1982 or in 1983, but the highest figure reported for total aid deliveries agreed to in Tunis in 1979 was around US$420 million.

By far the most reliable of the donors was the UAE. It had pledged US$45.7 million a year and met its 1980 and 1981 commitments in full, in addition to the US$13 million first-quarter contribution in 1982. At the opposite extreme was Libya, which had pledged US$62.84 million a year but had provided nothing by the end of 1982 (except covert arms deliveries to pro-Libyan militia groups). Algeria, which had pledged US$28 million a year, later declared that it could not comply because of financial difficulties. The remaining donors agreed to meet Algeria's commitments, but there is no evidence that they ever provided the funds.

Saudi Arabia, with the largest annual commitment—US$114.3 million—began its disbursements late. In 1980 it provided one-third of the amount due and in 1981 two-thirds. The Saudis made no further payments before the 1982 invasion. Iraq met its 1980 annual commitment of US$59.4 million but made no further contributions because of its war with Iran. Kuwait furnished US$25 million in 1980 and then in 1981 provided US$67.8 million—US$5 million more than what was due. But it, too, failed to pay anything in the first half of 1982. Qatar provided no assistance in 1980 and in 1981 provided only half of its pledged US$26.8 million.

After the Israeli invasion, the Arab donors provided about US$40 million. They indicated that they would contribute more funds to the reconstruction effort as funds from the World Bank and the industrialized countries became available. In July 1983, a US$229 million aid package was put together by representatives of major donor countries and organizations. Attending the meeting in Paris were officials from Austria, Belgium, Canada, France, West Germany, Italy, the Netherlands, Japan, Britain, the United States, and Sweden. Participating donor agencies included the World Bank, the IMF, the Saudi Development Fund, the UNDP, and the EC and its principal financial arm, the European Investment Bank.

Specific aid agreements were subsequently reached with most, if not all, of the participants at the Paris meeting, which marked the high point in Lebanon's search for orthodox sources of reconstruction finance. But Arab aid was given neither on the scale envisaged at the Tunis summit nor on the more limited scale supplied in 1980 and 1981. Falling oil prices in 1983 caused producers to cut back production to maintain prices. The cutbacks resulted in lost revenue, not only for themselves but indirectly for Lebanon. Some Saudi money did arrive in Lebanon, but only on an ad hoc basis. Some of it, reputedly from King Fahd, was given to charities and for education. Organized financial assistance, however, dried up by the mid-1980s. In early 1985, President Jumayyil appealed to the Saudis for US$500 million in economic aid, but the response did not match the request. The Arab nations, in essence, had lost interest in Lebanon.

Still, the Tunis aid pledge led Lebanon to believe that it could mobilize reconstruction funds if it could come up with practical projects. The CDR viewed the aid pledged as encouragement to

The Economy

intervene in the economy. The CDR's interventionist attitude ran counter to the Lebanese government's long-standing commitment to free-market principles. As a result, the CDR was criticized in government and financial circles for pursuing too interventionist a policy. Thus, in the months before the Israeli invasion, the old politics that had so bedeviled Lebanon were threatening to destroy the new economics on which those who opposed Lebanon's confessional (see Glossary) structure were placing considerable hope.

After the 1982 Israeli invasion, however, the argument became academic. Damage to Beirut and the devastation of communities in the south ushered in a new acceptance of greater state involvement in the reconstruction of the country.

Post-Israeli Invasion Reconstruction, 1982-84

When Amin Jumayyil took office in 1982, he assumed leadership of a country that, although stunned and paralyzed by the Israeli invasion, still had some positive economic forces at work. The Arab states were still providing financial assistance, although not as much as they had promised or as much as Lebanon needed. The four powers (Britain, France, Italy, and the United States) whose troops comprised the Multinational Force (MNF) in Beirut, created after the invasion, were all eager to see Lebanon regain its commercial prominence. International financial institutions, most notably the World Bank, believed that comprehensive reconstruction was possible. Even though the central government controlled only about a fifth of the national territory—Israel and Syria controlled the rest—there was an air of energy and determination in Beirut in the midst of apparently insuperable obstacles.

It was in this atmosphere that the CDR was to fashion its most ambitious reconstruction program. The program was projected in late 1982 to cost US$16.3 billion for the 9-year period 1982-91 (a revised 1983-92 version was estimated at US$17 billion in the spring of 1983). Once again, the plan proved overambitious. The CDR initially proposed that US$1.1 billion be spent in 1983, the first full year of reconstruction. In March 1983, however, the CDR proposed a much more modest start, entailing expenditure of just US$594 million during the year.

Housing was to get the largest share of reconstruction funds— about 35 percent of all spending. The emphasis on Al Janub Province was to be maintained, although the previous "50 percent rule" no longer seemed to apply following the devastation of other parts of the country by the Israeli assault and continuing occupation. UNICEF was to administer US$15.8 million in project funds for rehabilitation of 200 schools.

In November 1982, a World Bank team visited Lebanon and presented a US$6.7 billion reconstruction program. But because of doubts about how much of the program could be implemented, in February 1983 the World Bank proposed a more limited reconstruction project designed to cover only the Greater Beirut area in which government or international forces were deployed.

The World Bank's program differed considerably from that of the CDR. The CDR emphasized that housing would account for 29.4 percent of all funding under the US$17 billion plan, whereas telecommunications would account for just 5.1 percent. Under the World Bank's US$6.4 billion program, housing was to get only 14.8 percent of all funds, while telecommunications would receive 16.3 percent. The World Bank's emphasis proved more relevant, and since 1982 there has been extensive repair, renovation, and replacement work on the country's shattered telecommunications systems.

There was a renewed emphasis on water management. Beirutis have long dug deep into the soil for fresh water. Digging accelerated during the bitter rounds of fighting in 1975–76 and in 1982. Sea water began seeping into the city's fresh water, and as Beirut's sanitary system disintegrated during the violence, unpurified water entered the drinking water system, resulting in considerable health hazards at times.

In 1982, before the Israeli invasion, the National Waste Management Plan was drawn up to provide the residents of 542 cities, towns, and villages—covering 83 percent of the population—with solid and liquid waste treatment and disposal plants by the year 2000. This plan was incorporated into both reconstruction programs, with priority being given to the construction of main sewers in the principal cities. Foreign consultants were hired to get the program off the ground, but progress was much slower then expected because of fresh waves of conflict.

Considerable efforts to reopen Beirut's port were supported by a World Bank loan of US$50 million and funds from Arab nations and the United States. Transit sheds and warehouses were erected and old and damaged ones repaired. In 1983 work started on a new container terminal and on the expansion of the eastern end of the port. In the city center, the Oger Liban Company boosted morale in the autumn of 1982 as its trucks carted away months of refuse. The company also performed restoration work in 1983 and early 1984 on the old *suqs* (markets) in the commercial district. But the heavy fighting that accompanied the renewed partition of Beirut in February 1984 destroyed much of this work.

Reconstruction and Chaos, 1984–87

Western indulgence with Lebanon ended in February 1984. The bombing of the United States Marines barracks in Beirut on October 23, 1983, with the loss of 241 American lives, and the death of some 59 French peacekeeping troops in a similar blast that day, proved how unstable the reconstruction environment was (see Internal Security and Terrorism, ch. 5). Fighting in the Shuf Mountains during the autumn of 1983 illustrated the difficulty of asserting government control even when occupying forces pulled back. Most of the MNF troops pulled out with the partition of Beirut and the renewed fragmentation of the Lebanese Army, although the French and Italians delayed their departure for humanitarian reasons.

The MNF withdrawal was accompanied by the effective termination of United States economic and military assistance programs. The AID program was frozen, and US$130 million in aid was suspended. One effect of the aid suspension was a halt in work on an AID-financed telecommunications rehabilitation project in Beirut. Officials from the United States embassy said, however, that the United States would honor its US$18 million development aid commitment.

Despite persistent instability, the CDR pressed ahead over the next three years with efforts to secure external financing for the country's reconstruction. Some L£4.3 billion was spent between 1982 and early 1986 on reconstruction (equivalent to between US$500 million and US$700 million).

In 1985 the CDR's new chief, Malak Salam, confirmed that Italy would make US$130 million available for reconstruction assistance, of which US$30 million would be on concessionary terms. The EC was to consider about US$15 million in funding and France around US$54 million. Some US$5 million was pledged by Belgium. Whereas United States and Arab aid rose and fell according to political circumstances and the vagaries of the international oil market, West European aid, usually given on a more modest basis, was fairly steady.

Between 1978 and 1985, Lebanon secured about US$76 million in grants and interest-free or low-rate loans from the EC's European Investment Bank and some US$85.5 million in special reconstruction aid. In March 1986, it secured a further US$15.4 million to upgrade schools. In April 1987, the EC agreed to provide Lebanon with US$84 million under a five-year protocol to run from 1987 to 1991, of which US$23 million would be grants and the balance concessionary loans.

President Jumayyil periodically urged the industrialized nations to draw up a "Marshall Plan" for Lebanon's reconstruction. He traveled extensively to Western capitals to secure assistance but generally received negative responses. EC officials noted in 1987 that their attempts to disburse existing aid funds had sometimes proved unsuccessful.

The CDR did not confine its efforts to the developed world's principal financial institutions. In 1982 the CDR held talks on reconstruction assistance with Hungary and in 1986 with Beijing's China Harbors Engineering Company on a possible US$500 million protocol for construction work. In 1985 Czechoslovakia promised US$50 million, mainly in tied aid, and Romania said it was willing to lend US$100 million in trade credits. Aid also trickled in from other sources. Iranian social relief funds were disbursed to largely Shia areas. The Pasdaran in Baalbek, their Martyr Foundation, and affiliated groups furnished health and social services.

The EC provided emergency food aid and funds for school repairs. The Netherlands pledged aid for a factory to make artificial limbs. Canada lent money for water projects in Beirut and Tripoli. Britain gave the Red Cross money for humanitarian assistance. In the southern border strip, Israeli forces provided some humanitarian assistance. The FAO provided emergency food aid. The UNIFIL provided extensive medical, social, and, in some cases, even infrastructure services during the years following the 1982 invasion. Overall, the relief effort was just as much a patchwork as Lebanon itself.

By late 1987, there were few signs of centralized reconstruction efforts. The assassination of Prime Minister Rashid Karami on June 1, 1987, led to the reappointment as prime minister of Salim al Huss (also seen as Hoss), a Lebanese politician with a reputation for personal and public integrity. Huss, an economist, moved immediately to develop a radical financial reform package, including the abolition of fuel subsidies and the pledging of 20 percent of the country's gold reserves as security for an international loan. His efforts were largely undermined by Minister of Finance Camille Shamun, who demanded that reductions in government spending include a reduction of the bread subsidy. Huss renewed his reform efforts after Shamun's death in August, but he and Naim were unsuccessful at getting banks to increase deposits with the Central Bank.

The reform spirit was clearly alive, but the government was unable to negotiate agreements with key sectors of Lebanese political and economic life or impose its will on any part of the country. As Jumayyil's unhappy period of office drew closer to its September

The Economy

1988 termination date, there were still a few who hoped that a new president might be able to forge ahead with reconstruction effort. But in late 1987, reconstruction seemed unlikely.

* * *

The most important sources available in 1987 were Marwan Iskandar and Elias Baroudi's *The Lebanese Economy in 1981-82* and *The Lebanese Economy in 1982-83*. The *Middle East Economic Digest* has been equally vital. Both these sources, it should be noted, depend on a wide range of information furnished by Lebanese journals, newspapers, banks, and institutions. The original sources, such as *Le Commerce du Levant* and the quarterly and annual reports of the Central Bank, should receive much of the credit for attempting to portray a coherent picture of the Lebanese economy during more than twelve years of civil and international strife. The data used originated in Lebanon itself; the analysis is written from safety outside.

Reporters such as Nora Boustany of the *Washington Post* and Peter Kemp of the *Middle East Economic Digest,* directly or indirectly, have furnished a mass of useful information under extremely trying circumstances. The work of the Centre for Lebanese Studies in Oxford, United Kingdom, also should be noted. (For further information and complete citations, see Bibliography.)

Chapter 4. Government and Politics

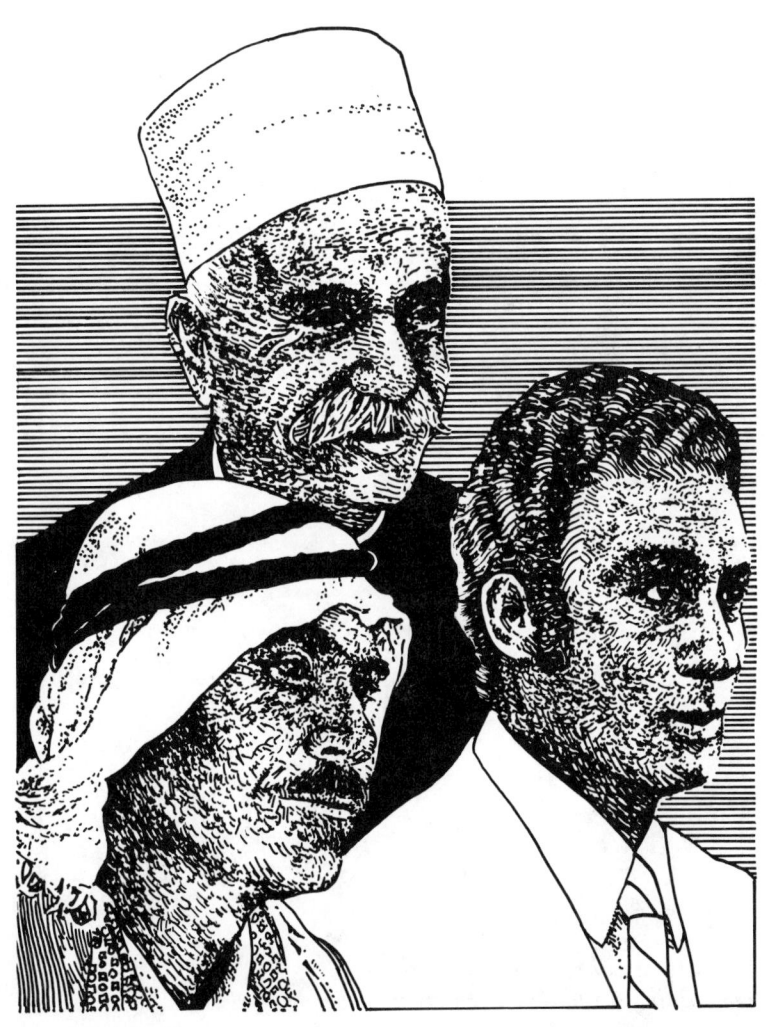

*A Muslim, a Druze, and a Christian,
representing the three major sects in Lebanon*

IN LATE 1987, after more than a dozen years of civil strife during which as many as 130,000 people may have died, Lebanese politics had become synonymous with bloodshed, and political power had come to be equated with firepower. Within this context, it was sometimes difficult to recall that Lebanon was once considered by some to be a model of pluralistic democracy in the Arab world.

Despite the widespread erosion of law and order and the reduced effectiveness of the central authorities, in 1987 some vestiges of the traditional political system persisted. The president, as provided for in the Constitution, had been elected by the legislature, or Chamber of Deputies. He presided over a carefully selected cabinet, commanded the Lebanese Armed Forces, and supervised the civil service. But at this point, much of the resemblance between this framework and the pre-1975 Civil War national-level political structure ceased. In 1987 the president controlled only a small portion of the country. The members of the Chamber of Deputies had been elected in 1972—as of 1987 the latest election—and some of the deputies no longer even lived in Lebanon. Many of the traditional *zuama* (sing., *zaim*—see Glossary) of the various sects who had formerly participated in Lebanon's many cabinets were dead. The confessionally split Lebanese Armed Forces were only the sixth or seventh most powerful military organization in the nation. And the civil service, which still collected taxes and provided services to some parts of the country, did so at greatly diminished levels.

Lebanon's political traditions—including its internal contradictions—can be traced back several centuries. Under Ottoman rule (1516-1916) Lebanon's multisectarian character was already in evidence as powerful Druze (see Glossary), Muslim, and Maronite (see Glossary) feudal lords extended their control over certain tracts of land in Mount Lebanon (see Glossary). They enjoyed a high degree of autonomy as long as taxes were paid to the Ottoman authorities. Likewise, under the short period of Egyptian control (1832-40), rule was relatively tolerant, both within the region and toward outside powers. It was during this era that European penetration helped Maronite Christians make gains against Druze landlords, and after the British and the Ottoman Turks drove out the Egyptians, Druze-Maronite antipathy turned violent. At the urging of the European powers, in 1842 the Ottoman Empire divided Mount Lebanon administratively, creating a Christian district in the north and an area under Druze control in the south. But this system, called the Double Qaimaqamate, did not change the fact that portions of the various populations were still integrated. For example, Maronite peasants worked for Druze overlords. In 1860, in response to peasant revolts, Maronite-Druze animosities again boiled over. Although both sides suffered, about 10,000 Maronites were massacred at the hands of the Druzes. As a result, at the instigation of the European powers, the Ottomans reunited the two sections of Mount Lebanon, this time under a single, non-Lebanese, Christian *mutasarrif* (governor), appointed by the Ottoman Sultan. The *mutasarrif* was assisted by a multisectarian council.

After World War I and the defeat of the Ottomans by the Allied Powers, the League of Nations granted France mandate authority over Greater Syria (see Glossary), an area that included present-day Lebanon. As a result of Lebanon's years under the French Mandate (1920-43), the Constitution enacted in 1926 is fashioned after that of the French Third Republic. Article 95, however, is unique in that it provides for "balanced" confessional (see Glossary) representation in government. In 1943 the provisions of this article were spelled out more clearly by unwritten agreements between Maronite and Sunni (see Glossary) leaders. These agreements came to be known as the National Pact. The balancing advocated in the National Pact was meant to be provisional and was to be discarded as the nation moved away from confessionalism (see Glossary).

This movement, however, never occurred; in fact, in the years between the National Pact and the start of the 1975 Civil War, sectarianism became even more entrenched, and the principle of balancing, which created multiple power centers, frequently inhibited the political process. Basic philosophical differences on political outlook often separated the various parties. Bickering among elites was common, not only between Christians and Muslims but also among sects within each religious group. Also during this period, the political system of *zuama* clientelism, whereby powerful heads of families (similar to the feudal warlords of the Ottoman era) who wielded considerable political influence and dispensed patronage, became institutionalized. As a consequence, loyalty to subnational entities, such as family or sect, took precedence over allegiance to the state.

Other problems impeded the smooth operation of government. Chief among them was that the National Pact was based on the 1932 census, which enumerated Christians (including even those who had emigrated) to Muslims in a six-to-five ratio. Because this census was never updated officially, the growing number of Muslims, especially Shias (see Glossary), was not taken into account, thus giving Christians disproportionate political power. Many observers believe that it was the inability of Lebanon's leaders to agree on a new power-sharing formula in line with demographic realities that led to the 1975 Civil War.

Although it no longer monopolized the means of coercion, the government survived this conflict. The destruction and brutality wrought by both sides were catastrophic, but, except for a few small extremist groups, none of the armed militias demanded the abolition of the state or the abrogation of the Constitution; instead, many of them called for meaningful reform.

To some extent, the state and governmental institutions were able to survive through the direct intervention of external powers. In 1976 Ilyas Sarkis was elected president while much of the country was subject to Syrian presence. Then, in 1982 Bashir Jumayyil (also seen as Gemayel) was elected president, largely under pressure from Israel, whose forces occupied most of southern Lebanon and Beirut. Because of the presence of a variety of armed militias throughout the country and the resulting "cantonization" of the state, in 1987 the term *government* had relevance only within the context of sectarian politics.

The Basis of Government

The Constitution and National Pact together form the framework of Lebanon's parliamentary democracy. The Constitution provides for three branches of government: an executive, a legislature, and an independent judiciary. The president of the republic, who appoints the prime minister, is elected by the Chamber of Deputies, the legislative body. Although this system resembles that of a Western democracy, because of the National Pact and its legitimization in the Constitution, the president, ministers, and deputies act as members of their respective confessional communities and not as at-large representatives (see Lebanese Confessional "Societies," ch. 2).

The Constitution

In the early 1920s, the League of Nations requested that the French Mandate authorities devise a law for Lebanon in cooperation with the native leaders and in harmony with the wishes and interests of the diverse religious sects. Accordingly, in July 1925 the French government appointed a commission, which by May 15, 1926, had prepared a draft constitution. The Representative

Council, an elected body of Lebanese leaders sitting as a constituent assembly, adopted the draft constitution on May 23.

Although many Lebanese historians and politicians have claimed that the Constitution was designed primarily by local leaders to reflect purely Lebanese interests, the minutes of the constituent assembly reveal the major role of the French representative. He had the power to veto any modification to the draft, and he also controlled the agenda. In reaction to France's dominance, Muslim representatives made it clear during the meetings that they were against the very idea of expanding the limits of mostly Christian Mount Lebanon to create Greater Lebanon incorporating Muslim areas and insisted that the record show their reservations.

When completed, the Constitution was divided into six parts, one of which contained four articles relating to the French Mandate and the League of Nations. By these articles, France retained full political control over the country. In theory, France's high commissioner was charged with advisory and supervisory functions in normal times; in practice, he exercised supreme power. Army troops under French control were stationed throughout the country. Although their ostensible role was to keep the high commissioner informed of the local political situation, in fact they exerted a great deal of influence on the local administration. Thus, between 1926, when the Constitution was adopted, and 1946, when the French finally handed over all functions of state, France, not local officials, exercised control over implementation of the Constitution. The high commissioner, in fact, suspended the Constitution several times during the 1932-37 period and again at the beginning of World War II.

The Constitution stresses freedom and equality, although with some limitations. All Lebanese are guaranteed the freedoms of speech, assembly, and association "within the limits established by law." There are also provisions for freedom of conscience and the free exercise of all forms of worship, as long as the dignity of the several religions and the public order are not affected.

Clearly, there are inherent contradictions within the Constitution. Even though articles 7 and 12 provide for equality of civil and political rights and equal access to public posts based on merit, Article 95 affirms the state's commitment to confessionalism, but without setting forth how it is to be applied. Article 95, in effect, legitimizes the National Pact.

Amendments to the Constitution may be initiated by the president of the republic or by a resolution of at least ten members of the Chamber of Deputies. The Chamber of Deputies, by a two-thirds majority, can recommend an amendment. However, the president and his cabinet, who together constitute the Council of Ministers, have veto powers, which can be overridden only by a complex procedure of the Chamber of Deputies. The most significant amendments were promulgated in 1943, when all references to the French Mandate were expunged and Arabic was designated the nation's official language.

Attempts to amend the Constitution have met with both favor and controversy. In 1949 the Constitution was amended to allow President Bishara al Khuri (also seen as Khoury) to succeed himself. Nine years later, however, when unpopular president Camille Shamun (also seen as Chamoun) sought an amendment that would allow him to succeed himself, vigorous opposition throughout the country prevented him from doing so.

The National Pact

The National Pact (al Mithaq al Watani), an unwritten agreement, came into being in the summer of 1943 as the result of numerous meetings between Khuri (a Maronite), Lebanon's first president, and the first prime minister, Riyad as Sulh (also seen as Solh), a Sunni. At the heart of the negotiations was the Christians' fear of being overwhelmed by the Muslim communities in Lebanon and the surrounding Arab countries, and the Muslims' fear of Western hegemony. In return for the Christian promise not to seek foreign, i.e., French, protection and to accept Lebanon's "Arab face," the Muslim side agreed to recognize the independence and legitimacy of the Lebanese state in its 1920 boundaries and to renounce aspirations for union with Syria. The pact also reinforced the sectarian system of government begun under the French Mandate by formalizing the confessional distribution of high-level posts in the government based on the 1932 census' six-to-five ratio favoring Christians over Muslims. Although some historians dispute the point, the terms of the National Pact were believed to have been enunciated by the first cabinet in a statement to the legislature in October 1943.

As noted, the confessional system outlined in the National Pact was a matter of expediency, an interim measure to overcome philosophical divisions between Christian and Muslim leaders at independence. It was hoped that once the business of governance got under way, and as national spirit grew, the importance of confessionalism in the political structure would diminish. Over the years, the frequent political disputes—the most notable of which were manifested in the 1958 Civil War, the Palestinian controversy of the 1960s and 1970s, and the 1975 Civil War—bear stark testimony to the failure of the National Pact as a means toward societal integration.

Moreover, some observers claim that the National Pact merely perpetuated the power of the privileged. The pact, combined with the system of *zuama* clientelism, guaranteed the maintenance of the status quo and the continuation of privilege for the sectarian elites.

The Practice of Government
Zuama Clientelism

In pluralistic societies, patronage is often a common feature of the political process; the promotion of the interests of a particular sect is frequently widespread. Although patronage is prevalent in developed and lesser developed countries alike, clientelism may be more entrenched in Lebanon than in most other nations. The pervasiveness of this system in Lebanon is easily traced to feudal times, wherein the overlord allowed peasants and their families the use of land in exchange for unquestioned loyalty. In more recent times, this social system has been translated into a political system; the overlord has become a political leader, or *zaim*, the peasants have become his constituents, and, instead of land, favors are exchanged for electoral loyalty. And although clientelism has its roots in the rural areas, it now pervades towns and large cities down to the neighborhood level.

A *zaim* is a political leader, and rather than being exclusively an officeholder, he may be a power broker with the ability to manipulate elections and the officials he helps elect. Accordingly, *wastah*—the ability to attain access to a power broker—is widely sought, but only achieved at some price.

There are those who believe that at the local level *zuama* clientelism may have reduced sectarian strife. Often, political competition was intrasectarian, rather than with members of different groups. And because only some of Lebanon's electoral districts were confessionally homogeneous (although most had a certain sectarian preponderance), a candidate often could not be elected unless he were supported by other confessional groups within his district. Once elected, however, the opportunity to augment his power was great. To ensure that constituents continued their support, *zuama* have been known to employ *qabadayat*, or enforcers, whose job it was to see that their chiefs were warmly supported at the polls or to discourage opponents from voting. In fact, in the post-World War II years, many *zuama* developed their own militias to safeguard their interests, often against rivals within their own sect. The development of these militias led to tragedy during the 1975 Civil

Some of Lebanon's most powerful zuama *in the mid-1980s*
Courtesy Lebanese Information and Research Center

War when these private armies were turned loose on members of opposing sects.

Another component of the Lebanese patronage system is the important role of family. The position of *zaim* is frequently hereditary, and politics is often treated like a family business. For example, almost one-fourth of the members of the 1960 Chamber of Deputies were the descendants of men who had been appointed to the legislative assemblies under the French Mandate. Furthermore, it was not uncommon for more than one member of the same family to hold office in the same government; for example, four different members of the Sulh family have held the position of prime minister. In the 1970s and 1980s, Amin Jumayyil (the Phalange Party—see Glossary), Dani Shamun (the National Liberal Party), and Walid Jumblatt (the Progressive Socialist Party) inherited their fathers' political mantles. Occasionally, the family of a *zaim* would control an entire sect, as the Asad clan did over the Shias of southern Lebanon in the first half of the twentieth century.

Thus, in 1987 Lebanon's constitutionally based political system had to be viewed through the overlay of clientelism, a system that had persisted in one form or another for over a hundred years. Even so, this system, although unlikely to disappear in the near term, perhaps was being challenged by a post-1975 Civil War development: the rise of the militias. Although some militias were still controlled by descendants of traditional *zuama*, others, like Amal, Hizballah (Party of God), and the Lebanese Forces, were led by figures who had arrived relatively late on the political scene (see Political Parties and Groupings, this ch.). These militias were not just military organizations; through military force they often gained control of revenues that formerly went to government coffers (see The Budget, ch. 3). In this way, by controlling armed might and the purse, the militias were appropriating the basic stock-in-trade of the traditional *zaim* system. The patron-client relationship, therefore, rather than dying out may merely have taken one more turn along an evolutionary track.

The Presidency

As might be expected because of the significance of the family with its strong father figure and the influential role of the *zaim*, Lebanese have come to accept a powerful national leader. Indeed, the Constitution consigns to the president vast authority. He is commander in chief of the army and security forces; he can appoint and dismiss his prime minister and cabinet; he promulgates laws passed by the Chamber of Deputies and may also propose laws, enact "urgent" legislation by decree, and veto bills; he can dissolve the Chamber of Deputies; and he exercises considerable influence throughout the bureaucracy.

His constitutional powers notwithstanding, the president is constrained by the necessity of obtaining cooperation from at least a majority of the *zuama* of the various confessional communities. In addition, he must accommodate an array of other competing interests, including those of religious, business, and labor leaders. Moreover, the president, who by custom is a Maronite, must try to work in harmony with the prime minister, who by custom is a Sunni Muslim. Together, they are the most eminent members of the executive and wield a direct and personal influence over the deputies and other political leaders.

The president is elected by the Chamber of Deputies, not by the general public. He is selected for a six-year term and may not succeed himself; he may serve any number of nonsuccessive terms, however. A sitting president steps down on September 23 of his sixth year in office. Thirty to sixty days before this, the speaker of the Chamber of Deputies calls for a special session to elect a new president. A quorum of two-thirds of the deputies is required to hold a special session. A two-thirds majority of deputies attending is needed to be elected on the first ballot; failing that, a simple majority is required on subsequent ballots.

In theory, anyone who meets the eligibility requirements for election to the Chamber of Deputies can be elected president; in reality, before the 1975 Civil War powerful Maronite *zuama* usually were elected. Exceptions were Fuad Shihab (also seen as Chehab) and Charles Hilu (also seen as Helou), leaders who unsuccessfully sought to diminish the power of the *zuama* (see The Rise of Shihabism, 1958-64; The Hilu Era, 1964-70, ch. 1). At times, political maneuvering and interconfessional wrangling have been intense; nonetheless, the reality has usually been that no one could be elected president without the support of a wide spectrum of confessional blocs.

Although the Constitution grants the president wide latitude in conducting the affairs of state, it is questionable whether the Lebanese leaders who negotiated the National Pact envisioned the growth in power that occupants of the office assumed in later years. For many Lebanese, especially Muslims, the presidency came to symbolize political tyranny and sectarian hegemony. In domestic matters involving regional interests, the powers of the local *zuama* always held sway. But on broader, national-level issues, the Maronite presidents tended to safeguard Maronite interests. This was certainly true with regard to the pan-Arab question and the events that led to the 1958 Civil War, with respect to the Palestinian controversy, and in response to any call for fundamental political reform, especially *musharaka*, i.e., a more equitable distribution of power between the president and prime minister.

Some presidents have viewed the office as a means for aggrandizement. Sulayman Franjiyah (also seen as Franjieh), for instance, a *zaim* from Zgharta who was elected through the efforts of traditional *zuama* by the margin of a single vote, is commonly regarded as having used his office to reward his family and constituency (see The Franjiyah Era, 1970–76, ch. 1). Many observers believe that nepotism and corruption—routine features of Lebanese politics—reached an intolerable level under Franjiyah's tenure.

The 1975 Civil War has left an indelible mark on the institution of the presidency. In the 1980s, the office no longer was viewed as a product of intersectarian consensus. The rise in sectarian consciousness has forced each president (and prime minister, for that matter) to be more accountable to the demands of his narrow community. At the same time, as external actors such as Syria and Israel have influenced elections, and as the power of the militias has increased, the status of the presidency has declined at home and abroad. In 1987 the authority of the president did not extend much farther than the confines of the Presidential Palace at Babda.

The Prime Minister and the Cabinet

As noted, the president is constitutionally empowered to appoint the prime minister and the cabinet. Although a prime minister need not be a member of the Chamber of Deputies, this has usually been the case, particularly because the president must consult with the deputies before naming a prime minister. The president and the prime minister deliberate over the composition of the cabinet and present the nominees to the Chamber of Deputies to solicit a vote of confidence.

As the highest Muslim political official, the prime minster can bring a significant amount of authority to his position, and indeed this may have been the intent of Lebanon's "founding fathers." In practice, however, the power of the prime minister has varied according to his personality, his base of support, and the preferences of the president he served. A distinguished prime minister can enhance the prestige of the president, and the office has been held by some fairly capable politicians, including Riyad as Sulh, Saib Salam, and Rashid Karami.

Clearly, a prime minister's constitutionally mandated power is small, and over the years his most effective methods of action have been informal. His resignation could embarrass a president, influence popular opinion, and increase Muslim opposition. He could induce the Chamber of Deputies to voice a vote of no confidence and force the president to reappoint a new list of ministers, thereby stalling for a time governmental operations. In the end, however, these informal weapons were virtually inconsequential in comparison with the arsenal at the president's disposal. If a prime minister's actions caused a president dismay, the minister could be dismissed and replaced with a more pliable individual. For example, in 1973 when Salam resigned as prime minister to protest the government's refusal to oppose Israeli attacks with force, President Franjiyah nominated a political unknown to the post. Although the nomination was defeated, the eventual replacement was decidedly less resistant than Salam. Since the 1975 Civil War, the president has been forced to treat his prime minister with greater deference, but in the late 1980s the balance of political power in what remained of the official government was essentially unchanged from the prewar status.

In theory, the cabinet is the vehicle through which the country is administered. It is supposed to set policy, prepare legislative bills, and appoint or dismiss top members of the bureaucracy. Historically, however, ministers have often used their positions to increase their patronage within their constituencies and to add to their personal wealth.

Unlike some other nations, in which the president appoints a group of like-minded officials to the cabinet, in Lebanon cabinets are often intricately formed bodies, designed to accommodate diverse sectarian interests. Consequently, they sometimes have degenerated into arenas for political sniping and backroom machinations, with ever-changing coalitions and factions being formed. It has not been uncommon for intracabinet antipathies to paralyze the business of government. In the late 1980s, some members of the cabinet were not even on speaking terms, and the Muslim members boycotted the president for more than a year.

Any Lebanese can be appointed as a minister, but most often influential *zuama* have held these positions. Less frequently, for example during the 1975 Civil War, technocrats have been called upon to serve as ministers. And, for a few days in 1975, military officers held ministerial slots (see The Military Cabinet, ch. 5). In general, certain ministries have been reserved for the various sects; as a consequence, cabinets have not been noted for their efficiency. One example of the anomalies that can develop because of these circumstances is the 1955 cabinet in which a Sunni exdiplomat headed the Ministry of Public Works, while a Maronite engineer became the foreign minister.

There is no set number of ministries, but historically it has fluctuated between four and twenty-two, expanding and contracting according to political exigencies. Sometimes a minister has held more than one portfolio; as of early 1987, there were ten ministers holding among them sixteen portfolios. And, as with much of Lebanese politics, members of the same privileged families have tended to hold cabinet positions. As an indication of postwar reform, however, and in recognition of the growing Shia population, in 1984 the Ministry of State for the South and Reconstruction was created.

Typically, because of constant political pressures, cabinets have been ephemeral. Between 1926 and 1964, the average life of each cabinet was less than eight months. Even though cabinets were in an almost constant state of dissolution and reformation, the same men tended to be reappointed to the same or other posts. For example, 333 ministerial posts were occupied by only 134 individuals from 1926 to 1963.

The Legislature

The Chamber of Deputies (sometimes called the parliament) has many responsibilities, but electing the president is its most important. Despite its legislative role, traditionally the Chamber of Deputies seldom has been involved in law making or policy formulation. The Constitution details the duties and procedures of the Chamber of Deputies and grants it considerable authority in such matters as budgetary oversight and amending the Constitution. But because of the strength of the presidency and the power of the *zuama,* the Chamber of Deputies generally has been a fragmented, inefficient body, playing an insignificant part in Lebanese politics. In effect, it has merely been an extension of the executive, rather than a separate, co-equal branch of government.

Deputies are elected every four years by popular vote, but only within the strictures of the confessional system. Each slot is assigned to one sect or another according to its size in any district. It should be noted, however, that party politics have played almost no part in Lebanon and candidates campaign as part of a "list" sponsored by a local *zaim*. In other words, competition within districts is intrasectarian, in which, for example, a Greek Catholic from one list would campaign against Greek Catholics from other lists. Even though it is possible to vote across lists, typically lists have been elected in toto. To ensure the success of his list, a *zaim* often enters into complex alliances with *zuama* supporting other lists in other districts. As a result, one *zaim* may support another *zaim* in a neighboring district but oppose him in another district.

Because of the 1975 Civil War and the subsequent political disintegration, as of late 1987 there had been no election since 1972. Elections have been somewhat chaotic, often characterized by the strong-arm tactics of *qabadayat*, vote buying, and general disruptions. Elections have been conducted in stages, as much to allow voters to return to their home towns to cast ballots as to permit the redeployment of security forces to limit disturbances.

Money, of course, has been at the core of this system. Regardless of confessional association, candidates have tended to be men of wealth, often landlords, lawyers, or businessmen with family connections to the local *zaim*. Not surprisingly, candidates have frequently spent large sums to win elections. Once in office, although he was still beholden to the *zaim*, a deputy could further his accumulation of wealth. In addition, this system has perpetuated the promotion of parochial interests over the national welfare.

Despite its obvious unrepresentativeness, little reform to this system has occurred. One important factor maintaining the system has been the government's voting regulations, which encourage an individual to vote in his home town or village, regardless of how long he may have lived elsewhere. This policy reinforced the political hold of the *zaim* and, at the same time, discouraged the emergence of modern political parties (see Political Parties and Groupings, this ch.).

Several other features characterized the Chamber of Deputies in 1987. By custom, its speaker (also referred to as its president), who was selected by the deputies, was a Shia Muslim. He presided over a body of fairly well-educated men, many of whom were related to one another. To be eligible for election, an individual had to be at least twenty-five years of age; still, most members of

*An example of the devastation of the 1975 Civil War
Courtesy United States Navy (Robert Feary)*

the Chamber of Deputies were over fifty years old. Only one woman, Mirna Bustani, had ever served in the Chamber of Deputies, and this was under unusual circumstances. Her father, Emile Bustani, a deputy, died in office, and, being an only child, Mirna was appointed to complete Emile's term in the 1960 Chamber of Deputies.

To accommodate the six-to-five formula for representation of Christians to Muslims, the number of deputies has always been a multiple of eleven, although the number has varied over time. In 1951 the Chamber of Deputies was increased from fifty-five to seventy-seven members, in 1957 it was reduced to sixty-six, and in 1960 it was raised to ninety-nine. In the latter year, the Chamber of Deputies was made up of thirty Maronites, twenty Sunnis, nineteen Shias, eleven Greek Orthodox, six Druzes, six Greek Catholics, four Armenian Orthodox, and three members of minority groups (see Lebanese Confessional "Societies," ch. 2).

Rather than trying to hold elections amid the chaos of the 1970s and 1980s, the Chamber of Deputies chose to renew its members' terms every two years until "appropriate conditions" would allow a free election. Moreover, it had not even been possible to hold by-elections to fill seats of deceased members. In the mid-1980s, government officials discussed appointing new deputies to these seats. In addition, during this time a national consensus developed to modify the formula of representation so that seats would be evenly distributed. Furthermore, some officials proposed that the size of the Chamber of Deputies be increased to 120. Nonetheless, by 1987 none of these ideas had been implemented, and, as a consequence, of the ninety-nine deputies elected in 1972, only seventy-seven remained.

The Judiciary

As with other branches of government, the judiciary suffered as a result of the 1975 Civil War and the ensuing disruptions. Prior to the war, the Lebanese justice system mirrored many features common to West European systems, especially that of France. The Ministry of Justice had official authority over the judicial system, but the Supreme Council of Justice, a body consisting of eleven judges appointed by the president in consultation with leaders of the sects, exercised actual jurisdiction over the various courts. It appointed judges to the several courts and could transfer or remove them. There were fifty-six courts of first instance, with seventeen in Beirut alone, and each was presided over by a single magistrate. Cases from these courts could be appealed to one of eleven courts of appeal, each of which had a three-judge panel. Above these were four courts of cassation, on which sat three judges each. Three of these courts adjudicated civil cases, and one heard criminal complaints.

Several other courts existed outside this general framework. The six-member Council of State functioned as an appeals court for administrative matters, and the Judicial Council, which included the most senior judge of the courts of cassation and four other judges appointed by the government, ruled on cases of public security. In addition, there were a few other special courts that heard questions relating to the military, the press, and business affairs.

Matters of personal status, dealing with such issues as marriage and inheritance, were in the domain of the various sects (see Lebanese Confessional "Societies," ch. 2). These cases sometimes involved complex layers of appeal. Maronites and Greek Catholics, for example, could appeal to the Vatican, whereas Greek Orthodox could look to the Patriarchal Court in Damascus for relief. Shias and Sunnis, in contrast, often dealt with appeals locally and based decisions on sharia (see Tenets of Islam, ch. 2).

As might be expected in a society based on patronage, political interference in judicial affairs was not uncommon, and pressures from *zuama* on judges often influenced rulings. Observers noted that confessionalism also marred the judicial system, not only in

Government and Politics

the selection of judges, some of whom were mediocre jurists, but also in the determination of criminal penalties.

As of 1987, the Ministry of Justice was an active portfolio, but there was little evidence that the judiciary resembled its prewar status; only a few government-run courts seemed to be in operation. These apparently handled only minor civil and criminal cases and ultimately were circumscribed by the desires of the local militias.

The Bureaucracy

In 1987 there were skeletal remains of the prewar bureaucracy. For example, although there were still many interruptions, telephone and postal service continued to function in many areas, and electric power and piped water still flowed to many users. But with the central authorities in a shambles, the bureaucracy was often more heavily influenced by the local militias than by the cabinet ministries.

Before the 1975 Civil War the bureaucracy, bloated by patronage, was noted for its slowness, inefficiency, and corruption. Favored clients of *zuama* often held important positions and, regardless of their competence, could not be fired. Given the low pay of many positions, it was not surprising that government employment did not attract the most capable people. Moreover, to make ends meet, many civil servants were prone to accepting bribes and spending only a few hours at the office so they could work at a second job.

Sectarianism has perhaps been stronger in the bureaucracy than in any other Lebanese political institution. President Shihab, one of the few national-level politicians to introduce reforms to the system, in 1959 enacted the Personnel Law. This statute technically abolished the practice of appointing officers on the basis of the six-to-five formula; instead, Christians and Muslims were to be appointed on an equal basis. Shihab also created the Civil Service Council to examine, train, and certify new appointees, and he established a school to provide such training.

But as with other reform measures that threatened the hold of the *zuama,* these efforts were largely ignored. An estimate of sectarian representation in 1955 among higher ranking civil servants put Maronites at 40 percent, Sunnis at 27 percent, and Shias at a mere 3.6 percent. Furthermore, by the start of the Civil War in 1975, these ratios remained relatively unchanged.

In the aftermath of the violence of the late 1970s and early 1980s, observers were uncertain of the exact functioning of local administration. As noted earlier, it was believed that, like much of Lebanese politics, local affairs had become the domain of the militias. In 1987 the country was divided into five provinces (*muhafazat*): Bayrut,

Lebanon: A Country Study

Al Biqa, Jabal Lubnan, Al Janub, and Ash Shamal (see fig. 1). A sixth province, Jabal Amil, was created in the 1980s. It was to be carved out of Al Janub Province, with its capital at An Nabatiyah at Tahta. In 1987, however, its exact boundaries could not be determined. All provinces except Bayrut were subdivided into districts. Prior to 1975, local administration was highly centralized, with the Ministry of Interior having oversight and fiscal responsibilities. The governor, who was appointed by the president with cabinet approval, was the highest-ranking official in each province. He headed the Provincial Council, which included a representative of the Ministry of Finance, and the deputy governors (*qaim maqams*), who were appointed in the same manner as the governor. Despite the elaborate infrastructure of the local administration, by virtue of its control over the purse strings, the Ministry of Interior exercised considerable authority.

Political Parties and Groupings

Historically, political parties in Lebanon have lacked traits common to parties in most Western democracies. Lebanese parties often have had no ideology, have devised no programs, and have made little effort at transcending sectarian support. In fact, despite their claims, most parties have been thinly disguised political machines for a particular confession or, more often, a specific *zaim*. Although nondescript, broad titles have been applied, such as National Bloc Party or Progressive Socialist Party, with the exception of a handful of left-wing movements, most parties have been the organizational personification of a few powerful politicians. Even Kamal Jumblatt (also seen as Junblatt), the most ideologically oriented of the *zuama*, derived his constituents' support principally because he was a Druze leader, not because of his political beliefs. For this reason, any one party could count on only a few votes in the Chamber of Deputies. This situation brought about a continuous stream of coalitions, each often created to represent a point of view on a particular issue. In this system, leaders could not even rely on the support of their coreligionists; in fact, some of the most severe acrimony has been intrasectarian. Nonetheless, in the face of challenges to fundamental issues—such as the six-to-five formula or the pan-Arab question—the various confessionally based parties generally closed ranks.

Before and during the 1975 Civil War, other political groupings were formed (see Appendix B). Although ideology played some role in their formation, for the most part these alliances—the Lebanese National Movement and the Lebanese Front—tended to be temporary associations of politically motivated militias under

Government and Politics

the leadership of powerful *zuama,* and divisions generally followed sectarian lines. So ephemeral were these associations, however, that after the heaviest fighting of the mid- and late 1970s ceased, several of the groups in these coalitions turned their guns on each other (see The Interwar Years, ch. 5).

Nonetheless, ideology, rather than the power and charisma of a *zaim,* has been the basis for the formation of a small number of political parties. These multisectarian groups have espoused causes ranging from Marxism to pan-Arabism. To a limited extent, several of these essentially leftist parties also participated in the fighting of the 1970s.

By 1987 political parties, in the sense of constitutionally legitimate groups seeking office, had almost become an anachronism. By virtue of armed strength, the various militias, surrogate armies, and foreign defense forces that controlled the nation had divided Lebanon into several semiautonomous "cantons," each having its own political, social, and economic structure (see fig. 8).

Sectarian Groups

Phalange Party

Formed in 1936 as a Maronite paramilitary youth organization by Pierre Jumayyil (who modeled it on the fascist organizations he had observed while in Berlin as an Olympic athlete), the Phalange, or Phalanxes (Kataib in Arabic), was authoritarian and very centralized, and its leader was all powerful. It quickly grew into a major political force in Mount Lebanon. After at first allying itself with the French Mandate authorities, the Phalange sided with those calling for independence; as a result, the party was dissolved in 1942 by the French high commissioner (it was restored after the French left Lebanon). Despite this early dispute, over the years the Phalange has been closely associated with France in particular and the West in general. In fact, for many years the party newspaper, *Al Amal,* was printed in Arabic and French.

Consistent with its authoritarian beginnings, Phalangist ideology has been on the right of the political spectrum. Although it has embraced the need to "modernize," it has always favored the preservation of the sectarian status quo. The Phalange Party motto is "God, the Fatherland, and the Family," and its doctrine emphasizes a free economy and private initiative. Phalangist ideology focuses on the primacy of preserving the Lebanese nation, but with a "Phoenician" identity, distinct from its Arab, Muslim neighbors. Party policies have been uniformly anticommunist and anti-Palestinian and have allowed no place for pan-Arab ideals.

Lebanon: A Country Study

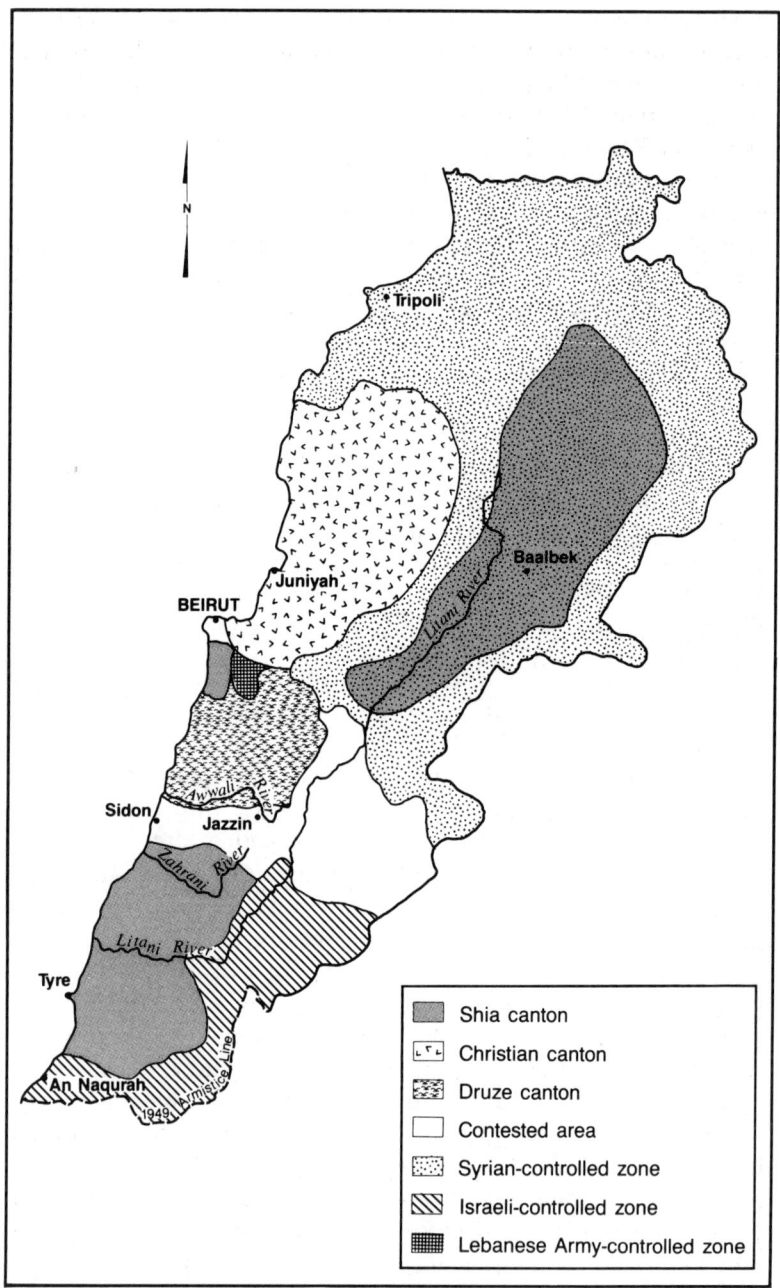

Figure 8. *The Cantons of Lebanon, 1986*

Government and Politics

Unlike many *zuama* who achieved their status by virtue of inheriting wealth, Jumayyil ascended because of his ability to instill discipline in his organization and, by the mid-1950s, through the accumulation of military might. By the outbreak of the 1958 Civil War, the Phalange Party was able to further its growing power by means of its militia. In that year, when President Shamun was unable to convince the army commander, Fuad Shihab, to use the armed forces against Muslim demonstrators, the Phalange militia came to his aid (see The 1958 Civil War, ch. 5). Encouraged by its efforts during this conflict, later that year, principally through violence and the success of general strikes in Beirut, the Phalange achieved what journalists dubbed the "counterrevolution." By their actions the Phalangists brought down the government of Prime Minister Karami and secured for their leader, Jumayyil, a position in the four-man cabinet that was subsequently formed.

The 1958 Civil War was a turning point for the Phalange Party. Whereas in 1936, the year of its formation, it had a following of around 300, by 1958 its membership had swelled to almost 40,000. Meanwhile, the French newspaper *L'Orient* estimated that the Phalange Party's nearest rival, the Syrian Socialist Nationalist Party, had a membership of only 25,000 (see Multisectarian Parties, this ch.). In addition, although until 1958 it had been able to elect only 31 percent of its candidates to the Chamber of Deputies, from 1959 through 1968 the Phalange placed 61 percent of its candidates in office. Moreover, by the start of the disturbances in 1975, the party's rolls may have included as many as 65,000 members, including a militia approaching 10,000 men.

Throughout the 1975 Civil War, the Phalange Party was the most formidable force within the Christian camp, and its militia shouldered the brunt of the fighting. As part of the Lebanese Front, the mostly Christian, rightist coalition, the power of the Jumayyil family increased considerably (see Appendix B). Ironically, as Pierre Jumayyil's son, Bashir, ascended as a national figure, the role of the Phalange Party diminished (see The Ascendancy of Bashir Jumayyil, ch. 5). This was true primarily because the relevance of political entities declined as the importance of armed power grew. Through a series of violent intrasectarian battles, Bashir seized control of the Lebanese Forces (not to be confused with the Lebanese Front), a conglomeration of the Phalange Party's military wing and some other Christian militias.

During the 1980s, the Phalange lost much of its credibility and political stature. In 1982, under pressure from Israel, which occupied a good deal of Lebanon, Bashir was elected president. Later that year, before talking office, Bashir was assassinated.

Subsequently, his brother Amin was elected president, again not so much for his Phalange Party connection as because of his support from Israel. With the death of Pierre Jumayyil in 1984, the role of the party declined further. When the deputy leader of the party, Elie Karamah, a Greek Catholic, was named as its new head, many Maronite members became disaffected. Maronite George Saadah succeeded Karamah in 1987 and strove to resuscitate the flagging Phalange by holding party meetings and by improving ties to the Lebanese Forces. The party, however, was factionalized, and many prominent members had left.

National Liberal Party

Established in 1958 by Camille Shamun after he left the presidency, the National Liberal Party (NLP) was a predominantly Maronite organization, although it had some non-Maronites and non-Christians in its leadership. More or less a political vehicle for Shamun, perhaps the most charismatic of all Christian leaders, the NLP lacked a coherent ideology or program. Although the NLP never matched the organizational efficiency of the Phalange Party, they shared many views, including favoring a free-market economy, anticommunism, close association with the West, and, most important, the continuation of Christian political advantage. In the early 1970s, the NLP claimed 60,000 to 70,000 members and controlled as many as 11 seats in the Chamber of Deputies, and Shamun had occupied several ministerial posts after his term as president.

During the 1975 Civil War, the NLP and its militia, the Tigers (Namur in Arabic), participated in the Lebanese Front, and Shamun, who was driven from his home district in the Shuf Mountains, was an active leader in the alliance. When, in July 1980, Bashir Jumayyil launched a surprise attack, defeating the Tigers, the political and military significance of the NLP declined. The party again suffered a severe setback in August 1987 when Shamun died. His son Dani assumed the chairmanship of the party, which still harbored hopes for the presidential election scheduled for 1988.

Lebanese Forces

The Lebanese Forces (LF) emerged as a political power in 1976 under the leadership of Bashir Jumayyil. At that time various Christian militias joined forces to bring about the destruction of the Palestinian refugee camp at Tall Zatar. In August of that year, a joint command council was established to integrate formally the several militias, but also to achieve a higher degree of independence from the traditional political leaders, whom many of the LF rank and

During a visit to Washington in 1983, President Amin Jumayyil meets with President Ronald Reagan. Courtesy Lebanese Information and Research Center

file regarded as too moderate. Jumayyil first took control of the military wing of his father's Phalange Party and then proceeded to incorporate other Christian militias. Those who resisted were forcibly integrated. In 1978 Jumayyil subjugated the Marada Brigade, the militia of former president Sulayman Franjiyah, killing Franjiyah's son, Tony, in the process. In 1980 the same fate befell Camille Shamun's Tigers militia.

Thus, by the early 1980s the LF controlled East Beirut and Mount Lebanon, and Jumayyil was its de facto president. But Jumayyil did not confine the LF to the military realm only; he created committees within the LF structure that had responsibility for health, information, foreign affairs, education, and other matters of public concern. Jumayyil established links with Israeli authorities, and he consistently battled with Syrian forces (see The Ascendancy of Bashir Jumayyil, ch. 5). Important features of the LF's operations were its legal (official) and illegal (unofficial) ports and the revenues generated by the transit trade (see The Budget, ch. 3). In this way, the LF took over the traditional role of the state as a provider of public services.

Following the 1982 assassination of Bashir Jumayyil, the LF suffered serious organizational cleavages. After numerous succession struggles, Elie Hubayka (also seen as Hobeika)—notorious for his role in the Sabra and Shatila massacres of 1982—assumed the leadership of the LF. But when Hubayka signed the

Syrian-sponsored Tripartite Accord in December 1985 against the wishes of President Amin Jumayyil, LF chief of staff Samir Jaja (also seen as Geagea) launched an attack on Hubayka and his loyalists and defeated them. Interestingly, Hubayka, who was once noted for his close ties to Israel, in late 1987 was headquartered in Zahlah, where he headed a separate pro-Syrian "Lebanese Forces" (see Chaos in Beirut and Syrian Peacemaking Efforts, ch. 5).

In 1987 the LF was one of the most important political and military actors on the Lebanese scene. As leader of the LF, Jaja wielded power rivaling that of President Jumayyil. Jaja embraced a hardline, anti-Syrian position and revived ties with Israel. The LF operated television and radio stations and published a weekly magazine.

Amal

The Amal movement was established in 1975 by Imam Musa as Sadr, an Iranian-born Shia cleric of Lebanese ancestry who had founded the Higher Shia Islamic Council in 1969. Amal, which means *hope* in Arabic, is the acronym for Afwaj al Muqawamah al Lubnaniyyah (Lebanese Resistance Detachments) and was initially the name given to the military arm of the Movement of the Disinherited. This latter organization was created in 1974 by Sadr as a vehicle to promote the Shia cause in Lebanon.

Sadr, who at first established his own militia, later resisted a military solution to Lebanon's problems, refusing to engage Amal in the fighting during the 1975 Civil War. This reluctance discredited the movement in the eyes of many Shias, who chose instead to support the Palestine Liberation Organization (PLO) or other leftist parties. Amal was also unpopular for endorsing Syria's intervention in 1976.

Nonetheless, several factors caused the movement to undergo a dramatic resurgence in the late 1970s. First, Shias became disillusioned with the conduct and policies of the PLO and its Lebanese allies. Second, the mysterious disappearance of Sadr while on a visit to Libya in 1978 rendered the missing imam a religious symbol; the significance attached to Sadr's disappearance was not unlike the significance attached to the occultational absence of the twelfth Shia Imam (see Muslim Sects, ch. 2). Third, the Iranian Revolution revived hope among Lebanese Shias and instilled in them a greater communal spirit. In addition, when the growing strength of Amal appeared to threaten the position of the PLO in southern Lebanon, the PLO tried to crack down on Amal by sheer military force. This strategy backfired and rallied even greater numbers of Shias around Amal.

By the early 1980s, Amal was the most powerful organization within the Shia community and perhaps was the largest organization in the country. Its organizational strength lay in its extension to all regions of the country inhabited by Shias.

Amal's ideology had evolved somewhat since Sadr's disappearance, when Husayn Husayni (also seen as Husseini) assumed leadership from April 1979 to April 1980 and was then followed by Nabih Birri (also seen as Berri). Although its charter considers the Palestinian cause a central issue for all Arabs, in the mid-1980s the Amal militia laid siege to Palestinian refugee camps in Beirut, in retribution for years of abuses at the hands of Palestinian liberation groups that operated in southern Lebanon. Amal stressed resistance to Israel, and Amal's leadership was perceived by many as being pro-Syrian. The Amal platform called for national unity and equality among all citizens and rejected confederation schemes. Amal was linked less closely to Iran than some other Shia organizations, and it did not propose the creation of an Islamic state in Lebanon.

Its broad geographical base notwithstanding, neither Amal's rank and file nor its leadership was especially cohesive. Amal's various geographic branches did not embrace a single position but were subject to particularist tendencies. Moreover, its two leading bodies—the Politburo, headed by Birri, and the Executive Committee, led by Daud Daud—appeared to effect a balance between two competing socioeconomic groups. The members of the first group, personified by Birri, were educated, upper middle class, and secularly oriented (in relative terms). The second, exemplified by Daud, was composed of members who had been in the movement since its inception, who generally were of peasant origins, and who were religiously oriented. In late 1987 the first group was in control of most of the movement, its radio and television stations, and its weekly magazine.

Hizballah

Established in 1982 at the initiative of a group of Shia clerics who were adherents of Shaykh Muhammad Husayn Fadlallah, by 1987 Hizballah (Party of God) was the second most important Shia organization. Fadlallah, who was born in southern Lebanon but educated in An Najaf, Iraq, moved to East Beirut, where he wrote books on Islamic jurisprudence. Having been evicted by Christian forces during the fighting in 1976, he relocated in Beirut's southern suburbs. Fadlallah continued his work and developed a following, which later evolved into Hizballah.

In 1987 Hizballah followed strictly the theological line of Iran's Ayatollah Sayyid Ruhollah Musavi Khomeini and called for the establishment in Lebanon of Islamic rule modeled on that of Iran. In pursuit of this goal, the party had developed close ties with Iranian representatives in Lebanon and Syria. In terms of secular policies, Hizballah rejected any compromise with Lebanese Christians, Israel, and the United States. This hardline approach appealed to many Shias, who abandoned the mainstream Amal movement to join Hizballah. These members tended to be young, radical, and poor.

The party's internal structure revolved around the Consultative Council (Majlis ash Shura), a twelve-member body, most of whom were clerics. The council divided among its members responsibilities that covered, among other matters, financial, military, judicial, social, and political affairs. The party's operations were geographically organized, with branches in Al Biqa and Al Janub provinces and in West Beirut and its southern outskirts. Among prominent Hizballah leaders in late 1987 were Shaykh Ibrahim al Amin, Shaykh Subhi at Tufayli, Shaykh Hasan Nasrallah, Shaykh Abbas al Musawi, and Husayn al Musawi; Fadlallah insisted that he had no formal organizational role but was merely Hizballah's inspirational leader.

Hizballah gained international attention in 1983 when press reports linked it to attacks against United States and French facilities in Lebanon, to the abduction of foreigners, and to the hijacking of aircraft (see Internal Security and Terrorism, ch. 5). Nonetheless, Fadlallah (who was himself a target of a terrorist assassination attempt) and Hizballah spokesmen continued to deny any involvement in anti-American attacks.

Islamic Amal

Based in Baalbek in the Biqa Valley, Islamic Amal was led by Husayn al Musawi, who was also a leading figure in Hizballah. The movement got its start in June 1982 when Nabih Birri, the head of Amal, agreed to participate in the Salvation Committee, a body set up by President Ilyas Sarkis following the Israeli invasion. The committee included Bashir Jumayyil, the much-despised Maronite commander of the LF. Musawi considered Birri's actions "treasonous" and Amal's orientation too secular. In response, Musawi broke from Amal and set up his own faction, which observers believed was organized primarily along family lines.

Islamic Amal was backed by officials in the Iranian government, and it coordinated with units of Iran's Pasdaran (Revolutionary Guards) stationed around Baalbek. Even so, in 1986 when Iranian

A demonstration by members of Amal
Courtesy As'ad AbuKhalil

officials pressured Musawi to dissolve his organization, he refused. He agreed, however, to remain part of Hizballah, and he reportedly served as a member of its Consultative Council. Press reports linked Islamic Amal, like Hizballah, to anti-Western violence in Lebanon (see Internal Security and Terrorism, ch. 5). Although Musawi's rhetoric was vehemently anti-Western, as of late 1987 he had not claimed any violence in the name of Islamic Amal.

Islamic Grouping

Founded during the 1975 Civil War by Lebanon's Sunni mufti, Shaykh Hasan Khalid, the Islamic Grouping (At Tajammu al Islami) was a loose confederation of Sunni political and religious notables. At one time it included most former or current Sunni prime ministers, ministers, deputies, and lesser politicians. It met weekly under the chairmanship of the mufti, it issued statements on current issues, and it was responsible for nominating Sunni representatives to fill official government posts. In 1987, with politics almost moribund and in the absence of a significant militia, the Islamic Grouping by default was the most important organization of the Sunni community.

Union of Muslim Ulama

The Union of Muslim Ulama emerged in 1982, when West Beirut was under siege by the Israel Defense Forces (IDF). It included Sunni and Shia clerics who shared the view that the application of sharia would solve Lebanon's problems and would end the IDF's occupation of Arab land. The union's fundamentalist line reflected its identification with the policies and objectives of Iran.

The Union of Muslim Ulama, which was unique because of its combined Sunni-Shia membership, strove to eliminate tensions between the two communities. For that reason, it organized mass rallies to propagate its views to the broadest audience possible. In 1987 the union was led by Shaykh Mahir Hammud (a Sunni) and Shaykh Zuhayr Kanj (a Shia).

Independent Nasserite Movement

The Independent Nasserite Movement (INM) was the oldest of several organizations in Lebanon that embraced the ideas of the late Egyptian president, Gamal Abdul Nasser. Despite its claims of nonsectarianism, the membership of the INM has been overwhelmingly Muslim; 1987 reports estimated it to be about 45-percent Sunni, 45-percent Shia, and 10-percent Druze. Its ideology was reflected by its motto: "Liberty, Socialism, and Unity."

The INM came to prominence in the 1958 Civil War and remained a strong force throughout the 1970s. At the height of the 1958 conflict, its militia, the Murabitun (Sentinels), clashed with the forces of pro-Western president Shamun. Consistent with its pan-Arab ideals, the INM was a firm supporter of the Palestinian movement in Lebanon in the late 1960s. During this time, it reenforced the Murabitun. When the 1975 Civil War began, it was well positioned to play an active part. The Murabitun engaged Phalangist fighters in the most severe combat during the early stages of the war, and absorbed many casualties (see Appendix B).

In the 1980s, the INM weathered difficult times. It fought with the Palestinians against the Israelis during the invasion of 1982 and with the Progressive Socialist Party (PSP) against the Lebanese Army in the Shuf Mountains in 1983. Its alliance with the PSP was short-lived, however. In 1985 a joint PSP-Amal campaign virtually eliminated the Murabitun as an important actor in Lebanon and forced INM leader, Ibrahim Kulaylat, into exile.

Progressive Socialist Party

Founded in 1949 by members of various sects who were proponents of social reform and progressive change, the Progressive Socialist Party (PSP) has been represented in the Chamber of Deputies since 1951. The party flourished under the leadership of Kamal Jumblatt, a charismatic—albeit somewhat enigmatic—character.

Jumblatt appealed to Druzes because of his position as *zaim,* to other Muslims who were disenchanted with the traditional political system, and to members of some other sects who were attracted by his secular and progressive rhetoric. By 1953 the PSP claimed some 18,000 adherents, and in the 1964 Chamber of Deputies it could count on as many as 10 deputies.

Despite its nonsectarian beginnings and secular title, by the early 1950s the party began taking on a confessional cast. By the 1970s, this tendency was unmistakably Druze; this point was demonstrated in 1977 when, after Kamal Jumblatt was assassinated (perhaps by pro-Syrian agents), his son, Walid, assumed the party leadership, continuing Druze control of the party.

Over the years the PSP has alternately cooperated with and opposed many of the same parties. For example, in 1952 it helped Camille Shamun unseat Bishara al Khuri as president; then, six years later, it was in the forefront of groups calling for Shamun's ouster. Moreover, from 1960 to 1964, when Jumblatt and Pierre Jumayyil served in the same cabinet, they spent much of their time vilifying each other in their respective party newspapers; yet in 1970, both Jumblatt and Jumayyil supported Franjiyah's candidacy for president, albeit for different reasons.

A reformer willing to work within the system, Kamal Jumblatt played an active role in politics, serving in the Chamber of Deputies and in several cabinets. Although philosophically opposed to violence, Jumblatt was not reluctant to pursue a military course when such action seemed necessary. The stalwart PSP militia was involved against the government during the 1958 Civil War, took a modest part in the Lebanese National Movement throughout the 1975 Civil War, and fought against Phalangist troops and the Lebanese Army in the 1983 battles in the Shuf Mountains (see The Israel Defense Forces Withdrawal and the Mountain War, ch. 5).

The Jumblatt family shared leadership of the Druze community with the Yazbak clan, led by Majid Arslan. Although divisions between these two branches have sometimes been wide, the coordinated Druze defense of the Shuf Mountains in 1983 and 1984 helped close the rift. In addition, the Yazbaks suffered several setbacks that drew them closer to the Jumblatt confederation. First, Arslan's son, Faysal, became discredited when he allied with Bashir Jumayyil and the LF before and during the 1982 Israeli invasion. Then, they lost their traditional leader, Arslan, who died in 1983. Consequently, by 1987 most Druze were united behind Walid Jumblatt as leader of the PSP and its formidable militia.

Minority Parties

Armenian Parties

In general, Armenian groups have supported whatever government was in power. They have tended to focus on issues of interest to the larger Armenian world community and not strictly domestic politics. The three most important Armenian parties have been the Tashnak Party, the Hunchak Party, and the Ramgavar Party. Of these the Tashnak Party has had the greatest political impact.

Founded in 1890 in Russian Armenia, the Tashnak Party sought to coordinate all Armenian revolutionary groups seeking to improve their conditions under Ottoman rule. Although the international Tashnak Party movement advocates socialism, the Lebanese branch of the party prefers capitalism. Since 1943 most of the Armenian deputies in the Chamber of Deputies (four in the election of 1972) have been members or supporters of the Tashnak Party. Prior to the 1975 Civil War, the mostly Christian Tashnak Party was an ally of the Phalange Party.

On the international level, the party has tended to be pro-Western, and during the 1950s and 1960s it took an anti-Nasser stance. As has been typical of Lebanon's Armenian community, the Tashnak Party has avoided sensitive and controversial domestic issues and has attempted to play a moderating role in politics. Like other Armenian groups, the Tashnak Party refrained from military activity during the 1975 Civil War. Because the party refused to come to the Christians' side, many Armenian quarters in Lebanese towns were subsequently attacked by Bashir Jumayyil's LF.

The Hunchak Party was organized in Geneva, Switzerland, in 1887. It has promoted the dual objective of liberating Turkish Armenia and establishing a socialist regime in a unified Armenian homeland. The Hunchak Party in Lebanon has advocated a planned economy and a just distribution of national income. In 1972, for the first time in its history, the Hunchak Party ran jointly for election to the Chamber of Deputies with the Tashnak Party.

Founded in 1921, the Ramgavar Party's ultimate goal was the liberation of Armenia. It has oriented its activities toward preserving Armenian culture among Armenian communities throughout the world. After a period of dormancy, the party was revived in the 1950s in the wake of increasing conflicts between the Tashnak Party and Hunchak Party. The Ramgavar Party presented itself as an alternative that avoided issues divisive to the Armenian community. The Ramgavar Party, sometimes considered the party of

Armenian intellectuals, also opposed what it considered the rightwing policies of the Tashnak Party.

The Armenian Secret Army for the Liberation of Armenia (ASALA) was not a political party but rather a highly secret organization that used violence to harm its political enemies, principally the government of Turkey. Established in 1975, ASALA used the Lebanese Civil War as an opportunity to put into practice without government interference its belief in armed struggle. Adhering to Marxism-Leninism, ASALA aligned with radical Lebanese and Palestinian groups against rightist forces during the fighting in the late 1970s.

Kurdish Parties

Kurdish parties have exerted little influence on Lebanese politics. In general, Kurds have been more concerned with international Kurdish matters than with internal Lebanese issues. In addition, Kurdish groups in Lebanon have been characterized by a high degree of factionalism.

Jamil Mihhu established the Kurdish Democratic Party in 1960, but it was not licensed until 1970. Mihhu, however, supported the Iraqi government against Kurdish rebels fighting in that country, and he was captured and imprisoned by the Kurdish resistance in Iraq. Consequently, the leadership of the party passed to Jamil's son, Riyad. Another son, Muhammad, disagreed with his family's position on several issues and therefore in 1977 started his own movement, the Kurdish Democratic Party—Temporary Leadership.

Riz Kari was another Kurdish group dissatisfied with the leadership of the Kurdish Democratic Party. Established in 1975 by Faysal Fakhu, Riz Kari supported the Kurdish forces fighting against the Iraqi regime. For a brief period during the 1975 Civil War, however, Riz Kari joined forces with the Kurdish Democratic Party to form the Progressive Kurdish Front in an effort to eliminate differences in the ranks of Lebanese Kurds. Riz Kari was weakened in the mid-1970s by the defection of part of its organization, which called itself the Leftist Riz Kari, or Riz Kari II. This organization, led by Abdi Ibrahim, a staunch ally of Syria, rejected the formation of the Progressive Kurdish Front because it included the "right-wing" leadership of Mihhu.

Multisectarian Parties

Multisectarian political groups have been primarily left-wing movements. Some groups have argued against the inertia of the *zuama* clientele system, while others espoused Marxist causes. Small parties sometimes have been externally controlled. In the 1970s, for example, the Popular Front for the Liberation of Palestine, under the leadership of George Habash, controlled the Arab Socialist Action Organization, which also fought on the side of the Lebanese National Movement during the 1975 Civil War. In 1987 the Baath (Arab Socialist Resurrection) parties in power in Syria and Iraq each had a faction operating in Lebanon. The late Egyptian president Nasser left a strong legacy in Lebanon. Many essentially pan-Arab parties have borne his name in their titles.

Although these groups have been characterized as multisectarian, this label may not be entirely accurate. In fact, over the years most have taken on narrower confessional patterns. For instance, Shias were dominant in the Lebanese Communist Party and Organization of Communist Action, whereas the Syrian Socialist Nationalist Party has been heavily represented by Greek Orthodox and Druze (of the Yazbak clan) members.

Lebanese Communist Party

One of the oldest multisectarian parties in Lebanon, the Lebanese Communist Party (LCP) was formed in 1924 by a group of intellectuals. Over the years, the LCP has had very little impact on Lebanese politics and has been unwavering in its support for Moscow. The party was declared illegal by the French Mandate authorities in 1939, but the ban was relaxed in 1943. For about twenty years, this single organization controlled communist political activity in both Lebanon and Syria, but in 1944 separate parties were established in each country.

During the first two decades of independence, the LCP enjoyed little success. In 1943 the party participated in the legislative elections but failed to win any seats in the Chamber of Deputies. The LCP again ran for election in 1947, but all of its candidates were defeated; in 1948 it was outlawed. During the 1950s, the party's inconsistent policies on pan-Arabism and the Nasserite movement cost it support and eventually isolated it. Surviving underground, the LCP in 1965 decided to end its isolation and became a member of the Front for Progressive Parties and National Forces, which later became the Lebanese National Movement under Kamal Jumblatt.

The 1970s witnessed something of a resurgence of the LCP. In 1970 Minister of Interior Kamal Jumblatt legalized the party. This allowed many LCP leaders, including Secretary General Niqula Shawi, to run for election in 1972. Although they polled several thousand votes, none of them succeeded in claiming a seat. But the LCP's importance grew with the arrival of the civil disturbances of the mid-1970s. The LCP, which had established a well-trained militia, participated actively in the fighting of 1975 and 1976.

Throughout the 1980s, the LCP has generally declined in power. In 1983 the Sunni fundamentalist movement in Tripoli, Tawhid (Islamic Unification Movement), reportedly executed fifty Communists. In 1987, in union with the PSP, the LCP fought a weeklong battle with Amal militants in West Beirut, a conflict that was finally stopped by Syrian troops. Also in 1987, the LCP held its Fifth Party Congress and was about to oust George Hawi, its Greek Orthodox leader, and elect Karim Murrawwah, a Shia, as secretary general when Syrian pressure kept Hawi in his position. Hawi, who had been a close ally of Syria, was reportedly unpopular for his lavish life-style and for spending more time in Syria than in Lebanon. Murrawwah was probably the most powerful member of the LCP and was on good terms with Shia groups in West Beirut. Nevertheless, between 1984 and 1987 many party leaders and members were assassinated, reportedly by Islamic fundamentalists.

Syrian Socialist Nationalist Party

The Syrian Socialist Nationalist Party (SSNP) has been one of the most influential multisectarian parties in Lebanon. Its main objective has been the reestablishment of historic Greater Syria, an area that approximately encompasses Syria, Lebanon, Jordan, and Israel. Over the years the SSNP has often resorted to violence to achieve its goals.

The SSNP was founded in 1932 by Antun Saadah, a Greek Orthodox, as a secret organization. His party, very much influenced by fascist ideology and organization, grew considerably in the years after independence. In fact, in a survey taken in 1958 by the French newspaper *L'Orient,* the SSNP was said to have 25,000 members—at the time, second only to the Phalange Party. Concerned by its strength, the government cracked down on the SSNP in 1948, arresting many of its leaders and members. In response, SSNP military officers attempted a coup d'état in 1949, following which the party was outlawed and Saadah was executed. In retaliation, the SSNP assassinated Prime Minister Riyad as Sulh in 1951.

In the 1950s, although still banned, the SSNP renewed its activities fairly openly. During the 1958 disturbances, the SSNP militia supported President Shamun, who rewarded it by authorizing it to operate legally. But in December 1961, when another attempted coup by SSNP members failed, it was again outlawed and almost 3,000 of its members imprisoned. In prison, the party underwent serious ideological reform when certain Marxist and pan-Arab concepts were introduced into the party's formerly rightwing doctrine.

Since the 1960s, the party has become more leftist. Most of its members joined the Lebanese National Movement and fought alongside the PLO throughout the 1975 Civil War. But during this period the party suffered internal divisions and defections, and since then party unity has been elusive. In 1987 there were at least four separate factions claiming to be the authentic inheritors of Saadah's ideology. The two most important were led by Issam Mahayri, a Sunni, and Jubran Jurayj, a Christian. Each faction was trying to settle disputes by means of violence.

Organization of Communist Action

In 1970 two minor extreme left-wing groups, the Organization of Socialist Lebanon and the Movement of Lebanese Socialists, merged to form the Organization of Communist Action (OCA). The organization, led since its inception by Muhsin Ibrahim, incorporated former cells of the Arab Nationalist Movement, which ceased to exist in the late 1960s. The OCA represented itself as an independent, revolutionary communist party and, in the early 1970s, strongly criticized the LCP, accusing its leaders of "reformist" tendencies. Differences between the LCP and OCA, however, shrank somewhat by the mid-1970s, but, although there was talk of unity between the LCP and the OCA, such a union never materialized. Ibrahim played an important role in the 1975 Civil War by virtue of his position as the executive secretary of the Lebanese National Movement and because his organization participated in the fighting. In 1987, however, the OCA was operating underground because Ibrahim refused to go along with the Syrian policy of opposition to PLO head Yasir Arafat. The OCA was also known to have a special relationship with the Democratic Front for the Liberation of Palestine.

Foreign Relations

For Lebanon's first three decades or so of independence, the outstanding feature of its foreign policy was its amicable relations with numerous countries. In the early 1970s, about eighty diplomatic representatives were accredited to Beirut. Not surprisingly, the Ministry of Foreign Affairs was one of the largest and most important ministries in the Council of Ministers.

Before the 1975 Civil War, foreign relations were based to a large extent on the National Pact. Under this covenant, Lebanon had to walk a thin line between the desires of the Christian communities to associate more closely with the West and the wishes of the

Government and Politics

Muslim communities to underscore Lebanon's Arab identity. Indeed, when major crises struck, as they did in 1958 and in the late 1960s, they were primarily generated by these sensitive foreign policy issues. Try though Lebanon did to walk this line, its geographic location near the center of the Arab-Israeli dispute has prevented it from striking what, for a pluralistic society, was a very difficult balance.

During the 1975 Civil War and afterward, the central government was only one of many domestic actors involved in the making of foreign policy. It shared this role with the various alliances and militias that were formed. In the late 1970s and throughout the 1980s, as central authority deteriorated, external actors, including Syria, Israel, Iran, and the Palestinians, also seized foreign-policy-making roles, although the first two were by far the most influential.

Syria

Historically under a variety of rulers, Syria and Lebanon (as well as some other countries) were considered one territory—Greater Syria. It was only in 1920, while under the French Mandate, that Greater Lebanon, which approximates the modern state, was separated from the larger entity. As a consequence, Lebanon and Syria traditionally have had strong bonds. Following World War II, after both had become independent, they shared a common currency and customs union and discussed economic union. In fact, the two had always been active trading partners, and when political disputes arose, each country often used economic means to pressure the other.

On a political level, the more powerful Syrian state has sometimes been viewed with suspicion in Lebanon. But because of intrasectarian feuds, no generalizations can be made in this regard; at one time or another, Syria has developed or dissolved friendships with a number of factions, Christian as well as Muslim.

In the 1950s and 1960s, Syria was wrestling with its own internal problems and was unable to focus on Lebanon's domestic ills. Even so, some sources have ascribed to Syria a prominent role in aggravating the 1958 disturbances, claiming that it worked to unseat the Shamun regime. Then, in the late 1960s the rise of Palestinian guerrilla activity in southern Lebanon contributed to tense relations with Syria. Although the Syrian government was reluctant to permit guerrilla attacks to originate from Syrian soil (for fear of Israeli reprisals), it was much less reticent to see such activity occur in southern Lebanon. Thus, in 1973, when the Lebanese

Army finally engaged in fighting against Palestinian guerrillas, Syria closed its borders in protest.

Since the start of the 1975 Civil War, Syrian involvement in Lebanon has been substantial, if inconsistent. On the one hand, the regime of President Hafiz al Assad has opposed the permanent fragmentation of Lebanon, fearing that the creation of a Maronite ministate would amount to the establishment of "another Israel." On the other hand, Syria has resisted the notion of the formation of a radical, left-wing state on its western border. Furthermore, after having to deal with its own Muslim fundamentalist rebellion in the late 1970s and early 1980s, Syria was concerned that a radical Islamic state in Lebanon would have negative domestic implications.

In the early stages of the Civil War, Syria acted as mediator, arranging several cease-fires. In February 1976 Syria helped formulate a political reform package, known as the Constitutional Document, that granted more power to Muslims; this compromise, however, was never implemented. When diplomacy failed, Syria intervened militarily (see Syrian Intervention, ch. 5). In March 1976, as the battle was going badly for the largely Christian Lebanese Front, Syria moved to prevent its total collapse, using Palestinian units under its control. In May Syria was instrumental in having Ilyas Sarkis, a pro-Syrian technocrat, elected president. By January 1977 about 27,000 Syrian troops were in Lebanon, technically as the largest part of the Arab Deterrent Force, set up by the League of Arab States (Arab League) in October 1976 (see The Riyadh Conference and the Arab Deterrent Force, ch. 5).

As the conflict wore on, the situation changed dramatically for Syria. In 1978 Bashir Jumayyil began his drive to incorporate all Christian militias under his LF (see Political Parties and Groupings, this ch.; The Ascendancy of Bashir Jumayyil, ch. 5). He provoked Syria's animosity by decimating in June 1978 the Marada Brigade, the pro-Syrian Franjiyah militia, and by his increasingly close ties to Israel. In response, Syria began to attack vigorously its erstwhile allies, the Christian forces, in effect making a complete about-face.

In the 1980s, Syria was the dominant external actor in Lebanon. It physically controlled much of the country, over which it imposed its will. At times, Syrian inaction, such as allowing one faction to war on another, had just as much impact as its active measures. Nonetheless, Syrian influence has had its limits. Its ability to impose stability—if, indeed, that was Assad's intention—has been frustrated by the multiplicity of factions, each with a different agenda. These limitations were visible during the 1982 invasion when Syria—alone among the Arab nations—opposed the Israel Defense Forces (IDF) on Lebanese soil. Although it acquitted itself well, the Syrian Army was unable to halt the IDF advance or to prevent its own ejection from Beirut. Later, the insertion of the Multinational Force (MNF) also reduced Syrian influence for a time. In 1983, when Israel pressured the government of Amin Jumayyil to sign an accord, called the May 17 Agreement, that normalized relations between the two countries, Syria vehemently objected. It sponsored the formation of the National Salvation Front, a coalition of pro-Syrian groups, both Christian and Muslim, to oppose the agreement. The Syrian effort eventually succeeded, and on March 6, 1985, Jumayyil abrogated the May 17 Agreement and Israel finally withdrew some of its forces from parts of Lebanon (see The May 17 Agreement, ch. 5).

There were additional examples of the strengths and limitations of Syrian influence in Lebanon. Syria brokered the Tripartite Accord, signed in late 1985 by the leaders of the main armed factions—Nabih Birri of Amal, Walid Jumblatt of the PSP, and Elie Hubayka of the LF. The accord's aim was to impose peace and to restructure the Lebanese Army (see Chaos in Beirut and Syrian Peacemaking Efforts, ch. 5). But when Jumayyil and anti-Syrian elements in the LF rebelled, the accord collapsed.

As of late 1987, Syrian troops were back in Beirut trying to keep peace, and Syrian influence was again significant. Even so, a true Syrian-imposed stabilty had not been achieved.

Israel

Although Lebanon joined with other Arab nations in the armed resistance against the creation of Israel in 1948, because of the small size of its armed forces Lebanon's action had little effect. Nonetheless, because of Lebanon's participation, in 1987 its southern border remained the line agreed to in the 1949 armistice (see fig. 1).

Throughout the 1950s and 1960s, Lebanese politicians for the most part sought to insulate Lebanon from the Arab-Israeli dispute. With its booming economy and high standard of living, the Lebanese elite had much to lose. Lebanon, therefore, abstained from the conflicts of 1956, 1967, and 1973.

Because Lebanon never presented a serious military threat, Israel has been mainly concerned about Palestinian guerrilla attacks launched from Lebanon, and, secondarily, about the presence of Syrian troops there. Since the 1960s, there has been a cyclical pattern of Palestinian guerrilla attacks on Israel and IDF attacks on Palestinian and Lebanese targets. After the 1975 Civil War, Palestinian guerrilla strength grew in southern Lebanon. At the same time, the breakdown of Lebanon's central government provided opportunities for Israel to act. Around 1975, Israel sponsored the creation of a surrogate force, led by Lebanese Christian Major Saad Haddad, based in a corridor along Lebanon's southern border. This force, which called itself the Free Lebanon Army (but was later renamed the South Lebanon Army [SLA] under leader Antoine Lahad), was intended to prevent infiltration into Israel of Palestinian guerrillas. In 1978 Israel invaded Lebanon, clearing out Palestinian strongholds as far north as the Litani River. Another consequence of the Israeli invasion was the establishment in southern Lebanon of the United Nations Interim Force in Lebanon, whose mission was to separate the various combatants.

As serious as the 1978 incursion was, it paled in comparison with the 1982 Israeli invasion, which affected all of the southern half of Lebanon as far north as Beirut (see The 1982 Israeli Invasion and Its Aftermath, ch. 5). This action had several direct consequences. First, it resulted in the deaths of several hundred Palestinian fighters and the expulsion of several thousand more, not to mention several thousand Lebanese and Palestinian civilian casualties and massive destruction. For a time, the invasion and occupation diminished Syrian influence, as the Syrian Army was forced north and east. The Israeli occupation promoted the creation of the MNF, made up of military units from Britain, France, Italy, and the United States, which supervised the Palestinian evacuation and later stayed to keep the peace. The IDF occupation also created an expedient climate for Bashir Jumayyil (and, subsequently, for his brother Amin) to win the presidency.

In addition, there were several less direct consequences. The occupation of Muslim West Beirut allowed Christian forces, on September 27-28, 1982, to enter the Palestinian refugee camps of Sabra and Shatila, where they massacred several hundred civilians. Lebanese Shias, who were severely affected by the invasion and occupation, turned their enmity on the Israelis. As a show of support for their coreligionists, the government of Iran, with Syrian approval, dispatched a contingent of the Pasdaran to the Biqa Valley. Anti-Israeli Shia opposition burgeoned during the occupation, and there were several suicide-bombing incidents perpetrated against IDF positions (see Suicide Bombings, ch. 5).

In 1987 Israel's relations with Lebanon continued to revolve around the issue of security. Israel retained its support of the SLA's activities in southern Lebanon, maintained its ties to the LF, and perpetuated its policy of attacking Palestinian and Lebanese targets that Israel labeled "terrorist" bases.

Palestinians

Palestinians have been an integral part of the Lebanese polity since the 1948 Arab-Israeli War. At that time, many fled to Lebanon. This refugee population increased after the June 1967 War and the 1970 eviction of the PLO from Jordan. By 1987 there were about 400,000 Palestinians in Lebanon (see The Palestinian Element, ch. 2).

As Palestinian guerrilla activity launched from Lebanon against Israel increased in the late 1960s, it gave rise to serious security and political problems for the Lebanese government. The PLO forces in southern Lebanon created what amounted to a distinct Palestinian entity, outside the control of the central authorities. PLO transgressions (*tajawuzat*) against the Lebanese populace and Israeli military attacks made the situation critical. Political battles between Christians and Muslims centered on the role in Lebanon of Palestinian guerrillas, who were effectively conducting foreign policy that had deep repercussions for the Lebanese government. The 1969 Cairo Agreement, brokered by other Arab states, was an attempt to reduce tensions by limiting the scope of Palestinian actions in Lebanon; this arrangement, however, was never successful.

During the 1975 Civil War, the Palestinian population in the Beirut area suffered extraordinarily, as urban refugee camps were besieged by Christian militias. In contrast, some Palestinian liberation groups were in the middle of the fiercest fighting and inflicted considerable damage on the Lebanese Front. Furthermore, the PLO increased its dominance because its forces controlled areas out of the reach of the Lebanese Front.

Throughout the 1980s, Palestinian fortunes in Lebanon dwindled. The Israeli invasion was a serious setback, followed closely by the Sabra and Shatila massacres (see The Siege of Beirut, ch. 5). In 1983 intra-Palestinian hostility was particularly pronounced, as factions battled near Tripoli; in the process, pro-Arafat forces were evicted by Syrian-backed elements. Moreover, the war of human attrition between Palestinians in the refugee camps of Beirut and the Amal militia that began in 1985 had not ceased by late 1987 (see Chaos in Beirut and Syrian Peacemaking Efforts, ch. 5). This tragic situation illustrated the complexity of Lebanese political events, showing that hostility to the PLO was not confined to Christian groups. Nonetheless, by late 1987 the PLO still enjoyed control of much of the Sidon region and retained a strategic foothold in Lebanon.

Iran

The importance of Iran to Lebanon's foreign relations increased in the 1980s. Following the success of the 1979 Iranian Revolution, the regime of Ayatollah Khomeini was anxious to spread its message to other Shias. This message found an audience in Lebanon's chronically downtrodden Shia community. Iran provided financial and inspirational support to several Lebanese Shia organizations in the early 1980s. Then, in 1982, as a show of solidarity against the Israeli invasion, a contingent of the Pasdaran arrived and established a base near Baalbek in the Biqa Valley. These units not only operated as a defense force but also set up medical facilities to serve the local populace.

In the late 1980s, Iranian-sponsored groups stepped up efforts to gain support among Lebanese Shias by providing sorely needed economic relief and social services. These groups (in particular Hizballah, which was reported to be receiving substantial financial aid from Iran) were able to use Iranian resources to run hospitals, pay families' school fees, remove refuse, and participate in housing reconstruction. These actions frequently drew supporters away from Amal, which for the most part was allied to Syria; Amal simply was unable to distribute the same level of aid as was Hizballah (see Sectarian Groups, this ch.).

For Western nations, the most significant aspect of Iran's influence in Lebanon has been the acceptance of the Islamic Republic's "antiforeign" rhetoric. In accordance with this principle, some extremist Shias, many acting under the name of the Islamic Jihad Organization, have carried out violent acts against the foreign community (see Internal Security and Terrorism, ch. 5).

United States

Before the 1975 Civil War, Lebanon enjoyed generally good official relations with the United States. In large measure, these ties were promoted by the sizable Lebanese-American community. One incident that weakened these relations was the United States role in the 1958 Civil War. At that time, the administration of President Dwight D. Eisenhower dispatched a unit of United States Marines to aid the government of President Shamun. Shamun's regime was under pressure from a part of the Lebanese community to strengthen ties to Egypt and Syria, which had just formed the United Arab Republic and were considered by some to be in the "radical Arab" camp. The Marines were never engaged in battle and were withdrawn soon after their arrival. Even so, many

Lebanese and other Arab states viewed the United States action as interference in Lebanon's internal affairs.

In the early 1980s, following the worst fighting of the 1975 Civil War, the United States became involved in Lebanon in several ways. On the political level, it sought to bolster the presidency of Amin Jumayyil and to broker a treaty between Lebanon and Israel. On the military level, the United States hoped to keep peace as part of the MNF (see The Multinational Force, ch. 5). On the economic level, the United States planned to assist in Lebanon's reconstruction (see Aid and Reconstruction, ch. 3). These tasks were never completed, however. The United States support for the pro-Jumayyil, Christian brigades of the Lebanese Army during the 1983–84 Mountain War turned into a fiasco (see The Lebanese Armed Forces in the 1980s, ch. 5). Not only did the United States lose two aircraft to ground fire, but the shelling of Druze and Shia population centers by the U.S.S. *New Jersey* convinced most Lebanese Muslims that the United States had taken the Christian side. Likewise, by 1984, in the face of renewed fighting, the business of reconstruction became a faint hope. The attacks on the United States embassy and annex, and on the MNF contingent, and the kidnapping of United States citizens eventually forced the administration of President Ronald Reagan to minimize United States involvement in the increasingly ungovernable Lebanese state.

Soviet Union

Lebanon's ties to communist nations have been amicable but lacking in depth. Its relations to the West and regional states have always been stronger. Although the Soviet Union maintained a visible diplomatic presence in Lebanon both before and after the 1975 Civil War, it has never exerted as much influence as has the United States or France.

Two major factors have limited the Soviet Union's influence in Lebanon. First, socialism has had little appeal to those who have benefited from the free-market economy. Second, the antireligious nature of Soviet communism is repugnant to Christians and Muslims alike.

During the 1975 Civil War, the Soviet Union kept a low profile, although it provided some military support to its leftist allies. When Syria intervened on the Christian side in 1976, the Soviet Union had the difficult task of trying to maintain good relations with Syria, its major regional ally, while at the same time sympathizing with the cause of the Lebanese left.

Lebanon has had no lack of parties displaying leftist orientations and Soviet influence. In addition to secular movements, the Soviet

Union has traditionally been involved with Palestinian groups. Perhaps its greatest influence has been in the LCP; but, as noted, the significance of this party has never been great (see Political Parties and Groupings, this ch.).

* * *

On the Lebanese political system and the events that provide the larger context of the 1975 Civil War, the following sources are the most useful: Michael C. Hudson's *The Precarious Republic,* Leonard Binder's *Politics in Lebanon,* Michael Suleiman's *Political Parties in Lebanon,* Enver M. Khoury's *The Crisis in the Lebanese System,* John Entelis's *Pluralism and Party Transformation in Lebanon,* Tabitha Petran's *The Struggle over Lebanon,* Roger Owen's *Essays on the Crisis in Lebanon,* Augustus Richard Norton's *Amal and the Shi'a,* Samir Khalaf's *Lebanon's Predicament,* B.J. Odeh's *Lebanon: The Dynamics of Conflict,* Walid Khalidi's *Conflict and Violence in Lebanon,* Elie Salem Adib's *Modernization Without Revolution,* Fouad Ajami's *The Vanished Imam,* David C. Gordon's *The Republic of Lebanon,* David Gilmour's *Lebanon: The Fractured Country,* and Wade Goria's *Sovereignty and Leadership in Lebanon, 1943-1976.*

For descriptions and discussions of the 1975 Civil War see Kamal S. Salibi's *Crossroads to Civil War,* Itamar Rabinovich's *The War for Lebanon, 1970-1985,* Marius Deeb's *The Lebanese Civil War,* P. Edward Haley and Lewis Snider's *Lebanon in Crisis,* and Helena Cobban's *The Making of Modern Lebanon.* (For further information and complete citations, see Bibliography.)

Chapter 5. National Security

A view of the Crusader Castle at Sidon

BY THE LATE 1980s, Lebanon's national security system had broken down almost completely. To the extent that a state's viability is defined by its government's ability to safeguard its borders against foreign incursions, enforce domestic security, and exert a monopoly on the use of armed force, Lebanon can no longer be considered a state. In 1987 the vestigial Lebanese government proved incapable of providing security to its citizens. Furthermore, most Lebanese do not identify themselves primarily with the state. A heterogeneous collection of mutually hostile religious and ethnic minorities, the Lebanese population has traditionally pledged its allegiance to sects rather than to the state (see Sectarianism, ch. 2). The fractious nature of the population was reflected in a weak central government, which maintained only a token national army in an environment where neighboring states supported formidable armed forces.

Lebanon's Civil War, which began in 1975, was the culmination of centuries of strife and conflict over sectarian issues and the resulting struggle for political and economic power. Over a decade of warfare took as many as 130,000 lives and caused an estimated US$100 billion in property damage. As of 1987, the basic issues had not been resolved; intermittent but chronic warfare continued. Because the numerous militias, each representing a sect, were approximately equivalent in strength, the conflict had reached a stalemate, with neither victor nor vanquished, only victims. And the overwhelming majority of victims in Lebanon's warfare have been civilians.

The Civil War has often been depicted as pitting leftist Muslims against rightist Christians. But there was considerable ambiguity as to the issues of contention. Although there were two main sides in the Civil War—the leftist Muslim Lebanese National Movement versus the rightist Christian Lebanese Front—each of these umbrella organizations was an uneasy coalition composed of scores of smaller groups (see Appendix B). Neither side was monolithic, and when fighting between the two sides slackened ephemeral alliances broke down and internecine warfare broke out. The Civil War has always been a multilateral rather than a bilateral conflict, with numerous protagonists.

By 1987 a dozen years of such conflict had fragmented the Lebanese polity. Lebanon has been divided since about 1976 into autonomous cantons and enclaves that function as small states within the matrix of the old state. Nevertheless, with near unanimity Lebanese politicians opposed partition, less from optimism than from conviction that only a unified Lebanon could justify the devastation and decimation the Lebanese people have suffered. To support this conviction, many Lebanese cited the prophetic writing of native poet Khalil Gibran: "Pity the nation divided into fragments, and each fragment deeming itself a nation."

Furthermore, foreign forces have been drawn into the Lebanese vortex by this vacuum of power, further complicating Lebanon's internal balance of power. In the 1960s, Palestinian guerrillas were the first interlopers, and their presence hastened the Civil War. The Syrian armed forces were invited by the Lebanese government as peacekeepers in 1976, but they later came to be regarded by some as a Trojan horse that would bring permanent Syrian occupation or annexation. The Israel Defense Forces invaded in 1978 and 1982 with the ostensible mission of expelling Palestinian guerrillas who had ensconced themselves in Lebanon. The Israelis managed ultimately to evict most Palestinian fighters, but many in Israel believed the moral and material cost of the campaign had been too high, and they cited the Old Testament warning, "The violence you do to Lebanon shall overwhelm you." In the 1980s, the United Nations Interim Force in Lebanon and also United States and West European contingents of the Multinational Force fought and died in Lebanon as peacekeeping troops invited by the government to enforce truces and cease-fires. Some Middle Eastern countries organized proxy forces or dispatched expeditionary forces into Lebanon for their own reasons. The Iranian Pasdaran (Revolutionary Guards), for example, entered Lebanon in 1982 as volunteers invited by Lebanese Shia (see Glossary) Muslims. Lebanon, therefore, became an arena for conflict among foreigners, and these conflicts were superimposed on the domestic conflict.

Searching for scapegoats, many Lebanese tended to attribute the war entirely to these foreign forces. As President Amin Jumayyil (also seen as Gemayel) said, "The current violence, while it is taking place in our country, is essentially a product of the interplay of foreign forces." The Lebanese Chamber of Deputies passed resolutions demanding the withdrawal of all foreign troops from Lebanon and insisting that the Civil War would end as foreigners evacuated the country.

Although the Lebanese have tended to look abroad for its cause, the perennial violence appeared to be endemic and indigenous. This admission was a difficult one for the Lebanese, who have regarded themselves as more cosmopolitan and modern than their Arab neighbors. Nevertheless, as one of Lebanon's leading sociologists,

Samir Khalaf, explained in 1986, the characteristics that account for the resourcefulness, prosperity, and cultural awakening in Lebanon were the same characteristics that fragmented the society and weakened its civic and national loyalties.

The Creation of the Army

Like most of the Middle East, Lebanon has a long history of conflict and conquest. Unlike other Middle Eastern nations, however, Lebanon also has a long history of inviting, or at the least acquiescing in, foreign military intervention. Lebanese leaders have traditionally traded sovereignty for security.

Prior to its establishment as a sovereign and independent state shortly after World War II, Lebanon had existed under centuries of foreign domination. Many Lebanese cities capitulated to the invasions of the Crusaders in the twelfth and thirteenth centuries, and Lebanon's Christians collaborated with the French Crusaders. In the early seventeenth century, the Druze (see Glossary) ruler Fakhr ad Din II concluded a secret treaty with Ferdinand I, duke of Tuscany in Italy, to oppose the Ottomans. Italian mercenaries helped to organize and equip his army on the European model. In 1840 the British and the Ottoman Turks bombarded Beirut at the behest of the Maronites (see Glossary) and the Druzes, who had united to fight the invasion of the Egyptian Muhammad Ali. In the 1850s, the Druzes cultivated a special relationship with the British, while the French maintained their traditional role as protectors of the Maronites. In 1860 European nations landed troops in Beirut to protect Christians and to end a massacre by the Druzes that had claimed over 10,000 Christian lives. And after World War I, Lebanese Christians supported the French Mandate.

The Ottoman Empire ruled Lebanon indirectly for almost 400 years (beginning in 1516) by delegating authority to local amirs (princes), who raised feudal armies consisting mainly of non-Lebanese mercenaries and some Lebanese conscripts. During this period, the amirs intentionally integrated their militia, and Christian Maronites and Druzes served side by side. In the settlement that followed the Druze massacre of Christians in 1860, Lebanon was made an autonomous province of the Ottoman Empire ruled by a Christian *mutasarrif* (governor) appointed by the Sublime Porte, i.e., the Ottoman sultan, but subject to the approval of the European powers that had intervened to help stabilize the area (see Religious Conflicts, ch. 1). The *mutasarrif* was empowered to establish a small local militia, whose officers were apportioned from religious groups in the area. The provincial militia was a voluntary organization, and it disintegrated with the advent of World War I.

After the establishment of the League of Nations mandate over Lebanon in April 1920, France formed the Troupes Spéciales du Levant (Levantine Special Forces), which were composed of Lebanese and Syrian enlisted personnel but commanded predominantly by French officers. The percentage of Lebanese and Syrian officers in the force increased gradually, however, especially after the outbreak of World War II. By 1945 approximately 90 percent of the officers in the Troupes Spéciales du Levant were Arabs, and the force had attained its maximum strength of about 14,000.

During World War II, Lebanese troops fought effectively in Lebanon with the Vichy French forces against British and Free French forces. After the surrender of Vichy forces in the Middle East in July 1941, volunteers from the Troupes Spéciales du Levant were enlisted in the Free French forces and participated in combat in North Africa, Italy, and southern France.

In June 1943, the French reconstituted units of the Troupes Spéciales du Levant, which were then attached to the British forces in the Middle East. In 1945, as the result of continuing pressure by Lebanese leaders for control of their own forces, the French turned over to them the Lebanese units of the Troupes Spéciales du Levant. These units totaled about 3,000 men and became the nucleus of the Lebanese Army.

Following independence, the government of Lebanon intentionally kept its armed forces small and weak—a "toy army," as one expert described it. Christian politicians, aware of the ubiquity of military dictatorships in Arab nations, feared that Muslims might use the armed forces as a vehicle for seizing power in a military coup d'état. Furthermore, as laissez-faire businessmen, the Christians appeared unwilling to incur the cost of maintaining a large standing army. Throughout the 1950s and 1960s, Lebanon never spent more than 4 percent of its gross national product on the military budget. Furthermore, many Christian Lebanese feared that a large army would inevitably embroil Lebanon in the Arab-Israeli conflict. Muslim politicians, on the other hand, were wary that a strong army, because it would be commanded by Christians, might be used prejudicially against Muslim interests. At the same time, however, they tended to feel that the military should be strong enough to play a part in the Arab-Israeli struggle. Finally, prominent politicians of all religious denominations have tended also to be feudal warlords commanding their own private militias and fearing that a strong army would erode their personal power.

Because of this disagreement over its role, the Lebanese Army has played little part in Lebanese politics. Furthermore, it has remained on the sidelines even with regard to issues within the scope of its mandate to preserve security. Consistent with this circumscribed role, the Lebanese Army's most salient mission has been to supervise and referee Lebanon's traditionally violent elections, which even in relatively peaceful times have been a volatile mixture of ballots and bullets.

The Lebanese Political-Military Situation: Independence to 1975

The 1948 Arab-Israeli War

Lebanon, alone among the Arab nations bordering Palestine, played no significant part in the 1948 Arab-Israeli War that led to the establishment of Israel. The Lebanese Army deployed four battalions along the border but withdrew them from combat, enabling the Israeli Army to capture a strip of eastern Lebanon in October 1948. The new state of Israel occupied this area until March 23, 1949, when Lebanon signed an armistice. Under the agreement, Lebanon and Israel gave mutual assurances that they would not embark on military offensives against each other and would respect each other's territory. The old Palestine-Lebanon border was accepted as the new "armistice demarcation line" but was not recognized as a legal political or territorial boundary (see fig. 1).

The Rosewater Revolution

In 1952 President Bishara al Khuri (also seen as Khoury) ordered the Maronite army commander, General Fuad Shihab (also seen as Chehab), to break a national strike of a coalition of Muslim and Christian leaders demanding Khuri's resignation. Shihab disobeyed Khuri's order to send the army into action, refusing, in his words, to order his troops to "shoot their fellow citizens." This paved the way for Khuri's resignation. Shihab was installed as prime minister in a caretaker government, and when Camille Shamun (also seen as Chamoun) was elected Lebanon's new president, Shihab characteristically relinquished his political position. In self-deprecation, Lebanese referred to the peaceful coup d'état as the Rosewater Revolution (see The Khuri Era, 1943–52, ch. 1).

The 1958 Civil War

The 1958 Civil War was instigated by Lebanese Muslims and Druzes who were inspired by the February 1958 unification of Egypt and Syria and agitated to make Lebanon a member of the new United Arab Republic (see The Shamun Era, 1952–58, ch. 1).

Although the war took a toll of some 2,000 to 4,000 lives, it was regarded by many as a comic opera, especially when 5,000 United States Marines were landed on the beaches near Beirut and waded ashore among sunbathers and swimmers. The Marines' role, in a situation described by the Department of Defense as "like war but not war," was to support the legal Lebanese government against any foreign invasion, specifically against Syria. The Marines were summoned because Shihab, believing that the army would mutiny and disintegrate if ordered into action, had disobeyed President Shamun's orders to send the army against Muslim rebels. Thus, Lebanon's army had once more proved unwilling to defend Lebanon's government.

Nevertheless, Shihab's reputation for evenhandedness was enhanced by his refusal to commit the army to ending the Civil War, and he succeeded Shamun as president. Shihab pictured himself as a military statesman like Charles de Gaulle. Although he relied heavily on the Deuxième Bureau (the military intelligence branch of the army) as his power base, he surrendered command of the Lebanese Army and did not rule as a military dictator. On the contrary, he was a reformer who made significant concessions to Muslims in an attempt to heal the wounds of the 1958 Civil War.

The Cairo Agreement and the Prelude to the 1975 Civil War

The army's inactivity continued under Shihab's successor, Charles Hilu (also seen as Helou), who became president in 1964. Hilu and his army commander refused to commit Lebanese troops to the June 1967 War, enraging many Lebanese Muslims. In the aftermath of that war, the army and its Deuxième Bureau turned a blind eye to Palestinian guerrillas infiltrating Lebanon from Syria, an attitude that angered Christians. But when the army did not interfere with commando raids and the Israelis launched attacks into Lebanon in retaliation against the Palestinian forces, the army and the Deuxième Bureau were charged with collusion with Israel. In December 1968, the government was humiliated when Israeli commandos landed at Beirut International Airport and destroyed Middle East Airlines aircraft with impunity.

In October 1969, the Lebanese Army took a more active role in fighting Palestinian forces. Nevertheless, it was clear that the army could decisively defeat the Palestinians only at the risk of splitting the nation. Therefore, army commander General Emil Bustani signed the Cairo Agreement in November 1969 with Palestinian representatives (see The Hilu Era, 1964–70, ch. 1). The Cairo Agreement remains officially secret, but it apparently granted to

The tragedy of war is reflected in the face of this Lebanese.
Courtesy United Nations

the Palestinians the right to keep weapons in their camps and to attack Israel across Lebanon's border. By sanctioning the armed Palestinian presence, however, Lebanon surrendered full sovereignty over military operations conducted within and across its borders and became a party to the Arab-Israeli conflict.

A turning point in Lebanon's modern history occurred in 1970. In that year, Sulayman Franjiyah (also seen as Franjieh) was elected president. Franjiyah, who came from the Christian enclave of Zgharta in northern Lebanon, was accused of promoting his own power and catering to the interests of his clansmen instead of confronting Lebanon's growing security problems. Believing that the Deuxième Bureau was staffed with Shihab loyalists, Franjiyah purged it and stripped it of its powers. But the Deuxième Bureau had been the only governmental entity capable of monitoring and controlling the Palestinians, and Franjiyah's action unintentionally gave the Palestine Liberation Organization (PLO) more freedom of action in Lebanon. Meanwhile, the PLO made a bid to topple Jordan's King Hussein, but it was crushed and evicted from the country—an event known in the Palestinian lexicon as "Black September." Therefore, the PLO leadership and guerrillas moved their main base of operations from Jordan to Lebanon, where the Cairo Agreement endorsed their presence. The influx of several hundred thousand Palestinians upset Lebanon's delicate confessional (see Glossary) balance and polarized the nation into two camps—those who supported and those who opposed the PLO presence.

Public order deteriorated with daily acts of violence between Christians and Palestinians. Meanwhile, the Israeli Air Force launched raids against the Palestinian refugee camps in retaliation for PLO terrorist attacks in Western Europe. On April 10, 1973, Israeli commandos infiltrated Beirut in a daring raid and attacked Palestinian command centers in the heart of the capital, killing three prominent PLO leaders. Once again, the conspicuous absence of the Lebanese Army during the Israeli attack angered Lebanese Muslims. Prime Minister Saib Salam claimed that army commander General Iskandar Ghanim—a Maronite—had disobeyed orders by not resisting the Israeli raid, and he threatened to resign unless Ghanim were stripped of his rank. Because Ghanim was allowed to remain as army commander (until he was replaced by Hanna Said in September 1975), Salam did resign and was succeeded by a series of weak prime ministers.

When the Lebanese Army finally went into action, it was against the PLO. In May 1973, fierce combat raged around the refugee camps for two weeks. When the dust settled, it became clear to all Lebanese that their army was not strong enough to control the PLO. To end the fighting, the government negotiated the Melkart Agreement, which on the one hand obligated the PLO to respect the "independence, stability, and sovereignty" of Lebanon but on the other hand ceded to the PLO virtual autonomy, including the right to maintain its own militia forces in certain areas of Lebanon. These provisions of the Melkart Agreement differed greatly from the Cairo Agreement, which preserved the "exercise of full powers in all regions and in all circumstances by Lebanese civilian and military authorities."

Lebanese Muslims believed that under the Melkart Agreement Palestinian refugees in Lebanon had been accorded a greater degree of self-determination than some Lebanese citizens. Inspired by this, they organized themselves politically and militarily and tried to wrest similar concessions from the central government. In 1974 Druze leader Kamal Jumblatt (also seen as Junblatt) established the Lebanese National Movement (formerly the Front for Progressive Parties and National Forces), an umbrella group comprising antigovernment forces.

The 1975 Civil War

The fuse that ignited the Civil War was finally lit in February 1975, when the Lebanese Communist Party and other leftists organized violent demonstrations in Sidon on behalf of fishermen who were threatened economically by a state-monopoly fishing company. The Lebanese Army was called in to restore order, but, in the volatile atmosphere, armed clashes erupted. Muslim politicians protested that use of the army was a violation of the demonstrators' democratic liberties and asked why the army was shooting at civilians rather than defending Lebanon's borders against Israeli incursions. Sunni leaders also faulted the channels used for ordering the army into action. General Ghanim had assumed charge of the army's conduct and reported directly to President Franjiyah, ignoring Sunni (see Glossary) Muslim Prime Minister Rashid as Sulh (also seen as Solh). Meanwhile, thousands of students in mainly Christian East Beirut demonstrated in support of the army. These serious splits were exacerbated when Maruf Saad, a Sunni populist leader, died in March of wounds suffered during the Sidon clashes. Long-standing concerns that the army would disintegrate if it were called into action were vindicated when intense fighting broke out between Maronite and Muslim army recruits.

The Military Cabinet

During the first months of intermittent combat between Muslims and Christians, Franjiyah refused to commit the army to separate the combatants. On May 23, however, he took the unorthodox and unprecedented step of appointing a military cabinet. Muslim Brigadier Nur ad Din Rifai, retired commander of the Internal Security Force, was named prime minister. Rifai selected the controversial Ghanim as his minister of defense; all other cabinet ministers except one were also military officers.

Franjiyah's motives were difficult to discern. Some believed his move was part of a plot to cement Maronite dominance of the government. Others believed he was attempting to force the recalcitrant army to intervene in the fighting. Perhaps Franjiyah sincerely thought that a strong interconfessional military government with unquestionable authority over the army could avert widespread conflict, although Lebanon's democracy would be sacrificed. Indeed, Syrian foreign minister Abdal Halim Khaddam reportedly warned Lebanese politicians that the Lebanese Army was capable of uniting its ranks, staging a coup d'état, and imposing a military dictatorship.

Nevertheless, Lebanon's first and last military government was short-lived, resigning two days after its inception. Even when installed in the government, the army proved unwilling or incapable of exerting authority in Lebanon. The resignation of the military government demonstrated the power vacuum in Lebanese politics and served as the catalyst to conflict. The rival military factions intensified their fighting, and full-fledged civil war began in earnest.

Lebanon: A Country Study

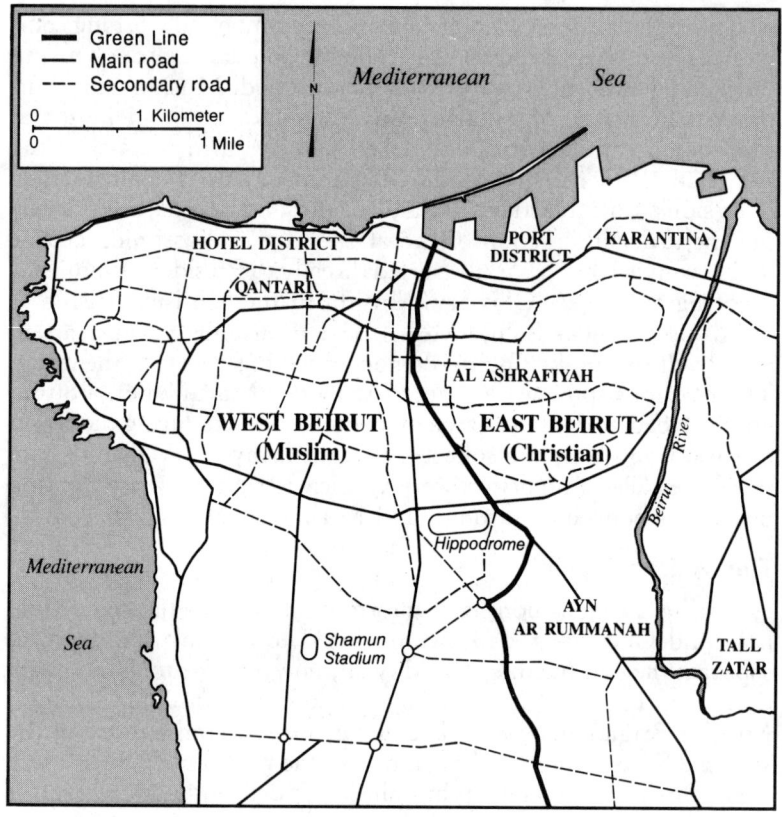

Figure 9. Beirut During the Civil War

The Early Stages of Combat

To many Lebanese, the complex 1975 Civil War can be summarized in only a few words. These words are place-names, such as Ad Damur or Karantina, which evoke traumatic memories of massacres and atrocities and need no further explanation. A narrative of the Civil War is therefore more a translation of this vocabulary of suffering and pain than a chronology of campaigns.

The Sarajevo of the Lebanese Civil War occurred on April 13, 1975, when unidentified gunmen opened fire at a congregation outside a Maronite church in Ayn ar Rummanah, a Christian suburb of Beirut (see fig. 9). In apparent retaliation, members of the Christian Phalange Party (see Glossary) ambushed a bus filled with Palestinians and shot the passengers. These events initiated the escalating cycle of retaliation and revenge that came to characterize Lebanon for the next decade.

The first six months of combat were desultory by subsequent Lebanese standards, with Phalangist and Palestinian forces exchanging small-arms and rocket-propelled grenade fire from their respective strongholds of Al Ashrafiyah and Tall Zatar. The Phalangist strategy was predicated on forcing the army to intervene on its side. Although over 1,000 people were killed in the early fighting, many Lebanese still viewed the nascent Civil War as a transitory phenomenon that would soon abate, like past security crises. Therefore, when well-organized Muslim militias attacked the downtown Qantari district in late October 1975, causing heavy loss of life and massive property damage, many inhabitants of Beirut realized for the first time that the war was a serious affair. The Muslim side eventually took Qantari and occupied the forty-story Murr Tower, the highest building in Beirut.

On December 6, 1975, "Black Saturday," Phalangists set up roadblocks on city streets, seized an estimated 350 Muslims, and murdered them. Muslims had been easily identifiable because Lebanese identification cards indicated religious affiliation. This was the first major massacre of civilians in the Civil War and started a vicious cycle of revenge and retaliation. From this point on, after combatants of each faction conquered territory from their rivals, they routinely killed civilians.

In late 1975 and early 1976, fierce fighting engulfed Beirut's high-rise hotel district. The hotels changed hands several times, with the Muslims ultimately securing control of the area. The expanded scope and intensity of the combat increased casualties greatly, with over 1,000 killed in the first weeks of the new year.

It was at this juncture that the Lebanese Army disintegrated completely. On January 16, 1976, Minister of Defense Shamun called in the mostly Christian-manned Lebanese Air Force to bomb leftist positions in Ad Damur. In response, Muslim troops rallied to the side of Lieutenant Ahmad Khatib, who split off and declared the creation of the Lebanese Arab Army (see Appendix B). In desperation, Beirut garrison commander Brigadier Aziz Ahdab seized Beirut's radio and television stations on March 11 and announced that the Lebanese Army was stepping in to take over the government and restore order. But Ahdab's move came too late, and he was derisively nicknamed "General Television" by militia leaders, who commanded far more men.

Karantina, a slum district named after the old immigration quarantine area, was the site of the next major episode in the war. Situated so that it controlled Christian access over the Beirut River

Lebanon: A Country Study

bridge to the strategic port area, it became a military target. Karantina was populated primarily by poor Kurds and Armenians but was controlled by a PLO detachment. On January 18, 1976, Christian forces conquered Karantina and massacred up to 1,000 civilians.

Two days later, revenge-seeking Palestinians and leftist Muslims attacked the Christian city of Ad Damur, located about 20 kilometers south of Beirut, and murdered between 200 and 500 Christians. The two consecutive massacres induced Muslims residing in Christian-dominated areas to flee to Muslim-held areas, and vice versa. Whereas most Lebanese towns and neighborhoods previously had been integrated, for the first time large-scale population transfers began to divide the country into segregated zones, the first step toward de facto partition.

The Christians were losing the Civil War as the Muslim-leftist side forced them to retreat farther into East Beirut. The Christians felt it imperative to retain control of Beirut's port district and constructed an elaborate barricade defense at Allenby Street. In May 1976, as the Christians tried to stave off the Muslim assault on the port district, the Lebanese Army finally entered the fray. Christian officers and enlisted men from the Al Fayadiyyah barracks outside Beirut came to the aid of their beleaguered coreligionists, bringing armored cars and heavy artillery. The Muslim advance was stopped, and the front at Allenby Street evolved into a no-man's-land, dividing Christian East Beirut from Muslim West Beirut. Vegetation that eventually grew in this abandoned area inspired the name *Green Line* (see Glossary), and in 1987 it still cut the city in two.

Syrian Intervention

The government of Syria, although in theory a socialist regime, feared that a leftist victory and the installation of a radical government in Lebanon would undermine Syrian security and provide Israel an excuse to intervene in the area. After repeated diplomatic efforts failed to quell the Lebanese Civil War, on June 1, 1976, Syria intervened on the side of the Christians. In the following months, the Syrian presence grew to 27,000 troops. By November the Syrians had occupied most Muslim-held areas of Lebanon, including West Beirut and Tripoli. Most Muslim forces capitulated without firing a shot, overwhelmed by the Syrian show of force. In Sidon, however, Palestinian and leftist forces fought off the Syrians for nearly six months before relinquishing their stronghold.

For nearly the entire first year of the Civil War, the Phalangists and the PLO had made a mutual attempt to avoid combat, even as smaller Christian and Palestinian splinter groups clashed. The PLO tried to enhance its reputation and credibility by playing the role of a neutral mediator between the Lebanese left and the Christians. For its part, the Phalange Party avoided antagonizing the PLO because it feared that the Palestinians would intervene on the Muslim side. After Syria had subdued the Muslim threat, however, the Phalangists turned their full attention to the Palestinians.

The battle for Tall Zatar was the final showdown of the Lebanese Civil War. Tall Zatar was a Palestinian refugee camp situated on the Christian side of the Green Line where about 1,500 Palestinian guerrillas defended a civilian population of roughly 20,000 against several thousand Christian militiamen. The Christians were supported and advised in their siege by the Lebanese and Syrian armies; Israeli advisers were also present on the Christian side.

Because Tall Zatar was honeycombed with bunkers and tunnels, the PLO was able to defend the camp from persistent Christian attacks for about six months, despite a nearly constant barrage of artillery fire that took a large toll. On August 12, Christian forces finally overran the camp and massacred many of the several thousand civilians who had remained there.

The Riyadh Conference and the Arab Deterrent Force

In October 1976, a League of Arab States (Arab League) summit conference was convened in Riyadh, Saudi Arabia, to resolve the Lebanese crisis. The conference did not address the underlying political and demographic problems, only the security situation. The resulting multilateral agreement mandated a cease-fire and, at the Lebanese government's behest, authorized the creation of the Arab Deterrent Force (ADF) to impose and supervise the cease-fire. In theory the ADF, funded by the Arab League, was to be a pan-Arab peacekeeping force under the supreme command of the Lebanese president. In reality, only about 5,000 Arab troops from Saudi Arabia, the Persian Gulf states, Libya, and Sudan augmented the existing Syrian forces. Moreover, Syria would not relinquish actual command over its soldiers. Therefore, the agreement in effect legitimized and subsidized the Syrian occupation of Lebanon. In the summer of 1977, Syria, the PLO, and the government of Lebanon signed the Shtawrah Accord, which detailed the planned disposition of the ADF in Lebanon and called for a reconstituted Lebanese Army to take over PLO positions in southern Lebanon.

The Red Line Arrangement

Meanwhile, Israel grew concerned over the Syrian military presence in Lebanon, particularly as the Syrian Army pursued retreating Palestinians and Muslim leftists into southern Lebanon. Israel believed that the Syrian forces, massed in southern Lebanon, might attack Israel across the unfortified Lebanese border and thus avoid the need to penetrate the heavily defended Golan Heights. Therefore, Israel enunciated its "Red Line" policy, threatening to attack Syria if it crossed a line identified geographically with the Litani River (see fig. 3). Thus, Syrian forces were generally precluded from moving south of the Litani. The Red Line was a geographic line, but it was also more subjective than a line on a map. Israeli prime minister Yitzhak Rabin identified the Red Line as a guideline for gauging Syria's overall military behavior in Lebanon, and he described several criteria Israel would use: the objectives of Syrian forces and against whom they were operating, the geographical area and its proximity to Israel's borders, the strength and composition of Syrian forces, and the duration of their stay in a given area.

The Interwar Years

Israel had cultivated a relationship with Lebanon's Christian community almost from the advent of the Zionist movement. Some Zionist politicians had envisaged a Jewish-Maronite alliance to counterbalance Muslim regional dominance. After Israel's independence in 1948, some Israeli leaders advocated extending the northern border to encompass Lebanon up to the Litani River and to assimilate the Christian population living there. In 1955 Prime Minister David Ben-Gurion and General Moshe Dayan conceived a plan to intervene in Lebanon and install a Lebanese Christian president amenable to improving bilateral relations.

The patriarchs of Lebanon's Christian community, particularly Pierre Jumayyil and Camille Shamun, were tempted by Israeli offers of assistance, but they nevertheless resisted entrusting the security of the Maronites to Israel and abjured close contact with Israel. But in 1976, threatened by the escalating Civil War, a new generation of Lebanese Christian leaders turned to Israel for military support against the ascendant PLO and the Muslim left. After a series of clandestine meetings between Mossad, the Israeli foreign intelligence agency, and militia leaders Bashir Jumayyil and Dani Shamun, Israel began supplying US$50 million per year to arm and equip the Christian fighters.

*The United Nations Interim Force in Lebanon had the difficult task of trying to separate the various combatants in southern Lebanon.
Courtesy United Nations*

Covert Christian-Israeli cooperation tapered off after Syria intervened on the Christian side in June 1976 and quelled the sectarian fighting. When the Syrian-dominated ADF began to act like an occupying army, however, the Maronites' fear of Muslim dominance was replaced by fear of Syrian dominance. Jumayyil, recognizing that only Israel was powerful enough to expel the Syrians, renewed contact with Israel; his initiative coincided with the victory of the Likud Party in Israel's 1977 elections. The new prime minister, Menachem Begin, was more inclined to support the Christians than his predecessor, both for ideological and for tactical reasons. Begin empathized with the Christians as a kindred, embattled religious minority and promised to prevent their "genocide." At the same time, he perceived the Maronites as a fifth column in Lebanon to check the power of the Palestinians. Arms shipments were stepped up, hundreds of Phalangist and Tigers militiamen were trained in Israel, and Israeli intelligence and security advisers were dispatched to East Beirut (see Appendix B).

Operation Litani

Because it was skeptical about the willingness and capability of the Lebanese Army to implement the Shtawrah Accord by displacing the PLO in southern Lebanon and securing the border area, in 1977 Israel started to equip and fund a renegade Christian remnant of the Lebanese Army led by Major Saad Haddad. Haddad's force, which became known as the Free Lebanon Army, and later as the South Lebanon Army (SLA), grew to a strength of about 3,000 men and was allied closely with Israel. Haddad eventually proclaimed the enclave he controlled "Free Lebanon." The insulation provided by this buffer area permitted Israel to open up its border with Lebanon. Under this so-called "Good Fence" policy, Israel provided aid and conducted trade with Lebanese living near the border.

On March 11, 1978, PLO terrorists made a sea landing in Haifa, Israel, commandeered a bus, and then drove toward Tel Aviv, firing from the windows. By the end of the day, the Israel Defense Forces (IDF) had killed the nine terrorists, who had murdered thirty-seven Israeli civilians. In retaliation, four days later Israel launched Operation Litani, invading Lebanon with a force of 25,000 men. The purpose of the operation was to push PLO positions away from the border and bolster the power of the SLA. The IDF first seized a security belt about ten kilometers deep, but then pushed north and captured all of Lebanon south of the Litani River, inflicting thousands of casualties.

Operations of the United Nations Interim Force in Lebanon

The United Nations Interim Force in Lebanon (UNIFIL) was established by the United Nations (UN) Security Council with Resolution 425 on March 19, 1978, "for the purpose of confirming the withdrawal of Israeli forces, restoring international peace and security, and assisting the government of Lebanon in ensuring the return of its effective authority in the area." Subsequent Resolution 426 defined UNIFIL's rules of engagement and instructed it to "use its best efforts to prevent the recurrence of fighting" and to ensure that its area of operation would not be used for hostile activities of any kind. UNIFIL consisted of approximately 7,000 men from 14 UN member states and between 30 and 90 military observers from the United Nations Truce Supervision Organization, headquartered in the town of An Naqurah.

UNIFIL, however, encountered difficulty in performing its mission. Resolution 425 made "full cooperation of all parties concerned" a prerequisite for UNIFIL's deployment. Although Israel had agreed formally to take the necessary steps for compliance with the resolution, it did not believe that UNIFIL could stop PLO incursions across the border. Therefore, when Israel started to withdraw in late March, it refused to relinquish all of the territory it had conquered in southern Lebanon to UNIFIL. Instead, Israel turned over an enclave to its proxy force, the SLA, increasing the area under Major Haddad's control. This area included not only the ten-kilometer-deep security belt adjacent to the Israeli border but also a vertical north-south corridor running from the border to the Litani River and splitting the UNIFIL area into two noncontiguous zones (see fig. 10).

Other parties frustrated the UNIFIL peacekeeping efforts. Although the PLO also had promised to cooperate with UNIFIL, it argued that the 1969 Cairo Agreement entitled it to operate in southern Lebanon, and it attempted to reoccupy areas after Israel withdrew. Furthermore, on the grounds that the IDF had not occupied Tyre, the PLO refused to allow UNIFIL to police the city, and Palestinian patrols attempted repeatedly to pass through UNIFIL lines. For its part, the SLA did not even make a pretense of cooperating with UNIFIL. Instead, it attacked UNIFIL personnel and encroached on UNIFIL's perimeter. Nevertheless, UNIFIL restored order to the areas under its control and served as an effective buffer force insulating Israel from the Palestinians. It set up roadblocks, checkpoints, and observation posts, interdicting approximately ten guerrilla patrols per month heading toward Israel. When UNIFIL apprehended Palestinian guerrillas, it confiscated their weapons but usually returned them later to PLO leaders. UNIFIL paid a price for performing its mission, however; between 1978 and 1982, thirty-six UNIFIL members were killed in action.

In late 1987 the future of UNIFIL was in doubt. Ironically, Israel, which had long considered UNIFIL a hindrance to its operations, changed its policy and in 1986 praised the positive role UNIFIL played in stabilizing the region. For its part, the government of Lebanon requested that UNIFIL be expanded to police almost the entire country. But at the same time, the Shias in southern Lebanon, who had traditionally supported UNIFIL, turned against the organization. In September 1986, Shia extremists started attacking UNIFIL's French contingent, and in five weeks of combat they killed four and wounded thirty. UNIFIL's casualty toll mounted and by mid-1987 stood at 139 killed and over 200 wounded. In 1986 the United States Congress cut the annual United States appropriation to UNIFIL from US$40 million to US$18 million, while France announced that it would withdraw its troops from UNIFIL in 1987.

The Ascendancy of Bashir Jumayyil

Emboldened by Israel's willingness to intervene militarily in Lebanon, Bashir Jumayyil exploited Israel's tacit guarantees to

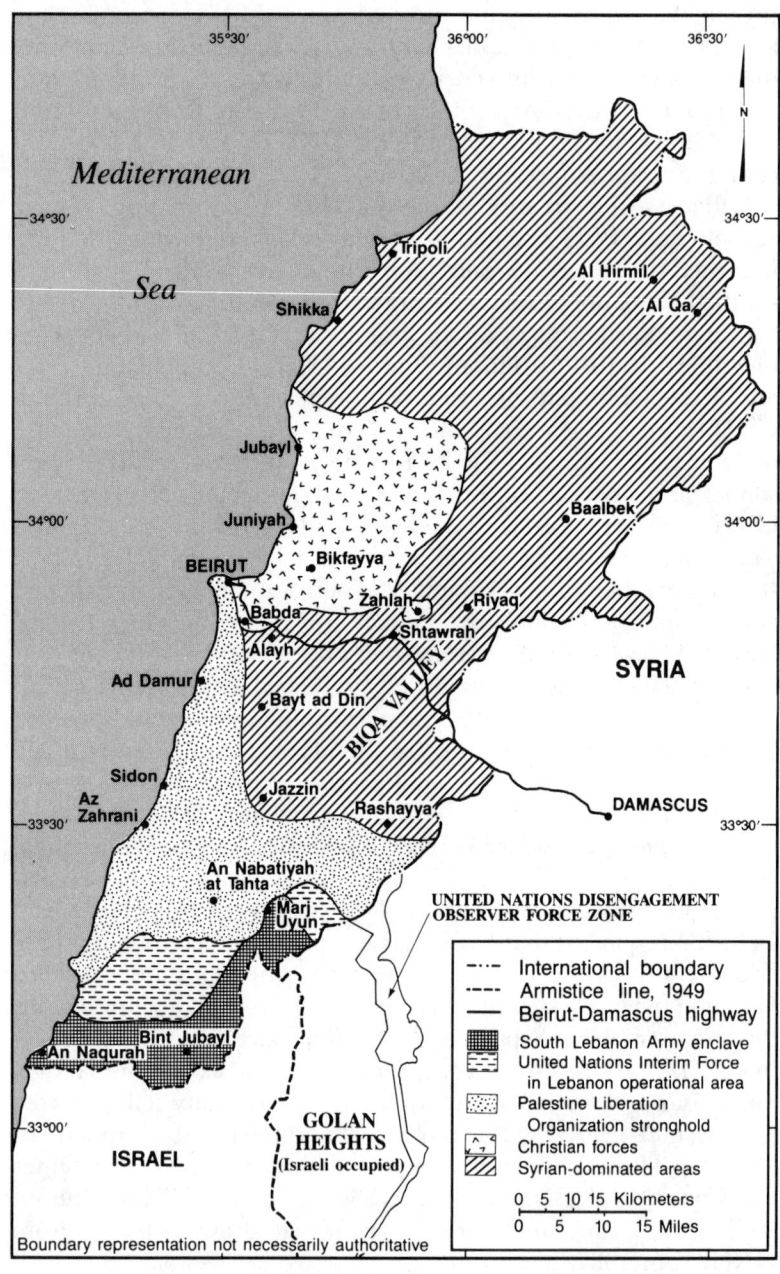

Figure 10. *Lebanon on the Eve of the 1982 Israeli Invasion*

consolidate his position within the fractious Maronite community. On June 13, 1978, he launched a surprise attack that decimated the Marada Brigade, the pro-Syrian Christian militia led by Tony Franjiyah (son of the former president), who was killed in the attack, and provoked the Syrians with direct attacks. In pitting his meager force of a few thousand fighters against three divisions of the Syrian Army, Jumayyil was taking a calculated gamble that Israel would come to his rescue and evict the Syrians. Syria rushed forces to Beirut and unleashed a devastating artillery attack on East Beirut, particularly the Phalangist stronghold of Al Ashrafiyah, in preparation for taking over the area. But Jumayyil's brinkmanship was vindicated. The IDF massed forces on the Golan Heights and threatened to go to war to preserve the Maronite community. To emphasize the point, Israeli jets overflew Syrian positions. The threat worked, and Syria withdrew its troops.

Once again, Jumayyil took the opportunity to strengthen his grip over the Maronites. On July 7, 1980, the Phalangists launched another surprise attack, wiping out Shamun's militia, the Tigers. Through this process of elimination, Jumayyil emerged as the dominant Maronite military leader.

Jumayyil persevered in his plot to embroil Israel in a full-scale war with Syria. In late 1980, after a series of meetings with Begin, he reportedly obtained a secret Israeli pledge to provide a defensive umbrella against a potential Syrian air attack. This pledge virtually committed Israel to fight Syria at Jumayyil's behest, although Israel admonished the Phalangists not to attack the Syrians.

In April 1981, Jumayyil decided to put Israel's promise to the test. Syria had launched its "Program of National Reconciliation," which was designed to install Sulayman Franjiyah as president. Jumayyil found the proposition unpalatable, but he was impotent to oppose it politically. Therefore, he staged an incident in the city of Zahlah deliberately calculated to flare into a major crisis. Zahlah, the capital of Al Biqa Province in eastern Lebanon, had never been a Phalangist base; its population was primarily pro-Syrian Greek Orthodox, and it was about fifteen kilometers west of the Syrian border in the heart of the Syrian-occupied zone of Lebanon. Jumayyil infiltrated approximately 100 Phalangist militiamen into the city to attack Syrian positions and to shell the Syrian headquarters in the adjacent town of Shtawrah. The Syrians responded by besieging Zahlah. Jumayyil then called an urgent meeting with Begin and convinced him that the Syrians intended to follow through on the siege with an all-out attack on the Christian heartland. Although Syrian president Hafiz al Assad had told Jumayyil he would lift the siege if the Phalangists evacuated the city, Jumayyil concealed this point from Begin and instead urged Israel to honor its promise and launch an air strike against the Syrians.

On April 28, the Israeli cabinet convened and authorized a limited air strike, but it did so over the strident objections of Israel's intelligence chiefs, who suspected that the crisis was a Phalangist ploy. Israeli fighters carried out the raid and downed two Syrian helicopter troop transports on Jabal Sannin, a strategic mountain overlooking Zahlah.

The Missile Crisis

The Israeli attack caught Assad by surprise. Syria had adhered to the so-called "Red Line" agreements by deliberately refraining from deploying antiaircraft missiles in the Biqa Valley and by not impeding Israeli photoreconnaissance overflights. Assad responded to the Israeli attack by stationing SA-6 surface-to-air missiles (SAMs) in the vicinity of Zahlah. Other SAMs and surface-to-surface missiles were deployed on the Syrian side of the border.

Begin vowed publicly that the IDF would launch an attack on the missiles. In response, President Ronald Reagan dispatched to the Middle East Special Ambassador Philip Habib, who averted the imminent Israeli strike. Meanwhile, the Phalangists abandoned Zahlah, and Syria reasserted its control over the Biqa Valley. The net effect of the crisis was that Syrian air defense missiles were deployed in Lebanon. Israel was forced to tolerate this situation in the short run, but it still regarded the missile deployment as an unacceptable shift in the balance of forces that could not be endured indefinitely. Therefore, Israel had reasons of its own for a future attack on the Syrians in Lebanon.

The Two-Week War

As the tension in the Biqa Valley subsided, IDF chief of staff Rafael Eitan urged Begin to mount an artillery bombardment of Palestinian bases in Lebanon. Israel routinely conducted preemptive artillery attacks and air strikes to deter PLO terrorist attacks against Galilee settlements in northern Israel. Then, on July 10, 1981, the IDF commenced five days of air strikes and naval bombardments against PLO strongholds in southern Lebanon.

The PLO fought back by shelling the Israeli resort town of Nahariyya on the Mediterranean coast. The conflict escalated as Israel launched a devastating air raid against the heavily populated Palestinian neighborhood of Fakhani in West Beirut, killing over 100 people and wounding over 600. By Israeli estimates, only thirty of those killed were terrorists. For ten days, the PLO then unleashed artillery fire against the upper Galilee. Six Israeli citizens were killed, and many Israelis were shocked and stunned by the PLO's capability to sustain such an attack.

On July 24, Ambassador Habib returned to Israel to negotiate an end to the artillery duel. Because the PLO was almost out of ammunition and most of its guns had been silenced, the IDF wanted to prolong the fighting until it could win a clear-cut victory. But the Israeli cabinet was eager to comply with Habib's cease-fire proposal, and Israel entered into a truce with the PLO.

PLO leader Yasir Arafat was determined not to break the cease-fire. On a political level, the truce enhanced the PLO's diplomatic credibility. Tactically, it allowed the PLO time to reinforce its military strength in southern Lebanon. The Soviet Union refused to provide the PLO with weapons, but PLO emissaries purchased arms from East European countries and the Democratic People's Republic of Korea (North Korea), acquiring Grad and Katyusha artillery rockets and antiquated but functional T-34 tanks. More significant, Arafat reorganized the command and control structure of his forces, transforming the Palestine Liberation Army (PLA) from a decentralized collection of terrorist and guerrilla bands to a disciplined standing army. By 1981 the Kastel, Karami, and Yarmuk brigades were established, and seven new artillery battalions were organized.

But on June 3, 1982, terrorists of the Abu Nidal Organization, a group that had split off from the PLO, attempted to assassinate Shlomo Argov, the Israeli ambassador to Britain. Israel seized on the attack as the pretext for launching its long-planned offensive. On June 4, IDF aircraft bombed Palestinian targets in West Beirut, and the PLO resumed artillery fire on Israeli settlements in the northern Galilee.

The Israeli cabinet convened and voted to authorize an invasion, named Operation Peace for Galilee, but it set strict limits on the extent of the incursion. The IDF was to advance no farther than forty kilometers, the operation was to last only twenty-four hours, Syrian forces were not to be attacked, and Beirut was not to be approached.

The 1982 Israeli Invasion and Its Aftermath
Operation Peace for Galilee

Because of the limits imposed by the Israeli cabinet, the IDF implemented its attack in increments, neither openly recognizing nor acknowledging its destination and objectives. Had it been ordered from the outset to secure Beirut, it could have done so in an effective and efficient manner. Instead, the IDF advance unfolded in an ad hoc and disorganized fashion, greatly increasing the difficulty of the operation.

When IDF ground forces crossed into Lebanon on June 6, they pursued a battle strategy that entailed a three-pronged attack conducted by five divisions and two reinforced brigade-size units. On the western axis, two divisions converged on Tyre and proceeded north along the coastal road toward Sidon, where they were to link up with an amphibious commando unit that had secured a beachhead north of the city. In the central sector, a third division veered diagonally across southern Lebanon, conquered the Palestinian-held Beaufort Castle, located a few kilometers southwest of Marj Uyun, and headed west toward Sidon, where it linked up with the coastal force in a classic pincer movement. The IDF advanced rapidly in the first day of the war, bypassing and enveloping pockets of PLO resistance. Most PLO military officers fled, abandoning their men, who split into small roving guerrilla bands. Moreover, it became clear that the PLO was fighting alone against the Israeli onslaught. The Shia Amal guerrillas had been ordered by their leaders not to fight and to surrender their weapons if necessary. Southern Lebanon's Shias had long suffered under Palestinian domination, and Shia villagers welcomed the advancing Israelis by showering them with rice and flowers. This traditional form of homage, later repeated by the Druze and Christian populations, lent credence to the Israeli claim that it was "liberating" Lebanon.

But Palestinian resistance proved tenacious, particularly in the sprawling refugee camps in the vicinity of Tyre and Sidon (see fig. 4). Staging hit-and-run operations and fighting in house-to-house and hand-to-hand combat, the Palestinians inflicted a high number of casualties on the IDF and impeded the progress of the Israeli advance. The IDF was further hampered because the refugee camps were inhabited by large numbers of civilian noncombatants who harbored the Palestinian fighters. Although the IDF made significant initial efforts to evacuate the civilians, it ultimately resorted to saturation bombing to subdue the camps. Palestinian resistance was especially fierce in the Ayn al Hulwah camp near Sidon, where several hundred Palestinian fighters fought to the last man, delaying the IDF advance for seven days. After the camp was leveled, the IDF stood poised to move against Beirut.

Two days later in eastern Lebanon, two divisions thrust directly north on parallel courses into Syrian-held territory with the mission of severing the strategic Beirut-Damascus highway. On June 8, the IDF evicted the Syrian Army from Jazzin and proceeded north. A brigade of Syrian commandos, however, ambushed the Israeli

*Israeli armored vehicles in Beirut during the 1982 invasion
Courtesy Lebanese Information and Research Center*

column in the mountainous terrain near Ayn Zhalta, approximately five kilometers short of the highway.

The IDF could not proceed further against the entrenched Syrian positions without close air support, but Syria's air defense systems threatened Israeli control of the skies. On June 9, the Israeli cabinet gave permission for an air raid against the Syrian antiaircraft missile batteries in the Biqa Valley. The Syrians, caught by surprise, sustained severe losses; of the nineteen missile batteries, only two were left intact by the Israeli attack. The Syrian Air Force made a desperate bid to protect the air defense system by sending up scores of interceptors and fighters, resulting in what both sides described as the biggest air battle in history, with over 200 aircraft engaged in supersonic dogfights over a 2,500 square kilometer area. The Israeli Air Force shot down twenty-nine Syrian aircraft that day (and later about fifty more) without a single loss. The devastation of the Syrian air defense system and the decimation of the Syrian Air Force provided the IDF with total air superiority in Lebanon and left the Syrian infantry exposed to air attack.

For three more days, the IDF mauled Syria's First Armored Division. The IDF was still stalled short of the Beirut-Damascus highway, but it was on the verge of breaking through the last line of Syria's defense. Bowing to political pressures, however, on June 11 Israel and Syria agreed to a truce under United States auspices.

The Siege of Beirut

The cease-fire signaled the start of a new stage in the war, as Israel focused on PLO forces trapped in Beirut. Although Israel had long adhered to the axiom that conquering and occupying an Arab capital would be a political and military disaster, key Israeli leaders were determined to drive the PLO out of Beirut. According to the original plan, the Phalangists were to move into West Beirut under the covering fire of Israeli artillery and reunite the divided capital. Bashir Jumayyil concluded, however, that such overt collusion with the IDF would prejudice his chance to become president, and he reneged on the promises he had made.

Israel maintained the siege of Beirut for seventy days, unleashing a relentless barrage of air, naval, and artillery bombardment. At times, the Israeli bombardment appeared to be random and indiscriminate; at other times, it was targeted with pinpoint precision. Israeli strategists believed that if they could "decapitate" the Palestinian movement by killing its leaders, Palestinian resistance would disappear. Therefore, the Israeli Air Force conducted what has been called a "manhunt by air" for Arafat and his top lieutenants and on several occasions bombed premises only minutes after the PLO leadership had vacated them.

If the PLO was hurt physically by the bombardment, the political fallout was just as damaging to Israel. The appalling civilian casualties earned Israel world opprobrium. Morale plummeted among IDF officers and enlisted men, many of whom personally opposed the war. Meanwhile, the highly publicized plight of the Palestinian civilians garnered world attention for the Palestinian cause. Furthermore, Arafat was negotiating, albeit through intermediaries, with Ambassador Habib and other United States officials. Negotiating with Arafat was thought by some to be tantamount to United States recognition of the PLO.

Arafat had threatened to turn Beirut into a "second Stalingrad," to fight the IDF to the last man. His negotiating stance grew tenuous, however, after Lebanese leaders, who had previously expressed solidarity with the PLO, petitioned him to abandon Beirut to spare the civilian population further suffering. Arafat informed Habib of his agreement in principle to withdraw the PLO from Beirut on condition that a multinational peacekeeping force be deployed to protect the Palestinian families left behind. With the diplomatic deadlock broken, Habib made a second breakthrough when Syria and Tunisia agreed to host departing PLO fighters. An advance unit of the Multinational Force (MNF), 350 French troops, arrived

*Lebanese wave to departing Palestinian fighters.
Courtesy Lebanese Information and Research Center*

in Beirut on August 21. The Palestinian evacuation by sea to Cyprus and by land to Damascus commenced on the same day. On August 26, the remaining MNF troops arrived in Beirut, including a contingent of 800 United States Marines. The Palestinian exodus ended on September 1. Approximately 8,000 Palestinian guerrillas, 2,600 PLA regulars, and 3,600 Syrian troops had been evacuated from West Beirut.

Taking stock of the war's toll, Israel announced that 344 of its soldiers had been killed and more than 2,000 wounded. Israel calculated that hundreds of Syrian soldiers had been killed and more than 1,000 wounded and that 1,000 Palestinian guerrillas had been killed and 7,000 captured. Lebanese estimates, compiled from International Red Cross sources and police and hospital surveys, calculated that 17,825 Lebanese had died and more than 30,000 had been wounded.

On August 23, the legislature elected Bashir Jumayyil president of Lebanon. On September 10, the United States Marines withdrew from Beirut, followed by the other members of the MNF. The Lebanese Army began to move into West Beirut, and the Israelis withdrew their troops from the front lines. But the war was far from over. By ushering in Jumayyil as president and evicting the PLO from Beirut, Israel had attained two of its key war goals. Israel's remaining ambition was to sign a comprehensive peace treaty with Lebanon that would entail the withdrawal of Syrian forces and prevent the PLO from reinfiltrating Lebanon after the IDF withdrew.

Jumayyil repudiated earlier promises to Israel immediately after the election. He informed the Israelis that a peace treaty was inconceivable as long as the IDF or any other foreign forces remained in Lebanon and that it could be concluded only with the consent of all the Lebanese.

But on September 14, 1982, President-elect Jumayyil was assassinated in a massive radio-detonated explosion that leveled the Phalange Party headquarters where he was delivering a speech to party members. The perpetrator, Habib Shartuni, was soon apprehended. Shartuni, a member of the Syrian Socialist Nationalist Party, was allegedly a Syrian agent. Jumayyil's brother, Amin, who was hostile to the Israeli presence in Lebanon, was elected president with United States backing.

On the evening of September 16, 1982, the IDF, having surrounded the Palestinian refugee camps of Sabra and Shatila, dispatched approximately 300 to 400 Christian militiamen into the camps to rout what was believed to be the remnant of the Palestinian forces. The militiamen were mostly Phalangists under the command of Elie Hubayka (also seen as Hobeika), a former close aide of Bashir Jumayyil, but militiamen from the Israeli-supported SLA were also present. The IDF ordered its soldiers to refrain from entering the camps, but IDF officers supervised the operation from the roof of a six-story building overlooking parts of the area. According to the report of the Kahan Commission established by the government of Israel to investigate the events, the IDF monitored the Phalangist radio network and fired illumination flares from mortars and aircraft to light the area. Over a period of two days, the Christian militiamen massacred some 700 to 800 Palestinian men, women, and children.

The Multinational Force

At the behest of the Lebanese government, the Multinational Force (MNF) was deployed again in Beirut, but with over twice the manpower of the first peacekeeping force. It was designated MNF II and given the mandate to serve as an "interpositional force," separating the IDF from the Lebanese population. Additionally, MNF II was assigned the task of assisting the Lebanese Army in restoring the authority of the central government over Beirut. The United States dispatched a contingent of 1,400 men, France 1,500, and Italy 1,400. A relatively small British contingent of about 100 men was added in January 1983, at which time the Italian contingent was increased to 2,200 men. Each contingent retained its own command structure, and no central command structure was created. The French contingent was assigned responsibility for the port area and West Beirut. The Italian contingent occupied the area between West Beirut and Beirut International Airport, which encompassed the Sabra and Shatila refugee camps. The 32d United States Marines Amphibious Unit returned to Beirut on September 29, where it took up positions in the vicinity of Beirut International Airport. The Marines' positions were adjacent to the IDF front lines.

The Marines' stated mission was to establish an environment that would permit the Lebanese Army to carry out its responsibilities in the Beirut area. Tactically, the Marines were charged with occupying and securing positions along a line from the airport east to the Presidential Palace at Babda. The intent was to separate the IDF from the population of Beirut.

The key to the initial success of MNF II was its neutrality. The Lebanese government had assured Ambassador Habib in writing that it had obtained commitments from various factions to refrain from hostilities against the Marines. The United States reputation among the Lebanese was enhanced when a Marine officer was obliged to draw his pistol to halt an Israeli advance, an event sensationalized in the news media. And, in the same month, Marines conducted emergency relief operations in the mountains after a midwinter blizzard.

At this juncture, the prevalent mood in Lebanon was one of cautious optimism and hope. The Lebanese Army was pressed into service to clear away the rubble of years of warfare. The government approved a US$600 million reconstruction plan. On October 1, President Jumayyil declared Beirut reunited, as the army demolished barricades along the Green Line that had been standing since 1975. Hundreds of criminals and gang leaders were rounded up and arrested. In the first months of 1983, approximately 5,000 government troops were deployed throughout Greater Beirut. Most important, the government began to build a strong national army (see The Lebanese Armed Forces in the 1980s, this ch).

Lebanese optimism was bolstered by changing Israeli politics and policies. Minister of Defense Ariel Sharon, the architect of Israel's war in Lebanon, had resigned in the wake of the Sabra and Shatila investigation, although he remained in the cabinet as a minister without portfolio. He was replaced by the former ambassador to the United States, Moshe Arens. Although Arens was considered a hawk in the Israeli political spectrum, he was not committed to Sharon's ambitious goals and wanted the IDF to withdraw promptly from Lebanon, if only to avoid antagonizing the United States, with which he had cultivated a close relationship. Accordingly, Israel withdrew its forces to the outskirts of the capital.

But the IDF had no clear tactical mission in Lebanon. Its continued presence was intended as a bargaining chip in negotiations for a Syrian withdrawal. While awaiting the political agreement, the IDF was forced to fight a different kind of war, which Israeli newspapers compared with the Vietnam War. The IDF had been turned into a static and defensive garrison force like the Syrians before them, caught in the cross fire between warring factions. When Phalangist forces tried to exploit the fluid situation by attacking the Druze militia in the Shuf Mountains in late 1983, the IDF had to intervene and separate the forces. In southern Lebanon, the IDF had to protect the many Palestinian refugees who had streamed back to the camps against attacks by Israel's proxy force, the SLA. In one of the bigger ironies of the war, the IDF recruited and armed Palestinian home guards to prevent a repetition of the massacres in Beirut.

The Rise of the Shias

The 1979 Iranian Revolution galvanized Lebanon's Shia community and inspired in it a new militancy. Iran sought to export Shia revolution throughout the Middle East, and in doing so it provided material support to an Amal terrorist campaign. From 1979 until the 1982 Israeli invasion, Shia terrorists hijacked six airliners, attempted to bomb several others, assassinated the French ambassador to Lebanon, blew up the French and Iraqi embassies, and committed numerous other violent acts.

The Israeli invasion served as a catalyst for a further upsurge in Shia militancy. In July 1982 Iran dispatched an expeditionary force of volunteer Pasdaran (Revolutionary Guards) to Lebanon, ostensibly to fight Israeli invaders. The approximately 650 Pasdaran established their headquarters in the city of Baalbek in the Syrian-controlled Biqa Valley. There they conducted terrorist and guerrilla training, disbursed military matériel and money, and disseminated propaganda.

The political fission that characterized Lebanese politics also afflicted the Shia movement, as groups split off from Amal. Husayn al Musawi, a former Amal lieutenant, entered into an alliance with the Revolutionary Guard and established Islamic Amal. Other Shia groups included Hizballah (Party of God), Jundallah (Soldiers of God), the Husayn Suicide Commandos, the Dawah (Call) Party, and the notorious Islamic Jihad Organization, reportedly headed by Imad Mughniyyah (see Internal Security and Terrorism, this ch.).

The May 17 Agreement

In April 1983, a terrorist attack destroyed the United States embassy, and the ambassador moved diplomatic operations to his official residence. The United States persevered in its efforts to broker an Israeli-Lebanese agreement, and Israel announced its willingness to negotiate. Although Israel had envisaged a treaty like the Camp David Agreements with Egypt, entailing full bilateral diplomatic recognition, it settled for mere "normalization." The military and security articles of the May 17 Agreement between the Israeli and Lebanese governments called for an abolition of the state of war between the two countries, security arrangements to ensure the sanctity of Israel's northern border, integration of Major Haddad's SLA into the regular Lebanese Army, and Israeli withdrawal.

The Israeli withdrawal was made contingent upon concurrent Syrian withdrawal, however. The United States had decided not to seek Syrian participation in the negotiations for the May 17 Agreement for fear of becoming entangled in the overall Syrian-Israeli imbroglio. Instead, the United States intended to seek Syrian endorsement after the agreement was signed. But Syria vehemently opposed the agreement, and because implementation hinged on Syrian withdrawal, Damascus could exert veto power. Although President Jumayyil made conciliatory overtures to Damascus, he also notified the Arab League on June 4 that the ADF was no longer in existence.

Syria responded by announcing on July 23, 1983, the foundation of the National Salvation Front (NSF). This coalition comprised many sects, including the Druzes led by Walid Jumblatt; Shias led by Nabih Birri (also seen as Berri); Sunni Muslims led by Rashid Karami; Christian elements led by Sulayman Franjiyah; and several smaller, Syrian-sponsored, left-wing political parties. These groups, together with Syria, controlled much more of Lebanon's territory than did the central government. Therefore, the NSF constituted a challenge not only to Jumayyil but also to his patrons, the United States and Israel. To emphasize their opposition to the May 17 Agreement, Syrian and Druze forces in the mountains above the capital loosed a barrage of artillery fire on Christian areas of Beirut, underscoring the weakness of Jumayyil's government.

By mid-1983 the mood of optimism that had flourished at the end of 1982 had disappeared. It became clear that the tentative alliance of Lebanon's rival factions was merely a function of their shared opposition to a common enemy, Israel. Terrorist activity resumed, and between June and August 1983, at least twenty car bombs exploded throughout Lebanon, killing more than seventy people. Lebanon's prime minister narrowly escaped death in one explosion. Targets included a mosque in Tripoli; a television station, hospital, and luxury hotel in Beirut; and a market in Baalbek.

The May 17 Agreement had significant implications for the MNF. As a noncombatant interpositional force preventing the IDF from entering Beirut, the MNF had been perceived by the Muslims in West Beirut as a protector. As the Israeli withdrawal neared, however, the MNF came to be regarded as a protagonist in the unfinished Civil War, propping up the Jumayyil government. In August militiamen began to bombard United States Marines positions near Beirut International Airport with mortar and rocket fire as the Lebanese Army fought Druze and Shia forces in the southern suburbs of Beirut. On August 29, 1983, two Marines were killed and fourteen wounded, and in the ensuing months the Marines came under almost daily attack from artillery, mortar, rocket, and small-arms fire.

The Israel Defense Forces Withdrawal and the Mountain War

On September 3, 1983, the Israel Defense Forces (IDF) began to evacuate the Shuf Mountains region and within twenty-four hours had completed its redeployment to south of the Awwali River. In the power vacuum resulting from the Israeli withdrawal, the Phalangist militia, no longer under Jumayyil's firm control, clashed with the Druze militia at Bhamdun, a town located where the Beirut-Damascus highway touches the edge of the Shuf Mountains. Simultaneously, the Lebanese Army sought to guard the cities of Suq al Gharb and Khaldah to prevent Druze forces from invading Beirut.

After several days of combat, the Phalangist militia was routed at Bhamdun and retreated to its stronghold of Dayr al Qamar, along with much of the Christian population. The Druzes surrounded and besieged Dayr al Qamar, which held 40,000 Christian residents and refugees and 2,000 Phalangist fighters. In other areas of the Shuf Mountains, the Druzes went on a rampage reminiscent of the 1860 massacres (see Religious Conflicts, ch. 1). The Catholic Information Center in Beirut reported that 1,500 Christian civilians were killed and 62 Christian villages demolished. The defeat of the Phalangists was expensive for the Christian community, which lost a large amount of territory.

The cost in political currency was even higher, however. Not only did the fighting deal a blow to Amin Jumayyil's credibility and authority in his dual role as chief of state and leader of the Christian community, it destroyed the myth shared by many different Lebanese factions that the Lebanese Civil War had been settled in 1976. Admittedly, Christians and Muslims had continued to fire on each other's neighborhoods on occasion, but this was perceived as part of Lebanon's environment, like the weather. In all the significant fighting between 1976 and 1982, the Syrians, Israelis, and Palestinians had been belligerents on either or both sides of the conflict. The Mountain War, as the 1983-84 fighting in the Shuf Mountains came to be called, however, was a purely Lebanese contest, and it dashed the hopes harbored by many that the withdrawal of foreign forces would end the Civil War.

In Suq al Gharb and Khaldah, it was the Lebanese Army rather than the Phalangists that confronted the Druze militias. On September 16, 1983, Druze forces massed on the threshold of Suq al Gharb. For the next three days the army's Eighth Brigade fought desperately to retain control of the town (see The Army, this ch.). The tiny Lebanese Air Force was thrown into the fray, losing several aircraft to Druze missile fire. United States Navy warships shelled Druze positions and helped the Lebanese Army hold the town until a cease-fire was declared on September 25, on which day the battleship U.S.S. *New Jersey* arrived on the scene.

The Multinational Force Withdrawal

Although the Lebanese Army had beaten the Druze forces on the battlefield, it was a Pyrrhic victory because the army was discredited if not defeated. Approximately 900 Druze enlisted men and 60 officers defected from the army to join their coreligionists. The Lebanese Armed Forces chief of staff, General Nadim al Hakim, fled into Druze territory, but he would not admit he had actually defected. Thus, the army again had split along confessional lines. Furthermore, the army had halted the Druzes only with United States armed intervention.

For its part, the United States had clearly inherited Israel's role of shoring up the precarious Lebanese government. On September 29, 1983, the United States Congress, by a solid majority, adopted a resolution declaring the 1973 War Powers Resolution to apply to the situation in Lebanon and sanctioned the United States military presence for an eighteen-month period.

Although the MNF remained in Lebanon after the October 1983 suicide truck bombings, the situation of the United States and French contingents was precarious (see Suicide Bombings, this ch.).

In early February 1984, Shia Amal militiamen clashed with the Lebanese Army in the southern suburbs of Beirut and after four days of heavy fighting gained control over Beirut International Airport, evicted the army from West Beirut, and reestablished the Green Line partitioning the capital. The decisive defeat of the army on two key fronts led to its gradual disintegration, as demoralized soldiers defected to join the opposition. United States Marines stationed near Beirut International Airport were surrounded by predominantly Shia militia groups. As the security environment in Lebanon deteriorated, Britain, France, Italy, and the United States decided to withdraw their MNF contingents.

The Bikfayya Accord

The withdrawal of the MNF left Syria as the dominant force in Lebanon, and Syria acted rapidly to consolidate its grip on Lebanese affairs. It pressured Jumayyil to abrogate the May 17 Agreement, and he did so on March 6, 1985. This event led to the resignation of the Council of Ministers and its replacement by a new government of national unity headed by Rashid Karami.

Syria hammered out yet another security accord, the Bikfayya Agreement of June 18. Muslim and Druze cabinet ministers had insisted on the creation of a military command council to replace the post of commander in chief of the armed forces, a proposal that was opposed by Christian cabinet ministers, who perceived it as a dilution of their control over the military. A compromise was reached providing for the continuation of the post of commander in chief, to be held by a Maronite as before, but also the establishment of a multiconfessional six-man military command council to have authority over appointments at the brigade and division levels (see Organization and Command Structure, this ch.). Major General Ibrahim Tannus, the army commander, was replaced by Major General Michel Awn (also seen as Aoun), who was somewhat more acceptable to Muslims. Furthermore, a new intelligence agency, the National Security Council, was established, with the stipulation that it be headed by a Shia Muslim. A Shia general, Mustafa Nasir, was named as the first director of the new agency. Nevertheless, the Maronite-commanded military intelligence apparatus remained intact as a separate but parallel institution. The agreement also called for a cease-fire, the withdrawal of heavy artillery and militiamen from the streets of East Beirut and West Beirut, the dismantling of barricades along the Green Line, and the reopening of the airport and port. The agreement formally took effect on June 23 and was implemented by July 6, 1985.

National Security

Optimistic predictions that the Bikfayya Agreement would end Lebanon's chronic conflict were dashed as sporadic battles and terrorist attacks resumed. The accord was criticized vehemently by elements among the Maronites as Druze, Shia, and Sunni militia fought one another in West Beirut. Armed Shias stormed and burned the Saudi Arabian embassy on August 24. On the same day, the Lebanese National Resistance Front, an umbrella organization fighting Israel in southern Lebanon, fired two rocket-propelled grenades at the British embassy. On September 20, in a replay of the April 1983 attack, a suicide vehicle bomber attacked the new United States embassy building in East Beirut, killing eight and wounding dozens. The mounting tension in Lebanon was exacerbated by Israeli air raids against Palestinian guerrilla camps of the Abu Musa faction. The Bikfayya Agreement suffered another blow on August 23, when General Hakim, the newly appointed Druze chief of staff of the Lebanese Armed Forces, died in an accidental helicopter crash. And, on August 30 Maronite patriarch and Phalange Party founder Pierre Jumayyil died of a heart attack, setting the stage for a power struggle in the Christian community.

Syria, determined to implement the security plans it had sponsored, attempted to restore order. It curbed the activities of the Iranian Pasdaran and Hizballah in Baalbek in the Biqa Valley, and it quelled the fierce fighting in the northern port city of Tripoli between the pro-Syrian Arab Democratic Party and the Sunni fundamentalist Tawhid (Islamic Unification Movement).

Events in Southern Lebanon

Some Israeli policymakers considered South Lebanon's Shias natural allies, especially because both Israel and the Shias wanted to prevent the PLO from returning to the area. Some Israelis envisioned a Shia buffer state modeled after "Free Lebanon," controlled formerly by Saad Haddad (Haddad died of cancer in January 1984 and was replaced by retired Lebanese general Antoine Lahad). Indeed, about 10 percent of the SLA was Shia, and the IDF armed and supported several Shia groups.

These hopes, however, were never realized. The Shias, in fact, turned out to be implacable foes, vehemently resisting the Israeli presence in southern Lebanon. Concerned about the growing number of casualties inflicted on the IDF by Shia militants, on February 16, 1985, the IDF implemented the first stage of a withdrawal from Lebanon, evacuating its troops from the northern front at the Awwali River to south of the Litani River, thus removing Sidon from Israeli control. Sidon's feuding factions, determined to avoid a flare-up of internecine violence in the wake of the Israeli withdrawal, formed a special committee to organize the smooth entry of Lebanese Army troops into the city. On February 17, a 3,000-man detachment of the army's predominantly Shia Twelfth Brigade took over the Israeli positions as the populace celebrated in the streets.

But the celebration was short-lived. In March and April, a new round of Christian-Muslim fighting pitting a Palestinian-Druze-Shia coalition against the Phalangists engulfed Sidon. The army was dispatched but appeared powerless to stop the combat. The Phalangists suffered a major defeat, as thousands of Christian civilians retreated east to Jazzin, where they were protected by Lahad's SLA. Others fled behind Israeli occupation lines.

Yet Israel's withdrawal gave it no respite from guerrilla attacks. On the contrary, the guerrilla campaign escalated into full-scale warfare, with most of the attacks occurring in the vicinity of Tyre. Frustrated by its inability to curb the resistance fighters, Israel resorted to what it called the "Iron Fist" policy, which entailed retaliatory and preemptive raids on villages suspected of harboring Shia guerrillas. On March 4, an explosion devastated a mosque in the village of Marakah—only hours after the IDF had inspected the site—killing at least twelve people, many of whom were Shia guerrilla commanders. On March 11, a large Israeli armored force wreaked vengeance on the village of Az Zrariyah, killing 40 people and detaining 200 men.

The IDF hastened its withdrawal from southern Lebanon, adhering to an accelerated deadline voted by the Israeli cabinet, and pulled its troops back to the armistice line on June 6, 1985. Israel also closed its detention center in Ansar and freed 752 of the inmates. But, in violation of the Geneva Conventions, which forbid transporting prisoners of war across international boundaries, 1,200 prisoners were transferred to Israel. Israel preserved a security zone approximately five to ten kilometers wide, which it handed over to the SLA. Some 150 Israeli combat troops and 500 advisers remained within the security zone.

Chaos in Beirut and Syrian Peacemaking Efforts

Internecine Battles in the Lebanese Forces

In early 1985, clashes erupted again in the capital, this time between rival Christian factions. Recognizing that Syria was now the dominant arbiter of Lebanese affairs, Jumayyil and senior Phalange Party members held conciliatory talks with Syria and attempted to obtain Syrian security guarantees for Lebanon's Christians. In

Lebanese Forces rivals, Samir Jaja (left) and Elie Hubayka

return, the Phalangists agreed to Syrian demands that the Christians make political concessions to the Muslims. However, a portion of the Lebanese Forces (LF) rebelled against the rapprochement with Syria. On March 13, 1985, Samir Jaja (also seen as Geagea), a pro-Israeli senior commander in the LF, ordered his followers to attack Jumayyil's loyalists, Lebanese Army units, and Muslim and Palestinian forces in Sidon and Beirut. Syria massed troops around the Christian heartland north of Beirut, but agreed to give Jumayyil time to neutralize the revolt before resorting to armed intervention. Jaja's relatively small force could not prevail against so many adversaries, and on May 10 he was replaced by Elie Hubayka, who was elected by Phalange Party executives as the new commander of the LF. Hubayka was notorious for his role in the 1982 Sabra and Shatila massacres but also had a reputation for being more pro-Syrian than Jaja (see The Siege of Beirut, this ch.).

The War of the Camps

Just as relative calm was restored to Christian East Beirut, fighting broke out again in Muslim West Beirut. Under Syria's aegis, the Shia Amal organization attempted to consolidate its control over West Beirut. Amal struck first in an April 15 assault that routed the once-formidable Sunni Murabitun militia of the Independent Nasserite Movement in a matter of days and sent its leader, Ibrahim Kulaylat, into exile. Then it turned its attention to the Palestinians in the refugee camps of Sabra, Shatila, and Burj al Barajinah. The Palestinians, with indirect support from the Druzes, put up stiff resistance against the Amal attacks, however. Although some 500 Palestinians were killed in the battles and about 25,000 took refuge in Druze-controlled areas, the Palestinians retained control of the camps. But the Palestinians were confined to their camps by an Amal siege that was to last on and off for another two years before Syrian forces dispersed the Shias.

The Tripartite Accord

In late 1985, Syria sponsored yet another agreement among Lebanon's factions aimed at ending the ongoing war. On December 28, the leaders of Lebanon's three main militias—Nabih Birri of Amal, Walid Jumblatt of the Druze Progressive Socialist Party, and Hubayka of the LF—signed the Tripartite Accord in Damascus. Although this agreement resembled many previous failed Syrian initiatives to restore order in Lebanon, it was more comprehensive. It provided for an immediate cease-fire and an official proclamation of the end of the state of civil war within one year. The militias would be disarmed and then disbanded, and sole responsibility for security would be relegated to the reconstituted and religiously integrated Lebanese Army, supported by Syrian forces. More broadly, the accord envisaged a "strategic integration" of the two countries in the spheres of military affairs, national security, and foreign relations. The accord also mandated fundamental, but not sweeping, political reform, including the establishment of a bicameral legislature and the elimination of the old confessional formula, which was to be replaced by majority rule and minority representation. The accord differed considerably from others inasmuch as the three signatories were the actual combatants in the war, rather than civilian politicians. This factor engendered considerable optimism in some quarters but great trepidation in others where it was viewed as an attempt to reconstruct Greater Syria (see Glossary). The most vehement protests came from the Sunni community, which was prominent in politics but had little military strength after its militia, the Murabitun, had been crushed earlier in the year.

Jumayyil refused to endorse the agreement, however, and solicited the support of Samir Jaja, who had been demoted only eight months earlier for his anti-Syrian, Christian-supremacist stance. Fierce fighting raged within the Christian camp between partisans of Hubayka and Jaja. On January 16, Hubayka fled to Paris, and then to exile in Damascus. Hubayka's defeat was a major blow to Syrian prestige, and Syria retaliated by urging the militias it controlled to attack Christian areas. The Presidential Palace and Jumayyil's home town of Bikfayya were shelled, and a series of car bombs were detonated in East Beirut. But the Christians closed ranks around their beleaguered president, and the Tripartite Accord was never implemented. Jaja, emboldened by his restored power, then challenged Jumayyil and the Phalange Party directly. In July he announced the creation of the Free Lebanon Army, which was to be under his sole command and was to serve as his personal power base. But LF loyalists fought this plan. On September 27, a 3,000-man force loyal to Hubayka launched a surprise attack across the Green Line from Muslim West Beirut against East Beirut. Hubayka's men, supported by Syria and their erstwhile Muslim adversaries, forced back Jaja's militiamen, and the invasion was stopped only when the Lebanese Army's Tenth Brigade and the Lebanese Air Force entered the three-way fray on the side of the president.

Pax Syriana

On July 4, 1986, Syrian troops entered West Beirut for the first time since being expelled during the 1982 Israeli invasion. Approximately 500 Syrian troops, working with the Lebanese Army and police, cleared roadblocks, closed militia offices, and collected weapons. In mid-February 1987, however, a new round of fighting broke out in West Beirut, this time between Druze and Shia militias, both of which were regarded as Syrian allies. The combat was described by witnesses as being of unrivaled intensity in twelve years of war, with the militiamen using formations of Soviet-made T-54 tanks that Syria had supplied to both sides. Five days of combat caused an estimated 700 casualties and set much of West Beirut aflame.

Syria acted decisively to stop the chaos in West Beirut, and it seized the opportunity to reimpose its hegemony over the areas in Lebanon from which it had been evicted by Israel in 1982. On February 22, 1987, it dispatched 7,500 troops, configured in two brigades and a battalion, from eastern Lebanon. The Syrian troops, most of whom were veteran commandos, closed down some seventy militia offices, rounded up and arrested militia leaders, confiscated arms caches, deployed troops along the major roads and at Beirut International Airport, established checkpoints, and sent squads on patrol in the streets.

The Syrian Army did not shy away from violence in its effort to restore order to the Lebanese capital. In the first two days of its police operation, Syrian troops shot some fifteen Lebanese of various militias. Then on February 24 a dozen trucks full of Syrian commandos entered the Basta neighborhood, a Shia stronghold, and attacked the Fathallah barracks, the headquarters of the Hizballah organization. There, Syrian troops killed eighteen Hizballah militants.

In mid-April the Syrian Army deployed troops south of Beirut. Approximately 100 Syrian commandos, fighting alongside soldiers of the Lebanese Army's Sixth Brigade, occupied key positions along the strategic coastal highway linking Beirut with southern Lebanon and took control of the bridge over the Awwali River, near Sidon.

By mid-1987 the Syrian Army appeared to have settled into Beirut for a protracted stay. Lebanon's anarchy was regarded by Syrian officials as an unacceptable risk to Syrian security. The government of Syria appeared prepared to occupy Beirut permanently, if necessary. The senior Syrian military commander in Lebanon, Brigadier General Ghazi Kanaan, said that militia rule of Lebanon had ended and that the Syrian intervention was "open-ended," implying that Syria would occupy West Beirut indefinitely. Meanwhile Syrian officials indicated that thousands of additional Syrian troops would probably be sent to Beirut to ensure stability. Kanaan declared that Syria would take full responsibility for the security of foreign embassies in West Beirut, and he invited foreign missions to return. Kanaan also promised that Syria would expend all possible efforts to secure the release of Western hostages held by Lebanese terrorists.

The Lebanese Armed Forces in the 1980s

After the 1982 Israeli invasion, President Amin Jumayyil, convinced that a strong and unified army was a prerequisite to rebuilding the nation, announced plans to create a 12-brigade 60,000-man army, equipped with French and American arms and trained by French and American advisers. In addition, he planned to increase the Internal Security Force to a strength of 20,000 men. But because the Lebanese Army could muster only about 22,000 men in 1982, the government decided on November 24, 1982, to impose the Law of Service to the Flag, a conscription law first enacted on the eve of the Civil War but never implemented. The conscription law mandated one year of military service for eligible males. Additionally, some 2,000 to 3,000 soldiers who were acting as aides to officers were transferred to combat units. As part of a shake-up in the command structure, gaps in rank between officers and soldiers were narrowed. In December 1982, long-time army commander General Victor al Khuri was retired and replaced by General Tannus. At the same time, about 140 field-grade officers

National Security

were purged from the ranks through forced retirements. Many, including the once-powerful military intelligence chief Johnny Abdu, were dispatched to diplomatic posts abroad. Hundreds of new appointments were made on a nonsectarian basis.

The United States was instrumental in helping the Lebanese government rebuild the armed forces. In 1982 the United States proposed a Lebanese Army Modernization Program to be implemented in four phases. The first three phases entailed organization of seven full-strength, multiconfessional army brigades, created from existing battalions. The fourth phase focused on rebuilding the navy and air force. The total cost of the first three phases was estimated at US$500 million. The United States pledged to pay US$235 million of this sum, with the Lebanese government paying the balance.

Initial progress was rapid. A new tank battalion equipped with M-48 tanks donated by Jordan was established. A new supply depot was built at Kafr Shima. About 1,000 vehicles, including hundreds of M-113 armored personnel carriers, were transferred from the United States to Lebanon. And at one point, new recruits joined so rapidly that not enough uniforms could be found to outfit them.

Lack of effective military leadership, however, remained the Achilles heel. United States experts were aware of this problem and devoted considerable attention to solving it. A cadre of Lebanese lieutenants was given infantry officer basic training in the United States. A team of eighty United States military advisers, including fifty-three Green Berets, provided officer training in Lebanon. Furthermore, Lebanese officers were attached to the United States MNF contingent for training in military unit operations.

Nevertheless, the Lebanese Army disintegrated in the 1983-84 battles in the Shuf Mountains (see Israel Defense Forces Withdrawal and the Mountain War, this ch.). Shortly after the MNF withdrawal in February 1984, precipitated in part by the eviction of the Lebanese Army from West Beirut by militia forces, the United States Congress slashed military matériel credits given to the Lebanese government from the 1983 level of US$100 million to US$15 million for 1984. In addition, the training grant was cut from US$1.8 million to US$800,000. And in late 1984, the United States decided to suspend further transfers of military matériel to Lebanon.

Organization and Command Structure

The New Defense Law

The 1926 Constitution designated the president of the republic as commander in chief of the armed forces, but it contained no other reference to the military establishment. On March 13, 1979,

Lebanon: A Country Study

the Chamber of Deputies passed the New Defense Law, which reorganized the command structure of the armed forces. The law created the Supreme Defense Council, consisting of the president of the republic as chairman, the prime minister as vice chairman, and the deputy prime minister and the ministers of defense, foreign affairs, interior, and finance as members. The commander of the armed forces attended Supreme Defense Council meetings in an advisory capacity. The Supreme Defense Council had a secretariat, whose secretary general was required to be an active officer of the rank of colonel or above and who reported to the prime minister.

The Supreme Defense Council

According to Articles 3, 5, and 6 of the New Defense Law, the Council of Ministers and the Supreme Defense Council were authorized to decide the nation's defense policies and to define their aims. Although the law reiterated the president's constitutional authority as supreme commander in chief of the armed forces, it also stipulated that he exercise this power through the Supreme Defense Council. Therefore, the law circumscribed the president's power over the armed forces and distributed some decision-making power to ministers. Article 17 of the New Defense Law placed the Ministry of Defense and all its attached organizations—such as the Military Bureau, the Lebanese Army, the General Administration Department, the Inspectorate General, and the Military Council—under the exclusive control of the minister of defense.

The New Defense Law also stipulated that the commander of the armed forces be appointed by the Council of Ministers from among staff officers nominated by the minister of defense, who supervised him in his duties, except for military and security operations, for which the commander of the armed forces had sole responsibility. The law designated the chief of staff as the second in command. The New Defense Law strengthened the position of the chief of staff by delegating to him some responsibilities previously belonging to the commander of the armed forces—including training and legal affairs. The New Defense Law also created slots for two deputy chiefs of staff.

The Military Council

Articles 29 and 30 of the New Defense Law established the Military Council, which was attached directly to the minister of defense. Its members were the commander of the armed forces, the secretary general of the Supreme Defense Council, the director of the General Administration Department, the inspector general, and two officers with the rank of colonel or above. By tacit agreement, the membership was allotted along confessional lines and required to include a representative of each of the prominent communities: Maronite, Sunni, Shia, Druze, Greek Orthodox, and Greek Catholic. The Military Council's duties consisted primarily of organizing the institutions attached to the Ministry of Defense and naming the commanders of military regions, divisions, and brigades; commanders of air force, military, and naval academies; and military attachés in embassy posts. Because these responsibilities previously had belonged to the commander in chief alone, the New Defense Law diminished his power.

Military Intelligence

On January 22, 1981, a presidential decree was promulgated to settle a long-standing dispute over the Deuxième Bureau, which had been under the exclusive control of the commander in chief and which Muslim politicians had sought to place under the authority of the Military Council. The law stipulated that the Deuxième Bureau was answerable directly to the commander in chief but would provide the chief of staff with all information available to it. Because the chief of staff is traditionally a Druze, this compromise allowed other communities to share in some prerogatives formerly reserved for the Christian community alone.

The Commander in Chief

The commander of the Lebanese Army in July 1987 was Major General Michel Awn, who was appointed in June 1984 after long negotiations in the national unity government of Prime Minister Rashid Karami. Awn, a Christian, was a career military officer who entered the military academy at Al Fayadiyyah in 1955 and graduated as a lieutenant in the artillery corps. He attended advanced courses in France and the United States and was promoted to commander of the artillery corps in 1976 during the Lebanese Civil War. Although the majority of Christian officers supported the Christian militia, Awn stayed aloof from factional politics during the Civil War and earned a reputation for neutrality and loyalty to the government. During the war, he was appointed to a military committee charged with rebuilding the army. Awn strongly advocated the need for an integrated, nonsectarian army. In 1977 he assembled a group of army officers and soldiers from different religious groups who had not participated in the sectarian fighting and founded the Eighth Brigade, which, under his command, suffered few defections.

In rising to the position of commander in chief, Awn succeeded his old rival, Major General Tannus. Tannus's resignation was demanded by Muslim politicians who believed him responsible for bombing Muslim areas while leaving Christian areas unscathed. Unlike Awn, Tannus had also favored the creation of four separate sectarian armies—Christian, Sunni, Shia, and Druze.

In 1987 the Lebanese Army consisted of 9 brigades containing a total of approximately 35,000 to 38,000 men, of whom only 15,000 to 18,000 were under the operational control of the central command structure. Many units existed only on paper, however, and soldiers who received paychecks were often in the service of the militias the army was intended to supplant. Under an informal agreement between the army and its renegade commanders, the ghost payroll was maintained to pump funds into Lebanon's war-torn economy. Additionally, the central government harbored hopes that the breakaway brigades eventually could be reunited with the official Lebanese Army.

Lebanon's governmental expenditures on its armed forces were estimated to be US$328 million annually and its expenditure on military matériel imports US$240 million in 1983, the most recent year for which statistics were available in late 1987. In addition, a 10-year US$955 million supplemental sum earmarked for rebuilding the armed forces was authorized in 1982, but the program was shelved when the army collapsed in 1984. Army equipment included 60 AMX-13 tanks, 137 M-48 tanks, 18 M-41 tanks, 100 Saladin armored cars, several hundred M-113 armored personnel carriers, an array of Western-supplied artillery, rocket launchers, antiaircraft artillery, and small arms.

The Army

In 1987 the order of battle of the Lebanese Army was in a state of flux. Officially, the army consisted of twelve nominal brigades. Most observers, however, omitted the first, second, and third brigades from the order of battle. The First Brigade, which was 100-percent Shia in composition, was stationed in the Syrian-controlled Biqa Valley, where it has been assimilated by the Syrian Army and Shia militias. The Second Brigade, which had been a mostly Sunni unit stationed in Tripoli, had dispersed. Likewise, the Third Brigade had disbanded. The remaining nine brigades were considered part of the Lebanese Army insofar as the soldiers were on the army payroll and followed orders from commanding officers. Not all of these brigades, however, were regarded as loyal to President Jumayyil.

National Security

The Fourth Brigade

The Fourth Brigade disintegrated during the Mountain War in February 1984 as Druze militiamen attempted to create a salient from Alayh to the coast at Khaldah, south of Beirut. Half of the soldiers deserted and joined the Druze forces, while the remainder fled to Christian East Beirut and enrolled in Christian-dominated brigades.

The Fifth Brigade

The Fifth Brigade in 1987 consisted of approximately 2,000 mostly Maronite troops under the command of Colonel Khalil Kanaan. The brigade's administrative headquarters was located in Sarba, north of Juniyah, an LF stronghold. It consisted of three infantry battalions and an artillery unit stationed in Brummana, east of Beirut. In 1987 Fifth Brigade units were deployed in the strategic town of Suq al Gharb to prevent Druze militiamen from shelling the capital. The Fifth Brigade was regarded as loyal to the president, but observers believed that if called upon to fight a Christian militia, it might remain neutral.

The Sixth Brigade

The mainly Shia Muslim Sixth Brigade had been commanded by a Christian officer, Colonel Lufti Jabar, and consisted of 1,600 soldiers and officers. Its mission had been to maintain order in West Beirut. It refused to participate in the February 1986 combat between the Shia Amal militia and the Lebanese Army, however; as a result, the Fifth Brigade was expelled from West Beirut. After the Sixth Brigade split off from the army command structure, it was taken over by a new officer, Major General Abd al Halim Kanj, and its ranks swelled to 6,000 men as Muslims from other army brigades deserted to join their coreligionists. In 1987 the Sixth Brigade was stationed in Shihab barracks in the southern suburbs of Beirut and was under the operational control of the Amal militia.

The Seventh Brigade

The Seventh Brigade was composed of 1,700 men in 1987. A contingent of the Seventh Brigade was stationed in the Jubayl district, north of Beirut. This contingent was regarded as loyal to former President Sulayman Franjiyah, whose feudal seat, Zgharta, is a few kilometers southwest of Tripoli. Consequently, the central government equipped this contingent with light weapons only. The brigade's headquarters was located in Amshit, just north of Juniyah. Units at Amshit were well equipped with United States-made tanks and armored personnel carriers but were

Lebanon: A Country Study

regarded as being under the sway of LF head Samir Jaja, who maintained his retinue in Amshit (see Chaos in Beirut and Syrian Peacemaking Efforts, this ch.).

The Eighth Brigade

The Eighth Brigade, commanded by Colonel Salim Kassis, was the strongest, best equipped, best trained, and most elite unit in the Lebanese Army in 1987. It was regarded as loyal to the president and the government. It consisted of 2,000 men, about 80 percent of whom were Christians from the northern region of Akkar, with the remaining 20 percent Sunni Muslims. It included a mechanized battalion equipped with ninety United States-made armored personnel carriers, an armored battalion with thirty-three United States-made M-48 tanks, and a missile battalion equipped with eighteen pieces of field artillery. It was stationed at the Presidential Palace at Babda and at the Ministry of Defense in the Yarzah section of Beirut. In 1983 the Eighth Brigade bore the brunt of fighting against Druze militia in Suq al Gharb and against leftist militia in West Beirut.

The Ninth Brigade

The Ninth Brigade, established in 1983, was commanded in 1987 by Colonel Sami Rihani, a Greek Orthodox. The majority of his soldiers were Christians from northern Lebanese cities, such as Tripoli, although the brigade also contained Sunni and Shia soldiers and officers. It was headquartered in Al Hazimiyah, and one of its battalions was deployed in the Beirut port area. The Ninth Brigade was regarded as being totally loyal to the government, and it fought successfully against Phalangist forces in East Beirut in January 1986.

The Tenth Brigade

The Tenth Brigade consisted of 1,800 soldiers, most of whom were Christians, under the command of Colonel Nassib Eid, and in 1987 it was stationed along the Green Line. Its troops manned the Beirut-Damascus highway to the Kafr Shima-Ash Shuwayfat front. The brigade was enlarged in 1984 when some soldiers and officers defecting from the Fourth Brigade joined it. The Tenth Brigade was composed of three airborne battalions and an artillery unit. The army's commando forces under Lieutenant Colonel Yusuf Tahan were attached to the Tenth Brigade. Tahan was an LF supporter, and observers doubted his loyalty to the government.

The Eleventh Brigade

The Eleventh Brigade, composed primarily of Druzes, had a strength in 1987 of about 900 men. Its commander, Colonel Amin

National Security

Qadi, ordered the unit confined to its Hammana garrison during the fighting between the Lebanese Army and the Druze militia in the Shuf Mountains in 1983 and 1984; this action was in response to a request from Druze leader Walid Jumblatt to neutralize the army. The Eleventh Brigade controlled the Hammana garrison and guarded the government radio station in West Beirut.

The Twelfth Brigade

Little was known in 1987 about the mostly Shia 1,300-man Twelfth Brigade. It was commanded by Colonel Muhammad Saad and was deployed in various positions in southern Lebanon, particularly along the coastal highway between Khaldah and Sidon.

The Air Force and Navy

In 1987 the Lebanese Air Force consisted of about 800 mostly Maronite enlisted men and officers under the command of General Fahim al Hajj. Its main base was Al Qulayat airfield, in the north near the Syrian border—an area under the control of Syrian forces. Additional military airfields were at Riyaq in the Biqa Valley and at Halat near Jubayl, where United States forces built an emergency landing strip using part of the coastal highway.

In 1987 the air force was composed of one helicopter attack squadron equipped with four French-made SA-342 Gazelle helicopters armed with SS-11 and SS-12 air-to-surface missiles, twenty-eight AB-212 transports, and SA-315 and SA-316 Alouette transport helicopters. These helicopters were capable of airlifting 300 men. In 1983 the air force had planned to increase its helicopter fleet to forty aircraft, and the Lebanese government signed an agreement with France to purchase about US$80 million worth of unspecified air force equipment. These plans were shelved after the French MNF contingent withdrew in 1984, however. The exact number of operational fixed-wing and jet aircraft in the air force inventory was not available in 1987. The air force apparently lost three of its ten semiobsolete British-made Hawker-Hunter F-70 fighter jets in the 1983–84 Mountain War, and only three of those remaining were reported to be serviceable. The air force was reported to have ten French-made Mirage fighter-bombers, of which only three were in commission. It also had eleven trainers—five Fouga Magisters and six propeller-driven Bulldogs.

In 1987 the Lebanese Navy consisted of 450 sailors and officers stationed at a naval base in Juniyah. Most personnel were Christians. The navy's fleet included six Aztec-class patrol boats, three Byblos-class patrol boats, and two French-made landing craft capable of transporting tanks and of being used in beachhead and evacuation operations.

Internal Security and Terrorism

By the mid-1980s, more than a decade of war had reduced drastically the authority and ability of the central government to enforce law and to implement justice. The unofficial militias and foreign occupying armies that governed much of Lebanon's civilian populace tended to enforce their own version of justice, without regard to the central government or legal norms. Nevertheless, Lebanese law still pertained in some limited venues. In 1987 Lebanon's police forces had been virtually assimilated into the armed forces and worked closely with the Syrian occupation force.

Under Lebanese law, a suspect must be arraigned before a committee composed of three judges and a prosecutor within forty-eight hours of being arrested. Nevertheless, government prosecutors sometimes held suspects for interrogation for indefinite periods of time without notifying judges. Every prisoner had the right to legal counsel, but there was no public defender's office. Bail was permitted in most cases. In practice and custom Lebanese law provided the right to a fair public trial, but many cases remained unadjudicated. Trial delays resulted from the difficulty of conducting investigations when most of the country remained outside government control, from a shortage of judges, and from the general breakdown in security. Courts existed in most parts of the country, but the disposition of criminal cases depended ultimately on the local power group. Militias frequently intervened to protect their members from prosecution and detention.

Common crime, to the extent that it could be distinguished from political violence, was rampant. In 1986 the Lebanese press described a surge in violent crime, including a rash of over eighty well-organized armed bank robberies in a two-year period and numerous kidnappings for ransom.

The definition of terrorism is fraught with controversy, particularly in the Middle Eastern context. But by almost any definition, Lebanon is an epicenter of terrorist activity. Assassination is an occupational hazard for politicians. The slaying of Prime Minister Karami on June 1, 1987, when a bomb exploded aboard his helicopter, was but another in a long string of political murders. Car bombings, known in the Lebanese lexicon as "canned death," were occurring almost on a daily basis. The United States embassy had twice been attacked by suicide truck-bombers. And the hijacking of TWA Flight 847 in June 1985 was only the most brazen of a long series of airliner hijackings originating in Beirut.

Over the years, literally hundreds of groups have claimed responsibility for various acts of terrorism committed against civilian targets. Most of the names of the groups claiming responsibility, however, were merely code words or noms de guerre meant to conceal the true identity of the organization behind the attack.

In the judgment of most informed observers, a few men or families have been responsible for masterminding the majority of terrorist operations. For example, the Lebanese Armed Revolutionary Faction, a terrorist organization that assassinated United States and Israeli officials in Western Europe in 1982 and 1984 and staged numerous other attacks, was revealed eventually to be run by a single Maronite extended family, the Abdallah clan from the northern Lebanese town of Al Qubayyat. In March 1987, ringleader George Ibrahim Abdallah was sentenced by a French court to life imprisonment. Likewise, virtually all of the Shia terrorist attacks against Western interests in Lebanon since 1982, claimed in the name of the Islamic Jihad Organization and a dozen other groups, have been attributed by intelligence experts to two related Shia families, the Mughniyyahs and the Musawis. Two leaders of these families, Imad Mughniyyah and Husayn al Musawi, were widely believed to be responsible for holding twenty-three Westerners hostage in 1987.

Suicide Bombings

One of the most spectacular terrorist tactics in the 1980s was a series of suicide vehicle bombings. The first occurred on April 18, 1983, when a pick-up truck driven by a suicide bomber exploded in the driveway of the United States embassy in West Beirut. The explosives detonated with a force equivalent to 2,000 pounds of trinitrotoluene and destroyed the chancery building, killing 63 people, including 17 Americans, and wounding 100, about 40 of whom were Americans. The Islamic Jihad Organization claimed responsibility for the attack. Informed sources believed that the Islamic Jihad Organization was a nom de guerre for Husayn Musawi's Islamic Amal organization, while others believed that it was a cover name for Hizballah.

On October 23, 1983, Shia terrorists struck the United States Marines compound and the French MNF headquarters in devastating, near-simultaneous suicide bombing attacks. The attack on the United States Marines compound took 241 lives and wounded over 100. The bombing was carried out by a lone terrorist driving a stakebed truck that penetrated the central lobby of the building and exploded. United States Federal Bureau of Investigation experts announced that the blast, with the force of over 12,000 pounds of trinitrotoluene, was the largest non-nuclear explosion ever detonated. The attack on the French contingent claimed fifty-eight dead. On November 4, 1983, the suicide bombing tactic was used once again. Near Tyre in southern Lebanon, an explosives-laden pickup truck crashed through an Israeli guard post and detonated near an IDF headquarters building, killing twenty-eight Israeli soldiers and thirty-two Lebanese and Palestinian prisoners. On September 20, 1984, a suicide vehicle bomber attacked the new United States embassy building in East Beirut, killing eight and wounding dozens. On March 10, 1985, Israel was struck again when a suicide bomber drove a car packed with explosives into an IDF convoy at the border crossing point, near the Israeli town of Metulla. Twelve Israelis were killed and fourteen wounded. The initial spate of Shia suicide bombings was so successful that it inspired other, secular organizations—particularly the Syrian Socialist Nationalist Party—to adopt the tactic in 1984 and 1985. As the frequency of suicide attacks rose, however, their effectiveness and impact waned. Lebanese groups abandoned the tactic and concentrated on a more effective technique—hostage-taking.

The Hostage Crisis

On June 14, 1985, American attention was riveted on Lebanon once again. A TWA airliner, Flight 847 en route from Athens to Rome, was hijacked by Shia terrorists of the Hizballah organization who demanded the release of Shia prisoners held in Kuwait, Israel, and Spain. The airliner was forced to fly to Beirut, where nineteen passengers were released, then to Algiers, where twenty-two more were freed. It then returned to Beirut where on June 15 one of the passengers, a United States Navy diver, was murdered. Seven American passengers, who, according to the terrorists, had Jewish-sounding surnames, were taken off the jet by Hizballah terrorists and sequestered in Beirut. Then, about a dozen Amal members joined the hijackers on the airplane, and the pilot was forced once again to fly to Algiers, where sixty more passengers were freed. On the following day the airplane returned to Beirut with the thirty-two remaining passengers. Approximately 200 Lebanese Army soldiers withdrew from the vicinity of Beirut International Airport, leaving the area in the control of Amal. In response to suspicions that the United States was planning a military rescue of the hostages, the terrorists moved the passengers off the airplane and sequestered them in various groups dispersed throughout Beirut. Amal and Hizballah members mined the runways at the airport to prevent a rescue attempt.

On June 17, the third day of the crisis, Amal leader and Lebanese minister of justice Nabih Birri agreed to "mediate" and take responsibility for the safety of the hostages. Birri's intervention appeared hypocritical because his men were holding most of the hostages and controlled the hijacked jet. Nevertheless, the Hizballah organization retained control of seven kidnapped Americans, leaving Birri unable to negotiate independently. Accordingly, Birri adopted a hardline stance and refused to release any hostages until Israel released 700 Shia detainees. Indeed, on June 24 Birri actually added another condition for the hostages' release, stipulating that United States warships leave Lebanese waters.

The deadlock was finally broken through a series of complex and controversial political maneuvers. The United States, determined not to concede to the terrorists' demands, refused to request Israel to release its Shia prisoners but acknowledged that it would welcome such a move. Israel, also unwilling as a matter of policy to negotiate with terrorists, refused to release its prisoners unless requested by the United States to do so. The thirty-nine hostages were ultimately freed on June 30. On July 1, Israel announced that it was ready to release the Shia detainees from its prison. Over the next several weeks, Israel released over 700 Shia prisoners, but Israel denied that the prisoners' release was related to the hijacking.

Hostage-taking has become commonplace in Lebanon. By 1987 the International Committee of the Red Cross estimated that 6,000 Lebanese had been kidnapped or had disappeared since 1975. The systematic kidnapping of Western civilians began a few years after the Civil War. Perhaps the first victim whose case was widely publicized was American University of Beirut president David Dodge, abducted by Shia terrorists in 1981 and freed in 1982. As of September 1987, twenty-three foreigners—most of whom were journalists, diplomats, or teachers—were believed to be held hostage by various terrorist organizations in Lebanon. Of this total, nine were American. Terry Anderson, chief Middle East correspondent for the Associated Press, had been in captivity the longest. Anderson, seized on March 16, 1985, by the Shia fundamentalist Islamic Jihad Organization, was one of six hostages who had been held for more than two years. American television correspondent Charles Glass was seized on June 17, 1987. A previously unknown group, the "Organization for the Defense of Free People," claimed responsibility. Three hostages were Britons, including Anglican Church envoy Terry Waite, who disappeared January 20, 1986, while on a negotiating mission to free the other kidnap victims. Other hostages included one of two citizens of the Federal Republic of Germany (West Germany) abducted in January 1987 by an organization calling itself "Strugglers for Freedom." The West Germans were seized shortly after the West German government arrested Muhammad Ali Hamadi, a Shia terrorist leader who allegedly masterminded the 1985 TWA hijacking. Six French citizens, two of whom were diplomats, also remained in captivity in late 1987, as did an Indian professor, an Irish professor, an Italian businessman, and a Republic of Korea (South Korea) diplomat.

Little information was available concerning the circumstances of the hostages: In late June 1987, the Lebanese magazine *Ash Shira* reported that some American hostages had been transferred from Beirut to Iran where they were being put on "trial" and that Imad Mughniyyah and Abdul Hadi Hamadi, security chiefs of the Hizballah organization, had visited Tehran to testify in the "trial."

Since 1982 seven kidnapped foreigners are believed to have been murdered by their captors. On October 3, 1985, the Islamic Jihad Organization claimed to have killed the United States Central Intelligence Agency Beirut chief of station, William Buckley, whom it had abducted on March 16, 1984. The Islamic Jihad Organization later released to a Beirut newspaper a photograph purporting to depict his corpse. Press reports stated that Buckley had been transferred to Iran, where he was tortured and killed. One of four Soviet diplomats kidnapped by the Islamic Liberation Organization on September 30, 1985, was killed by his captors; the other three were released a month later. On February 10, 1986, the Islamic Jihad Organization released a photograph that claimed to show the body of French citizen Michel Seurat, who had been kidnapped earlier. On April 17, 1986, the bodies of three American University of Beirut employees, American citizen Peter Kilburn and Britons John Douglas and Philip Padfield, were discovered near Beirut. The Revolutionary Organization of Socialist Muslims claimed to have "executed" the three men in retaliation for the United States air raid on Libya on April 15, 1986. On April 23, 1986, a Beirut newspaper received a videotape film showing a man being hanged. The Revolutionary Organization of Socialist Muslims claimed the man was British citizen Alec Collet, who had been kidnapped more than a year earlier.

A few fortunate Western hostages have escaped from their captors. American citizen Frank Regier, engineering professor at the American University of Beirut, was freed after several months in captivity by Amal militiamen, who raided the Beirut hideout of his extremist captors on April 15, 1984. On February 14, 1985, American journalist Jeremy Levin escaped from his captors in the Biqa Valley. On April 11, 1986, French captive Michel Brillant escaped several days after his abduction when his captors were surprised by a party of hunters in the Biqa Valley. On July 16, 1986, a Saudi Arabian diplomat was freed when the Lebanese Army caught his captors. On September 26, 1986, British journalist David Hirst escaped by bolting from his captors' automobile in a Shia neighborhood of Beirut, and several days later French television correspondent Jean-Marc Sroussi escaped from a locked shed days after his capture. American Charles Glass escaped in August 1987, two months after his capture.

Only a few hostages have been released by their captors. On May 20, 1985, Saudi Arabian consul Husayn Farrash was released by Muslim fundamentalists after over a year in captivity. In mid-September 1985, the Reverend Benjamin Weir, a Presbyterian minister held hostage since May 1984, was freed by the Islamic Jihad Organization; on July 26, 1986, the same group released Father Lawrence Martin Jenco, who had been held since January, 1985; and on November 2, 1986, American University of Beirut hospital administrator David Jacobsen was released after more than a year and a half in captivity. Americans Weir, Jenco, and Jacobsen had been held by the same Islamic Jihad Organization cell as Terry Anderson and Thomas Sutherland, who in September 1987 remained in captivity. Several other hostages have been released by various groups, including a Spanish diplomat, a French journalist, two British women, a West German Siemens employee, and two Cypriot students.

* * *

A wide variety of published sources discuss Lebanese national security issues, although information on the armed forces is fragmentary. Several impressionistic but vivid accounts of Lebanon's war, based on the authors' firsthand observations, provide a good introduction to the topic. The most prominent among these are *Going All the Way* by Jonathan C. Randal; *Final Conflict* and *Death of a Country* by John Bulloch; and *Israel's Lebanon War* by Ze'ev Schiff and Ehud Ya'ari. David C. Gordon's books, *The Republic of Lebanon* and *Lebanon: The Fragmented Nation*, provide a good general overview. For a scholarly treatment of Lebanese political-military affairs, Michael C. Hudson's dated but seminal *The Precarious Republic* is useful for background information. More current scholarly works include *The War for Lebanon, 1970-1983* by Itamar Rabinovich, *The Lebanese Civil War* by Marius Deeb, and *Conflict and Violence in Lebanon* by Rashid Khalidi. The contributions on Lebanon by Itamar Rabinovich and Yosef Olmert in the annual *Middle East Contemporary Survey* are a useful reference source. Other sources focus on more specific issues. Rashid Khalidi concentrates on the Palestinian presence in Lebanon in *Under Siege*. The Syrian role in Lebanon is explored in *Syria and the Lebanese Crisis* by Adeed I. Dawisha and *Syrian Intervention in Lebanon* by Naomi J. Weinberger. *Middle East Insight,* a periodical, frequently publishes articles about Lebanon, including Augustus Richard Norton's work on the Shia community. Journalistic coverage of Lebanese affairs by the international news media is comprehensive. In addition, Lebanon has a relatively large domestic press, although much of its coverage represents partisan viewpoints. Among the most authoritative English-language Lebanese publications is the *Middle East Reporter.* (For further information and complete citations, see Bibliography.)

Appendix A

Table

1 Metric Conversion Coefficients
2 School Enrollment by Province, 1981–82
3 Principal Institutions of Higher Learning, 1981–82
4 Hospitals, Beds, and Dispensaries by Province, 1982
5 Port Activity, Selected Years, 1974–83
6 Production of Main Crops, 1970–85

Appendix A

Table 1. Metric Conversion Coefficients and Factors

When you know	Multiply by	To find
Millimeters	0.04	inches
Centimeters	0.39	inches
Meters	3.3	feet
Kilometers	0.62	miles
Hectares (10,000 m^2)	2.47	acres
Square kilometers	0.39	square miles
Cubic meters	35.3	cubic feet
Liters	0.26	gallons
Kilograms	2.2	pounds
Metric tons	0.98	long tons
	1.1	short tons
	2,204	pounds
Degrees Celsius (Centigrade)	9 divide by 5 and add 32	degrees Fahrenheit

Table 2. School Enrollment by Province, 1981-82

Province	Preprimary	Primary	Intermediate	Secondary	Total	Percentage of Total School Enrollment
Bayrut	53,750	157,820	78,712	34,829	325,111	42
Jabal Lubnan	15,450	50,311	26,868	8,960	101,589	13
Ash Shamal	20,037	78,876	28,993	10,848	138,754	18
Al Biqa	16,261	59,308	20,169	5,987	101,725	13
Al Janub	14,924	55,905	24,166	10,496	105,491	14
TOTAL	120,422	402,220	178,908	71,120	772,670	100

Source: Based on information from Lebanon, Ministry of National Education and Fine Arts, Educational Center for Research and Development, *Al Ahsa'at al Awwaliyyah lil 'Am ad Dirasi, 1981–82* (Basic Statistics for the 1981–82 School Year), Beirut, n.d., 5–7.

Appendix A

Table 3. *Principal Institutions of Higher Learning, 1981-82*

Institutions	Males	Females	Total Number of Students	Lebanese Students as Percentage of Total
Lebanese University	15,190	13,858	29,048	93
Beirut Arab University	19,734	5,122	24,856	11
St. Joseph's University	2,851	2,530	5,381	94
American University of Beirut	2,813	1,896	4,709	76
Holy Spirit University	1,274	970	2,244	97
Beirut University College	815	998	1,813	76

Source: Based on information from Lebanon, Ministry of National Education and Fine Arts, Educational Center for Research and Development, *Al Ahsa'at al Awwaliyyah lil 'Am ad Dirasi, 1981-82* (Basic Statistics for the 1981-82 School Year), Beirut, n.d., 37.

Table 4. *Hospitals, Beds, and Dispensaries by Province, 1982*

	Bayrut	Jabal Lubnan	Ash Shamal	Al Janub	Al Biqa
Hospitals					
Private	22	23	15	15	6
Public	1	4	3	5	4
Total hospitals	23	27	18	20	10
Beds					
Private	2,119	1,663	784	824	324
Public	20	160	130	170	210
Total beds	2,139	1,823	914	994	534
Dispensaries	48	187	61	133	78

Source: Based on information from World Health Organization, *Reconstruction of the Health Services in Lebanon*, Geneva, 1983, 35-36.

Table 5. *Port Activity, Selected Years, 1974-83*
(in thousands of tons of goods unloaded)

Port	1974	1978	1979	1980	1981	1982	1983
Beirut	3,411	n.a.	2,480	2,732	2,195	1,789	2,546
Tripoli	587	825	922	625	722	591	n.a.
Sidon	n.a.	174	88	73	20	n.a.	105

n.a.—not available.

Table 6. *Production of Main Crops, 1970–85*
(in thousands of tons)

	1970	1971	1972	1973	1974	1975	1976	1977	1978	1979	1980	1981	1982	1983	1984	1985
Wheat	41	64	55	n.a.	n.a.	n.a.	40	50	45	40	35	22	23	20	18	15
Citrus fruit	272	278	296	307	n.a.	n.a.	289	309	314	340	350	365	315	322	310	270
Potatoes	93	109	116	116	n.a.	n.a.	85	45	70	112	145	140	126	125	120	120
Sugar beets	100	146	190	139	n.a.	n.a.	36	123	98	108	30	100	61	55	50	80
Apples	154	220	166	n.a.	n.a.	n.a.	n.a.	85	106	109	79	n.a.	130	126	100	117
Grapes	115	109	107	n.a.	n.a.	n.a.	70	71	100	135	125	150	161	160	165	n.a.
Tobacco	7	8	10	4	n.a.	n.a.	n.a.	n.a.	n.a.	n.a.	n.a.	n.a.	4	4	4	4

n.a.—not available.

Appendix B

The Contending Sides in the 1975 Civil War

THE TWO COMBATANT coalitions in the 1975 Civil War were the right-wing Christian Lebanese Front, sometimes called the Kufur Front, and the left-wing Muslim Lebanese National Movement (formerly the Front for Progressive Parties and National Forces). Combined Lebanese Front forces totaled about 30,000 fighting men and women. Total Muslim-leftist forces were slightly fewer, but they were occasionally allied with Palestinian forces totaling some 20,000. The Syrian Army deployed about 30,000 men in Lebanon and intervened first on the Christian and then on the Muslim side. The Lebanese Army numbered about 18,000 men at the outset of the Civil War. It split quickly along confessional (see Glossary) lines, with about 3,000 officers and men joining the Lebanese Front and an approximately equal number joining the Lebanese National Movement. These defections, as well as widespread desertions, left the Lebanese Army with a primarily Christian rump force of about 10,000 men. Commanded by General Hanna Said, the Lebanese Army was officially neutral and followed the orders of the government but provided tacit and active support to the Lebanese Front.

The Lebanese Front
The Phalange Party

Known in Arabic as the Kataib, the Phalange Party (see Glossary) was the mainstay of the Lebanese Front and bore the brunt of the fighting for the Christian side. The party was founded by Christian patriarch Pierre Jumayyil (also seen as Gemayel) in 1936 and was modeled on the German and Italian fascist parties. The Phalangist militia called itself the Lebanese Forces (LF). It could muster up to 20,000 troops, of which a core of 3,000 were full-time soldiers. Under the leadership of William Hawi, and then of Bashir Jumayyil, it evolved into a formidable and highly organized fighting force. The Phalange Party practiced conscription in the areas it controlled, drafting eligible young men to swell its ranks. In internecine fighting throughout the Civil War and up to 1982, the LF consolidated its leadership of the Lebanese Front by assimilating other Christian militia, often by force of arms.

The Tigers

A 500-man militia that was the armed force of the National Liberal Party of former President Camille Shamun (also seen as Chamoun). The Tigers (Namur) were more aggressive than the Phalangists, often initiating hostilities with the Muslim side. On July 7, 1980, the Tigers were virtually wiped out by Phalangist forces in a surprise operation known as the "Day of the Long Knives."

The Marada Brigade

This 3,500-strong unit, also called the Marada (Giants), named after Byzantine border guards in ancient Lebanon, represented the interests of Sulayman Franjiyah (also seen as Franjieh), president of Lebanon at the outbreak of the Civil War. It was also called the Zghartan Liberation Army after Zgharta, Franjiyah's home town. It operated mainly out of Tripoli and other areas of northern Lebanon, but it also fought in Beirut. The alliance between the Phalangists and the Marada ended on June 13, 1978, with a surprise LF attack on Ihdin, the Marada headquarters, during which the Marada commander, Tony Franjiyah (Sulayman's son), was killed.

The Guardians of the Cedars

This was an extremist Maronite (see Glossary) militia and terrorist organization led by a former police officer, Etienne Saqr. Named after Lebanon's national symbol, it consisted of about 500 men and cooperated with the Phalangists during the Civil War.

The Order of Maronite Monks

An order of militant monks with a militia of 200 priests led by Father Sharbal Qassis, it fought alongside the other Christian forces.

At Tanzim

At Tanzim (The Organization) was originally a small secret society of Christian officers within the Lebanese Army who supported the Phalangists. At Tanzim helped split the army early in the Civil War and attempted to incorporate defectors from the army into its ranks. At Tanzim also accepted members from outside the army, mostly from the upper and professional classes. It fielded its own militia of about 200.

The Lebanese National Movement

The Progressive Socialist Party

Lebanon's Druze (see Glossary) community, led first by Kamal Jumblatt (also seen as Junblatt) and, after his assassination in 1977, by his son Walid, provided the titular leadership of the

Appendix B

Muslim-leftist coalition in the Civil War. The party's militia of approximately 2,500 men played only a small role in the actual combat, however, limiting its involvement to fighting in the Mount Lebanon (see Glossary) area.

The Syrian Socialist Nationalist Party

The Syrian Socialist Nationalist Party (SSNP) was established in Lebanon in 1932 by Antun Saadah, who hoped to unite the Levantine nations and recreate Greater Syria (see Glossary). Even though it fought in alliance with the Muslims and leftists in the Civil War, its membership was primarily Christian and its political stance right wing; in fact, its red hurricane symbol was modeled after the Nazi swastika. The SSNP has a long history of terrorism and subversion in Lebanon. Saadah was executed by the Lebanese government in 1949, after launching an abortive coup attempt. The SSNP was active in the 1958 Civil War, where it fought on the pro-Western side. In December 1961, an SSNP armored battalion commander staged the Lebanese Army's only significant attempted coup d'état against the government and managed to arrest a half-dozen high-ranking officers before he was stopped. During the 1975 Civil War, the SSNP fielded a militia of about 3,000 men. After the 1976 Syrian intervention, it split into anti-Syrian and pro-Syrian factions. The latter group reportedly assassinated Druze patriarch Kamal Jumblatt in 1977 and President-elect Bashir Jumayyil in 1982. Since March 1985, the SSNP has dispatched about a half-dozen suicide vehicle-bombers against Israeli positions in southern Lebanon.

Amal

The word for *hope* in Arabic, Amal is also an acronym for Afwaj al Muqawamah al Lubnaniyyah (Lebanese Resistance Detachments). Amal, with a strength of approximately 1,500 men, played only a marginal role in the 1975 Civil War. Nevertheless, many Shias (see Glossary) fought for other leftist organizations and were the cannon fodder of the Civil War. The Shia renaissance was initiated by Imam Musa as Sadr, a charismatic Iranian religious figure of Lebanese ancestry who founded a *husayniyyah* (Shia religious site) in Sidon in 1959. In 1974, on the eve of the Civil War, Sadr established the Movement of the Disinherited to represent Shia interests. In 1975, with the help of the Palestine Liberation Organization, he organized the Amal militia as the military arm of The Movement of the Disinherited. Sadr disappeared and was presumed murdered while on an official visit to Libya in August 1978, and leadership of Amal was assumed by Nabih Birri (also seen as Berri), a secular-oriented Beirut lawyer. In 1987 Birri continued to lead Amal, but several fundamentalist splinter groups had broken away from his organization.

Communist Organizations

The Lebanese Communist Party (LCP), led by George Hawi, had a membership of about 3,000, mainly Greek Orthodox and Armenian Orthodox. Its militia, the Popular Guard, played a significant role in the Civil War, fighting on the Muslim-leftist side despite its Christian membership. The Organization of Communist Action, a dissident, radical splinter group of the LCP, was led by Muhsin Ibrahim and had a membership of about 2,000.

The Najjadah

Led by Adnan Hakim, the Najjadah was established in the 1930s as a Sunni (see Glossary) Muslim counterpart of the Christian Phalange Party, although it was not as successful. Its militia numbered about 300.

The Lebanese Arab Army

The establishment of the Lebanese Arab Army (LAA) was announced on January 21, 1976, by Lieutenant Ahmad Khatib, a Sunni Muslim officer in the Lebanese Armed Forces. Khatib urged his fellow Muslims to mutiny and desert the army. Within several days, he rallied 2,000 soldiers, including the members of 40 tank crews, to his side. At the zenith of its power, the LAA controlled three-quarters of all army barracks and posts in Lebanon.

The Baath (Arab Socialist Resurrection) Party

Both the Syrian and the Iraqi governments were, and in 1987 continued to be, run by rival wings of the pan-Arab socialist Baath Party, and each government supported a Lebanese branch. The pro-Iraqi branch in Lebanon was headed by Abdal Majid ar Rifai and fielded a militia of about 3,000 men. The pro-Syrian branch in Lebanon was headed by a Shia, Issam Qansuh, and had a militia of similar size. The two militias fought each other in proxy battles for their sponsors.

Nasserite Organizations

Several Nasserite organizations, which adhered to the socialist ideals of the late Egyptian president Gamal Abdul Nasser, fought in Lebanon's Civil War. The largest was the Independent Nasserite Movement led by Ibrahim Kulaylat. Its 3,000-man militia, the Murabitun (Sentinels), was one of the mainstays of the

Appendix B

anti-establishment side. The Union of Toiling People's Forces, led by Kamal Shatila, was tied closely to Syria. Its 1,000-man militia, called the Firqat an Nasr (Victory Divisions), played an active part in the Civil War. Another group, the Nasserite Correctionist Movement, was led by Issam al Arab and had a militia called the Quwwat an Nasir (Nasser's Forces). The Popular Nasserite Forces (led by Mustafa Saad), the Arab Socialist Action Organization, and the 24 October Movement were also active in the war.

Palestinians

Dozens of Palestinian military entities operated in Lebanon during and after the Civil War. Most of these groups were controlled by the mainstream, moderate Palestine Liberation Organization, which maintained its neutrality during the first year of the Civil War. Other groups in the radical Rejectionist Front fought on the Muslim-leftist side. Still others, such as Saiqa, the Arab Liberation Front, and the Popular Front for the Liberation of Palestine— General Command were essentially mercenary armies for foreign governments (Syria, Iraq, and Libya, respectively). About 25,000 Palestinians were under arms during the Civil War.

* * *

Journalists and scholars have written extensively on the various militias that participated in the 1975 Civil War. Many of the sources used for the national security chapter were also used in the preparation of Appendix B. Particularly useful are the works of John Bulloch, Marius Deeb, David Gilmour, David C. Gordon, Michael Jansen, Itamar Rabinovich, Jonathan C. Randal, and Ze'ev Schiff and Ehud Ya'ari. A report by Paul A. Jureidini, R.D. McLaurin, and James M. Price on military operations in urban terrain is also useful. In addition, the periodical *Middle East Reporter* frequently spotlights individual militias, providing information on a group's ideology, leadership, and combat capability. (For further information and complete citations, see Bibliography.)

Bibliography

Chapter 1

Al-Bustani, Fuad Afram. "Notes on Lebanon under the Emirs, 1516-1842." Pages 237-39 in Beirut College for Women (ed.), *Cultural Resources in Lebanon.* Beirut: Libraire du Liban, 1969.

Bulloch, John. *Death of a Country.* London: Weidenfeld and Nicholson, 1977.

_____. *Final Conflict: The War in the Lebanon.* London: Century, 1983.

Christopher, John B. *Lebanon: Yesterday and Today.* New York: Holt, Rinehart, and Winston, 1966.

Cobban, Helena. *The Making of Modern Lebanon.* Boulder, Colorado: Westview Press, 1985.

Deeb, Marius. *The Lebanese Civil War.* New York: Praeger, 1980.

Fisher, W.B. "Lebanon." Pages 554-82 in *Middle East and North Africa, 1988.* London: Europa, 1987.

Gilmour, David. *Lebanon: The Fractured Country.* New York: St. Martin's Press, 1983.

Glubb, John Bagot. *Syria, Lebanon, Jordan.* New York: Walker, 1967.

Gordon, David C. *Lebanon: The Fragmented Nation.* London: Croom Helm, 1980.

_____. *The Republic of Lebanon: Nation in Jeopardy.* Boulder, Colorado: Westview Press, 1983.

Hitti, Philip K. *History of the Arabs.* New York: Macmillan, 1956.

_____. *Lebanon in History: From the Earliest Times to the Present.* New York: St. Martin's Press, 1957.

_____. *The Origins of the Druze People and Religion.* New York: AMS Press, 1966.

_____. *A Short History of Lebanon.* New York: St. Martin's Press, 1965.

Hourani, Albert H. *Syria and Lebanon.* London: Oxford University Press, 1946.

Hudson, Michael C. *The Precarious Republic.* New York: Random House, 1968.

Ismail, Adel. *Le Liban: Histoire d'un Peuple.* Beirut: Dar al Makhouf, 1968.

Kerr, Malcolm H. *Lebanon in the Last Years of Feudalism, 1840-1868.* Beirut: Catholic Press, 1959.

Khalaf, Samir. *Persistence and Change in 19th Century Lebanon: A Sociological Essay.* Beirut: American University of Beirut, 1979.

Khalidi, Rashid. *Under Siege: PLO Decisionmaking During the 1982 War.* New York: Columbia University Press, 1986.

Khalidi, Walid. *Conflict and Violence in Lebanon: Confrontation in the Middle East.* Cambridge: Harvard University Press, 1979.

Longrigg, Stephen H. *Syria and Lebanon under French Mandate.* London: Oxford University Press, 1968.

Lyautey, Pierre. *Le Liban Moderne.* Paris: Julliard, 1964.

Mayer, Thomas. "Lebanon." Pages 663-86 in Colin Legum (ed.), *Middle East Contemporary Survey, 1980-81.* New York: Holmes and Meier, 1982.

Olmert, Yosef. "Lebanon." Pages 702-33 in Colin Legum (ed.), *Middle East Contemporary Survey, 1981-82.* New York: Holmes and Meier, 1983.

Peretz, Don. *The Middle East Today.* New York: Praeger, 1983.

Rabinovich, Itamar. *The War for Lebanon, 1970-1983.* Ithaca: Cornell University Press, 1984.

Rabinovich, Itamar, and Hanna Zamir. "Lebanon." Pages 492-525 in Colin Legum (ed.), *Middle East Contemporary Survey, 1976-77.* New York: Holmes and Meier, 1978.

_____. "Lebanon." Pages 603-27 in Colin Legum (ed.), *Middle East Contemporary Survey, 1977-78.* New York: Holmes and Meier, 1979.

Randal, Jonathan C. *Going All the Way.* New York: Viking Press, 1983.

Salibi, Kamal S. *Crossroads to Civil War: Lebanon, 1958-76.* Delmar, New York: Caravan Books, 1976.

_____. *Maronite Historians of Medieval Lebanon.* New York: AMS Press, 1980.

_____. *The Modern History of Lebanon.* Delmar, New York: Caravan Books, 1977.

Seeden, Helga. "Coastal Lebanon." Pages 56-70 in Beirut College for Women (ed.), *Cultural Resources in Lebanon.* Beirut: Libraire du Liban, 1969.

Ward, William A. "Ancient Lebanon." Pages 11-32 in Beirut College for Women (ed.), *Cultural Resources in Lebanon.* Beirut: Libraire du Liban, 1969.

Yazbek, Yusif I. "Lebanese History Between 1841 and 1920." Pages 240-42 in Beirut College for Women (ed.), *Cultural Resources in Lebanon.* Beirut: Libraire du Liban, 1969.

Zamir, Meier. *The Formation of Modern Lebanon.* London: Croom Helm, 1985.
Ziadeh, Nicola A. *Syria and Lebanon.* New York: Praeger, 1957.

Chapter 2

AbuKhalil, As'ad. "Druze, Sunni, and Shi'ite Political Leadership in Present-Day Lebanon," *Arab Studies Quarterly,* 7, No. 4, Fall 1985.
Ajami, Fouad. *The Vanished Imam: Musa al Sadr and the Shia of Lebanon.* Ithaca: Cornell University Press, 1986.
Alamuddin, Nura, and Paul Starr. *Crucial Bonds: Marriage among the Druze.* Delmar, New York: Caravan Books, 1980.
Al-Bustani, Fuad Afram. *Ittijahat Lubnaniyyah* (Lebanese Attitudes). Beirut: ad Da'irah, 1982.
'Amil, Mahdi. *Taqdim lil Nafi at Takfir at Ta'ifi* (An Introduction to the Negation of Sectarian Thought). Beirut: Dar al Farabi, 1985.
Armstrong, Lincoln. "Demographic Characteristics of Beirut as a City in 1970," *Population,* 5, July 1973, 32-62.
_____. "Social Differentiation in Selected Lebanese Villages," *American Sociological Review,* 21, No. 4, 1956, 425-34.
_____. "A Socio-Economic Poll in Beirut-Lebanon," *Public Opinion Quarterly,* 12, No. 1, 1959, 17-27.
_____. "Sociological Patterns and Value Orientation in Rural Lebanon," *Public Opinion Quarterly,* 22, No. 3, 1958, 22-32.
Asad, Talal, and Roger Owen (ed.). *The Middle East.* (Sociology of the Middle East Series.) New York: Monthly Review Press, 1983.
Baer, Gabriel. "Religious and Ethnic Groups." Pages 250-66 in Jacob M. Landau (ed.), *Man, State, and Society in the Contemporary Middle East.* New York: Praeger, 1972.
Barakat, Halim. *Al Mujtama' al Arabi al Hadith* (Contemporary Arab Society). Beirut: Center for Arab Unity Studies, 1984.
_____. *Lebanon in Strife: Student Preludes to the Civil War.* Austin: University of Texas Press, 1977.
_____. "Social and Political Integration in Lebanon: A Case of Social Mosaic," *Middle East Journal,* 27, Summer 1973.
_____. "The Social Context." Pages 3-20 in Lewis Snider and Edward Haley (eds.), *Lebanon in Crisis.* Syracuse: Syracuse University Press, 1979.
Beirut College for Women (ed.). *Cultural Resources in Lebanon.* Beirut: Libraire du Liban, 1969.

Betts, Robert C. *Christians in the Arab East: A Political Study.* Athens: Lycabettus Press, 1975.

Bilani, Bashir. *Al Qawanin al Mita' ash Shakhssiyah fi Lubnan* (Personal Status Laws in Lebanon). Beirut: Dar al 'Ilm lil Malayin, 1982.

Binder, Leonard. *Politics in Lebanon.* New York: John Wiley and Sons, 1966.

Chamie, Joseph. *Religion and Fertility.* Cambridge: Cambridge University Press, 1981.

_____. "Religious Groups in Lebanon: A Descriptive Investigation," *International Journal of Middle East Studies,* 2, 1980, 175-87.

Chevallier, Dominique. *La Société du Mont Liban à L'Epoque de la Révolution Industrielle en Europe.* Paris: Libraire Orientaliste Paul Geuthner, 1971.

Churchill, Charles. *The Druze and the Maronites under the Turkish Rule from 1840 to 1860.* New York: Cambridge University Press, 1973 (Reprint.).

Cobban, Helena. *The Making of Modern Lebanon.* Boulder, Colorado: Westview Press, 1985.

_____. *The Shi'ite Community in Lebanon.* Washington: Islamic Institute, The American University, 1984.

Dahir, Mas'ud. *Al Asas at Tarikhiyah lil Qanun at Ta'ifi* (The Historical Roots of the Lebanese Confessional Question). Beirut: Institute for Arab Development, 1986.

_____. *Lubnan: At Tahrir al Qa'ida wa al Mithaq* (Lebanon: Independence, the Formula, and the Pact). Beirut: Dar al Matbu'at ash Sharqiyyah, 1984.

Enayat, Hamid. "The Guardianship of the Jurisconsult." In James Piscatori (ed.), *Islam in the Political Process.* Cambridge: Cambridge University Press, 1983.

Evans, Louella. *Portrait of a People: Lebanon.* New York: Graphic Society, 1972.

Farsoun. Samih. "Family Structure and Society in Modern Lebanon." Pages 257-307 in Louise Sweet (ed.), *Peoples and Cultures of the Middle East,* II. New York: Natural History Press, 1970.

Fuller, Anne. *Buarij: Portrait of a Lebanese Moslem Village.* Cambridge: Harvard University Press, 1966.

Gibb, H. (ed.). *Shorter Encyclopedia of Islam.* Ithaca: Cornell University Press, 1984.

Gordon, David C. *Lebanon: The Fragmented Nation.* London: Croom Helm, 1980.

_____. *The Republic of Lebanon: Nation in Jeopardy.* Boulder, Colorado: Westview Press, 1983.

Bibliography

Gubser, Peter. "The Zu'ama of Zahleh: The Current Situation in a Lebanese Town," *Middle East Journal,* 27, No. 2, 1973, 173-89.

Gulick, John. *Social Structure and Culture Change in a Lebanese Village.* New York: Viking Fund, 1955.

———. *Tripoli: A Modern Arab City.* Cambridge: Harvard University Press, 1967.

Harik, Iliya. "The Ethnic Revolution and Political Integration in the Middle East," *International Journal of Middle East Studies,* 3, July 1972.

Hatab, Zuhayr. *Tatawwur at Tashkilaat min al 'Ailah al Arabiyyah* (The Development of the Structures of the Arab Family). Beirut: Institute for Arab Development, 1976.

Hess, Clyde, and Herbert Bodman. "Confessionalism and Feudality in Lebanese Politics," *Middle East Journal,* 8, Winter 1954.

Hitti, Philip K. *Lebanon in History: From the Earliest Times to the Present.* New York: St. Martin's Press, 1957.

———. *The Origins of the Druze People and Religion.* New York: AMS Press, 1966.

Hourani, Albert H. *Minorities in the Arab World.* London: Oxford University Press, 1947.

———. *Syria and Lebanon.* London: Oxford University Press, 1946.

Hudson, Michael C. *The Precarious Republic.* New York: Random House, 1968.

Ismail, Adel. *Le Liban: Histoire d'un Peuple.* Beirut: Dar al Makhouf, 1968.

Keehn, J.D., and Edwin T. Prothro. "The Structure of Social Attitudes in Lebanon," *Journal of Abnormal Social Psychology,* 53, 1956, 157-60.

Khalaf, Samir. *Lebanon's Predicament.* New York: Columbia University Press, 1987.

———. *Persistence and Change in 19th Century Lebanon: A Sociological Essay.* Beirut: American University of Beirut, 1979.

———. "Primordial Ties and Politics in Lebanon," *Middle East Studies,* 4, April 1968.

Khalid, Mufti Hasan. *Al Muslimun fi Lubnan wa al Harb al Ahliyyah* (The Moslems in Lebanon and the Civil War). Beirut: Dar al Kindi, 1978.

Khalidi, Rashid. *Under Siege: PLO Decisionmaking During the 1982 War.* New York: Columbia University Press, 1986.

Khuri, Fuad I. "The Changing Class Structure in Lebanon," *Middle East Journal,* 23, No. 1, 1969, 29-44.

———. "A Comparative Study of Migration Patterns in Two Lebanese Villages," *Human Organization,* 26, Winter 1967, 206-13.

_____. *From Village to Suburb: Order and Change in Greater Beirut.* Chicago: University of Chicago Press, 1975.

Labaki, Georges. "On the Air: The Rise of Private Radio and T.V. Stations in Lebanon," *Lebanon Monitor,* 2, No. 4, December 1986, 1-2.

Lebanon. Ministry of Education. *At Ta'lim fi Lubnan* (Education in Lebanon). Beirut, 1985.

_____. Ministry of National Education and Fine Arts. Educational Center for Research and Development. *Al Ahsa'at al Awwaliyyah lil 'Am ad Dirasi, 1981-82* (Basic Statistics for the 1981-82 School Year). Beirut: n.d.

Lerner, Daniel. *The Passing of Traditional Society.* Glencoe, Illinois: Free Press, 1958.

McLaurin, R.D. (ed.). *The Political Role of Minority Groups in the Middle East.* New York: Praeger, 1979.

Makarem, Sami Nasib. *The Druze Faith.* Delmar, New York: Caravan Books, 1974.

Naji, Amin. *La Na'ish ka Dhimiyyin* (We Will Not Live as Dhimmi People). Beirut: al Mutba'ah al Hadithah, 1979.

Najjar, Abdallah. *The Druze.* n.p., n.d.

Nasr, Salim, and Claude Dubar. *At Tabaqat al Ijtima'iyyah fi Lubnan* (Social Classes in Lebanon). Beirut: Institute of Arab Research, 1984.

Norton, Augustus Richard. *Amal and the Shi'a.* Austin: University of Texas Press, 1987.

Odeh, B.J. *Lebanon: The Dynamics of Conflict.* London: Zed Press, 1984.

Owen, Roger (ed.). *Essays on the Crisis in Lebanon.* London: Ithaca Press, 1976.

Patai, Raphael. *Society, Culture, and Change in the Middle East.* Philadelphia: University of Pennsylvania Press, 1971.

Prothro, Edwin Terry. *Child Rearing in the Lebanon* (Harvard Middle Eastern Monographs, 8). Cambridge: Harvard University Press, 1961.

Rondot, Pierre. *At Tawa'if fi ad Dawlah al Lubnaniyyah* (Sects in the Lebanese State). (Arabic trans. by Elias Abboud of Les Communautés dans L'Etat Libanais.) Beirut: Dar al Kitab al Hadith, 1984.

Salem, Elie. *Modernization Without Revolution: Lebanon's Experience.* Bloomington: Indiana University Press, 1973.

Salibi, Kamal S. "The Lebanese Identity," *Journal of Current History,* 6, 1961, 76-86.

_____. *The Modern History of Lebanon.* Delmar, New York: Caravan Books, 1977.

Bibliography

Schmida, Leslie C. (ed.). *Education in the Middle East.* Washington: AMIDEAST, 1983.
Spillman, Kathy. "The Concept of al-'Ard in Arab Society." (Unpublished paper.) 1984.
Stewart, Bonnie Ann. "A Vanishing Lifestyle: The Nomads in Lebanon Search for Their Future in the 20th Century." (Unpublished paper.) 1985.
Taqi-y-Yiddin, Sulayman. *Al Mas'alah at Ta'ifiyyah fi Lubnan* (The Sectarian Question in Lebanon). Beirut: Dar Ibn Khaldun, 1986.
Touma, Toufic. "Reading and Education in a Lebanese Village." Pages 327-31 in Jacob M. Landau (ed.), *Man, State, and Society in the Contemporary Middle East.* New York: Praeger, 1972.
_____. *Un Village de montagne au Liban.* Paris: Mouton, 1958.
United States. Central Intelligence Agency. *Who's Who in Lebanon.* Washington: 1986.
United States. Department of State. *Country Reports on Human Rights Practices for 1983.* (Report submitted to United States Congress, 98th, 2d Session, House of Representatives, Committee on Foreign Affairs, and Senate, Committee on Foreign Relations.) Washington: GPO, 1984.
United States. Department of State. Bureau of Public Affairs. *Background Notes: Lebanon.* Washington: GPO, September 1984.
Al-Waqi'. Vols. 1-9. Beirut: Lebanese Institute for Thought and Culture, 1982-1984.
World Health Organization. *Reconstruction of the Health Services in Lebanon.* Geneva: 1983.
Ziadeh, Nicola. *Syria and Lebanon.* New York: Praeger, 1968.
Zurayk, Huda, and Haroutune Armenian. *Beirut 1984: A Population and Health Profile.* Beirut: American University of Beirut, 1984.

Chapter 3

Alamuddine, Najib. *The Flying Sheikh.* London: Quartet Books, 1987.
Azar, Edward E., and Robert F. Haddad. "Seminar on the Reconstruction of the Lebanese Economy: Plans for Recovery." (Unpublished research paper.) College Park, Maryland: Center for International Development and Conflict Resolution, University of Maryland, n.d.
Boustany, Nora. "A Few Lebanese Cling to Homes Inside Israel's 'Security Zone'," *Washington Post,* June 23, 1987.
Bulloch, John. *Death of a Country.* London: Weidenfeld and Nicolson, 1977.

———. *Final Conflict: The War in the Lebanon.* London: Century, 1983.
Gilmour, David. *Lebanon: The Fractured Country.* New York: St. Martin's Press, 1983.
Gordon, David C. *The Republic of Lebanon: Nation in Jeopardy.* Boulder, Colorado: Westview Press, 1983.
Hamdan, Kamal. "The Lebanese Economy in 1985: Eminent Disaster." n.p.: Middle East Council of Churches, 1986.
Iskandar, Marwan, and Elias Baroudi. *The Lebanese Economy in 1981-82.* Beirut: Middle East Economic Consultants, 1983.
———. *The Lebanese Economy in 1982-83.* Beirut: Middle East Economic Consultants, 1984.
Labaki, Georges. "The Lebanese Economy: Miracle or Debacle," *Lebanon Monitor*, 2, No. 2, October 1986, 1-2, 8.
Maroun, Ibrahim. *L'Economie Libanaise, Le Marché Arabe, et la Concurrence Israélienne.* Beirut: Publishing and Marketing House, 1984.
Munro, John. "The Future of Lebanon's Economy." Pages 139-58 in John Munro (ed.), *Trade and Peace in the Middle East.* New York: Paragon House Press, 1984.
Norton, Augustus Richard. *Amal and the Shi'a.* Austin: University of Texas Press, 1987.
Petran, Tabitha. *The Struggle over Lebanon.* New York: Monthly Review Press, 1987.
Randal, Jonathan C. *Going All the Way.* New York: Viking Press, 1983.
Saidi, Nasser H. *Economic Consequences of the War in Lebanon.* Oxford, United Kingdom: Centre for Lebanese Studies, 1986.
United States. Congress. House of Representatives. Committee on Foreign Affairs. *Report of the United States Narcotics Control Program Overseas: A Continuing Assessment.* Washington: GPO, March 1987.
Yassen, Ahmad. "Lebanon." Pages 46-47 in *Arab Agriculture 1987 Yearbook.* Manama, Bahrain: Falcon, 1987.

(Various issues of the following publications were also used in the preparation of this chapter: *An Nahar Arab Report and Memo* [Nicosia, Cyprus]; Banque du Liban (Central Bank), *Quarterly Report* [Beirut]; Economist Intelligence Unit, *Quarterly Economic Review of Lebanon and Cyprus, Lebanon and Cyprus: Annual Supplement*, and *Country Report: Lebanon and Cyprus* [London]; International Monetary Fund, *International Financial Statistics Yearbook*; *Middle East Economic Digest* [London]; *Middle East Economic Survey* [Nicosia, Cyprus]; *New York Times*; *Wall Street Journal*; and *Washington Post.*)

Bibliography

Chapter 4

Abu Fadil, Munir (ed.). *Lubnan: Al Qadiyyah* (Lebanon: The Cause). Beirut: al-Khalil, 1984.
Ajami, Fouad. *The Vanished Iman: Musa al Sadr and the Shia of Lebanon.* Ithaca: Cornell University Press, 1986.
Al-Jisr, Basim. *Mithaq 1943* (The 1943 Pact). Beirut: Dar an Nahar, 1978.
'Amil, Mahdi. *Bahith fi Asbab al Harb al Ahliyyah fi Lubnan* (A Study of the Causes of the Civil War in Lebanon). Beirut: Dar al Farabi, 1979.
Arab Information Center (ed.). *Jenef-Lusan: Al Mahadir as Sirriyya al Kamilah* (Geneva-Lausanne: Complete Secret Minutes). Beirut: 1984.
'Atiyyah, Najlah. *Lubnan: Al Mushkilah wa al Ma'sat* (Lebanon: The Problem and the Tragedy). Beirut: n.p., 1977.
Azar, Edward E. (ed.). *The Emergence of a New Lebanon: Fantasy or Reality?* New York: Praeger, 1984.
———. *Lebanon and the World in the 1980s.* College Park, Maryland: Center for International Development and Conflict Resolution, University of Maryland, 1983.
"Background to the Lebanese Communist Party," *Middle East Reporter* [Beirut], December 12, 1987, 13–16.
Ball, George. *Error and Betrayal in Lebanon.* Washington: Foundation for Middle East Peace, 1984.
Barakat, Halim. *Lebanon in Strife: Student Preludes to the Civil War.* Austin: University of Texas Press, 1977.
Bashir, Iskandar. *Civil Service Reforms in Lebanon.* Beirut: American University of Beirut Press, 1977.
Beirut College for Women (ed.). *Cultural Resources in Lebanon.* Beirut: Libraire du Liban, 1969.
Binder, Leonard. *Politics in Lebanon.* New York: John Wiley and Sons, 1966.
Bourgi, Albert, and Pierre Weiss. *Les Complots Libanais: Guerre ou Paix au Proche-Orient.* Paris: Berger-Lerrault, 1978.
Cobban, Helena. "Lebanon's Chinese Puzzle," *Foreign Policy,* No. 53, Winter 1983–84, 34–48.
———. *The Making of Modern Lebanon.* Boulder, Colorado: Westview Press, 1985.
Crow, Ralph E. "Parliament in the Lebanese Political System." Pages 273–302 in E. Kornberg and L.D. Musolf (eds.), *Legislatures in Developmental Perspective.* Durham: Duke University Press, 1970.

_____. "Religious Sectarianism in the Lebanese Political System," *Journal of Politics,* 24, 1962, 489-520.
Dawisha, Adeed I. *Syria and the Lebanese Crisis.* New York: St. Martin's Press, 1980.
Deeb, Marius. *The Lebanese Civil War.* New York: Praeger, 1980.
Dekmejian, Richard. "Consociational Democracy in Crisis: The Case of Lebanon," *Comparative Politics,* 10, No. 2, 1978, 251-65.
Dhibyan, Sami. *Al Haraka al Wataniyyah al Lubnaniyyah* (The Lebanese National Movement). Beirut: Dar al Masirah, 1977.
Entelis, John. *Pluralism and Party Transformation in Lebanon: Al-Kata'ib, 1936-1970.* Leiden: Brill, 1974.
Gemayel, Amine. *Peace and Unity.* United Kingdom: Colin Smythe, 1984.
Gemayyel, Pierre. *Lubnan: Waqi' wa Murtaja* (Lebanon: Reality and Aspiration). Beirut: Lebanese Phalange Party, 1970.
Gilmour, David. *Lebanon: The Fractured Country.* New York: St. Martin's Press, 1983.
Gordon, David C. *Lebanon: The Fragmented Nation.* London: Croom Helm, 1980.
_____. *The Republic of Lebanon: Nation in Jeopardy.* Boulder, Colorado: Westview Press, 1983.
Goria, Wade. *Sovereignty and Leadership in Lebanon, 1943-1976.* London: Ithaca Press, 1985.
Haddad, Wadi. *Lebanon: The Politics of Revolving Doors.* New York: Praeger, 1985.
Hagopian, Elaina (ed.). *Amal and the Palestinians.* Belmont, Massachusetts: Association of Arab-American University Graduates, 1981.
Haley, P. Edward, and Lewis Snider (eds.). *Lebanon in Crisis: Participants and Issues.* Syracuse: Syracuse University Press, 1979.
Harik, Iliya. *Lebanon: Anatomy of Conflict.* Hanover, New Hamsphire: American Universities Field Staff, 1981.
"How Presidents Are Elected in Lebanon," *Lebanon Monitor,* 3, No. 2, October-November 1987, 4.
Hudson, Michael C. "The Breakdown of Democracy in Lebanon," *Journal of International Affairs,* 38, Winter 1985, 277-82.
_____. "The Electoral Process and Political Development in Lebanon," *Middle East Journal,* 20, No. 2, 1966, 173-86.
_____. "The Lebanese Crisis: The Limits of Consociational Democracy," *Journal of Palestine Studies,* 5, Spring-Summer 1976, 109-22.
_____. "The Palestinian Factor in the Lebanese Civil War," *Middle East Journal,* 32, Summer 1978, 261-78.
_____. *The Precarious Republic.* New York: Random House, 1968.

_____. *The Precarious Republic Revisited: Reflections on the Collapse of Pluralist Politics in Lebanon.* Washington: Center for Contemporary Arab Studies, 1977.

Hurewitz, J.C. "Lebanese Democracy in Its International Setting," *Middle East Journal,* 27, No. 5, 1963, 487-506.

Iskandar, Marwan. "Constitutional Features of Lebanese Democracy," *Middle East Forum,* 37, 1961, 31-34.

Al Harakat al Islamiyyah fi Lubnan (Islamic Movements in Lebanon). Beirut: ash-Shira, 1984.

Jansen, Michael. *The Battle of Beirut.* Boston: South End Press, 1983.

Joumblatt, Kamal. *I Speak for Lebanon.* London: Zed Press, 1982.

Khalaf, Samir. *Lebanon's Predicament.* New York: Columbia University Press, 1987.

Khalid, Mufti Hasan. *Al Muslimun fi Lubnan wa al Harb al Ahliyyah* (The Muslims in Lebanon and the Civil War). Beirut: Dar al Kindi, 1978.

Khalidi, Rashid. "Lebanon in the Context of Regional Politics," *Third World Quarterly,* 7, July 1985, 495-514.

_____. "The Palestinians in Lebanon," *Middle East Journal,* 38, Spring 1984, 255-66.

_____. "Problems of Foreign Intervention in Lebanon," *American-Arab Affairs,* No. 7, Winter 1983-84, 24-30.

_____. *Under Siege: PLO Decisionmaking During the 1982 War.* New York: Columbia University Press, 1986.

Khalidi, Walid. *Conflict and Violence in Lebanon: Confrontation in the Middle East.* Cambridge: Harvard University Press, 1979.

Khoury, Enver M. *The Crisis in the Lebanese System: Confessionalism and Chaos.* Washington: American Enterprise Institute, 1976.

Khuri, Fuad I. *From Village to Suburb: Order and Change in Greater Beirut.* Chicago: University of Chicago Press, 1975.

Labaki, Georges. *The Lebanon Crisis.* College Park: Center for International Development, University of Maryland, 1986.

Mallison, Sally V., and Thomas Mallison. *Armed Conflict in Lebanon, 1982: Humanitarian Law in a Real World Setting.* Washington: American Educational Trust, 1985.

"Moslem and Leftist Organizations: Al Murabitoun," *Middle East Reporter* [Beirut], November 28, 1987, 7-9.

"Moslem and Leftist Organizations: The Amal Movement," *Middle East Reporter* [Beirut], October 31, 1987, 7-9.

"Moslem and Leftist Organizations: Communist Organizations," *Middle East Reporter* [Beirut], November 14, 1987, 9-10.

"Moslem and Leftist Organizations: Hizbullah," *Middle East Reporter* [Beirut], November 7, 1987, 8-10.

"Moslem and Leftist Organizations: The National Syrian Social Party," *Middle East Reporter* [Beirut], November 21, 1987, 7-9.

Muir, Jim. "Buying Hearts and Minds," *Middle East International,* December 19, 1987, 6-7.

_____. "Lebanon: Arena of Conflict," *Middle East Journal,* 38, Spring 1984, 204-19.

Norton, Augustus Richard. *Amal and the Shi'a.* Austin: University of Texas Press, 1987.

Odeh, B.J. *Lebanon: The Dynamics of Conflict.* London: Zed Press, 1984.

Owen, Roger (ed.). *Essays on the Crisis in Lebanon.* London: Ithaca Press, 1976.

Petran, Tabitha. *The Struggle over Lebanon.* New York: Monthly Review Press, 1987.

Qubain, Fahim. *Crisis in Lebanon.* Washington: Middle East Institute, 1961.

Rabinovich, Itamar. *The War for Lebanon, 1970-1983.* Ithaca: Cornell University Press, 1984.

Randal, Jonathan C. *Going All the Way.* New York: Viking Press, 1983.

Rizq, Charles. *Le Régime Politique Libanais.* Paris: R. Pichon et R. Durand-Auzias, 1966.

Salam, Nawaf, and Lina Sadaka. *The Civil War in Lebanon: A Bibliographical Essay.* Beirut: American University of Beirut, 1982.

Salem, Elie. "Cabinet Politics in Lebanon," *Middle East Journal,* 21, No. 4, Autumn 1967, 485-502.

_____. "Lebanon's Political Maze," *Middle East Journal,* 33, Autumn 1979, 444-63.

_____. *Modernization Without Revolution: Lebanon's Experience.* Bloomington: Indiana University Press, 1973.

Salibi, Kamal S. *Crossroads to Civil War: Lebanon, 1958-1976.* Delmar, New York: Caravan Books, 1976.

Schiff, Ze'ev, and Ehud Ya'ari. *Israel's Lebanon War.* New York: Simon and Schuster, 1984.

Shamun, Camille. *Crise au Moyen-Orient.* Paris: Gallimard, 1963.

Shararah, Waddah. *As Silm al Ahli al Barid* (The Cold Civil Peace). Beirut: Arab Development Institute, 1980.

_____. *Fi Usul Lubnan at Ta'ifi* (On the Roots of Sectarian Lebanon). Beirut: Dar at Tali'ah, 1975.

_____. *Hurub al Istitba'* (Wars of Followership). Beirut: Dar at Tali'ah, 1979.

Shruru, Fadl. *Al Ahzab wa at Tanzimat wa al Quwat as Siyasiyyah fi Lubnan, 1930-1980* (Political Parties, Organizations, and Forces in Lebanon, 1930-1980). Beirut: Dar al Masirah, 1981.

Bibliography

Smock, David, and Audrey Smock. *The Politics of Pluralism: A Comparative Study of Lebanon and Ghana.* New York: Elsevier, 1975.
Suleiman, Michael. *Political Parties in Lebanon.* Ithaca: Cornell University Press, 1967.
Vocke, Herald. *The Lebanese War: Its Origins and Political Dimensions.* London: C. Hurst, 1978.
Zamir, Meier. *The Formation of Modern Lebanon.* London: Croom Helm, 1985.

Chapter 5

Bavly, Dan, and Elihu Salpeter. *Fire in Beirut: Israel's War in Lebanon with the PLO.* New York: Stein and Day, 1984.
Berlin, Michael J. "Funding Cutbacks Threaten UNIFIL," *Washington Post,* April 4, 1987.
Bernstein, Richard. "Trial of Suspected Terrorist Leader Opens in Paris Today," *New York Times,* February 23, 1987, A6.
"Bloody Beirut: Trading in Lives," *U.S. News and World Report,* February 9, 1987, 24-29.
Bouhabib, Abdallah. "Lebanon: A Fuse Instead of a Buffer," *Arab-American Affairs,* No. 15, Winter 1986-87, 13.
Boustany, Nora. "Syrians Deploy Southward in Lebanon," *Washington Post,* April 15, 1987, A23.
Bulloch, John. *Death of a Country.* London: Weidenfeld and Nicholson, 1977.
_____. *Final Conflict: The War in the Lebanon.* London: Century, 1983.
Clyde, Mark. "Lebanon: The Remaining U.S. Hostages. A Chronology, 1984-1986." (Library of Congress, Congressional Research Service, No. 87-322-F.) 1987.
Creed, John. *Lebanon: Developments Between February 1984 and July 1985.* (Library of Congress, Congressional Research Service, No. 85-885-F.) 1985.
Dawisha, Adeed I. *Syria and the Lebanese Crisis.* New York: St. Martin's Press, 1980.
Deeb, Marius. *The Lebanese Civil War.* New York: Praeger, 1980.
"Details on Bank Attacks in Lebanon," *Middle East Reporter* [Beirut], October 18, 1986, 7.
"Diverse Allegiance of the Army," *Middle East Reporter* [Beirut], May 17, 1986, 8-14.
"Dollar Rate, Crime, and Unemployment on the Rise," *Monday Morning* [Beirut], June 9-15, 1986, 10.

Dunn, Michael Collins. "Rebuilding Lebanon's Army," *Defense and Foreign Affairs Monthly*, June 1983, 16-19.

———. "Return to Reality on Lebanese Hostages?" *Defense and Foreign Affairs Daily*, January 30, 1987, 3.

Economist Intelligence Unit. *Quarterly Economic Review of Lebanon and Cyprus* [London], No. 2, 1984, 7-10.

———. *Quarterly Economic Review of Lebanon and Cyprus* [London], No. 3, 1984, 6-8.

———. *Quarterly Economic Review of Lebanon and Cyprus* [London], No. 3, 1985, 11.

Fisher, W.B. "Lebanon." Pages 556-95 in *Middle East and North Africa, 1987.* London: Europa, 1986.

"Future of U.N. in Lebanon in Doubt Again," *Jane's Defence Weekly* [London], September 27, 1986.

Gabriel, Philip Louis. *In the Ashes: A Story of Lebanon.* Ardmore, Pennsylvania: Whitmore, 1978.

Gainsborough, J. Russell. *The Arab-Israeli Conflict: A Politico-Legal Analysis.* Brookfield, Vermont: Gower Press, 1986.

Gammer, Moshe. "The War in Lebanon: The Course of the Hostilities." Pages 128-48 in Colin Legum (ed.), *Middle East Contemporary Survey, 1981-82.* New York: Holmes and Meier, 1983.

Gemayel, Amin. "The Prince and the Promise," *Foreign Affairs,* 63, Spring 1985, 773.

"Ghazi Kenan Takes on West Beirut," *Defense and Foreign Affairs Weekly*, March 9-15, 1987, 2.

Gibran, Khalil. *The Prophet.* New York: Phoenix Press, 1986.

Gilmour, David. *Lebanon: The Fractured Country.* New York: St. Martin's Press, 1983.

Gordon, David C. *Lebanon: The Fragmented Nation.* London: Croom Helm, 1980.

———. *The Republic of Lebanon: Nation in Jeopardy.* Boulder, Colorado: Westview Press, 1983.

Herzog, Chaim. *The Arab-Israeli Wars.* New York: Random House, 1982.

Hijazi, Ihsan. "U.N. Forces Battle Lebanese Militia," *New York Times,* August 13, 1986.

———. "Unrivaled Clashes Raging in Streets of West Beirut," *New York Times*, February 19, 1987, A1.

Houghton, Robert, and Frank G. Trinka. *Multinational Peacekeeping in the Middle East.* Washington: Foreign Service Institute, 1984.

Hudson, Michael C. *The Precarious Republic.* New York: Random House, 1968.

Hurewitz, J.C. *Middle East Politics*. New York: Octagon Books, 1974.
International Institute of Strategic Studies. *The Military Balance, 1986-1987*. London: 1986.
James, Alan. "Painful Peacekeeping: The United Nations in Lebanon, 1978-1982," *International Journal*, Autumn 1983, 613-34.
Jansen, Michael. *The Battle of Beirut*. Boston: South End Press, 1983.
Jureidini, Paul A., and R.D. McLaurin. "Army and State in Lebanon," *Middle East Insight*, 3, No. 2, 1983, 31.
Kechichian, Joseph A. "The Lebanese Army: Capabilities and Challenges," *Conflict Quarterly*, 5, No.1, Winter 1985, 15-39.
Khalaf, Samir. *Lebanon's Predicament*. New York: Columbia University Press, 1987.
Khalidi, Rashid. *Conflict and Violence in Lebanon: Confrontation in the Middle East*. Cambridge: Harvard University Press, 1979.
_____. *Under Siege: PLO Decisionmaking During the 1982 War*. New York: Columbia University Press, 1986.
Laffin, John. *The War of Desperation: Lebanon, 1982-85*. London: Osprey, 1985.
Lamb, Franklin P. (ed.). *Israel's War in Lebanon*. Boston: South End Press, 1984.
Lebanese Center for Documentation and Research. *Mufawazat al Lubnaniyyah al Isra'iliyyah* (Lebanese-Israeli Negotiations). Antilyas, Lebanon: 1984.
"Lebanon: Why Hobeika's East Beirut Raid," *Defense and Foreign Affairs Daily*, October 7, 1986.
Longva, Wilhelm Hans. "UNIFIL: Objectives and Prospects," *Middle East Insight*, 3, No. 5, 1984.
Mauer, Robert J. "Peacekeeping in Lebanon: Lessons Learned." (Unpublished paper, written for Naval War College.) 1984.
Norton, Augustus Richard. "Making Enemies in South Lebanon: Harakat Amal, the IDF, and South Lebanon," *Middle East International*, 3, No. 3, 1984, 13-20.
Olmert, Yosef. "Lebanon." Pages 657-702 in Colin Legum (ed.), *Middle East Contemporary Survey, 1982-83*. New York: Holmes and Meier, 1985.
Podesta, Don. "Ethnic Conflicts; Toll Mounts," *Washington Post*, May 26, 1987, A17.
"Profiles: Brigadier General Kenaan," *Middle East Reporter* [Beirut], March 7, 1987, 12.
Rabinovich, Itamar. "Israel and Lebanon in 1983." Pages 135-49 in Colin Legum (ed.), *Middle East Contemporary Survey, 1982-83*. New York: Holmes and Meier, 1985.

_____. *The War for Lebanon, 1970-1983.* Ithaca: Cornell University Press, 1984.

_____. "The War in Lebanon: An Overview." Pages 109-27 in Colin Legum (ed.), *Middle East Contemporary Survey, 1981-82.* New York: Holmes and Meier, 1984.

Randal, Jonathan C. *Going All the Way.* New York: Viking Press, 1983.

Schiff, Ze'ev, and Ehud Ya'ari. *Israel's Lebanon War.* New York: Simon and Schuster, 1984.

Sivard, Ruth L. *World Military and Social Expenditures, 1986.* Washington: World Priorities, 1986.

TWA Hijacking: A Chronology of Events. (Library of Congress, Congressional Research Service, No. 85-845-F.) July 1986.

Tyler, Patrick. "Lebanon's Soldiers Fight for Militia," *Washington Post,* March 5, 1985.

United States. Department of Defense. *Report of the DOD Commission on Beirut International Airport Terrorist Act, 23 October 1983.* Washington: GPO, December 20, 1983.

_____. Department of State. *Country Reports on Human Rights Practices for 1986.* (Report submitted to United States Congress, 100th, 1st Session, Senate, Committee on Foreign Relations, and House of Representatives, Committee on Foreign Affairs.) Washington: GPO, February 1987.

Weinberger, Naomi J. *Syrian Intervention in Lebanon.* Oxford: Oxford University Press, 1986.

Zamir, Meier. *The Formation of Modern Lebanon.* London: Croom Helm, 1985.

Appendix B

Bulloch, John. *Death of a Country.* London: Weidenfeld and Nicholson, 1977.

_____. *Final Conflict: The War in the Lebanon.* London: Century, 1983.

Creed, John. "Lebanon." (Library of Congress, Congressional Research Service, Major Issues System, 85-885-F.) July 31, 1985.

Deeb, Marius. *The Lebanese Civil War.* New York: Praeger, 1980.

Gilmour, David. *Lebanon: The Fractured Country.* New York: St. Martin's Press, 1983.

Gordon, David C. *Lebanon: The Fragmented Nation.* London: Croom Helm, 1980.

_____. *The Republic of Lebanon: Nation in Jeopardy.* Boulder: Westview Press, 1983.

Bibliography

Jansen, Michael. *The Battle of Beirut.* Boston: South End Press, 1983.
Jureidini, Paul A., R.D. McLaurin, and James M. Price. *Military Operations in Built Up Areas, 1975-78.* (Technical Memorandum, No. 11-79.) Aberdeen, Maryland: United States Army, Human Engineering Laboratory, Aberdeen Proving Ground, June 1979.
Norton, Augustus Richard. "Political Violence and Shi'a Factionalism in Lebanon," *Middle East Insight,* 3, No. 2, 1983, 9-16.
Rabinovich, Itamar. *The War for Lebanon, 1970-1983.* Ithaca: Cornell University Press, 1984.
Randal, Jonathan C. *Going All the Way.* New York: Viking Press, 1983.
Ya'ari, Ehud. "Behind the Terror," *Atlantic Monthly,* June 1987, 18-22.

Glossary

barrels per day (bpd)—Production of crude oil and petroleum products is frequently measured in barrels per day. A barrel is a volume measure of forty-two United States gallons. Conversion of barrels to tons depends on the density of the special product. About 7.3 barrels of average crude oil weigh one ton. Heavy products would be about seven barrels per ton. Light products, such as gasoline and kerosene, would average close to eight barrels per ton.

confessional, confessionalism—In its broadest sense, refers to adherence to a faith or religion, such as Christianity or Islam. In Lebanon, however, it more often connotes identification with narrower affiliations, such as sect or clan. Often used interchangeably with *sectarian*.

Druze(s)—Religious community generally considered to be Muslim but whose practices also contain elements of Christianity and paganism. The religion was brought to Lebanon around the eleventh century by Darazi (hence the name *Druze*), a disciple of Al Hakim, the Fatimid caliph of Egypt who considered himself the final incarnation of God. The religion is secretive, and very few members are masters. The Druze community lives primarily in West Beirut, the Shuf Mountains, the Al Matn district and the regions around Hasbayya and Rashayya.

Greater Syria—Term used by historians and others to designate the region that includes approximately the present-day states of Jordan, Israel, Lebanon, and Syria before those states were formed.

Green Line—A no-man's-land created in Beirut during the 1975 Civil War by the forward lines of advance of the contending forces. The vegetation that grew in this abandoned area gave rise to the name *Green Line*. In 1987 it still separated Christian East Beirut from Muslim West Beirut.

Gross domestic product (GDP)—A value measure of the flow of domestic goods and services produced by an economy over a period of time, such as a year. Only output values of goods for final consumption and investment are included because the values of primary and intermediate production are assumed to be included in final prices. The word *gross* indicates that deductions for depreciation of physical assets have not been made. Because of the turmoil in Lebanon since 1975, GDP estimates are very imprecise.

International Monetary Fund (IMF)—Established along with the World Bank (*q.v.*) in 1945, the IMF is a specialized agency affiliated with the United Nations and is responsible for stabilizing international exchange rates and payments. The main business of the IMF is the provision of loans to its members (including industrialized and developing countries) when they experience balance of payments difficulties. These loans frequently carry conditions that require substantial internal economic adjustments by the recipients, most of which are developing countries.

Lebanese pound (L£)—The unit of currency, which is divided into 100 piasters. Before the outbreak of the 1975 Civil War, the pound was strong, and it required only L£2.3 to buy a United States dollar. During and immediately after the worst fighting, confidence in the pound dropped, but in 1982 the exchange rate was still fairly firm at L£3.81 to the dollar. During the chaos from 1983 to 1987, however, the pound rapidly depreciated, so that by August 1987 it was nearly worthless, trading at more than L£250 to the dollar.

Maronites—The largest Christian sect in Lebanon, the Maronite Church is one of a group of Christian churches known as Uniate, which are in full communion with the Holy See in Rome but are separately organized and adhere to an Eastern rite. Maronites settled in the mountains of northern Lebanon in the mid-seventh century; many continue to live there and in East Beirut. Maronites traditionally have looked to the West for cultural inspiration. Maronites tend to be better educated and wealthier than other segments of Lebanese society. By custom, the president of the republic is a Maronite.

Mount Lebanon—A term first used during the Ottoman era to designate the central part of the Lebanon Mountains inhabited mostly by Maronites and Druzes. After 1864 the area was administered as a separate entity and Christians prospered. Most of the region surrounding Mount Lebanon (often called simply "the Mountain") was considered part of Greater Syria, an area that encompassed present-day Syria, Lebanon, Israel, and Jordan. In 1920, while under the French Mandate, parts of Greater Syria (*q.v.*) were annexed to Mount Lebanon to create Greater Lebanon. This newly established territory eventually became the present-day state of Lebanon.

Phalange Party—Founded in 1936 by Pierre Jumayyil (also seen as Gemayel), the Phalange, or Phalanxes (Kataib in Arabic), was a mostly Maronite organization whose followers were known as Phalangists. Its policies were Western oriented and

Glossary

right wing. Its powerful militia, which was supported by Israel, participated heavily on the Christian side in the 1975 Civil War. Beginning in the late 1970s, as its militia, led by Pierre's son Bashir, seized control of other Christian forces, it became known as the Lebanese Forces (LF). By the mid- to late 1980s, however, after Bashir's assassination and Pierre's death, Phalange power ebbed, and it lost control of the LF.

Shia(s)—The largest Muslim sect in Lebanon. The word *Shia* comes from Shiat Ali, or party of Ali. Those who believed that Ali, Muhammad's cousin and son-in-law, should have succeeded the Prophet have come to be known as Shias. Those who thought that the successor should have been chosen by the community came to be known as Sunnis (*q.v.*). This dispute created the first great division in Islam. Most Lebanese Shias are Twelver Shias (also known as Imami Shias), believing that the twelfth imam (divinely appointed religious leader) is in hiding and will reappear. Shias live in West Beirut and its southern suburbs, southern Lebanon, and in parts of the Biqa Valley. Shias have tended to have less education and to be poorer than most other segments of society.

Shiite(s)—*See* Shia(s).

Sunni(s)—The second largest Muslim sect in Lebanon. After Muhammad's death, those followers who supported a traditional method of election based on community agreement became known as Sunnis; those who supported Ali as successor became known as Shias (*q.v.*). Sunnis primarily inhabit parts of West Beirut, the south-central coast, and the north. By custom, the prime minister is a Sunni.

World Bank—Informal name used to designate a group of three affiliated international institutions: the International Bank for Reconstruction and Development (IBRD), the International Development Agency (IDA), and the International Finance Corporation (IFC). The IBRD, established in 1945, has the primary purpose of providing loans to developing countries for productive projects. The IDA, a legally separate loan fund but administered by the staff of the IBRD, was set up in 1960 to furnish credits to the poorest developing countries on much easier terms than those of conventional IBRD loans. The IFC, founded in 1956, supplements the activities of the IBRD through loans and assistance designed specifically to encourage the growth of productive private enterprises in the less developed countries. The president and certain senior officers of the IBRD hold the same positions in the IFC. The three institutions are owned by the governments of the countries that subscribe their capital. To participate in the World Bank group, member states must first belong to the International Monetary Fund (IMF—*q.v.*).

zaim (pl., *zuama*)—Believed to be a vestige of feudal times, the *zaim* (Arabic for leader) is a political leader, either an officeholder or a power broker, whose followers are usually of the same religious sect. Within his district, the *zaim* is all powerful, and his clients promise electoral loyalty in exchange for favors.

Index

Abbas, Abul, 8
Abbasids, 8, 10, 12
Abdallah, George Ibrahim, 227
Abdallah clan, 227
Abdul Hamid II, 17
Abu Bakr, Caliph, 7
Abu Haydar, Munir, 114
Abu Nidal Organization, 201
Abu Sharqa, Shaykh Muhammad, 66
Achaemenids, 5
Acre, 11, 13-14
Acre Armistice, 19
Ad Damur, 120, 190, 192
ADF. *See* Arab Deterrent Force (ADF)
Administration for Tobacco and Tombacs, 119
administrative system, 20
Agha Khan, 63
agriculture, xvi, xxiii; in Biqa Valley, 44; effect of landholding shifts on, 118; impacts on crop production, 118
Ahdab, Aziz, 191
Ahmose I, 4
AID. *See* United States Agency for International Development (AID)
air traffic, 112-14
airports, xvii, 112-14
Akkar region, 56, 123
Alamuddin, Najib, 112
Al Ashrafiyah, 191, 199
Alawi Muslims, 59, 64-65
Al Biqa Province, 49, 56, 154, 199
Alexander the Great, 5
Al Fatah, 26, 36
Al Fayadiyyah, 192, 221
Al Hakim, Caliph, 10, 65
Al Hirmil, 120
Al Janub Province, 26, 49, 56, 118, 126, 131, 154
Allenby Street, 192
Al Matn region, 65
Al Qulayat, 225
Al Walid, Khalid ibn, 7
Amal (*see also* Islamic Amal; Islamic Jihad Organization): anti-Israel position of, 161; anti-PLO position of, 160-61; effect of Iranian Revolution on, 208; effect of political fragmentation in Lebanon on, 208; effect of presence of Pasdaran, 208; efforts to attract Lebanese Shias, 176; establishment of, 160; evolution of philosophy of, 161; Husayn Suicide Commandos splinter, 208; Islamic Jihad Organization splinter, 208-9; Jundallah (Soldiers of God) splinter, 208; Movement of the Disinherited militia, 241; reestablish Green Line, 212; rise of militia of, 145; Shia military force of, 35
American University of Beirut (AUB), 16, 75, 83-84
Amin, Ibrahim al, 162
Anderson, Terry, 229, 231
An Nabatiyah at Tahta, 154
An Naqurah, 196
Antigonus I, 5
Anti-Lebanon Mountains, 44-47
Aoun, Michel. *See* Awn, Michel
Arab, Issam al, 243
Arab Democratic Party, 213
Arab Deterrent Force (ADF) (*see also* Shtawrah Accord): role and activities of, 325, 193, 195; Syrian troops in, 172, 195
Arabic: official language of Lebanon, xxii, 71-72, 143; unifying role in Arab world, 72
Arab-Israeli War (1948), 173, 175, 185
Arab-Israeli War (June 1967): effect on Lebanon of, 25
Arab-Israeli War (October 1973), 25, 29
Arab League: Arab Deterrent Force (ADF) of, 32; Cairo meeting (October 1976), 31; Lebanon becomes member of, 21; Riyadh Conference (1976), 193
Arab Liberation Front, 243
Arab nationalists, 17
Arab rule, 3, 8, 10
Arabs, 7, 53
Arab Socialist Action Organization, 243
Arab states: reconstruction aid to Lebanon after Civil War, 128-31
Arafat, Yasir, 26, 28, 170, 201; in negotiations for Beirut 1982 cease-fire, 204; preference for Amin Jumayyil by, 36
Arens, Moshe, 207-8

267

Argov, Shlomo, 201
armed forces (*see also* Lebanese Air Force; Lebanese Army; Lebanese Navy; militia), xviii, 184, 211; under New Defense Law, 220
Armenian groups: Catholics, 71; language, 72-73; in Lebanon, 57, 70; Orthodox members of Lebanese Communist Party (LCP), 242; Orthodox religion of, 69-70, 242; political parties, 166-67
Armenian Secret Army for the Liberation of Armenia (ASALA), 167
army. *See* Lebanese Army
Arslan, Faysal, 165
Arslan, Majid, 165
Arslan family, 21, 145
Asad family, 21, 145
ASALA. *See* Armenian Secret Army for the Liberation of Armenia (ASALA)
Ash Shamal Province, 49, 56, 154
Assad, Hafiz al, 33; position on Lebanon of, 172; preference for Amin Jumayyil by, 36
Assyrian language, 73
Assyrian religion, 70
Assyrian rule, xxii, 3, 4
At Tanzim, 240
Austria, 14, 16
aviation, 112-15
Awn, Michel, xxiv, xxv, 212, 221-22
Ayn al Hulwah (refugee camp), 202
Ayn ar Rummanah, 50, 190
Az Zahrani, xvii, 109, 125-26

Baalbek, 49-50, 62, 208; base of Islamic Amal and Pasdaran in, 162
Baath (Arab Socialist Resurrection) Party, 168, 242
Babylonians, xxii, 3, 4, 5
Bahais, 71
balance of payments: in 1985, 96; in mid-1980s, 97
balancing principle, 140
Bank Al Mashrek, 102-3, 105
banking (*see also* Central Bank; Intra Bank) domestic, xxiii, 89-92, 101-5; international, xxiii, 96, 103, 105-6
barley production, 120
Bashir II, 13-14
Bashir III, 14

Battle of Yarmuk, 7-8
Bayhum family, 62
Bayrut Province, 154
Beaufort Castle, 202
Begin, Menachem: perception of Christians and Maronites, 195; promise of defense of Lebanon, 199-200; promises to defend Lebanon against Syria, 199
Beirut (*see also* Green Line) xvii, 3, 7, 11, 16, 42, 111; as capital of Greater Lebanon, 18; demographic expansion in, 49, 52; at end of Civil War (1976), 32; as health care center, 84; as model city, xxi; partition by Green Line of, 32, 50, 192, 207, 212; population distribution of, 49; reconstruction in 1982 of, 207; siege of, 80, 204-6; Sunnis in, 62; violence under Bikfayya Agreement in, 213
Beirut, East: Christian enclave, 50, 215; fighting in (1989), xxv; Israeli intelligence in, 195; Maronite enclave, 67
Beirut, West: clashes (1981-82), 35; fighting in (1989), xxv; Muslim enclave, 50, 215
Beirut Arab University, 83
Beirut-Damascus highway, 15, 106-7, 202, 203, 210
Beirut International Airport, xvii, 25
belt of misery, 41, 50
Ben-Gurion, David, 194
Berri, Nabih. *See* Birri, Nabih
Bikfayya Agreement (1985), 212
Biqa Valley, 10, 11, 14, 43, 44, 46-47; agricultural production in, 44, 120; Syrian controlled, 208, 222; watering of, 47
Birri, Nabih, 161, 173, 209, 241-42
Bizri family, 62
Brillant, Michel, 230
Britain, 14, 16
British Bank of the Middle East, 106
Buckley, William, 230
budget deficit, 97
bureaucracy: influence of militia and zuama on, 153-54; local administration and, 153-54
Burj al Barajinah (refugee camp), 216
Bustani, Emile, 21, 151
Bustani, General Emil, 26
Bustani, Mirna, 151
Byblos (formerly Gubla), 3-4, 7
Byzantine Empire, 7

268

Index

cabinet (*see also* Council of Ministers; military cabinet), 18, 148-49
Cairo Agreements (1969 and 1976), 26, 31-32, 34, 175, 186; control of guerrilla activity under, 28; effect on PLO of, 26, 187; invoked by PLO, 197
Cambyses, 5
Canaanites, 3
cantonization, 141, 155, 181-82
car bombings, 36, 210
Carthage, 4
Casino du Liban, 98
Catholics. *See* Armenian groups; Chaldean Catholics; Greek Catholics; Roman Catholics
Catroux, General Georges, 19
CDR. *See* Council for Development and Reconstruction (CDR)
cement industry, 124-25
census of 1932, xvii, xxiii, 48, 140
Central Bank: establishment and function of, 101; foreign assets in, 97; Intra Bank controversy of, 102-3; and public debt controversy, 103-5, 123
Chaldean Catholics, 71
Chamber of Deputies, xxiii-xxiv, 18, 149-52; ends French mandate, 20; insignificant role in politics of, 149-50; role in electing president, 146; speaker of, 21
Chamoun, Camille. *See* Shamun, Camille
Chamseddine, Shaykh. *See* Shams ad Din, Shaykh Muhammad Mahdi
Chehab, Fuad. *See* Shihab, Fuad
child-rearing, 77-78
Christians, 8, 10, 14-16, 17; conflict with Druzes, 14-16; disproportionate political power, 141; distribution among fighting groups in Civil War (1975), 239-40, 242; effect of Shuf Mountains war on, 210-11; in Lebanese Army, 224; in Lebanese Navy, 225; relations with Israel of, 195-96; supported by Syria in Civil War (1975-76), 31; violence in Beirut among (1985), 214; weapons supplies from Israel to, 194
Circassians, 71
cities: population influx, 50; population of, 49-50; religious distribution in, 49-50
citrus fruit production, 119-20
civil code: improved under French Mandate, 20; sectarian nature for personal status, 55-56

Civil Service (*see also* bureaucracy), 139
Civil War (1958), 24, 143, 185-86; Phalange Party in, 157; Progressive Socialist Party in, 165; United States in, 176, 186
Civil War (1975), 29-32, 94, 143; effect on economy of, 94-95; Guardians of the Cedars in, 240; impact on family of, 78-81; impact on office of president, 147; Independent Nasserite Movement (INM), 164, 215; issues unresolved, 181, 211; Lebanese Front in, 30, 36, 154-55; Lebanese National Movement in, 30, 154-55; Mountain War as continuation of, 211; National Liberal Party in, 158; opposing coalitions in, 239; Phalange Party in, 157-58, 190-91, 239; Progressive Socialist Party in, 165, 240-41; Soviet Union in, 177; start of, 29; Syrian role in, 172; United States in, 177
clans. *See* family networks; *zuama* clientelism
climate, xvi, 45-47
coalition (*see also* Lebanese Front; Lebanese National Movement), importance in political system of, 154
Collet, Alec, 230
commonality: Arabic language as symbol of, 71-72; within family networks, 21, 56-57; of national loyalty, 92; with Syria, 171
compressed wood industry, 123
confessional system (*see also* sectarianism): communities of, xxii-xxiii, 42, 55-56; continuation to present of, 42; outlined in National Pact, 143-44; of personal status laws, 55-56; principle of balancing in, 140; specified in National Pact of 1943, 140
conscription: Law of Service to the Flag, 218; practiced by Lebanese Forces (LF), 239
consensus: to implement change in system of representation, 151-52; lacking on national issues, 42; of sectarianism in office of president, 147
Constantinople, 7, 10, 13
Constitution: amendments to, 19-20, 142-43; contradictions in, 142; first Lebanese (1926), 18-19, 140; history of, 141-42; legitimizes National Pact, 141; principles of, xvii, 141-43

269

Constitutional Document, 172
Constitution of 1926, 18-19, 140; specified in National Pact of 1943, 140
Consultative Council, 162
Copts, 71
Council for Development and Reconstruction (CDR), 94, 128-32
Council of Ministers, 18, 143
Council of State, 152
courts, 152, 226
Crete, 4
crime, 226
Crusades, 10-11, 12
currency value, xvii, 89, 90-91, 96, 104, 119
current account, 97
custom duties, 97-98, 100
Cyprus, 4, 111
Cyrus, 5

Dabbas, Charles, 18
Daud, Daud, 161
Dauq family, 62
Dawah (Call) Party, 208
Dayan, Moshe, 194
Dayr al Qamar, 210
de Gaulle, General Charles, 19
de Martel, Comte Damien, 19
debt, external, 98
deficit, public, xxiii, 96, 97, 103-5
Democratic Front for the Liberation of Palestine, 170
demographics: of Beirut, 49; characteristics, 49-50; lack of official statistics for analysis of, 48
Dentz, General Henri-Fernand, 19
Deuxième Bureau, 186, 187, 221
Directorate of Posts, Telephone, and Telegraph, 115
Directorate of Waqfs, 61
displacement of population, 51, 52
divisive forces, xxi-xxii
Dodge, David, 229
Double Qaimaqamate, 15, 140
Douglas, John, 230
drug economy, 120, 122
Druze militia (*see also* Progressive Socialist Party): in Lebanese Army, 224-25; in Shuf Mountains war, 210-11
Druzes, 10, 12, 17; conflict with Christians, 14-16, 53; in National Salvation Front (1983), 209; offshoot of Ismaili

Islam, 65-66; in Progressive Socialist Party, 165

EC. *See* European Community (EC)
economic development and recovery, 94
economy (*see also* banking, Central Bank) xxiii; in 1987, 92-93; benefits from increased security, 89-90; effect of sectarianism on, 53; failure to function efficiently, xxiii; fragmentation of, 89; official, 89; pre-Civil War (1975), 93
Edde, Emile. *See* Iddi, Emile
education, xvi, 16, 81-84; arguments over questions of curriculum, 55; higher, 83-84; intermediate, 82; primary, 81-82; secondary, 82; technical and vocational, 82-83
Egyptian rule (1832-40), xxii, 4, 139
Eid, Nassib, 224
Eisenhower, Dwight D., 176
Eisenhower Doctrine, 23
Eitan, Rafael, 200
election system: interruption of, 150; intrasectarian nature of, 150
electric power (*see also* oil industry): dependence on oil for, 125; effect of war on generation of, 125-27
Electricity of Lebanon, 125
emigration, 16, 50, 52; among religious groups, 50; of Jews, 71
English language, 73
Esarhaddon, 4
Eternit Libanaise, 124
ethnic groups (*see also* Arabs; Armenian groups; Jews in Lebanon; Kurds): xxvii, 57
European Community (EC), 126, 134
European Investment Bank, 130

Fadlallah, Shaykh Muhammad Husayn, 63, 161-62
Fakhr ad Din I, 12
Fakhr ad Din II, 12-13, 183
Fakhu, Faysal, 167
family (*see also* child-rearing; marriage customs): effect of Civil War on structure of, 78-79; structure and customs in, 73-74, 75, 76, 77-78
family networks, 21, 56-57, 145
Farrash, Husayn, 231
Fatahland, 32
Fatamids, 8

Index

Firqat an Nasr, 243
foreign domination, 183
foreign interests in Lebanon. *See* Britain; France; Iran; Israel; Soviet Union; Syria; Turkey; United States
foreign intervention, 141, 171-73, 182, 183, 192-93
foreign relations, xviii, 170-71; with Iran, 176; with Syria, 171-73; with United States, 176-77
foreign trade, xxiii, 3, 10, 11-12, 42, 93, 95; in cement, 124; with Syria, 171
fragmentation: economic, 89; political, 29
France (*see also* Vichy government): Crusaders' interest in Lebanon, 11; end of Mandate of, 20; forms Levantine Special Forces, 184; influence under Mandate of, 61; interest in Lebanon, 16; Mandate for Greater Lebanon (1920-43), xxii, 3, 14, 18-21, 41, 140, 142
Franco-Lebanese Treaty (1946), 21
Franjieh, Sulayman. *See* Franjiyah, Sulayman
Franjiyah, Sulayman, 26, 28-29, 199, 209; actions in 1975 Civil War, 189; administration of, 26-29, 30, 94, 187; interest in Marada Brigade, 240
Franjiyah, Tony, 199
Franjiyah family, 21
Free Lebanon Army (*see also* South Lebanon Army), 174, 196, 217
French language, 73
Front for Progressive Parties and National Forces. *See* Lebanese National Movement

GDP. *See* gross domestic product
Geagea, Samir. *See* Jaja, Samir
Gemayel, Pierre. *See* Jumayyil, Pierre
General Administration Department, 220
geography, xxii, 3, 42-45
Ghandur family, 62
Ghanim, Iskandar, 188
Glass, Charles, 229, 231
Good Fence policy, 34, 196
Gouraud, General Henri, 18
government, central, xvii
Greater Lebanon, 14, 18, 41, 171
Greater Syria, xxii, 14, 42, 140, 169, 171
Greco-Persian War, 5
Greek Catholics, 10, 16, 68

Greek civilization in Lebanon, xxii, 3, 5
Greek Orthodox, 16, 17, 69, 242
Green Line, 32, 50; barricades down at, 207; origin of, 192; reestablished by Shia Amal, 212
Green Plan land reclamation project, 117
Gregorians. *See* Armenian Orthodox
gross domestic product (GDP), xvi, 90, 93
Guardians of the Cedars, 240
Gubla (Jubayl), 3-4
guerrilla tactics (*see also* Palestinian guerrillas): Lebanese government attempts to curtail, 26; of Palestinians, 25-26, 28-29; of Amal, 202, 214

Habib, Philip, 207; averts Israeli air strike, 200; negotiates cease-fire between Israel and PLO, 201; negotiates cease-fire in 1982 war, 204
Haddad, Saad, 119, 174; Christian militia leader, 34-35; dies (1984), 213; "Free Lebanon" buffer area of, 34, 196-97; relation with Israel of, 174
Hajj, Fahim al, 225
Hakim, Adnan, 242
Hakim, Nadim al, 211, 213
Halat, xvii, 114, 225
Hamada family, 21
Hamadi, Abdul Hadi, 230
Hamadi, Muhammad Ali, 230
Hammud, Mahir, 164
Hariri, Rafiq, 125
hashish production, xxiii, 120, 122
Hawi, George, 169, 242
Hawi, William, 239
health (*see also* medical services; public health): xvi
Helou, Charles. *See* Hilu, Charles
Higher Shia Islamic Council, 63, 160
Hilu, Charles, 28, 146; administration of, 25-26, 94, 186
Hirst, David, 231
Hizballah (Party of God): established as Shia organization, 161; Fadlallah as spiritual leader of, 63, 161; follows theology of Khomeini, 162; headquarters attacked by Syrian troops, 218; hijack TWA airliner, 228; link to Iran of, 176; purported leaders of, 162-63; splinter of Amal, 208; Syria curbs activities of, 213; theological foundation of, 162
Hobeika, Elie. *See* Hubayka, Elie

271

Holy Spirit University, 67
Hoss, Salim al. *See* Huss, Salim al
hostages, Western: purported holders of, 227; Syrian promise to help secure release of, 218
hostage-taking, 229
Hubayka, Elie, 159-60, 173, 206, 215, 216
Hunchak Party, 166
Husayn Suicide Commandos, 208
Husayni, Husayn, 161
Huss, Salim al, 32, 35, 134; forms own cabinet (1988), xxiv
Hussein (king of Jordan), 187
Husseini, Husayn. *See* Husayni, Husayn
Hyksos, 4
hyperinflation, 96

Ibrahim, Muhsin, 170, 242
Ibrahim Pasha, 14
Iddi, Emile, 18-19
IDF. *See* Israel Defense Forces (IDF)
Imami Shias. *See* Twelver Shias
immigrants, 52-53, 175
independence, 19-21, 184
Independent Nasserite Movement (INM), 164, 215; formation and power of, 164; Murabitun militia of, 164
industrial capacity, 123
industry, xvi, xxiii, 121-27
inflation (*see also* hyperinflation), 28, 96, 99-100
INM. *See* Independent Nasserite Movement (INM)
Inspectorate General, 220
Internal Security Force, 189, 218
International Monetary Fund, 98, 130
Intra Bank (later Intra Investment Company), 101-2
Intra Investment Company, 98, 102-3, 114
investment, 123-24, 126
IPC. *See* Iraq Petroleum Company (IPC)
Iran, 24; Ismaili Muslims in, 63; relations with Lebanon of, 176; sends Pasdaran volunteers to Lebanon, 208; ties of Hizballah with, 162
Iranian Revolution (1979), 208
Iraq: revolution in, 23; supports a Lebanese branch of Baath Party, 242
Iraq Petroleum Company (IPC), xvii, 127
irrigation, 115, 117

Islam: in areas around Lebanon, 7; Sunni and Shia as major divisions of, 61; tenets of, 59-61
Islamic Amal: link with Iranian government through Pasdaran, 162; splinter of Amal, 208
Islamic Grouping, 61-62, 163
Islamic Jihad Organization, 176; splinter of Amal, 208-9; terrorist tactics of, 227
Islamic Unification Movement (Tawhid), 213
Ismaili Muslims (*see also* Druzes): Shia sect known as, 59, 63-64
Israel: actions after 1978 invasion of Lebanon, 196-97; air strike against pro-Syrian forces, 200; attacks in Lebanon of, 26, 28; effect of raid on Beirut International Airport, 25; gains from 1982 offensive, 205-6; intelligence in East Beirut, 195; interference in shipping by, 111-12; Iron Fist policy of, 214; leaders plan to intervene in Lebanon, 194; leaves Lebanon in 1984, 111; Lebanon's opposition to establishment of, 173; military supplies to Lebanon, 194-95; Operation Litani, 196; Red Line policy of, 194; relations with Haddad's South Lebanon Army, 196; relations with Lebanese Christian community, 194; relations with Lebanon of, 173-74; siege of Beirut by, 204; transfers Lebanese prisoners to Israel, 214
Israel Defense Forces (IDF), 163-64; actions of Operation Peace for Galilee (1982), 201-6; against PLO invaders, 196; defends Maronite community, 199; invasion of Lebanon by, 35, 95, 173; offensive against PLO, 201; role in Lebanon after 1982 offensive, 206-8; withdrawal, 210, 213-14
Israeli invasion (1978), 174, 182
Israeli invasion (1982) (*see also* Operation Peace for Galilee), xxi; Arab states' reaction to, 129-30; cease-fire, 203, 204, 211; effect on agriculture, 118-19; effect on Amal, 208; effect on economy of, 95; effect on PLO of cease-fire, 201; impact of, xxi, 174; opposition by Syria for, 173; role of Independent Nasserite Movement in, 164; role of Progressive Socialist Party in, 165
Israeli raids: against Palestinian guerrilla activity, 26, 28, 188

Index

Jabal Amil Province, 41, 154
Jabal Lubnan Province, 154
jabaliyyun, 44
Jabar, Lufti, 223
Jacobites, 69
Jacobsen, David, 231
Jaja, Samir, xxv, 215-17; leader of Lebanese Forces (LF), 160
Jamal Pasha, 17
Jazzin, 47, 202, 214
Jenco, Lawrence M., 231
Jet Holdings, 114
Jews in Lebanon, 57, 70-71; hostility toward, 71
Jisr, Muhammad al, 19
Jisr family, 62
Jubayl, 3, 106, 115
Judicial Council, 152
judicial system, 20, 150-53, 226
Jumayyil, Amin, 37, 74, 90, 96, 130, 134, 158, 173, 174; abrogates the May 17 Agreement (1985), 212; against Tripartite Agreement, 216; appoints Awn, xxiv; budget of administration of (1987), 100; cost of Shuf Mountains war for, 211; inherits family political role, 145; National Salvation Front challenge to, 209; succeeds assassinated brother, 206
Jumayyil, Bashir, 33, 36-37, 141, 157, 158-59, 162, 172, 174; asks Israel for military aid, 194-95; attempts to get Israel into war with Syria, 199-200; as example of new social stratum, 57; heads Lebanese Forces (LF), 239; as president of Lebanon, 205-6; rise to power of, 198-200; strengthens leadership of Maronites, 199
Jumayyil, Pierre, 22, 29, 74, 155, 157, 158; effect of death of, 213; founder of Phalange Party, 155, 239; interest in Israeli offer of intervention, 194
Jumayyil family, 21
Jumblatt, Kamal, 21, 29, 154; as leader of Lebanese National Movement, 30, 240; leader of Progressive Socialist Party, 164-65; and Lebanese Communist Party (LCP), 168; opposes Shamun, 22
Jumblatt, Walid, 165, 173, 209, 240; inherits family political role, 145
Jumblatt family, 21, 66
Junblatt, Kamal. *See* Jumblatt, Kamal

Jundallah (Soldiers of God), 208
Juniyah, 98, 106-7, 111-12, 225
Jurayj, Jubran, 170

Kahan Commission, 206
Kanaan, Ghazi, 218
Kanaan, Khalil, 223
Kanj, Abd al Halim, 223
Kanj, Zuhayr, 164
Karamah, Elie, 158
Karami, Rashid, 29, 104, 134, 148, 209, 212, 226
Karami family, 21, 62
Karantina, 190-92
Kasrawan region, 11, 15
Kassis, Salim, 224
Kataib. *See* Phalange Party
Khaldah, 210
Khalid, Shaykh Hasan, 61, 163
khamsin, 45-46
Khatib, Ahmad, 31, 191, 242
Khaybar Brigades, 71
Khomeini, Ayatollah Sayyid Ruhollah Musavi, 162
Khoury, Bishara. *See* Khuri, Bishara al
Khuri, Bishara al, 18, 19, 143, 185; administration of, 21-22; and Rosewater Revolution, 22, 185
Khuri, Victor al, 218
Khuri family, 21
Kilburn, Peter, 230
Kufur Front. *See* Lebanese Front
Kulaylat, Ibrahim, 164, 215, 242
Kurdish political parties, 167
Kurds, 57, 62

LAA. *See* Lebanese Arab Army (LAA)
labor force: in agriculture, service sector and industry, 80; emigration, 52; women's participation in, 80
Lahad, Antoine, 213
lakes, 47-48
land: policy and use, 115, 116-17; tenure system, 117
landholders, 117-18
languages, xvi, 71-73
Law of Service to the Flag, 218
LCP. *See* Lebanese Communist Party (LCP)
League of Arab States. *See* Arab League
League of Nations, 14, 41, 140, 141-42, 184

273

Lebanese Air Force, xviii, 225
Lebanese-Americans, 176
Lebanese Arab Army (LAA), 31
Lebanese Armed Forces, xxiv
Lebanese Armed Revolutionary Faction, 227
Lebanese Army: against PLO, 188; allocation and disposition of brigades of (1987), 222-23; at beginning of Civil War (1975), 189; development and role of, 183-85; disintegration in Civil War (1975), 191; encounters with Arab Deterrent Force (ADF), 33; factional division in, 30-31; fights Palestinians (1969), 186-87; history of, 183-84, 217; losses in siege of Beirut, 205; role in Arab-Israeli War (1948), 185-86; role in Civil War (1975), 239; role in Israeli raids (1973), 188; role in politics of, 184-85; in Shuf Mountains war, 210-11; South Lebanon Army splinter of, 196
Lebanese Army Modernization Program, 219
Lebanese Cement Company, 124
Lebanese Christians: emigration compared to other groups of, 16, 50; fear of Turkish policies, 17; position on presence of Palestinians in Lebanon, 25
Lebanese Communist Party (LCP), 168-69, 188-89, 242
Lebanese Forces (LF), 215, 239; establishment and power of, 158-60; formal name of Phalangist militia, 239; operating illegal Beirut port, xxv; port control and revenue collection by, 100
Lebanese Front, 154-55; coalition in Civil War (1975), 239; groups in Civil War of 1975-76, 30; internal disagreements of, 36
Lebanese National Movement, 30-31, 154-55, 239; established by Kamal Jumblatt, 188; Lebanese Arab Army (LAA) joins, 31; Syria against, 31
Lebanese National Resistance Front, 213
Lebanese Navy, xviii, 225-26
Lebanese University, 83
Lebanon: added to Roman Empire, 7; formation of, 41; link with Syria of, xxii; separated from Syria (1861), 16
Lebanon Mountains, 44
Lebanonization, xxi
legislature. *See* Chamber of Deputies

Levantine Special Forces (Troupes Spéciales du Levant), 184
Levin, Jeremy, 230
LF. *See* Lebanese Forces (LF)
Likud Party, Israel, 195
literacy rate, xvi, 81
living conditions, prewar and war time, 79-81
London Treaty (1840), 14

Maan family, 12-13
majlis, 15
Mamluks, 11-12
Marada Brigade: pro-Syrian Christian militia, 172, 199; role in Civil War (1975), 240
Marada incursions, 8
Maronite archdioceses and dioceses, 67
Maronite Christians, 8, 10-11, 14, 16-17; Begin perception of, 195; communion with Roman Catholic Church, 66; conflict with Druzes, 53; fear of Muslim dominance, 195; in Lebanese Air Force and Navy, 225; in Lebanese Army, 223; tenets of religion of, 66-68
marriage customs, 75-77, 78
Martyrs' Day, 18
May 17 Agreement, 173; effect of abrogation (1985) of, 212; between Israel and Lebanon, 209
Mayhayri, Issam, 170
medical services, 84-85
Mediterranean Refining Company, 126
Melchites, 10
Melkart Agreement, 188
Middle East Airlines (MEA), 112-14, 186
migration (*see also* displacement of population), 50-52; effect of, 41; precipitated by war, 26, 51-52; from rural areas, 50
Mihhu, Jamil, 167
military budget, 184, 222
Military Bureau, 220
military cabinet, 189
Military Council, 220-21
military government, interim, xxiv
militia, armed (*see also* Lebanese Forces (LF)), xviii, xxiv; of Amal, 161; assuming government functions, 89, 97, 100; coalition among, 154-55; development by *zuama* of, 144-45; effect of presence of, 141; effect on Ministry of Justice, 152-53; force cantonization, 155;

Index

influence on bureaucracy of, 153-54; Lebanese Forces (LF), 158-60, 239; Muslim, 191; role of Amal and Hizballah as, 145-46; support by Israel of Christian, 34
millet system, 10
Ministry of Defense, 220-21
Ministry of Education, 83
Ministry of Finance, 100, 129, 134, 154
Ministry of Interior, 154
Ministry of Public Health, 84
Ministry of State for the South and Reconstruction, 149
Ministry of Transport, 114
missile crisis, 34, 200
MNF. *See* Multinational Force (MNF)
MNF II. *See* Multinational Force II (MNF II)
modernization, 41, 80
Mongols, 11
Mossad, 194
Mountain War (1983-84) (*see also* Shuf Mountains region), xxi, 210-11; role of United States in, 177
Mount Lebanon, xxii, 14, 31, 41, 44, 139, 159
Movement of the Disinherited, 241
Movement of Lebanese Socialists. *See* Organization of Communist Action (OCA)
Muawiyah, Caliph, xxii, 8
Muez-Aibak, 11
Mughniyyah, Imad: connected to Islamic Jihad Organization and Hizballah, 227, 230; reported leader of Islamic Jihad, 208-9
Multinational Force (MNF), 131, 133, 173, 174; action in siege of Beirut, 204-5; implications under May 17 Agreement for, 210; withdrawal from Lebanon (1983) of, 133, 212
Multinational Force II (MNF II), 206-7
Munif Pasha, 17
Muqaddam family, 62
Murabitun militia, 242-43; of Independent Nasserite Movement, 164; rout of, 215, 216
Murrawwah, Karim, 169
Musa, Al Ashraf, 11
Musawi, Abbas al, 162
Musawi, Husayn al: connected to Islamic Jihad Organization, 227; leader in Hizballah and Islamic Amal, 162-63; leader of Islamic Amal, 208

musharaka, 147
Muslims (*see also* Alawi Muslims): ask for increased representation, xxiv; distribution among fighting groups in Civil War (1975), 240-43; sects, 61-65
mutasarrif, 16-17, 140, 183
mutasarrifiyah, 16, 41
Naccache, Alfred. *See* Naqqash, Alfred
Naccash, Alfred. *See* Naqqash, Alfred
Naim, Edmond, 97, 102, 124
Najjadah, 242
Napoleon, 13-14
Naqqash, Alfred, 19
narcotics industry, 120-21
Nasir, Mustafa, 212
Nasrallah, Hasan, 162
Nasser, Gamal Abdul, 23, 55
Nasserite Correctionist Movement, 243
National Bloc Party, 26
National Cotton Mill, 123
National Covenant. *See* National Pact
National Liberal Party (NLP), 240; Tigers militia of, 158
nationalization of industry, 127
National Pact (1943), xxiii, 20-21, 22, 29, 140; basis for foreign relations before 1975, 170-71; effect of sanction by Constitution, 141, 142; formal announcement and effect of, 143-44; as means to reduce Christian-Muslim division, 55, 143-44; representation based on 1932 census, 140-41; unwritten agreement between Christians and Muslims, 20, 143
National Salvation Front (NSF) coalition, 209
national security, xxiv, 181
National Security Council, 212
National Waste Management Plan, 132
Nebuchadnezzar, 5
Nestorian Church. *See* Assyrian religion
New Defense Law (1979), 219-20
Njaim, Jean, 26
NLP. *See* National Liberal Party (NLP)
NSF. *See* National Salvation Front (NSF)

OCA. *See* Organization of Communist Action (OCA)
October 1973 War, 29
Ohannes Pasha, 17

275

oil industry: finance and irregularity of supplies, 126; nationalization of Tripoli refinery, 127; revenues from, 93-94
OPEC. *See* Organization of Petroleum Exporting Countries (OPEC)
Operation Litani, 195-96
Operation Peace for Galilee, 201
opium production, xxiii, 121
Order of Maronite Monks, 240
Organization for the Defense of Free People, 229
Organization of Communist Action (OCA) (*see also* Democratic Front for the Liberation of Palestine), 168, 170, 242
Organization of the Oppressed of the Earth, 71
Organization of Petroleum Exporting Countries (OPEC), 93, 128-31
Organization of Socialist Lebanon. *See* Organization of Communist Action (OCA)
Ottoman Empire, 16
Ottoman rule (*see also* Turkish occupation, World War I), xxii, 3, 10, 12, 16, 139-40, 183

Padfield, Philip, 230
Palestine Liberation Army (PLA), 30-31; transformed in standing army, 201
Palestine Liberation Organization (PLO) (*see also* Al Fatah): 26; activities in Lebanon of, 175; activity in Jordan (1970), 187; areas of control in 1987, 175; buys arms from North Korea and Eastern European countries, 201; transformed into standing army, 201
Palestinian forces: in Civil War (1975), 243; losses in Israeli offensive, 205
Palestinian guerrillas: attacks from Lebanon, 173, 175; effect of presence in Lebanon of, 25-26, 28, 173; expulsion from Jordan of, 52; struggle against Israel of, 25-26, 28-29, 182
Palestinian refugee camps (*see also* Burj al Barajinah refugee camp; Sabra refugee camp; Shatila refugee camp; Tall Zatar), 30, 52-53, 174, 175, 188, 193, 202; Burj al Barajinah, Sabra, and Shatila massacres, 206, 216; function in Israeli 1982 offensive, 202
Palestinian Resistance Movement, 28

Palestinians: effect of influx to Lebanon of, 187-88; effect of presence in Lebanon of, 25, 175; refuge in Lebanon of, 52-53, 175
pan-Arabism, 22-23, 55
parliament. *See* Chamber of Deputies
partition (*see also* Double Qaimaqamate; Green Line): in 1842, 14-15; in 1984, 96; origin of Green Line (1976), 192
Party of God. *See* Hizballah (Party of God)
Pasdaran (Iranian Revolutionary Guards): headquarters in Lebanon of, 120, 208; Iran sends volunteers to Lebanon, 208; in Lebanon, 120, 176; link with Islamic Amal, 162; Syria curbs activities of, 213
patronage. *See* family networks; *zuama* clientelism
Pax Romana, 7
peacekeeping forces, 89, 196-97; in Lebanon after Israeli 1982 offensive, 182, 205-8
Persian Empire, xxii, 3, 5
Personnel Law of 1959, 153
Phalange Party, 22, 24, 29, 35-36; armed militia of, 157; in Civil War (1975), 157; founding and philosophy of, 155; growth of power in 1958 and 1975 Civil Wars, 157-58; role in 1975 Civil War, 190-91, 239
Phalangist militia: called Lebanese Forces (LF), 239; decimate Tigers, 199; massacre at Palestinian refugee camp by, 206; in Shuf Mountains war, 210-11; training in Israel of, 195
Phoenicians, xxii, 3-7
pipelines, xvii, 126
PLA. *See* Palestine Liberation Army (PLA)
PLO. *See* Palestine Liberation Organization (PLO)
police, xviii, 226
political nature of religious conflict, 22, 47
political parties, 17; dependence on sectarianism, 154; ideology as basis for some, 155; lack of significance of, 150; multisectarian, 167-70; sectarian composition of, 56-57
political system, xviii; in 1987, 139; effect of sectarianism on, 53; history of multisectarianism, 139-40; importance of coalition in, 154; inadequacies of, 29;

Index

Maronites in, 68; role of *zuama* in, 56–57, 139, 140, 144–46, 150
Pompey, 7
Ponsot, Henri, 19
Popular Front for the Liberation of Palestine, 168
Popular Front for the Liberation of Palestine—General Command, 243
Popular Guard, 242
Popular Nasserite Forces, 243
population (*see also* emigration; migration), xvi, xxii, 3, 48–50, 48–53; effect of decline in Christian, 3; effect of displacement of, 42, 51; effect of increase in Muslim, 3
ports (*see also* foreign trade), xvii, 42, 110; control by militias of illegal, xxv, 100, 110–11
power-broker system (*see also* family networks; patronage; *zuama* clientelism), xxiii
president: power and role of, 21, 146–47; power in 1987, 139, 147
prime minister, 21, 147–48
Program of National Reconciliation, 199
Progressive Socialist Party (PSP), 21, 164–65, 240–41
Prophet Muhammad, 7, 59–61
Protestants, 70
Provincial Council, 154
Prussia, 14, 16
PSP. *See* Progessive Socialist Party (PSP)
Ptolemy, 5
public health, 84–85

qabadayat, 144
Qadi, Amin, 224–25
Qansuh, Isam, 242
Qassis, Father Sharbal, 240
Quwwat an Nasir, 243

Rabin, Yitzhak, 194
railroads, xvii, 109–10
Ramadan, 60
Ramgavar Party, 166–67
Reagan, Ronald, 177, 200
reconstruction: after Civil War (1975), 94–96; after 1982 Israeli invasion, 131–36; under French Mandate, 20; of roads, 108–9
reconstruction aid, xxiii, 128–31; after Civil War, 96, 127–31; lack of guarantees for, 133–35; from United States, 177
Red Line policy: of Israel, 194; Syria adheres to, 200
refugee camps. *See* Palestinian refugee camps
Regier, Frank, 230
reinforcement of, 42
Rejectionist Front, 243
religions, xvi, 57–71
religious conflicts, 14–17
religious leaders, 61, 68
Representative Council, 142
reserves, external, 98–99
Revolutionary Organization of Socialist Muslims, 230
Rhodes, 4
Rifai, Abdal Majid ar, 242
Rifai, Nur ad Din, 189
Rihana, Sami, 224
rivers, 47–48
Riyadh Conference (1976), 31–32, 193
Riyaq, xvii, 109, 225
Riz Kari, 167
roads, xvii, 20, 106–9
Roman Catholics, 68–69
Roman Empire, xxii, 3, 7
Rosewater Revolution, 22, 185
Russia, 14

Saad, Habib as, 19
Saad, Muhammad, 225
Saad, Mustafa, 243
Saadah, Antun, 169, 241
Saadah, George, 158
Sabra refugee camp: massacre in, xxi, 159, 175, 206, 207, 215; siege by Amal, 216
Sadr, Imam Musa as, 63, 65, 241; establishes Amal movement, 160
sahil, 43–44
Said, Hanna, 188, 239
St. Joseph's University, 16, 83
Saiqa, 243
Salam, Saib, 28, 148, 188
Salam family, 62
Salvation Committee, 162
San Remo Conference, 18
Saqr, Etienne, 240
Sargon II, 4
Sarkis, Ilyas, 28; administration of (1976–82), 31–36, 141; support by Syria for, 172

277

Saudi Development Fund, 130
sectarianism, xxii-xxiii, 3, 41, 53, 55, 56-57, 140; after Civil War (1975), 141; in Chamber of Deputies, 149-52; Civil War (1975) intensifies, 140; dependence of political parties on, 154; effect of National Pact tenets on, 143-44; sects, 42, 59, 152
Seleucid dynasty, 5-7
Seleucus I, 5
Seurat, Michel, 230
Seveners. *See* Ismaili Muslims
sexes. *See* family structure; population; women
Sfeir, Nasrallah. *See* Sufayr, Nasrallah Butrus
Shams ad Din, Shaykh Muhammad Mahdi, 36, 63
Shamun, Camille, 21, 36, 134; administration of, 22-24, 176; founder of National Liberal Party (NLP), 158, 240; interest in Israeli offer to intervene, 194; pro-Western administration of, 55; role in Arab-Israeli War (1948), 186
Shamun, Dani, 158, 194; inherits family political role, 145
Shamun family, 21
Sharon, Ariel, 207
Shartuni, Habib, 206
Shatila, Kamal, 243
Shatila refugee camp: massacre in, xxi, 159, 175, 206, 207, 215; siege by Amal, 216
Shayah (section of Beirut), 50
shaykh, 61
Shias (*see also* Twelver Shias), 11, 17, 41; attraction to Amal, 160-61; in belt of misery, 41, 50, 62; Fadlallah as leader of, 63; followers attracted to Amal, 160-61; followers in Lebanon, 176; geographic locations of, 62-63; growing importance of, 35, 36; in Lebanese Army, 222-25; in National Salvation Front (1983), 209; leadership in, 62; leaving Amal for Hizballah, 162; position in society of, 62
Shihab, Fuad, 22, 24, 94 146, 185; role in Arab-Israeli War (1948), 186
Shihab family, 12, 13-14, 21
Shihabism, 24-25, 28
shipping, 110-12

Shtawrah, 106, 109, 123, 199
Shtawrah Accord, 34, 193, 195
Shuf Mountains region: fighting in 1989, xxv; Lebanese Army and Druze fighting in, xxi; power vacuum after IDF withdrawal (1983), 210
Shuf Mountains, 44
Siblin Cement Company, 125
Sidon, xvii, 3, 7, 11, 36, 42, 49, 95, 111, 188-89, 192, 202; population distribution of, 49-50; Sunnis in, 62
SLA. *See* South Lebanon Army (SLA)
SNF. *See* Social National Front (SNF)
Social National Front (SNF), 21-22; formation of, 21
social structure: (*see also* child-rearing); education; family; health; living conditions; marriage; women, 73-81; divisions in, xxi-xxii, 53; fragmentation of, 41; Maronites at top of, 67-68
Solh, Rashid. *See* Sulh, Rashid as
Solh, Riyad. *See* Sulh, Riyad as
South Lebanon Army (SLA) (*see also* Free Lebanon Army): 117; formerly Free Lebanon Army, 196; lack of cooperation with UNIFIL, 197; Lahad as head, 213-14
Soviet Union, 177-78
Sroussi, Jean-Marc, 231
SSNP. *See* Syrian Socialist Nationalist Party (SSNP)
Statute of 1861, 16
Strugglers for Freedom, 230
subsidies, 100-101
Suez Canal crisis, 22-23
Sufayr, Nasrallah Butrus, 67
suicide bombings: by Syrian Socialist Nationalist Party (SSNP), 241; terrorist tactics using, 226, 227-28; of Western government installations, xxi
Sulh, Rashid as, 29, 189
Sulh, Riyad as, 19, 143, 148
Sulh family, 21, 62, 145
Sunni Muslims, 17; comprise the Najjadah and Lebanese Arab Army (LAA), 242; growing power of, 36; in Lebanese Army, 224; in Lebanon, 61-62; Murabitun militia of, 215, 216; in National Salvation Front (NSF) (1983), 209; orthodox, 61; Tawhid (Islamic Unification Movement), 213
Supreme Council of Justice, 152
Supreme Defense Council, 220

Supreme Islamic Council: source of Sunni religious leadership, 61
Suq al Gharb, 210, 223
Sutherland, Thomas, 231
Syria: added to Roman Empire, 7; Alawi faction in, 64; Arab Democratic Party and, 213; in Civil War (1975), 30, 192-93; influence in Lebanon of, xxii, 171-73; initiatives to restore order in Lebanon, 216; interest in Lebanese Civil War, 30-31; interference in Lebanese politics, 199; intervenes in 1975 Civil War, 192; link with Lebanon of, xxii; military intervention against Lebanese National Movement, 31; presence in Lebanon of, 31-32; Program of National Reconciliation, 199; relations with Lebanon after Civil War (1975), 32-34; relations with Lebanon of, 171-73; responds to Jumayyil attack on Marada Brigade, 199; role in Lebanon after Civil War (1975-76), 32; separated from Lebanon (1861), 16; sponsors Tripartite Accord, 216; supports a Lebanese branch of Baath Party, 242; violence diminished by (1985), 213; violence initiated by, 216-17
Syrian Army: attempts to restore order in Lebanon, 217-18; losses in Israeli offensive, 205; and Red Line policy, 194, 200; role in Civil War (1975), 239; troops enter West Beirut (1986), 217
Syrian Monophysites or Syrian Orthodox. *See* Jacobites
Syrian Orthodox or Syrian Monophysites. *See* Jacobites
Syrian Socialist Nationalist Party (SSNP), 157, 169-70, 206, 241; role in Civil War (1975), 241; suicide bombings by, 228

Tahan, Yusuf, 224
Tall Zatar, 30, 158, 191, 193
Tamraz, Roger, 102-3, 114
Tannus, Ibrahim, 212, 221-22
Tapline. *See* Trans-Arabia Pipeline
taqiyya, 64
Tashnak Party: domestic activity of, 166; international activity of, 166
Tawhid (Islamic Unification Movement), 169, 213

telecommunications, xvii, 115
terrorist activity (*see also* car bombings; Hizballah; Islamic Jihad Organization; suicide bombings), 36, 176, 210, 226-27, 228-29; against foreign diplomats, Muslim and Christian leaders, 36, 201; of Amal, 208; of Syrian Socialist Nationalist Party (SSNP), 241
textile industry, 123
Theodusius I, 7
Thutmose III, 4
Tigers militia: of National Liberal Party (NLP), 158, 240; training in Israel of, 195
Tiglath-Pilesar, 4
TMA. *See* Trans Mediteranean Airways
tobacco production and marketing, 119
topography, 43-45
tourism, xxiii, 95
Trans-Arabia Pipeline (Tapline), xvii, 126
Trans Mediteranean Airways (TMA), 114
transportation, conventional and ad hoc, 106-14
Tripartite Accord (1985), 173, 216
Tripoli, xvii, 8, 10, 11, 35, 42, 49, 95, 111, 222
Tripoli Oil Installation, 127
Troupes Spéciales du Levant, 184
Tufayli, Subhi at, 162
Tunisia, 204
Turkey, 24
Turkish occupation, World War I, 17-18
Turkomans, 71
TWA airliner: hijack of, 228-29
Twelver Shias, 62, 63
24 October Movement, 243
Two-week war, 200-201
Tyre, xvii, 3, 7, 10, 11, 42, 49-50, 111, 202

Umar, Caliph, 8
Umayyads, 8
unemployment, 28, 90
UNIFIL. *See* United Nations Interim Force in Lebanon (UNIFIL)
Union of Muslim Ulama, 163-64
Union of Toiling People's Forces, 243
United Arab Republic, 23
United Nations (UN), 21
United Nations Development Program (UNDP), 128

United Nations Interim Force in Lebanon (UNIFIL), 117, 126-27, 174; current problems and lack of support, 197; establishment and mission of, 35, 196; exodus from Beirut, 205; Lebanese Army against, 188; in Lebanese Civil War, 30; peacekeeping efforts of, 196-97
United Nations International Children's Emergency Fund, 128, 131
United Nations Relief and Works Agency (UNRWA) for Palestine Refugees in the Near East, 52-53
United Nations Resolution 425 (1978), 196
United Nations Truce Supervision Organization, 196
United States Agency for International Development (AID), 128, 133
United States: aid in rebuilding Lebanese armed forces, 219; embassy destroyed (1983), 209; military intervention in 1958, 24; relations with Lebanon of, 176-77; War Powers Resolution sanctions military presence, 211
United States Marines: bombardment in Beirut of, 210; return to Beirut, 207; role in Civil War (1958), 186; at siege of Beirut, 205; suicide bombing of barracks, 133, 227-28; surrounded by predominantly Shia militia groups, 212
United States Navy, 211
universities, 83-84
UNRWA. *See* United Nations Relief and Works Agency (UNRWA) for Palestine Refugees in the Near East
urbanization, 41, 50, 56

Vichy government, 19, 184
violence (*see also* suicide bombings; terrorist activity): among Christian Lebanese factions, 214; in Beirut under Bikfayya Agreement, 213; role of Syria in, 213, 216-17

Waite, Terry, 229
waqf, 61
war: effect on Lebanon of, 41-42; effect on quality of life during, 79-81
War Powers Resolution (1973): sanction for presence of United States military, 211
water sources, 47-48
Wazzan, Shafiq al, 35
wealth: concentration of, xxiii
Weir, Benjamin, 231
wheat production, 120
women, 52, 74-75, 76, 77
World Bank: loan to open Beirut's port, 132; reconstruction program of, 132
World War I, 17-18
World War II, 19-21

Yafi family, 21
Yarzah (section of Beirut), 224
Yazbak family, 21, 66, 165
Yemen Arab Republic (North Yemen): Ismaili Muslims in, 63
Young Turks, 17

Zahlah, 33, 50, 95, 160, 199-200
zaim, 56-57, 139, 145; as political leader, 144-46, 150
Zghartan Liberation Army. *See* Marada Brigade
zuama clientelism (*see also* clans, family networks), 56-57, 139, 140, 144-46, 150
zuama: influence on bureaucracy, 153; influence on judiciary, 152-53

Published Country Studies

(Area Handbook Series)

550-65	Afghanistan	550-153	Ghana
550-98	Albania	550-87	Greece
550-44	Algeria	550-78	Guatemala
550-59	Angola	550-174	Guinea
550-73	Argentina	550-82	Guyana
550-169	Australia	550-151	Honduras
550-176	Austria	550-165	Hungary
550-175	Bangladesh	550-21	India
550-170	Belgium	550-154	Indian Ocean
550-66	Bolivia	550-39	Indonesia
550-20	Brazil	550-68	Iran
550-168	Bulgaria	550-31	Iraq
550-61	Burma	550-25	Israel
550-37	Burundi/Rwanda	550-182	Italy
550-50	Cambodia	550-30	Japan
550-166	Cameroon	550-34	Jordan
550-159	Chad	550-56	Kenya
550-77	Chile	550-81	Korea, North
550-60	China	550-41	Korea, South
550-26	Colombia	550-58	Laos
550-33	Commonwealth Caribbean, Islands of the	550-24	Lebanon
550-91	Congo	550-38	Liberia
550-90	Costa Rica	550-85	Libya
550-69	Côte d'Ivoire (Ivory Coast)	550-172	Malawi
550-152	Cuba	550-45	Malaysia
550-22	Cyprus	550-161	Mauritania
550-158	Czechoslovakia	550-79	Mexico
550-36	Dominican Republic/Haiti	550-76	Mongolia
550-52	Ecuador	550-49	Morocco
550-43	Egypt	550-64	Mozambique
550-150	El Salvador	550-88	Nicaragua
550-28	Ethiopia	550-157	Nigeria
550-167	Finland	550-94	Oceania
550-155	Germany, East	550-48	Pakistan
550-173	Germany, Fed. Rep. of	550-46	Panama

550-156	Paraguay	550-89	Tunisia
550-185	Persian Gulf States	550-80	Turkey
550-42	Peru	550-74	Uganda
550-72	Philippines	550-97	Uruguay
550-162	Poland	550-71	Venezuela
550-181	Portugal	550-32	Vietnam
550-160	Romania	550-183	Yemens, The
550-51	Saudi Arabia	550-99	Yugloslavia
550-70	Senegal	550-67	Zaire
550-180	Sierra Leone	550-75	Zambia
550-184	Singapore	550-171	Zimbabwe
550-86	Somalia		
550-93	South Africa		
550-95	Soviet Union		
550-179	Spain		
500-96	Sri Lanka		
550-27	Sudan		
550-47	Syria		
550-62	Tanzania		
550-53	Thailand		

☆U.S. GOVERNMENT PRINTING OFFICE: 1989-242-444/00013

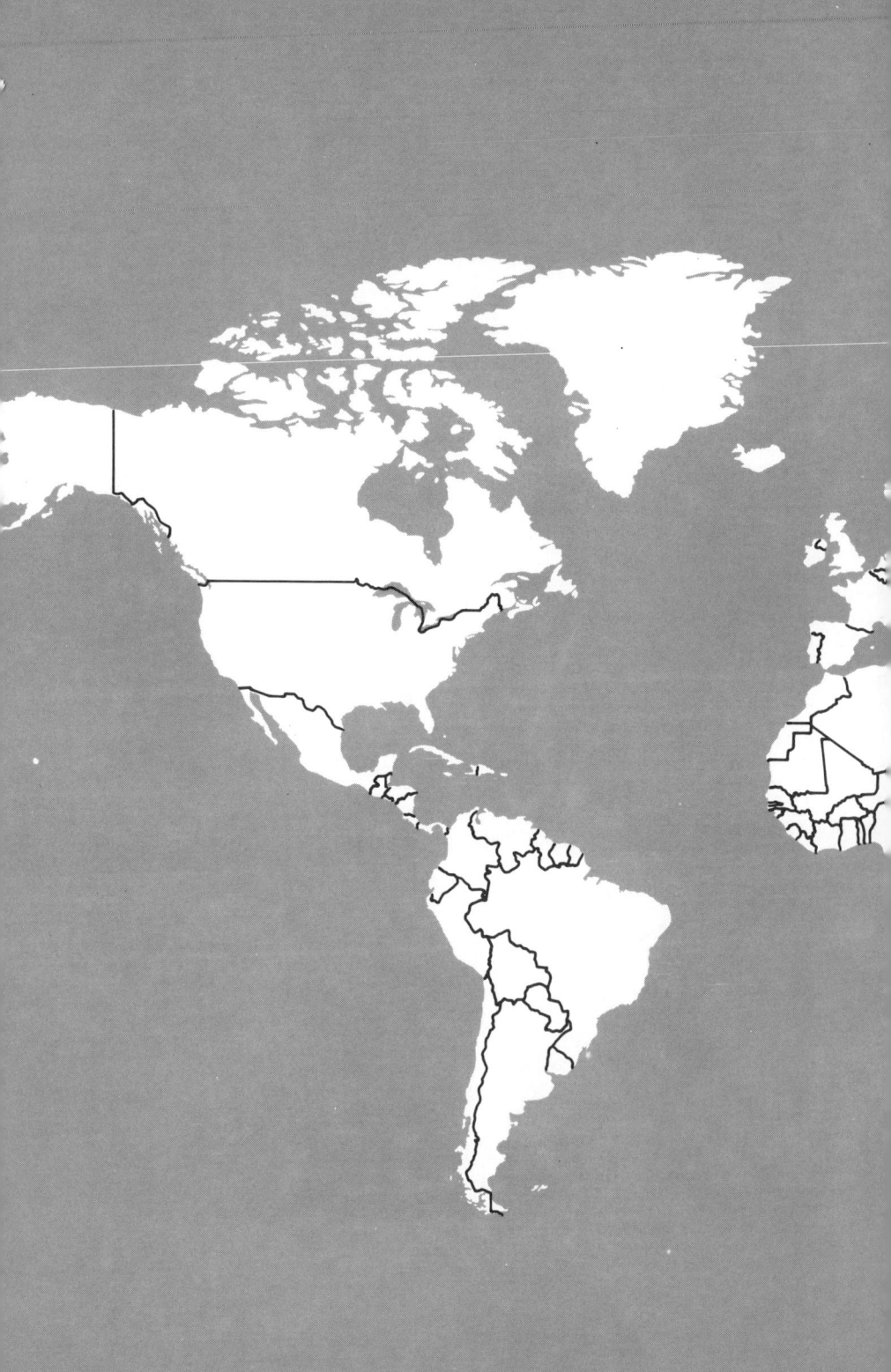